WASHINGTON'S
SECRET WAR

⊛ Smithsonian Books

 Collins

An Imprint of HarperCollins*Publishers*

WASHINGTON'S SECRET WAR

THE HIDDEN HISTORY OF VALLEY FORGE

THOMAS FLEMING

For my two Alices

HarperCollins books may be purchased for educational, business, or sales promotional use. For information please write: Special Markets Department, HarperCollins Publishers, 10 East 53rd Street, New York, NY 10022.

First Smithsonian Books edition published 2005.

Designed by Nicola Ferguson

Library of Congress Cataloging in Publication Data has been applied for.

ISBN-10: 0-06-082962-1
ISBN-13 978-0-06-082962-9

05 06 07 08 09 WBC/RRD 10 9 8 7 6 5 4 3 2 1

Contents

Picture Credits

Acknowledgments

Many people have made this book possible. High on the list are the members of the National Park Service at Valley Forge, notably Assistant Superintendent Barbara Pollarine, archivist Scott Houting, and Ranger William Trottman, who gave me access and guidance to the Valley Forge National Park Library and its many specialized books and collections. An exceptional thanks must go to retired park librarian Joseph Lee Boyle, whose series of books, Writings from the Valley Forge Encampment, and other compilations of source material such as the letters of Deputy Commissary of Purchases Ephraim Blaine and his staff, have frequently been useful. Mr. Boyle has also compiled a computerized collection of diaries and letters pertinent to Valley Forge which I have found very helpful. Another person to whom I am indebted is my son, Richard Fleming, whose computer and library expertise has been invaluable. My thanks also go to the staffs of the New York Society Library and the Yale University Library, who were invariably helpful in my research. Dr. Roger W. Moss, head of the Philadelphia Athenaeum, advised me on the history of the city's mansions and neighborhoods. Special thanks must go to my wife, Alice Fleming, whose computer expertise helped me navigate the journals of Congress and other online sources. Similar gratitude goes to my agent, Ted Chichak, who has, as usual, been supportive and encouraging, as well as an astute reader of the manuscript. Finally, renewed thanks to my editor, Don Fehr, whose wise counsel remains one of my major resources.

Timeline

1775

APRIL 19   Battles of Lexington and Concord

JUNE 17   Battle of Bunker Hill

JULY 2   George Washington takes command of the Continental Army

1776

MARCH 17   British evacuate Boston

JULY 4   Congress declares independence

AUGUST 27   British win battle of Long Island

SEPTEMBER 15   British land at Kips Bay and seize New York City

DECEMBER 26   Washington wins crucial victory at Trenton

1777

JANUARY 3   Washington wins battle of Princeton

JUNE 27   British under Burgoyne invade New York from Canada

AUGUST 27   British under Howe invade Pennsylvania

AUGUST 16   Americans win battle of Bennington

SEPTEMBER 11   British win battle of Brandywine

SEPTEMBER 19   Americans win first battle of Saratoga

SEPTEMBER 21   British win battle of Paoli

SEPTEMBER 26   British capture Philadelphia

OCTOBER 4   Washington attacks at Germantown and is defeated

OCTOBER 7   Americans win second battle of Saratoga

OCTOBER 17   Burgoyne surrenders to General Gates

NOVEMBER 15–21   British capture Delaware River forts

DECEMBER 19   Washington retreats to Valley Forge

1778

FEBRUARY 7   Lafayette leaves Valley Forge to lead invasion of Canada

FEBRUARY 23   Baron von Steuben arrives at Valley Forge

MARCH 2   Congress abandons invasion of Canada

MAY 1   News of the French alliance reaches Valley Forge

MAY 20   Battle of Barren Hill

JUNE 17   British evacuate Philadelphia

JUNE 19   Americans march out of Valley Forge

JUNE 28   Battle of Monmouth

Introduction

After forty years of reading and writing about the American past, I have reached one undebatable conclusion: history is full of surprises. Not many readers realize that historians are sometimes among the surprised. A book that seems relatively simple to create turns out to have hidden conflicts and unexpected insights into major characters that seldom appear in previous accounts of the drama. That is the story behind this book on Valley Forge, which I think will surprise readers as much as it has surprised me.

As I began to research the subject, I assumed my theme would be the clash between history and memory. With more than a dozen books on the American Revolution on my escutcheon, I already knew more than a little about Valley Forge. I looked forward to reporting on recent research that exploded myths about the freezing weather, the reasons for the soldiers' nakedness and starvation, and the ethnic composition of Washington's army.

The overarching drama, as I saw it, was still the stubborn endurance of Washington's soldiers and their emergence from the ordeal with their patriotism enriched by a new sense of solidarity. I hoped to enlarge this portrait with fresh, presumably vivid details.

As my files began to bulge with data from diaries and letters, archives and collections, the surprise began to emerge before my disbelieving eyes.

There was another explanation for the Continental Army's survival at Valley Forge—one that added an unexpected personal element to the story.

A new George Washington—or at least a new side of this often oversimplified man—gathered force and substance in my flies. This Washington was not the long-suffering general who did little in the six months at Valley Forge but bemoan the condition of his starving half-naked army in letters to state governors and Continental congressman. He was a man who confronted not only the threat of his army's collapse, he also resisted the ruin of his reputation as a leader and a patriot, and struck back at his enemies with ferocity and guile.

Even before his shoeless, shirtless, blanketless soldiers trudged to Valley Forge, General Washington was under savage attack by critics in the Continental Congress and in the upper ranks of his army. While the Americans headed for their bare bones winter camp in the bleak hills, twenty miles away the British army was luxuriating in Philadelphia, the American capital that Washington had failed to defend.

More and more people concluded it was time to replace this fallen idol with a more reliable and experienced general. How Washington responded to these attacks, the way he identified and challenged or outmaneuvered his clandestine enemies, and found allies in the Continental Congress began to evoke a word in my mind: *politician*. It troubled me at first. Washington is usually portrayed as a man who transcended politics. For too many Americans, politician connotes trickster, grandstander, schemer.

The political Washington who was emerging from my research was none of the above. He was a good politician in every sense of the word. Shrewd and tough when he needed to be, he was also adept at forming alliances with men like Henry Laurens, the president of the Continental Congress, who began as one of his critics.

Washington never lost sight of his goal, which was not a petty personal triumph over his adversaries but the rescue of his army, which he rightly saw as America's sole hope of victory in a long, bloody war. To achieve that aim, he had to out think the conspirators who sought to destroy him and persuade others to out vote the congressional ideologues whose wrongheaded policies were the source of the Continental Army's woes.

In the end, Washington forced the naysayers and name callers to accept new men and new measures, selected and conceived by the embattled commander in chief. He also put an end to the slanderous campagin against his personal reputation, which was endangering the army almost as much as incompetence and ignorance in high places.

Washington's success in this secret war is all the more amazing because he achieved it while managing to keep the Continental Army from dissolving into mutiny and dispersal at Valley Forge. His political skills were bolstered by the power of his personality and his intelligence. This big Virginian not only looked like a leader, he understood and accepted leadership's responsibilities. He devoted serious amounts of time and energy to this secret war, often keeping several contentious balls in the air at the same time.

George Washington's political performance at Valley Forge is nothing less than a tour de force that adds a new dimension to his historical portrait. To my continuing surprise, it has become the heart of this book. Among other things, I hope it will restore respectability to that much misunderstood word, *politician*.

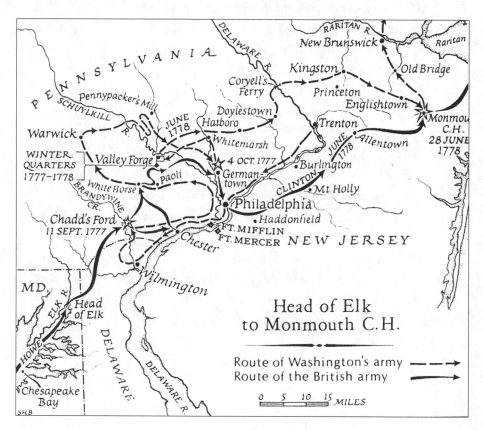

Head of Elk to Monmouth C.H.

Route of Washington's army — — — →
Route of the British army ———→

0   5   10   15 MILES

1. This overview of the 1777-1778 struggle in Pennsylvania tracks the British landing at Head of Elk on Chesapeake Bay and the battles and maneuvers that led to the capture of Philadelphia, followed by Washington's decision to winter at Valley Forge. Six months later the British retreated from the American capital and the two armies clashed again at Monmouth Court House in New Jersey.

ONE

GENERAL GEORGE
WASHINGTON: LOSER

O N DECEMBER 19, 1777, beneath lowering gray skies, with snow swirling in a savage north wind, soldiers of the Continental Army of the United States of America trudged up the narrow sloping Gulph Road—a rutted dirt track whose modern concrete descendant bears the same eerily symbolic name. Their destination was a mix of wooded tableland and forbidding hills called "the Valley-Forge."

The marchers were coming from the very Gulph itself, a name 1726 roadbuilders had fastened on a brooding chasm in the southeastern Pennsylvania hills where the army had spent the previous five days.[1] Connecticut surgeon's mate Albigence Waldo thought it was "not an improper name . . . for this Gulph seems well adapted . . . to keep us from the pleasures & enjoyments of this world."[2]

Behind the marchers in the wintry Pennsylvania countryside lay a landscape of defeat. At Brandywine Creek and Germantown, these soldiers had given battle to George III's redcoated battalions and lost. They had marched and countermarched across the autumn countryside until they were groggy with fatigue—while their shoes disintegrated and their rations dwindled to the vanishing point. Now, while these half-starved sons of liberty bent into the icy wind, their misery was redoubled by

thoughts of the victorious devotees of royal authority in Philadelphia,
feasting and drinking at its numerous taverns, enjoying the comforts of
feather beds and warm fires in its hundreds of handsome houses.

This city of more than thirty thousand wealthy merchants and prosperous artisans and charming women had been the prize that the Americans had struggled to defend—and failed. It was a painful, demoralizing
loss. Philadelphia was the largest city in America and the third largest in
the British empire. Only Dublin and of course London were bigger and
more splendid examples of Great Britain's global wealth and power.

In the previous three tumultuous years, the City of Brotherly Love, as
its Quaker founders had optimistically christened Philadelphia, had become the capital of the rebellious American confederacy. From the redbrick
Pennsylvania statehouse, eighteen months ago the Continental Congress
had issued the Declaration of Independence, creating a new country out of
thirteen disparate and often disputatious colonies—and inspiring many
people to begin calling Philadelphia "the Rome of America."

Almost as important as its political significance was Philadelphia's role
as the engine of a regional economy that included the farmers of western
New Jersey, southeastern Pennsylvania, Delaware, and northern Maryland. In the early 1770s, the city had exported staggering amounts of
wheat—as much as fifty-seven thousand tons (114 million pounds) in a
single year—to a Europe struggling with growing populations and poor
harvests. (This was enough flour to feed an army of 240,000 men.) Add to
this annual avalanche of grain thousands of tons of salted meat and bar
iron from numerous nearby forges, plus lumber and other products.
Philadelphia's exports frequently totaled $40 million (roughly $600 million in modern money) a year—a potent glimpse of why an overtaxed England thought it was time for the Americans to pay a share of the costs of
running the empire. More pertinent to the fate of the plodding soldiers on
the Gulph Road was the likelihood that a British grip on Philadelphia
could lead to the demoralization—even the capitulation—of the entire
region, which had become dependent on the city's ability to turn farm and
forge surpluses into ready money.[3]

This dismaying possibility was not a primary or even a secondary thought in the minds of the trudging rank and file. They were concerned with more mundane matters, such as the bitter cold and the absence of food in their gnawing bellies. One of the youngest marchers, seventeen-year-old Private Joseph Plumb Martin of Connecticut, remembered the Gulph as a place where "starvation *rioted* in its glory."[4]

While the army camped in this chasm in the hills, the Continental Congress ordered the men to join the rest of their embryo nation in a day of Thanksgiving on December 18, 1777. The reason for this seemingly improbable summons? Two months earlier, near Saratoga in the state of New York, a British army led by an overconfident general named John Burgoyne had been defeated and forced to surrender by a "Northern" American army, led by a British-born general named Horatio Gates. The men on the march from the Gulph felt scarcely a glimmer of gratitude for this victory. They were too acutely conscious of their own military disappointments. Along with the two battlefield defeats, they had lost painful lesser encounters. At Paoli, an American division had been ambushed and massacred. On the Delaware River, two forts that had tried to deny the Royal Navy access to Philadelphia had been blasted into rubble by British men-of-war after weeks of heroic resistance.

A glum Lieutenant Colonel Henry Dearborn of Massachusetts told his journal: "God knows we have little to keep it [Thanksgiving] with this being the third day we have been without flour or bread—& are . . . laying on the cold ground, upon the whole I think all we have to be thankful for is that we are alive and not in the grave with most of our friends."[5]

Lieutenant Samuel Armstrong of the Ninth Massachusetts Regiment was no less unhappy but took a more positive approach toward rectifying his discontents. "We had neither bread nor meat 'till just before night when we had some fresh beef, without any bread or flour. . . . Mr. Commissary did not intend we shou'd keep a day of rejoicing—but however we sent out a scout for some fowls and by night he return'd with one dozen: we distributed them among our fellow sufferers three we roast'd two we boil'd and borrowed a few potatoes upon those we supp'd without any bread or anything stronger than water to drink!"[6]

Private Joseph Plumb Martin was not so fortunate as Armstrong and his fellow officers. "We had nothing to eat for two or three days previous," he recalled, "except what the trees of the fields and forests afforded us. But now we must have what Congress said: a sumptuous thanksgiving." With savage sarcasm, Martin reported what the brigade commissary gave him and his fellow privates. It was, he recalled, something that "our country, ever mindful of its suffering army, opened her sympathizing heart" to procure: two ounces of rice and (to prevent dysentery) a tablespoon of vinegar.

Following this feast, the men were marched to an open field to listen to a Thanksgiving sermon, while Martin's stomach kept reminding him of bountiful Thanksgivings past in his native Connecticut. These memories only became more acute when he and the rest of his regiment trudged back to their tents for a supper that consisted of "a leg of nothing and no turnips."[7]

II

The day before the soldiers endured this hollow Thanksgiving celebration, their commander in chief, George Washington, had addressed them in his general orders. He had thanked them for the "fortitude and patience with which they have sustained the fatigues of the campaign." With a candor rare among generals and even rarer among politicians, Washington ruefully admitted that "in some instances we unfortunately failed."

Yet on the whole, he added, "heaven has smiled on our arms and crowned them with signal success"—a generous tribute to the victors at Saratoga. There was good reason to hope that the "end [goal] of our warfare—Independence—Liberty and Peace" was within reach. While the power of America alone, if fully exerted, was enough to challenge the force of Britain, there was an added reason for hope: "France yields us every aid we ask" and there were "reasons to believe" she would soon join them "in war against the British crown." Most of the men knew that American diplomats, led by Benjamin Franklin, had been in Paris for more than a year, trying to persuade the French to sign a treaty of alliance.

Next Washington confessed that "the General ardently wishes it were now in his power to conduct the troops to the best winter quarters." Alas, this ideal refuge did not exist. Nearby towns were crowded with refugees from British-occupied Philadelphia. It was vital for the army to remain close to the capital. Otherwise a "vast extent of fertile country" would be "despoiled and ravaged" by the enemy. So they were going to camp in the vicinity of the Gulph, in a place where "huts may be erected that will be warm and dry." He was referring to Valley Forge—a name that at this point meant nothing to 95 percent of the men in the ranks.

General Washington closed this frank message by exhorting officers and soldiers to be "of one heart and one mind . . . to surmount every difficulty with a fortitude and patience becoming their profession and the sacred cause to which they are engaged."[8]

III

To not a few members of the army, the commander in chief was whistling in the dark. Few were more saturnine than Major General Johann de Kalb, the burly fifty-six-year-old German-born professional soldier who had crossed the Atlantic at the behest of the French government, hoping to lend military expertise to the Americans' revolution. After four months with the Continental Army, de Kalb was a disillusioned man, and the choice of Valley Forge for winter quarters seemed to signal the final ruin of his hopes. He condemned the site as a "wooded wilderness, certainly one of the poorest districts in Pennsylvania; the soil thin, uncultivated, and almost uninhabited, without forage and without provisions!"[9]

Worse, as far as de Kalb was concerned, "we are to lie in shanties, generals and privates." He grimly concluded that "the idea of wintering in this desert can only have been put in the head of the commanding general by an interested speculator or a disaffected man."

That comment revealed General de Kalb's low opinion of George Washington. He had characterized him in recent letters to France as "the weakest general" he had ever seen, a man who let Congress or close advisers among his aides and subordinate generals persuade him to succumb to bad advice, again and again.[10]

General de Kalb was not the only French officer with a negative opinion of the faltering revolution. On November 12, 1777, Brigadier General Louis Duportail, a gifted engineer, had written to the French minister of war: "Such are the people that they move without spring or energy . . . and without a passion for the cause in which they are engaged, and in which they follow only as the hand which puts them in motion directs. There is a hundred times more enthusiasm for this Revolution in any one coffee house at Paris than in the thirteen provinces united."[11]

Still another French volunteer, the tall, angular Marquis de Lafayette, was equally shocked by the widespread lack of enthusiasm for the Revolution. Unlike de Kalb and Duportail, who were agents of the French government, this immensely wealthy twenty-year-old idealist had come to America as a volunteer in the cause of liberty. He had been elevated to the rank of major general because his father-in-law, the Duc D'Ayen, was an influential figure at the court of King Louis XVI.

"When I was in Europe," Lafayette told George Washington in labored, recently acquired English, "I thought here almost every man was a lover of liberty and rather die free than live [a] slave. You can conceive my astonishment," he continued, when he discovered that loyalty to George III was as frequently professed by many Americans as devotion to the newborn republic. Lafayette had also arrived under the illusion that "all good Americans were united together." Instead, he had discovered "dissensions in Congress, parties who hate one another as much as the enemy itself."[12]

The champion in any competition for foreign disillusion was Brigadier General Thomas Conway. This pop-eyed forty-four-year-old Irish-born French colonel could talk war and battles with almost overpowering verbiage. He had impressed Lafayette with his military expertise and his readiness to impart it to the youthful volunteer. But Conway's prissy mouth and patronizing manner had failed to charm most American officers. Conway was not only disillusioned with Valley Forge and the American war effort; he had become convinced that George Washington was incompetent and had to be replaced as commander in chief as soon as possible. He was working hard to spread this message to the Continental Congress and anyone else who would listen.

IV

There was another explanation for this Gallic gloom, beyond the choice of Valley Forge and the lackluster performance of Washington's army. The British triumph in the Seven Years' War (1754–61), which was called the French and Indian War in America, had stripped France of Canada and other colonies and elevated Britain to the status of the premier world power. Paris had been waiting fifteen years for revenge.

Marshal Victor Francois de Broglie, the French commander in that lost war, had sent de Kalb, Duportail, and a dozen other officers to America with orders to persuade Congress to appoint him commander in chief of the American army. From a French point of view, that would not only guarantee victory, but might turn the thirteen colonies into a satellite from which large military and political advantages could be gained, not to mention satisfying amounts of money for all concerned.

De Kalb had been in this covert game for quite a while. In 1768, when the American colonies were growing restive, he had visited America incognito and toured the main centers of resistance. He had reported to his superiors that the moment had not yet come: the Americans had too many Protestant prejudices and hostile memories of French and Indian ferocity in the Seven Years' War and earlier colonial wars to consider an alliance with Catholic France. Morever, the revolutionary movement was still disorganized and incoherent.

Not until 1775, after gunfire at Lexington and Concord, the all-out battle on Bunker (actually Breed's) Hill, and the rapid spread of a shooting war north into Canada, did Paris decide that secret intervention might be worth a try. Through dummy companies in Paris, they began shipping weapons and ammunition to the rebels. When 1776 produced a series of British victories that seemed to presage an imminent American collapse, the French had second thoughts—until George Washington temporarily rescued the situation with his Christmas night raid across the Delaware River. The Americans captured almost a thousand men at Trenton and followed it with another triumph at Princeton a week later. Paris decided maybe a victory was still possible—if the Americans took orders from French professional soldiers.

Unfortunately for French dreams of glory (and cash), the Americans had proven to be averse to foreign military guidance. American generals, having risked their necks and reputations on numerous battlefields in the previous two years, were unenthused by the prospect of taking orders from Frenchmen who stepped off ships with contracts signed by American diplomats in Paris, declaring them brigadiers and major generals. The reception from the American generals was so hostile that all thoughts of pushing Marshal de Broglie into a commander in chief's role were abandoned. This left more than a few of these French warriors in a very disgruntled mood.

Lafayette was a wild card in this Gallic dissonance. He was not part of his government's plan to take charge of the American Revolution. In fact, he had defied and ultimately evaded King Louis XVI's orders to abandon his impulse to fight in the cause of liberty. A French contemporary critical of the Marquis would later say liberty was the only idea Lafayette ever had, but fortunately for him it was the idea of the century.

The Marquis' father had been killed fighting the English when Lafayette was two. His mother had abandoned him in the Lafayette chateau in Auvergne to be raised by his grandmother, and departed for Paris. When both his mother and her father died unexpectedly, the Marquis had inherited an immense fortune at the age of thirteen. By this time he was in Paris, where he grew into a gangling youth with a long nose and sloping chin who could not seem to do anything right. He became the laughingstock of the city when he fell on his face while dancing a quadrille with Queen Marie Antoinette.

The Marquis compounded this social disaster by entering an arranged marriage with wealthy Adrienne de Noailles at the age of fifteen—and falling in love with his wife. No self-respecting French aristocrat of the era would have been guilty of such a gaffe. To rescue the shreds of his reputation, Lafayette challenged his best friend to a duel over a French beauty who would not even speak to him. The Duc D'Ayen soon concluded his son-in-law was hopeless. Lafayette's mission to America was in equal parts a desire to escape the sneers of sophisticated Paris and a determination to win fame as a soldier and make his critics squirm.

The Marquis' complicated past was undoubtedly a strong influence on his growing friendship with George Washington. The commander in chief was beginning to emerge as the father Lafayette never had. For the childless forty-five-year-old Washington, the ebullient Frenchman was becoming a kind of son. He had proven his courage at Brandywine, the first of the major clashes in the campaign for Philadelphia, staying on the battlefield in spite of a painful leg wound. He also wrote a stream of letters to his father-in-law and others in and around Louis XVI's court, defending Washington's role in this embarrassing defeat.

Washington's own past had some interesting similarities to Lafayette's. His father had died when George was eleven, leaving him at the mercy of a domineering mother with a viper's tongue and a fierce temper. He grew up to be amazingly tall (six two and a half in an era when most men averaged five seven). He too had been something of a bumpkin when he began living at Mount Vernon, then owned by his older brother Lawrence. Sophisticated neighbors left him feeling awkward and tongue-tied with women. He had gravitated to a military career to prove himself—which he soon did in sensational fashion in the French and Indian War.

General Washington took Lafayette's letter about American disunity seriously. He admitted there were dissensions swirling through Congress and the army. Drawing on the worldly wisdom he had acquired in his mature years, Washington urged the Marquis not to lose faith in the cause of liberty. "We must not, in so great a contest, expect to meet with nothing but sunshine." He was certain they would "triumph over all our misfortunes," and afterward Lafayette would join him at Mount Vernon, where they would "laugh at our past difficulties and the folly of others." [13]

Lafayette's reply was nothing less than fervent. He had not thought the commander in chief would have time to answer his letter, but now he had to tell Washington how much pleasure the reply gave him. "Every assurance and proof of your affection fills my heart with joy." There is no doubt that the sentiment was genuine on both sides of this paternal equation. Neither man realized at the time that their friendship would soon have a profound impact on Washington's survival as leader of the Continental Army.[14]

V

There were plenty of Americans who thought General Washington's choice of Valley Forge for a winter camp was a terrible idea. Brigadier General James Mitchell Varnum of Rhode Island, a loquacious lawyer in civilian life, viewed the place "with horror." Working himself into a hyperbolic fury, Varnum declared it was "unparalleled in the history of mankind to establish winter quarters in a country[side] wasted and without a single magazine."[15]

Brigadier General Jedediah Huntington of Connecticut, who usually struggled to see the bright side of a situation, was another officer who admitted doubts about Valley Forge. "I hope it is for the best that we are stationed here though I must say I do not see it," he told his father the day after he and his men arrived. "We are watching [guarding] a country that has little to reward us." He meant that the surrounding countryside, which included some of the most productive soil in America, had been ransacked by both armies during the campaign for Philadelphia. It seemed all but devoid of supplies for the army.[16]

Several other American generals had been inclined to retreat deeper into Pennsylvania, to Reading or Lancaster, where the army would be in a position to protect warehouses full of ammunition and other crucial war matériel. But the problem Washington pointed out in his general orders— these towns were already full of refugees from Philadelphia and could not possibly house another fourteen thousand military strangers—cast doubt on this idea. Other generals pushed for Wilmington, Delaware, a pleasant town of fine brick houses at the mouth of the Delaware River. They pointed out that Valley Forge, twenty miles west of Philadelphia, was not close enough to prevent the British from foraging for supplies in other parts of the rich agricultural arc around the city.

Also in the argument were the leaders of the revolutionary government of Pennsylvania, who let it be known that they wanted the army to stay close enough to Philadelphia to mount an attack on the British in the city or at least contend with their attempts to forage in the countryside. General Washington, after consulting with Brigadier General Anthony Wayne, who had been born a few miles away, had opted for Valley Forge as the best available compromise.

VI

In his memoirs of Washington, a best seller in the nineteenth century, the general's stepgrandson, George Washington Parke Custis, described a touching scene on the march from the Gulph. When Washington and his usual mounted escort rode to the head of the plodding column, the colonel of the leading regiment ordered his men to halt and present arms to salute the general. As Washington rode slowly past them, returning the salute, he beckoned the colonel to join him. "How comes it sir," he asked, "that I have tracked the march of your troops by the bloodstains of their feet upon the frozen ground? Were there no shoes in the commissary stores, that this sad spectacle is to be seen along the public highways?"

The officer replied: "Your Excellency may rest assured that this sight is as painful to my feelings as it is to yours; but there is no remedy within our reach. When the shoes were issued, the different regiments were served; and the stores became exhausted before we could obtain even the smallest supply!"

Washington was "observed to be deeply affected" by this report, Custis wrote. "His compressed lips, the heaving of his manly chest, betokened the powerful emotions that were struggling in his bosom." Washington turned away and "with a voice tremulous yet kindly" exclaimed, "Poor fellows," and rode on. The soldiers, hearing these compassionate words, replied: "God bless your excellency, your poor soldiers' friend." It was, Custis concluded, a glimpse of Washington's "native goodness of heart." [17]

There is a core of truth in this story. George Washington did feel deep sympathy for his suffering men, and they knew it. There was a bond between these soldiers and the tall, seemingly aloof Virginian that had spiritual as well as patriotic dimensions. It will play a large part in the hidden story of Valley Forge. But the encounter on the Gulph Road never happened. The story is typical of the way nineteenth-century writers attempted to dramatize Valley Forge as a place of pathetic misery for the enlisted men—while distancing General Washington and the Continental Congress from their pain.

By December 19, 1777, Washington knew that far more than one unlucky regiment in his army lacked shoes. He had been receiving cries of distress about disintegrating footwear (and clothing) for months. On December 1, 1777, Brigadier General George Weedon of Virginia told Washington his men lacked shoes, as well as warm clothing and blankets. On the same day, Major General John Sullivan of New Hampshire reported that a third of his men were "without shoes, stockings or breeches."

Two days later, Major General William Alexander (also known as Lord Stirling—he claimed the title of a Scottish ancestor) told the American commander that half the men in his division were "walking barefooted on the ice or frozen ground." On the same day, Major General Nathanael Greene of Rhode Island made an identical estimate—half his men were "without breeches shoes or stockings."

Private Joseph Plumb Martin confirmed these cries of alarm in his memoir. "The greatest part" of the army "were . . . shirtless and barefoot." Martin told how he fashioned crude moccasins from a piece of "raw cowhide," but he soon gave them up because the hard edges cut deep ridges in his ankles. Thereafter he went barefoot "as hundreds of my companions had to."

As for the army distributing shoes to barefoot regiments, on December 3, James Mease, the clothier general, sent Washington a report of the warehouses in Lancaster: there was a smattering of coats (two hundred), breeches (thirty), and hats (fifty), and a grand total of ninety pairs of shoes. In a follow-up letter on December 16 Mease added that he had a terrible cold and his generally "weakened" constitution made it necessary for him to quit his job.[18]

Was America incapable of producing shoes for its soldiers? By no means. The image of the primitive frontier clings to the American Revolution. In fact, America had been settled for 150 years, and a surprisingly mature economy had long since evolved. On October 19, 1777, Elias Boudinot, a wealthy New Jerseyan from Elizabethtown, wrote to Timothy Pickering, the Continental Army's adjutant general, about the soldiers' shoelessness. "I have an offer from three substantial men immediately to erect a large tannery in a secure place." These men were prepared to tan from 1,500 to 2,000 hides a year and make shoes out of them. "Had attention been paid to this last spring many thousands of pairs of shoes might have now been ready."[19]

Why was no attention paid to this the previous spring? The answer was the wrongheaded policies of the Continental Congress, which insisted on trying to manage all aspects of running the war, without the knowledge or skill to do the job. The congressmen appointed second- or third-raters like James Mease to clothe and feed the army and never bothered to find out if they were doing it. Worst of all, they did not think anyone should make money out of the war. Patriotism should be the only emotion motivating everyone from politicians to army privates.

Congress's reaction to every problem was to give it to a committee. In 1777 the solons created 114 of these creatures, and in 1778 the number was 253. Before the war ended, the total hit 3,249. Most were three-man affairs, with members chosen with little or no reference to their expertise or abilities, which meant they were usually incapable of getting much done. As early as 1775, Congress had to appoint a committee on committees to keep track of who was doing what. General Washington often complained of being bombarded with queries from so many different committees that he wondered if he would have time to fight the war.[20]

This fundamental flaw had been identified by many participants in Congress. Merchant Robert Morris summed it up bluntly in a 1776 letter to Benjamin Franklin and his fellow diplomats in Paris. "As long as [Congress] persist[s] in the attempt to execute as well as deliberate on their business, it will never be done as it ought. . . . this has been urged many a time by myself and others, but some of them do not like to part with power."[21]

Meanwhile, the congressmen carped at General Washington's performance. From the temporary capital of York, Pennsylvania, after the

American army had suffered a second major defeat at the Battle of Germantown, Henry Laurens of South Carolina wrote his twenty-two-year-old son John who was serving as one of the commander in chief's aides.

"I am writing in Congress & in the midst of much talk . . . buz! [*sic*] says one:

"'I would if I had been commander of that army with such powers have procured all necessities which are said to be wanted without such whining complaints.'

"'I would, says 2nd, have prevented the amazing desertions which have happened, it only takes proper attention at fountain head' 3d 'It is very easy too to prevent intercourse between the army and the enemy & as easy to gain intelligence but we never mind who comes in & who goes out of our camp.'

"In short our army is under no regulation nor discipline &c &c &c." [22]

Adding to this negative chorus were members of the revolutionary government of Pennsylvania, which had fled to Lancaster after the fall of Philadelphia. One of their leaders, Christopher Marshall, informed his diary that many people were unhappy with the "weak conduct of General Washington." They said his "slackness and remissness" in the management of the army were so conspicuous that there was growing fear of a "general langor" that would lead to a total collapse. [23]

VII

The almost unbelievable destitution of the American army was the chief reason why the weary soldiers were marching to Valley Forge. It was literally impossible for men verging on nakedness to undertake winter combat with the warmly clothed enemy, something that both the Continental Congress and Pennsylvania's revolutionary Assembly wanted them to do. Major General John Sullivan opined that the army would barely survive, even if "placed in the warmest houses during the winter." All of them lacked heavy "watch coats," half had no blankets, and not a few were without shirts. The voluble General Varnum for once put it succinctly in another letter to Washington: "I am fully convinced that your troops should immediately go in to quiet peaceable winter quarters. . . . The hospitals are crouded [sic] with sick and invalids, occasioned in a great measure by the want of cloathing [sic] and rest." Virginia's General Weedon told Washington that a third of the army was "more fitting for a hospital than the camp." The soldiers were "destitute of every comfort."[24]

As early as September 21, 1777, Washington was writing to his aide, twenty-two-year-old Lieutenant Colonel Alexander Hamilton, "The distressed situation of the army for want of blankets and many necessary articles of clothing is truly deplorable." But there was little or nothing he could do about it. For one thing, he was heavily involved in a campaign with a well-equipped, resourceful enemy who was trying to destroy his army or capture Philadelphia, or both.[25]

Washington got no help from the Continental Congress. On November 14, 1777, the politicians had piously informed him that they had "long since" written to France ordering eighty thousand complete uniforms which had, alas, not yet arrived. They also reported they had sent a circular letter to the governors and assemblies of the thirteen states, urging them to persuade their citizens to contribute clothing and blankets to the army. This plea also had no delivery date attached to it. Since "the wants of the army are immediate," the solons authorized Washington to seize clothing from the "disaffected inhabitants" of Pennsylvania.[26]

"Disaffected" was a polite term for loyalist. This in itself was an embarrassing admission—there were enough people loyal to George III in the second largest state in the shaky American union to relieve the clothing problems of an army of fourteen thousand men. The solution also omitted exactly how this requisition from an unwilling populace was to be managed while face-to-face with an enemy army. Further boggling the process was a dolorous fact pointed out by Major General Arthur St. Clair: the politicians "seem to have forgotten how much the inhabitants of this state have already been stripped."[27]

Another complication was Washington's reluctance to use the power of search and seizure that the Continental Congress had given him. He was always aware that he was fighting a war for civilian hearts and minds as well as for military victory. When he sent Colonel Hamilton to Philadelphia with orders to seize whatever was portable for the use of the army shortly before the city fell, the general urged him to utilize "as much delicacy and discretion as the business demands." Washington did not agree with Congress's smug assumption that the "well-disposed" people would "rather be pleased than dissatisfied" with plundering the disaffected. These people were neighbors and friends and often members of the same family. Moreover, as Washington politely pointed out to Henry Laurens, now the president of Congress, Americans had become accustomed to obeying civil authorities, but they had a tradition of viewing military power "with a jealous & suspicious eye." [28]

VIII

While Washington was deciding to winter at Valley Forge, he was also continuing to fight a war for a continent. Letters poured into his headquarters at the Gulph, where he remained until December 20 (further invalidating George Washington Parke Custis's story about his encounter with shoeless soldiers on December 19). From New York, Major General Israel Putnam reported on a disastrous expedition across Long Island Sound to British-held Long Island in which sixty men and numerous officers from colonels to lieutenants were captured by a Royal Navy frigate. The aging hero of Bunker Hill, whose wife had recently died, requested permission to go home to Connecticut to settle his affairs. Washington told him he could not be spared. [29]

Meanwhile, Washington was reading a long letter from Governor George Clinton of New York, which the commander in chief had solicited. It was a confidential report on the inadequacies of "Old Put" as the general in command of the vital forts in the Hudson Highlands and the lines around British-held New York City. The British had captured the Highlands forts with almost ridiculous ease when they sent a force up the Hudson to try to help the trapped Burgoyne. In the lines around New

York City, things were much too relaxed. People came and went virtually at will under innumerable flags of truce. It was all too clear that Putnam was not up to the job.[30]

William Shippen, the director of the American army's hospitals, wanted to know if he should set up a hospital in Princeton, New Jersey. With scarcely concealed impatience, Washington replied that Princeton was a poor idea because a British foray could capture the sick men in a day's march from Philadelphia. Shippen set it up anyway.

The recently captured General Burgoyne requested permission to sail home to England in advance of his troops, who under the surrender terms signed at Saratoga were to return to Europe. Washington forwarded his letter to Congress, which was already at work on repudiating the peculiar "convention" that Burgoyne had worked out when he surrendered to General Horatio Gates. Under its terms, the captives were to be permitted to go home, with a promise not to fight in North America again. It seems never to have occured to General Gates that they could be switched with troops in Ireland or England, and British strength in North America would be undiminished.[31]

Loyalist leader Joseph Galloway wrote to Washington, asking permission for his wife, Grace, to join him in Philadelphia. She was living at their country house, and Galloway hoped she could bring her "household furniture and effects" with her. Washington replied that he would immediately prepare a passport for Mrs. Galloway but she could not bring furniture or anything else with her. The Pennsylvania Assembly had decreed that all loyalists had forfeited their property to the state. It was a graphic glimpse of the savage civil war that was raging throughout Pennsylvania, immensely complicating the problem of feeding Washington's army.[32]

Another letter revealed a primary Washington worry, the haphazard way the states were filling their quotas for troops. Washington told Richard Peters, secretary of the Board of War, an entity created by Congress to help them administer the army, that most of the men of nine Virginia regiments had been permitted to return home on furloughs because their one-year enlistments were expiring in February. He hoped this considerate gesture would encourage them to reenlist for three years or the duration of the war, the terms on which most of the men in the army were serving. Also a worry were a "considerable number" of troops from Massachusetts and Connecticut who had been drafted for eight months and would go home on January 1. These departures would "weaken us more than is proper" now that the Americans had decided to winter near the enemy to protect the countryside around Philadelphia.[33]

IX

Also on Washington's crowded desk were numerous secret service reports. The American commander in chief was on his way to becoming an accomplished spymaster. Perhaps the most interesting was a letter from the Continental Navy Board. Francis Hopkinson, who combined poetry and songwriting with radical politics (he was a signer of the Declaration of Independence) wrote from Bordentown, New Jersey, on the Delaware River above Philadelphia that "we have done everything in our power to forward the work in hand," and he had the pleasure of reporting that "everything goes on with secrecy and dispatch, to the satisfaction of the Artist."[34]

The Artist was David Bushnell, an engineering genius who had built the world's first submarine, the *Turtle*, in 1775. The vessel had attacked a British ship of the line in New York Harbor in the fall of 1776 but had failed to sink her. Bushnell was hard at work on another nautical device which he hoped would spread havoc among the British men-of-war in the Delaware off Philadelphia.

Across Washington's desk also flowed report after report from Major John Clark Jr., who was sending spies into Philadelphia on a daily basis to find out what the British were thinking and doing. Most of the agents went into the city carrying provisions provided by Clark to sell to the British. It was hazardous work for Clark and his operatives. He reported that one man came within an ace of being seized by a British sentry when another would-be food seller pointed him out as "a damned rebel." The spy put spurs to his horse and escaped. Later in the day, the spy came upon his betrayer being questioned by a patrolling American horseman. The rattled squealer made the mistake of asking the spy to confirm his loyalty to the American cause. Clark forwarded the double-talker's name to Washington, hoping that an example would be made of him.[35]

Clark also complained mightily about another spy, a woman, who was taken by an American patrol that apparently ignored the passes Clark gave his agents. The officer in command of the patrol told one of his men to escort her to the colonel of their regiment for questioning. On the road the man suggested he was ready to let her go into the city with her provisions if she would "permit him to use *certain freedoms* with her (which her modesty and virtue would not admit)." The indignant Clark wanted to know if Washington thought this was "conduct becoming freemen." If the licentious culprit was not punished, "farewell Virtue—Religion & Liberty!"

The protest was a glimpse of how some Americans saw the Revolution as a kind of spiritual as well as military package, with virtuous individual conduct a crucial part of the enterprise. Others, such as the amorous escort, were much less idealistic about their roles.[36]

By and large, Clark's spies reported good news about the British in the City of Brotherly Love. They were showing no inclination to make a foray in Washington's direction. ("There is no talk at present of their moving.") Instead they were ringing the outskirts of the city with formidable redoubts. But a very large problem remained: "The country people carry in provision constantly." While this made it easy for Clark to send in spies, he knew that Washington was determined to put the enemy on rations as short as the Continental Army's, if possible.[37]

From Major General John Armstrong, an old Washington friend from the French and Indian War, now commander of the Pennsylvania militia, came a worrisome epistle. Armstrong had been assigned the task of blockading Philadelphia. He reported that the Continental Army's quartermaster department had left muskets, tents, empty wagons, and entrenching tools (ten or fifteen wagonloads of the latter) scattered all over the landscape, and Armstrong was trying to collect them before the British did.

The biggest worry in General Armstrong's letter was geographic. There were nine "capitol" [sic] roads to Philadelphia, plus numerous byroads, to be guarded. This meant he had to divide his militiamen into small groups, making them vulnerable to British attacks. Meanwhile the country people were "beginning to crowd upon me" in their eagerness to sell food to the British, who paid for it in "hard money" instead of the paper dollars printed by Congress in ever increasing—and depreciating—millions.[38]

Yet another Washington worry was Wilmington, Delaware. Should he occupy it? Major John Clark Jr.'s intelligence system may have helped him make up his mind. On December 19, before the army departed from the Gulph, Washington wrote to George Read, the temporary president of Delaware's ruling council, that he had "rec'd information" that the British planned to seize the town to bolster the numerous loyalists in the tiny state. Washington decided to send Continental troops under Brigadier General William Smallwood of Maryland to occupy Wilmington.

The troops were few and the chances were good that the British might try to attack them. Washington urged Read to call out the Delaware militia to bolster Smallwood's force. There was no time to be lost. He advised Read to order the militia to march by companies or even parts of companies to Wilmington. This letter was a gesture Washington probably knew was futile. Militia seldom turned out in Delaware, because they were liable to get their houses burned down and their cattle slaughtered. Congressman John Harvie of Virginia told Thomas Jefferson: "Two thirds of the state of Delaware are notoriously known in their hearts to be with our enemys." Delaware seldom sent delegates to Congress.[39]

When General Smallwood and his 1,200-man brigade reached Wilmington, the reception they received was grim proof that Washington had made the right decision. The men in the lead regiment were wearing red coats captured from the British. A large number of Wilmingtonians rushed to greet them with cheers and cries of "God save the king!" Several mistook Smallwood for a British general and eagerly informed him that they had hidden plenty of "good mutton and fine fat Hogs," which they were ready to sell. The loyalists swiftly learned the newcomers were not British and found themselves in jail, while their hidden mutton and pork made a nice Christmas dinner for the rebels. For once, the Continental Army's shortage of clothing had paid a positive dividend.[40]

X

By the end of snowy December 19, the bedraggled, freezing Continentals had completed their trek up the Gulph Road to Valley Forge. The place did not look much more encouraging than the Gulph. Thick woods, many of them filled with ancient oaks five feet in circumference, surrounded the elongated plateau on which the army was to camp. Here and there were patches of farmland, long since harvested of their wheat, rye, or corn. A scattering of small houses offered no hope of refuge from the cold. Looming over the plateau was a steep-sided hill christened Mount Joy by William Penn a hundred years before. Behind it, on the other side of Valley Creek, was another mountain, with a more appropriate name: Mount Misery. The mountains, the creek, the nearby Schuylkill River to the east, were ready-made defenses, and the slope to the plateau could be fortified with redoubts and trenches that would guarantee reasonable security against an enemy assault.

None of these positive features were visible to the exhausted Continentals on that first bitterly cold night. Most of them huddled in icy tents; many without blankets dozed beside hastily built fires. Not only were they short of food, but many were thirsty. In the darkness few realized that Valley Creek, which had powered the forge that gave the place its name, was a half mile away.

Private Joseph Plumb Martin recalled "perishing with thirst" and "search[ing] for water till I was weary without finding any." The ground was coated with snow but it was too thin to collect and melt as a substitute for water. When Martin saw two soldiers from another regiment swigging from their canteens, he asked them where they had gotten the water. They told him they had located Valley Creek, but it was too dark for him to repeat their journey. Martin asked them for a drink. They shook their heads, "rigid as Arabs," obviously determined to share their liquid find with no one. A desperate Martin finally offered to buy a drink and gave them a threepenny paper note in Pennsylvania currency, which he wryly observed was "every cent of property I could then call my own."

When General Washington arrived the next day, he pitched his large marquee tent for himself and his aides instead of taking shelter in one of the nearby houses. He wanted to show the men his readiness to share their suffering. Many of his brigadiers and major generals felt no such compunction. They had sent scouts ahead and quickly took over a dozen of the scattered civilian houses, some as many as three miles from camp. In his letters to France, General de Kalb severely criticized this pursuit of creature comforts. He declared himself determined to build a hut and stay close to his men. Washington said nothing. He needed the support of his native-born generals.

Meanwhile, the men went to work on their huts. In general orders the day before they marched, Washington had issued detailed plans for these shelters. They were to be "fourteen by sixteen each—sides, ends and roofs made with logs and the roof made tight with split slabs . . . the sides made tight with clay." The fireplace was to be made of wood covered with eighteen inches of clay, and was to be in the rear of the hut. Twelve men were assigned to each hut. Officers' huts would have fewer tenants. Engineers were ordered to mark the ground where each brigade would build. The goal was a compact community with each hut facing a brigade "street."[41]

The work went slowly. It was complicated by the men's exhaustion and lack of shoes and clothing—and by a shortage of axes and other tools, and the absence of nails. But the primary problem was lack of food. For two days and a night, Joseph Plumb Martin did not have "a morsel of anything to eat all that time save a small pumpkin" which he probably purloined from a farmer's barn and cooked in a fire he built on a rock.

In one Massachusetts brigade, the commissaries distributed meat—but it was so rotten that the men refused to eat it. A committee of three captains was appointed to inspect it, and they reported to General Washington that they "judge it not fit for the use of human beings, unwholesome and destructive to nature for any person to make use of such fude [sic]." At the bottom of the report, Major General de Kalb scrawled that "the same complaints" were made in another Massachusetts brigade. "They all complain also that the flour being sour is of no use."[42]

The weather remained brutally cold. The second night was a repetition of the first, with blanketless men dozing around fires while those with blankets shivered in unheated tents. The huts Washington described in general orders soon proved to be an ideal not easily attained. Washington offered twelve dollars to the twelve-man team who finished their hut in "the quickest and most workmanlike manner." There is no record of the prize being collected.

Roofing the huts turned out to be a major problem. Splitting slabs to fit with an ax or handsaw was slow work. Washington offered a hundred dollars to anyone who came up with a solution that would be cheaper and faster—another prize that went uncollected. Some men used branches from felled trees, others used sod; many cut canvas strips from tents, which ruined these valuable summer shelters.[43]

Colonel Henry Beekman Livingston of New York wrote wryly to his older brother, Robert, a powerful Hudson River valley politician. "We are now building huts for our winter quarters without nails or tools so that I suppose we may possibly render ourselves very comfortable by the time the winter is over." Livingston added that all but eighteen of his men were unfit for duty "for want of shoes stockings and shirts, breeches and coats."[44]

Officers below the rank of colonel built their own huts. On Christmas Day, Surgeon's Mate Jonathan Todd of the Seventh Connecticut Regiment told his father he, two doctors, the chaplain, and seven other staff officers were trying to build their hut with "one dull ax." Three weeks later, he reported they were in their "hutt," which was eighteen feet long and sixteen feet wide. It was divided into two rooms and had two fireplaces. They had completed the job with the same "poor ax." The roof was "not the best in wet weather" but otherwise they were comfortable.[45]

Generals, who could command a construction crew, produced even more comfortable quarters. General de Kalb stayed close to his men, as he had promised. But his home away from home was thirty-two feet long and had three fireplaces, as well as a kitchen, a dormitory for servants, and a stable. His aides would live in a nearby hut, similar to those the troops were building.[46]

By and large, officers seemed reasonably satisfied with their quarters.

Captain William Gifford of New Jersey reported that his men were now "pretty comfortable." But they had "lay in tents until January 20—an instance of the kind hardly known in any country whatever, but what can't brave Americans endure." Among the few surviving letters of the enlisted men, there was no talk of being comfortable. John Buss of Connecticut told his family "our Chimbly is made of wood and roof covered with tirfe [turf] and dirt . . . & find it much better . . . living than it was in tents these cold nights."[47]

For mattresses in both enlisted men's and officers' huts, there was only one solution: straw. Large quantities would have to be found in the countryside. It would have to be replaced regularly. Otherwise the stuff would soon be crawling with vermin. General Washington hastily prepared a proclamation to be issued in English and German (many of Pennsylvania's farmers spoke only the latter) ordering "all persons residing within seventy miles of my headquarters" to thresh half their grain by the first day of February, which would theoretically create an ample supply of straw. The decree was rushed to Lancaster, where it was published in Dunlap's *Pennsylvania Packet, or, The General Advertiser.* Three hundred broadsides were also printed for distribution in the wintry countryside.[48]

This sudden call for straw is a glimpse of one of the least understood aspects of the Continental Army's ordeal at Valley Forge. Wintering there was a decision for which little or no preparation had been made. It was not what Washington—or most of his generals—wanted to do. Until the last possible moment, they had hungered for another battle with the British and a victory that would rescue their sinking reputations and drive the royal army out of Philadelphia. Only the threat of the American army's imminent collapse forced the generals to abandon this forlorn ambition.

XI

For the moment, there was no room or time for second thoughts. The food shortage rapidly went from acute to disastrous. On December 21, only a few brigades received some salt pork—never a welcome ration. The rest got nothing. The next day, there was no food whatsoever for anyone. As it dawned on the troops that they faced starvation, a mutinous spirit swept the camp. One regiment after another began chanting, "NO MEAT! NO MEAT!"

Other regiments began giving very good imitations of screeching owls and cawing crows, suggesting that they were thinking of flying their coops like these winged predators and marching into the countryside to find food at the points of their bayonets. Officers raced up and down the regimental streets, their swords drawn, ordering the soldiers to desist. After strenuous shouting, the men in authority produced silence. But it was a sullen, ominous quiet, during which little work was done on the huts.

The next day, hunger's impact became starkly visible when Major John Clark Jr., still spying on the fringes of Philadelphia, reported at noon that "a large body of the enemy are on their march to Darby." The British had crossed the Schuylkill River at a ford called the Middle Ferry and were headed toward this fertile countryside southwest of Philadelphia. They were obviously intent on acquiring large amounts of meat and grain for their soldiers and hay for their horses. "If a corps is thrown immediately toward Middle Ferry their retreat is inevitably cut off," Clark wrote.

The spymaster forwarded another letter at two o'clock, reporting that one of his agents had learned the British commander in chief, Sir William Howe, and several other generals were with this foraging expedition. "They have a very formidable body [of troops] with them," Clark wrote. Another spy reported they had at least 200 wagons. Howe was hoping this foray would solve his forage and food problems for a long time.

Washington immediately ordered the Continental Army to prepare to do battle with this bold enemy thrust. He got a response that shook him to the core of his being. Not a morsel of food was available to give the men for a long winter march, possibly followed by a battle. The commissary department reported that it did not have a single animal for slaughter, and there were only twenty-five barrels of flour in the camp, with no prospects of resupply.[49]

Brigadier General Varnum told General Washington the bad news in his usual over-the-top style. "According to the saying of Solomon, hunger will break through a stone wall. . . . Three days successively we have been destitute of bread. Two days we have been intirely [sic] without meat. . . . the men must be supplied or they cannot be commanded." With bleak ferocity, Varnum warned the commander in chief: "If you expect the exertion of virtuous principles while your troops are deprived of the essential necessaries of life, you[r] final disappointment will be great." There it was again, the dwindling faith that the Revolution would be won by pure patriotism.[50]

Brigadier General Jedediah Huntington told Colonel Timothy Pickering, the army's adjutant general, "I have used every argument my imagination could invent to make the soldiers easy but I despair of being able to do it much longer." Huntington added another possibility to the list of impending disasters: "[Among] men who have been used to be full fed, the spirit of stealing and robbing, which God knows was great enough before, must increase if no other bad consequences follow."[51]

A shaken Washington could only order parties of fifty "pickt men" from each brigade, led by a "good partizan captain" to muster and march to Darby to harass the enemy's flanks. He also organized twenty-man parties from each brigade to begin foraging in the countryside in search of food, and summoned Charles Stewart, the commissary general of issues, and his deputy, Thomas Jones, to a meeting with him and his generals.

The generals ranted about their men being meatless and breadless for two days and their struggle to avert a mutiny. New Jerseyan Stewart listened impassively. He seldom visited the army, leaving the day-to-day business of issuing food to Jones. Stewart later admitted he was shocked to discover "not a barrel of flour or one fatt ox or cow on hand" when he arrived at Valley Forge. With Stewart and Jones came an assistant deputy commissary general of purchases, John Chaloner, who was frankly terrified. "Lucky for me Colonel Stewart was present," he wrote Ephraim Blaine, deputy commissary general of purchases for the Middle States, who was his boss. Chaloner added that Blaine was lucky to be absent, because "the facts were against us."

Apparently Stewart, as commissary general of issues, was able to talk himself and Thomas Jones off the hook by blandly reporting that there were no cattle in the camp, so Jones was unable to issue any meat rations. He claimed that the generals were wrong about the absence of bread—some had been issued in the previous two days. Admittedly, there was no more available, but that too was not the fault of the issuing department. No flour had arrived in camp to issue. Chaloner was there to represent the guilty parties, the commissary general of purchases and his deputies. But he was a small fish, and all but vibrating with fright. The disgusted generals stomped out without bothering to talk to him. As far as they were concerned, all commissaries were liars and crooks.[52]

Washington and his generals were face-to-face with the bureaucratic never-never land created by the Continental Congress when they reorganized the Commissary Department in the spring of 1777, dividing it into commissaries of issue and of purchases. The commissary general of purchases, William Buchanan, a Baltimore merchant, was an even bigger zero than Stewart. The two groups frequently acted as if they operated on separate planets.

In his letter to Blaine, Chaloner included a glimpse of the dimensions of the food shortage. From various deputy commissaries of purchase, he had hopes of receiving 1,200 head of cattle in the next few days. This would keep the army eating meat for only ten days. The soldiers consumed an average of 34,577 pounds of meat per day—a million pounds a month. Their appetite for bread was equally immense. They chomped down a million pounds of the staff of life each month.[53]

XII

Toward the close of this harrowing December 22, General Washington wrote to Henry Laurens, the president of Congress. "With infinite pain and concern," he enclosed Varnum's and Huntington's letters and assured Laurens that their description of the "state of the commissary department" was not exaggerated. Sorrow mingling with bewilderment, the commander in chief confessed: "I do not know from what cause this alarming deficiency, or rather total failure of supplies arises." Unless something was done immediately, "this army must dissolve."

There was an even starker possibility. At four o'clock that morning, the general had received a warning from Major John Clark that made Washington fear an attack on Valley Forge. "Had a body of the enemy crossed [the] Schuylkill this morning, the divisions which I ordered to be in readiness to march & meet them could not have moved," Washington wrote.[54]

In the midst of this crisis, Washington received a letter from President Laurens, enclosing a peremptorily worded resolution passed by Congress, informing the commander in chief that the state of New Jersey was an "object demanding attention and protection." With it was a "Remonstrance" passed by the assembly and ruling council of Pennsylvania, rebuking Washington for going into winter quarters and demanding that he consider it his responsibility to make sure the eastern part of Pennsylvania was not "left in the power of the enemy." Unless Washington attended to these matters, the state would be unable to raise taxes for the war effort or enlist men in the Continental Army's regiments. In a word, it would virtually abandon the contest.

In long, defensive paragraphs, Washington struggled to answer these thinly veiled accusations that he was not doing his job. It would give him "infinite pleasure" to protect "every individual and every spot of ground in the whole of the United States." But it simply was not possible with the sickly, unclothed army under his command. He rehearsed all the options he had considered before going to Valley Forge. Never in the war or "in my whole life" had he devoted more thought to a problem.

As for New Jersey, there was no state which he was more willing to protect. But he refused to compromise the central principle of his military thinking: "I cannot divide the army." If Congress insisted on his doing so, he would not be "answerable for the consequences." When and if he got things under control in Valley Forge, he would detach a "small force" of Continentals to encourage New Jersey's part-time soldiers, the militia. That was all he could safely promise.[55]

XIII

Meanwhile, the British continued their leisurely foraging in the vicinity of Darby. Letters poured into Washington's headquarters from commanders of the Pennsylvania militia, who were trying to cope with the situation. With them was Colonel Daniel Morgan and his regiment of Virginia riflemen. The huge, combative Morgan was already a legendary figure. He and General Benedict Arnold had stormed British-held Quebec at dawn on January 1, 1776. The attack had failed and the "Old Wagoner," as he called himself, had been taken prisoner. Exchanged, he had played a crucial role in the victory at Saratoga.

Morgan and the militia generals told Washington little that Major Clark had not already communicated in his letters. The militia were almost as short of food as the Continentals. The countryside had little to offer. Major General Armstrong told Washington that there was no hope of finding food for the Continental Army "from this quarter." In fact, "the support of the militia would soon fail" if the army's commissary department did not extend them some help. The idea must have inspired a dry laugh—or a curse—from the harassed commander in chief.[56]

The fifty-man detachments of picked men Washington had dispatched on December 22 were also on the scene. Colonel Morgan did not think much of them. For one thing, each considered itself a separate command, and most showed no inclination to take orders from Morgan or anyone else. "They are by no means fit for scouts," Morgan wrote, "being taken promiscuously from the regiments, when they ought to have been pick'd men." The words must have made Washington writhe. Picked men was precisely what he had specified. In the chaos and starvation of mutinous Valley Forge, the commander in chief's orders obviously did not count for much.

Worse, Morgan added, the detachments "all came out without provisions which renders them almost useless." Instead of fighting, they spent most of their time straggling in search of food.[57]

General James Potter, also operating around Darby with some Pennsylvania militia, was equally unimpressed with the Continental detachments. "I have no great expectation from these partys," he told Washington."[58]

XIV

On the same day—December 23—that he received these disheartening letters, General Washington revealed a side of his character that many people had thus far failed to detect: an instinct to strike, and strike hard, at men who were opposing him. In warfare, this tactic is called seizing the initiative. Washington had demonstrated his ability to manage this feat on the battlefield in 1776, when he rescued the collapsing Revolution with his Christmas night foray across the Delaware River. The shaken British had retreated to an enclave along the Raritan River. Throughout the spring of 1777, Washington surrounded them with aggressive raiding and skirmishing parties, costing them hundreds of men. He eventually intimidated General Howe into abandoning New Jersey and its numerous loyalists.

Now his opponents were the carping politicians in Congress and in the Pennsylvania state government. Washington's counterattack against these gentlemen was a letter to Henry Laurens, which Washington knew would be passed on to Congress and by them to the Pennsylvania Assembly and Supreme Executive Council. The commander in chief began with a rhetorical salvo that might be called shock treatment. He reiterated in more vivid terms the warning he had sent Laurens the previous day. If the commissary department continued to fail, there was no doubt in his mind that the army would have only three choices: "starve, dissolve, or disperse."

He described in detail his inability to do anything to stop the huge British foraging expedition around Darby. He excoriated the commissary and the quartermaster departments, both of which were apparently doing nothing to prevent the impending disaster at Valley Forge. With brutal candor, he told the politicians the facts and figures that he had gotten from the adjutant general on the condition of his army. No fewer than 2,898 men in camp were unfit for duty because they were "barefoot and otherwise naked." That left little more than 8,200 infantry to fight a British army that was well over 10,000 men. He told them how "numbers" of his men were still sitting up before campfires in Valley Forge because they had no blankets.

Then Washington turned his verbal artillery directly on the politicians, with much of the salvo directed at the Pennsylvanians. Without bothering to find out where the army was going into winter quarters, they had sent their obnoxious Remonstrance, which spoke of the soldiers as if they were "made of stocks or stones, and equally insensible of frost or snow." Washington assured these gentlemen that "it is a much easier and less distressing thing, to draw remonstrances in a comfortable room by a good fire side, than to occupy a cold bleak hill, and sleep under frost and snow without cloaths [sic] or blankets." If these gentlemen had little feeling for the naked and distressed soldiers, Washington felt "superabundantly for them, and from my soul pity those miseries which it is neither in my power to relieve or prevent."

The attitude of the gentlemen by their firesides "adds not a little to my other difficulties and distress," Washington continued. Above all, it was disturbing to find that "much more is expected of me than it is possible to perform." Meanwhile he had to conceal the true state of the army from "public view" and "thereby expose myself to detraction and calumny." [59]

These words make it clear that General Washington was all too aware that the Pennsylvania Remonstrance and the hectoring tone in Congress's resolution were not accidents. They were part of the widespread whispering campaign that was undermining the prestige and admiration he had won in 1776. From a victorious hero, whom some people had begun calling the father of his country, General Washington sensed he was in danger of being considered a loser who could be denigrated and ordered about with impunity. He was not going to let this happen without defending himself.

At the time, no one, including Washington, realized that this letter was the beginning of a political struggle that would pit the commander in chief and his allies against detractors and intriguers in Congress and in the Continental Army. This anti-Washington circle soon revealed a hostility that was both personal and ideological. The nature and direction of the

American Revolution become involved in the fray, which has been dismissed by too many historians as a mere ripple of dissension that Washington brushed aside as a passing annoyance. We will also see how serious and how intricately involved with the Continental Army's survival the dispute became.

XV

For the moment, after mailing his letter to Congress, Washington could do little but hope that the Pennsylvania militia, Morgan's riflemen, and the detachments of unpicked Continentals could accomplish something on the fringes of the British army around Darby. Washington asked Major General Lord Stirling to take charge of the militia. These officers all did their best to harass the British, but their reports were a study in frustration. "We keep close round them," Morgan wrote on December 24. But "they don't offer to come far out side of thair pequets [pickets] so that we have little chance to take any of them." Stirling's reports were equally glum.[60]

On Christmas Eve the skirmishers dispatched some Pennsylvania militia with a few cannon to the outskirts of Philadelphia. At 6:30 p.m. the amateurs opened fire, shooting at nothing in particular. The goal was to disrupt the enemy's holiday festivities and make the foraging force around Darby fear for its communications with the city. The militia commanders proudly reported that they had "made a good retreat . . . without the loss of a man." This was not the sort of victory General Washington needed and wanted.[61]

On Christmas Day it began to snow heavily. The ever enterprising Major John Clark stayed close to the enemy foragers, ignoring the weather and the calendar, even though he had barely recuperated from a shoulder wound received at the Battle of Brandywine. Wistfully he told Washington that "if we had 200 light dragoons [horsemen] we might catch the enemy by the dozens" as they wandered down byroads in search of remote farms to plunder. But the 515 cavalrymen at Valley Forge were in no shape to fight. They and their horses were starving, along with the rest of the army. Washington had decided to send them to New Jersey in the hope that they could subsist there. Clark added a by now all too familiar complaint: "The wretched situation of the troops here is much to be lamented, no provisions provided for them, ill clothed and many of 'em no shoes."[62]

XVI

The heavy snow forced Washington to abandon his marquee tent and move into a small stone house owned by Quaker Isaac Potts, one of the original owners of the forge which gave the valley its name. A Potts relative, twice widowed Deborah Hewes, was the current tenant. She agreed to rent the house to the general for one hundred pounds in Pennsylvania state currency. Washington took over one of the upstairs rooms as a bedroom and a downstairs room for an office.

Struggling to establish a semblance of hospitality, Washington provided a spartan Christmas dinner for his aides. Beginning a routine that he would follow for the rest of his time in Valley Forge, he invited the five officers of the day, led by General de Kalb, and two officers from the commander in chief's guard. Also on the list as a personal guest was the Marquis de Lafayette. The meal was as plain and rough as the surrounding landscape: unadorned mutton, veal, potatoes, and cabbage, washed down by water.[63]

After dinner, Washington went to his office and renewed his campaign to awaken Congress to the army's plight. He wrote a letter to Elbridge Gerry of Massachusetts, urging him to persuade his New England colleagues to arrange for a committee to visit Valley Forge and join him and his staff in a comprehensive overhaul of the way the army was being supplied and recruited. He hoped the committee's powers would be "general and extensive." The "whole military system" needed to be rethought and reconsidered. Gerry had visited the army early in December and discussed the possibility of such a committee with Washington.[64]

XVII

The snow and the militia's pathetic pseudoattack of Christmas Eve reminded more than one man in the Continental Army of Christmas a year before. The memory of the Trenton victory was tinged with melancholy now. No one's emotions on this score were keener than George Washington's. In his files was a document titled "Plan to Attack Philadelphia" dated "Valley Forge, c. 25 December, 1777." The date makes it especially poignant—Washington or the aide who filed it was thinking of the previous year, when the password was "Victory or Death," and snow and sleet and the ice-choked Delaware had lulled the enemy into a false sense of security.

Almost certainly they were also thinking of how Trenton had turned General Washington into a hero of almost mythic proportions. The commander in chief was hailed as a military genius on a par with the great generals of history. From Boston to Savannah, American morale rebounded from the depths to the heights. Poets gushed tributes:

> Our object was the Hessian band
> That dared invade fair freedom's land
>   And quarter in that place.
> Great Washington he led us on
> Whose streaming flag in storm or sun
>   Had never known disgrace.[65]

The plan in the file at Valley Forge envisioned an even greater triumph. It was the boldest imaginable assault on British-held Philadelphia. While Morgan's men and Stirling's militia kept up "an appearance of an attack upon the enemy" around Darby, cavalry would patrol west of the Schuylkill to prevent any intelligence from reaching Howe. Meanwhile picked groups of sixty men commanded by "spirited and enterprising" officers would storm the enemy redoubts around Philadelphia. Simultaneously, the right wing of the Continental Army under General Sullivan would seize the four bridges that the British had built at the fords across the lower Schuylkill and capture more redoubts in that quarter.

Under Washington's personal command, the army's left wing would storm into the city, release prisoners, and demand the immediate surrender of the men Howe had left behind as a garrison. They would be threatened with no quarter if they tried to fight. The sailors and ships at the docks would be menaced with fire and sword if they resisted. Four brigades were to form a reserve corps on the Philadelphia common. Militia, already alerted, would pour in from New Jersey, Delaware, Maryland, and Pennsylvania to bolster the Continentals. The goal was "to crush Howe before he could recover from the suprize [sic] or regain his ships."[66]

It was a fierce, beautiful dream that revealed the warrior side of its creator. But reality was a letter Washington's aide Tench Tilghman wrote to Lord Stirling on Christmas Day, telling him they had received his latest report. "His Excellency seems to be of the opinion with you that while the enemy remain in their present position nothing further can be done than is done." Tilghman could not resist adding a personal message that summed up the melancholy that swirled through Valley Forge on this traditional day of joy: "I WISH WE COULD PUT THEM IN MIND TOMORROW MORNING, OF WHAT HAPPENED THIS TIME TWELVE MONTH."

Stirling knew exactly what Tilghman meant. He mournfully replied that he knew of "no way of putting them in mind of last year." The only thing that occurred to him was "making a grand bonfire" in the camps from which the Pennsylvania militia and Morgan's riflemen and the Continental detachments were trying to harass the enemy foragers.[67]

The bonfire was a way of saying, "Look—we're still here!" Otherwise the gesture was as feckless as the militia's cannonade of Philadelphia. The Continental Army of the United States of America—and its commander in chief—seemed in danger of becoming bad, sad jokes.

TWO

※

REVELS AND REDCOATS

I F WASHINGTON'S STARVING, half-naked soldiers at Valley Forge
could have seen the letters eighteen-year-old Rebecca Franks was writing in Philadelphia, they would have concluded that their envious fantasies were correct: the British were having a wonderful time in the
American capital. Rebecca and her loyalist family were among the wealthiest people in Philadelphia. For her and many other young women of her
social class, the city, crowded with British officers, had become a veritable
pleasure palace. Here is how she described her daily routine to Anne Harrison Paca, wife of wealthy Maryland congressman William Paca, with
whom Rebecca had grown friendly during Congress's sojourn in the City
of Brotherly Love.

"You can have no idea of the life of continued amusement I live in. I can
scarce have a moment to myself . . . and most elegantly am I dressed for a ball
this evening at Smith's [the City Tavern] where we have one every Thurs-
day." No one, she assured her friend, was ever at a loss for partners. She her-
self was engaged to dance with seven gentlemen that night. There was a
"fixed rule never to dance more than two dances with the same person."

Rebecca wished Congressman Paca would let Anne join the fun for a
week or two. "I know you are as fond of a gay life as myself. You'd have an

opportunity at rakeing [looking stylish] as much as you choose, either at plays, balls, concerts or assemblies. I've been but three evenings alone since we moved to town."[1]

Another wealthy young lady who participated in the high life that the British brought to the staid Quaker city was Margaret "Peggy" Shippen, whose father, Edward Shippen, maintained a nervously neutral stance toward the war. His son was married to Alice Lee, sister of Continental Congressman Richard Henry Lee of Virgina. His cousin, William Shippen, was the director of the Continental Army's hospitals. But Edward Shippen did not have the courage to join either side. All the family's decisiveness and daring, the talents that had made them rich, seemed to have been inherited by Shippen's daughter Peggy. Blond and beautiful, she had just turned sixteen, the age when young women came out socially in Philadelphia. Her two older sisters were also considered attractive, though not in Peggy's league.

Balls were held in the private homes of the rich and at assembly halls and taverns. One letter from a young woman who claimed to be a rebel reported that the officers did not care two pins about her politics. It was seldom discussed. More genteel topics and some not so genteel were preferred. A great many of the officers were aristocrats, which added a special thrill to flirtations with them.

II

Rebecca seemed to prefer playing the field, but Peggy Shippen soon became attracted to Captain John André. Brown-haired and almost exotically handsome, he was the product of a marriage between a French beauty and an English merchant. André spoke fluent French and German and wrote more than passable poetry. He could sketch himself and others with considerable skill. At times he emanated a subdued melancholy which undoubtedly intrigued his numerous women friends. Two centuries later, one is tempted to wonder if he somehow sensed the tragic fate that awaited him in the shadowy future.

At the age of nineteen André had fallen violently in love with a blond English beauty who inspired him to abandon his boyhood dreams of military glory and become a merchant to support her in grand style. When she changed her mind the heartbroken André bought a commission in the army to forget her. After a tour of Europe, he joined his regiment in Canada in 1775, just in time to be captured by the Americans who invaded the vast colony, hoping to make it the fourteenth state. André spent more than a year of unhappy captivity in western Pennsylvania, frequently insulted and threatened with physical violence by hotheaded frontier rebels.[2]

By the time André was exchanged, he thoroughly hated Americans. He saw them as a cultural as well as a political enemy, a tribe of ignoramuses who threatened to destroy the upper-class British world of gentility and culture that he treasured. The young captain soon became an aide to Major General Charles Grey, who also thought American rebels should be subdued by the application of maximum brutality.

Captain André helped Grey plan a ferocious attack on General Anthony Wayne's brigade of 1,500 Pennsylvania troops at Paoli, shortly before the British seized Philadelphia. Striking at midnight, using only the bayonet, Grey's men rampaged through the American camp, showing no quarter to anyone. Even musicians, traditionally spared in battle, were bayoneted repeatedly. The British boasted they had killed 500 men. A more likely figure was 150; many were left bleeding from as many as a dozen bayonet wounds. André never expressed the slightest regret for this slaughter.[3]

Off the battlefield, a different André emerged. He selected Benjamin Franklin's comfortable house as quarters for himself and General Grey and sought the company of Philadelphia's prettiest women. He was polite and amusing to all the young ladies, including Peggy Shippen. But he was far more attracted to another beauty, Peggy Chew, who lived in Cliveden, a handsome mansion in Germantown, about seven miles west of Philadelphia. Her father, Benjamin Chew, had been chief justice of Pennsylvania during its colonial years.

One day, seeing Peggy in Cliveden's garden, André dashed off a poem:

The Hebrews write and those who can
Believe an apple tempted man
To touch the tree exempt;
Tho' tasted at a vast expense
'Twas too delicious to the sense
Not mortally to tempt.

But had the tree of knowledge bloomed
Its branches by much fruit perfumed,
As here enchants my view—
What mortal Adam's taste could blame,
Who would not die to eat the same,
When gods might wish a Chew?[4]

III

A British officer with less appeal to wellborn ladies such as Misses Shippen, Franks, and Chew was Banastre Tarleton, a burly, thick-necked cavalryman who had wildman written all over him. He had gambled away a modest inheritance and joined the army mostly to escape his creditors. In America, while still a cornet (second lieutenant), he had demonstrated an aggressive style that won the attention of his superiors. On December 13, 1776, he had been part of a patrol behind rebel lines in New Jersey that captured Major General Charles Lee, second in command of the American army. For this feat of daring and courage, Tarleton won promotion to captain.

In Philadelphia, Tarleton and his friends were more interested in the numerous less genteel women who were looking for an officer to protect them. Whether they were streetwalkers by profession or servant girls who found themselves abandoned by their rebel employers when they fled Philadelphia was seldom clear. Few questions were asked. "Ban" and his good friend and immediate commander in the cavalry, Major Richard Crewe, were soon equipped with complaisant mistresses. But Ban had a wandering eye. One night, Major Crewe strolled into his quarters and found Ban in bed with the major's charmer. The story made the London papers, and the two bravos came perilously close to a duel.[5]

A summary of this approach to enjoying Philadelphia was an ad placed in a loyalist newspaper: "Wanted to live with two single gentlemen, a young woman to act in the capacity of a housekeeper, and who can occasionally put her hand to anything. Extravagant wages will be given and no character required. Any young woman who chooses to offer may be further informed at the bar of the City Tavern."[6]

IV

Sally Logan Fisher was another well-to-do Philadelphia woman who had outspoken loyalist views. A Quaker, she (and her husband, Samuel) refused to participate in the war. When the Americans celebrated the first anniversary of the Declaration of Independence in 1777, Mrs. Fisher declined to illuminate her house to testify to her support for the Revolution. Some of the city's rebels demolished her windows with rocks.

Next, the Pennsylvania government arrested Samuel Fisher and nineteen other prominent Quakers as suspected traitors and exiled them to western Virginia. The contrast between this behavior and a royal government that (in her opinion) "breathe[d] liberty and peace" soon had Sally referring to British commander in chief Sir Willliam Howe as "our beloved general." In September she welcomed the news that Sir William and his army had invaded Pennsylvania as "an event I had so long wished to take place."

By the time Washington's army retreated to Valley Forge, and the British became an occupying army in Philadelphia, Mrs. Fisher's political opinions had undergone a drastic change. Sir William Howe was no longer beloved and the British army no longer represented liberty and peace. Mrs. Fisher was dismayed to see local women living with officers such as Captain Tarleton and Major Crewe and shamelessly strolling the streets, arm in arm with them. The poorly paid British enlisted men were prone to petty thievery. Worst of all, in the countryside around Philadelphia, the British and their German allies indiscriminately plundered rebels and loyalists alike.[7]

On November 22, 1777, Quaker Robert Morton recorded in his diary that the British had burned seventeen houses on the city's outskirts, including the beautiful mansion known as Fair Hill, because rebel snipers used them to fire on their pickets. Morton was particularly enraged because Howe's men did not bother to remove valuable furniture before putting the houses to the torch. Some of the homes had belonged to loyalists. Young Morton bitterly noted that Washington's men had not "wantonly destroyed and burned their friends' property."[8]

Less than two weeks later, on December 4, 1777, most of the British army marched out to try to draw Washington into a pitched battle. Washington declined to take the bait, and the British soon returned. Along the line of march, Morton gloomily noted, the German troops "committed great outrages." They drove off seven hundred cattle from one wealthy farmer's fields and burned a well-known tavern. Morton wondered if "the sole purpose" of the expedition was "to destroy and spread desolation and ruin," convincing more people that the British were the enemies of all Americans.[9]

V

Elizabeth Drinker was another affluent Quaker wife who had good reason to dislike the American cause. Her husband had also been arrested and deported to western Virginia, leaving her more than a little apprehensive about her safety. Her household consisted of her sister, her two daughters and two young sons, and an indentured servant named Ann.

One night in November her daughter saw Ann in the yard with a British officer. Mrs. Drinker's sister held a candle to the man's face and asked him who he was. "What's that to you?" he snarled.

The intruder followed Ann and the sister into the kitchen, and they could not get rid of him. He was drunk and abusive, claiming he had come into the yard by mistake. The guilty expression on Ann's face made that an obvious lie. She introduced him as Captain John Tape. When a Quaker male friend who was visiting came into the kitchen, Tape threatened him with his sword and a wrestling match ensued, which the Quaker won.

After a great deal more swearing and arguing, Tape finally departed with "saucy Ann," as Mrs. Drinker called her, promising that he would pay the money she owed on her indenture. Mrs. Drinker tried to calm her terrified children and lay awake until 1 a.m. trying to recover from her own fright.

About a month later Mrs. Drinker found another officer at her door, a major named Crammond, who said he wanted to rent quarters in her house. She refused him at first, but he made two more visits, assuring her that he would not cause any trouble. He seemed "a sober thoughtful young man," and she reluctantly said yes. Other friends had been threatened with violence when they turned away would-be officer boarders.

Soon Crammond had parked three horses, three cows, two sheep, and two turkeys in the Drinker barn, plus two servants and a black boy named Damon, who spent much of the day in the Drinker house. The major took over the two front parlors, an upstairs bedroom, and part of the kitchen, and began giving dinner parties for as many as twelve fellow officers. He also stayed out late on many nights and was neither sober nor quiet when he came home. But he and his entourage did not otherwise misbehave, and Mrs. Drinker endured his lifestyle as the lesser evil.[10]

On January 4, Mrs. Drinker encountered Captain Tape passing her house. She called to him and he said he was in a hurry. In stentorian tones she ordered him to stay where he was until a noisy wagon lumbered past. Then she lit into him. If neither religion nor honesty troubled his conscience, she wondered if "what you soldiers call honor" would disturb him when he saw her house and remembered his atrocious behavior several weeks earlier.

"Who me?" replied Tape in his usual style.

"I have been careful about exposing thee," Mrs. Drinker said. But if the captain did not pay for Ann's "time" [her indenture], she would tell all the officers who were quartered nearby in the houses of her numerous friends about his misdeeds.

Captain Tape stuttered and finally exclaimed: "I haant got your servant. I don't care who has her!"

"If you don't bring the money or send it over, you'll hear from me!" Mrs. Drinker stormed.

"Well—well—well," Tape muttered, and hurried off looking "confused."

Although Mrs. Drinker had the satisfaction of humbling Captain Tape, she never got the money. Face-to-face, even a Quaker lady could stand up to her country's conquerors when they turned girl chasers. But Mrs. Drinker's disillusion with the British army did not change her Quaker conviction that the revolutionists were the tyrants.[11]

VI

Presiding over these revels and wrangles was the British commander in chief, General Sir William Howe. He had acquired the "Sir" when George III made him a Knight of Bath for his victory over General Washington's army in the August 1776 Battle of Long Island. Sir William was popular with the rank and file and the army's junior officers because he often declared that no soldier's life would be wasted "wantonly." That meant he preferred flanking maneuvers to costly frontal assaults.

In his youth, Howe had been a daring infantryman who had been ready and even eager to take risks. In 1759, he had led a storming party up a secret path from the St. Lawrence River to establish a foothold on the Plains of Abraham that led to the capture of the fortress city of Quebec and the capitulation of Canada. He had fought with equal distinction on other battlefields. But in private, he often revealed a lack of self-confidence and a dependence on the approval of his older brother, Admiral Lord Richard Howe.[12]

In America, this lack of self-confidence had been compounded by Howe's first battlefield experience as a general, on the hilly Charlestown Peninsula opposite Boston. On June 17, 1775, he confronted some two thousand entrenched rebels in and around a fort on Breed's Hill. Forced to make a frontal assault, he won the contest (usually known as the Battle of Bunker Hill) at horrendous cost—half his small army were killed or wounded. There was, Howe later admitted, "a moment [I] never felt before."

A genial six-footer with a face that some people described as "coarse," the forty-nine-year-old general took over a handsome house on Market Street that belonged to the prewar governor, Richard Penn. There he gave splendid dinners and balls where the wine flowed freely. Sir William loved a bottle of port as much as any officer in his army.[13]

To the dismay of the Quakers and other loyalists, Howe made no attempt to set a moral tone that might have influenced his men. On his arm at his revels, Sir William displayed to all and sundry blond and beautiful Mrs. Joshua Loring Jr., formerly Elizabeth Lloyd of New York. Her family owned Lloyd's Neck on Long Island, a large peninsula that contained a fine mansion, three thousand acres of prime farmland, and miles of shoreline. She was an American aristocrat, and so was her handsome husband, whose father owned an estate in Roxbury, Massachusetts, and a mansion in Boston. Joshua Junior's marriage to Elizabeth had been one of the social events of 1769. Like his father, who had commanded a fleet on the Great Lakes during the Seven Years' War, Joshua Junior acquired a number of cushy government jobs, such as surveyor of the woods in New Hampshire and sheriff of Suffolk County, which included Boston.

On April 19, 1775, after the Battles of Lexington and Concord, Joshua and his father had fled to Boston, leaving behind Elizabeth, who was pregnant. She lost the child in the ensuing emotional and political turmoil. In Boston the elder Loring said: "I have always eaten the king's bread and I always intend to." Joshua Junior adopted the same creed, and the Lorings became loyalists with a capital L.

When the British evacuated the city and retreated to Halifax, Nova Scotia, the Lorings were among the 1,100 loyalists who went with them. A few months later, General Howe embarked his army to assault New York City, and the Lorings joined him. Joshua formed a company to which General Howe granted a license to import wine and rum for the army's thirsty officers. Loring also became commissary of prisoners, a job which he had reportedly won by exhibiting a talent for mistreating rebels captured at the Battle of Bunker Hill. This accusation may be a Yankee canard; more friendly sources claim the future commissary had met Howe while Joshua was in the British army during the Seven Years' War and they had become friends.

Aside from his legal right to a percentage of the cash flow, a hard-hearted commissary could make thousands of pounds by stealing from the money advanced to feed hungry captives. Ethan Allen, who was in Joshua's clutches for a while, called him "a monster." In a quid pro quo that was by no means unique in the British army (General Burgoyne had a similar arrangement with his paymaster's wife), Joshua enjoyed piling up cash while Sir William enjoyed Mrs. Loring. There was, it perhaps should be added, a Mrs. Howe, an attractive woman who often testified to her love for her dashing soldier and had hoped to go to America with him.[14]

For most of the army, the center of the social whirl was the City Tavern, on Walnut Street not far from the Pennsylvania State House, where the Continental Congress and the Pennsylvania Assembly had held forth. A group of field rank officers (colonels and majors) became managers of the place, and officers who sought membership paid two days pay per month to support it. There was a ball a week, and dinners were available on other nights. But the great attraction of the City Tavern was its faro bank.

General Howe loved to gamble, and he led a brigade of his officers to the tables. Captain Johann Ewald of the Hessian army, a sober thoughtful man, visited the gambling rooms and came away appalled by the recklessness with which many of the English wagered. The bank, set up by another German captain, began with a thousand guineas in it. Before the end of the occupation, the bank had raked in another six thousand. "More than once," Ewald wrote in his diary, "I have seen ten thousand guineas [fifty thousand dollars] change hands" in a single night.[15]

Some people made fortunes, but many more officers were ruined. They were forced to sell their commissions to pay their gambling debts and return to London. Not a few high-ranking British officers deplored

Howe's indifference to losing talented men this way. True, the lifestyle that Sir William personified in Philadelphia was not much different from other garrison towns in England and Ireland. In upper-class Great Britain at the time, gambling was close to a national disease. Huge amounts were won and lost each night at Boodles, the premier gaming club in London. But Sir William was also fighting a war for American hearts and minds— something he seemed to prefer to forget in Philadelphia.

VII

Behind this facade of aristocratic joie de vivre, Sir William Howe was even more beleagured than George Washington by politicians in London who had become disillusioned with his leadership. These critics blamed him for the surrender of General John Burgoyne's army in northern New York. It was a complicated story, in which Burgoyne himself was one of the principal blunderers. But Howe was the commander in chief in America, and the ultimate responsibility for the stunning capitulation landed on his doorstep.

Howe's obsession with capturing Philadelphia to the virtual exclusion of concern for Burgoyne's fate was closely related to the victory Washington had won at Trenton in 1776. This lightning stroke had reversed the momentum of the war and made a mockery of Howe's policy of attempting to pacify New Jersey by issuing thousands of pardons to those who swore they would remain in "peaceable obedience to His Majesty." After Trenton, not a few of these pardon takers sallied forth, muskets in hand, to snipe at British outposts and foraging parties.

This dismaying reversal of fortune would never have happened had Howe crossed the Delaware and taken Philadelphia in 1776, various people on his staff told Sir William. The city and the entire state of Pennsylvania were reportedly a vast storehouse of supporters of the king, eager to fight on George III's behalf. Capture it and Howe would soon have a loyalist American army at his disposal, ready to attack Washington's demoralized battalions. That would permit the British commander to take his professional soldiers elsewhere, to assault New England or Virginia, where defiant rebels were in control.

Alas for Sir William's hopes, nothing of the sort had happened. The American army had not crumpled with the loss of Philadelphia. For two full months, its forts along the lower Delaware had prevented the British from getting more than a dribble of supplies into the city. Attempts to capture these forts by frontal assault and by bombardment from the fleet had been beaten off with heavy losses in ships and men. Until November 21, 1777, the British army in Philadelphia ate reduced rations, and anxiety pervaded the ranks. Worse, the turnout of loyalists was pathetically small. Only a few hundred volunteered to form provincial cavalry regiments.

VIII

By that time, in the London newspapers and in Parliament, Sir William was being savaged for losing Burgoyne's army. More directly critical were the dispatches he received from his immediate boss, Lord George Germain, the secretary of state for American affairs. The two men were never friendly, politically or personally. Germain was a dour loner, who had been cashiered from the army during the Seven Years' War for disobeying a direct order in a major battle. This hard fate had won him the sympathy of the Prince of Wales, the future George III.

As king, George backed Germain, apparently in the belief that he was righting a great injustice. Few people agreed with his royal highness. But in 1775, when Germain came to power, he was one of the few who claimed to have an answer to the defiant Americans: to exert "the utmost force of this kingdom to finish the rebellion in one campaign." This Sir William Howe had signally failed to do.[16]

Sir William and his brother Admiral Lord Richard Howe were fighting the war in America as military leaders and as peace commissioners. Behind this strange combination lay George III's struggle to satisfy those in Parliament who wished for reconciliation with the Americans and his own inclination to use Germain's "utmost force." Sir William seldom seemed to take his role as peace commissioner seriously, except for his bid to woo New Jerseyans with pardons. Admiral Lord Richard Howe, a very different personality, made a number of attempts to persuade Washington and members of Congress to negotiate a reconciliation.

The admiral was a severely moral man who preferred shipboard life to the pleasures of land. Sir William, a classic younger brother, seemed to prefer letting Lord Richard do the political thinking for both of them. Temporarily, the Howes had satisfied both sides in the clashing politics of the home front. They were vocal friends of the Americans, in part because their oldest brother, Lord George Augustus Howe, had been killed there, fighting the French in the Seven Years' War. At the same time, they were talented military leaders, with a firm devotion to king and country.

IX

From London, Lord George Germain relentlessly criticized the Howes' performance. Reports convinced him that they could have destroyed Washington's army several times during the fighting around New York in 1776, but they had allowed the Americans to escape to fight another day, hoping Washington would agree to a negotiated peace. (Some historians, including this one, think this is true.) Lord George found issuing pardons especially reprehensible. He condemned "this sentimental way of waging war." He also acerbically suggested that Sir William might send him reports of his plans and progress more often.

The conflict reached the crisis stage when Germain sent Howe a letter that Burgoyne had written in August 1777, when he was beginning to realize his invasion of New York was not going to be a leisurely promenade from Canada to Albany. The self-serving "Gentleman Johnny" complained that he was alone and neglected in the northern wilderness without a word of advice or a smidgen of support from Howe. The letter arrived on Howe's desk while he was still struggling to clear the Delaware and supply his army, and rumors of Burgoyne's imminent surrender were swirling through the city.

Germain also accused the Howes of opening the campaign for Philadelphia much too late in 1777 and waging a halfhearted war based on his fatuous belief in a loyalist majority. Germain wanted an intensified war—raids on New England seaports from which privateers were ravaging British shipping, an all-out blockade that would prevent the Americans from catching so much as a single fish to feed their people.

An infuriated General Howe abandoned the politeness that had masked his dislike of Germain. He defended himself against Burgoyne's accusation, which was not hard to do. Gentleman Johnny had talked loudly and vaingloriously about his prospects of painless victory until things started going wrong. Howe also claimed a personal affront over Germain's failure to promote Lieutenant Colonel William Harcourt, commander of the Sixteenth Light Dragoons, ignoring the general's personal recommendation. Sir William took even greater offense at being reprimanded for failing to keep the American secretary fully informed of his operations. It all added up to a dismaying lack of "the necessary confidence and support" from his government that every commander expected.

General Howe threw in a reminder that he had repeatedly warned Germain there was no hope of subduing the rebellion without at least ten thousand more troops. The British commander in chief no longer intended to put up with the irony and sarcasm with which the American secretary harassed him. There was only one way to end this intolerable situation: the resignation of his command.[17]

This burst of defiance was not as definitive as it looked on paper. The Howes knew they had numerous supporters in the cabinet and in Parliament. They also had royal blood, being descended from an illegitimate offspring of King George I and his German mistress. Resignation was a kind of trump card that dared George III to choose between Sir William and the unpopular Germain.

A glimpse of the game the Howes were playing emerges from a look at Lord Richard Howe's correspondence with Germain at this time. The colonial secretary had also sent him one of his sarcastic letters. Germain had wryly congratulated the admiral for the humane policy he had been pursuing—permitting the Americans to continue "subsistence fishing" in small boats that were clearly not warships or merchantmen. Refusing to lose his cool as his brother had done, Lord Howe answered Germain's sarcasm with verbal acid of his own. He wrote that he was "very happy to find the motive for my conduct with respect to the inhabitants of the sea coasts of this continent, appear to have met with your Lordship's approbation." [18]

This high-level sparring remained confidential. But there was little Sir William could do to mitigate the dolorous impact of Burgoyne's surrender on his men's morale. Not a few higher-ranking officers blamed the disaster on Sir William. Ironically, one of the bluntest condemnations came from Colonel Harcourt, whose promotion Howe was so assiduously pursuing. The cavalryman wrote to his father, Earl Harcourt, that Philadelphia should never even have been "thought of " until Howe had joined forces with Burgoyne and ensconced him safely in Albany.

Lieutenant Colonel Richard Fitzpatrick was so dismayed that he told his brother, the Earl of Upper Ossory, "I grow every day more disgusted with the folly and iniquity of the cause in which I am condemned to serve." The adjutant general of the Hessian troops, Major Leopold Baurmeister, wryly informed his superiors in Europe: "The English army . . . has got no farther than Philadelphia [and] is master only of some parts of the banks of the Delaware and Schuylkill." [19]

X

The letters of two British junior officers reveal a decline in the army's morale for reasons more complex than the defeat at Saratoga. Loftus Cliffe was a lieutenant in the Forty-sixth Infantry Regiment. Early in the war, he wrote enthusiastic letters to his brother, his mother, and other family members full of vivid details of the fighting in and around New York in 1776 and in Pennsylvania in 1777. He told them how rebel corpses "stunk of rum" after one battle. When the Americans burned New York in September 1776, he saw a "rebel captain" hanged with an effigy of George Washington looming over him. Almost certainly, this was Nathan Hale.

Cliffe endured the winter of 1776–77 in New Brunswick, New Jersey, fighting American patrols and snipers revived by the victory at Trenton. There were scouting parties and skirmishes every night. In spite of having his baggage captured by an enterprising American patrol, Cliffe seemed to thrive on the excitement. He remained cheerfully confident of beating the Americans anytime he and his men got close to them.

In Pennsylvania, the tone of his letters began to change. The hard marching in the countryside followed by short rations in the captured city drained everyone's enthusiasm. Cliffe noted that one man in the Thirty-third Regiment dropped dead of exhaustion on a march. He expressed sympathy for the Americans who were bayoneted to death in General Grey's surprise attack on Anthony Wayne's men at Paoli. "Four hundred of the poor wretches fell without firing a shot. This was done for our own protection but I'm glad it was not my duty to see it done."

The battle of Germantown was even more troubling. The light infantry, the army's elite corps, panicked and ran. For a while Cliffe and his regiment experienced "the devil of a fire" on their front and flanks. "I never felt so disagreeably in my life." The lieutenant called the American attack "silent and well concerted."

For the next few weeks, Cliffe and his men labored at building a string of fourteen redoubts north and west of the city. It was wearying work—and did nothing for his or his men's morale. They had come to America to beat the Americans in one or two glorious battles. Here they were, on a dull, depressing defensive.

Eventually, they marched into Philadelphia to spend the winter. Cliffe was impressed by the city. The streets and the people were "remarkably clean." He called the Quakers "respectable people" and sympathized with those the rebels had exiled to western Virginia, where the Indians were probably "cutting their throats."

Everything in the city was expensive, and Cliffe had to borrow thirty or forty guineas from the wife of a corporal to enjoy himself. (He makes no attempt to explain how this lady acquired so much cash—the probable explanation is loot from American houses on the march to Philadelphia.) The cash did little to console him when the news of Burgoyne's surrender reached town. A stunned Cliffe thought it would "derange our operations" in the next campaign. If the rebels were wise, he added, they would sue for an advantageous peace. From ebullient confidence, the young lieutenant was virtually admitting defeat.

In a letter to his brother, a discouraged Cliffe declared that if he did not get promoted soon, he was going to sell his commission and quit the army. Several people like him, "with equal or superior claims," were infuriated to see "a parcel of boys jumping over our heads." This was a comment on General Howe's fondness for surrounding himself with younger officers and promoting those who pleased or flattered him.[20]

XI

Another series of letters from Captain William Dancey, commander of a light infantry company, shows a similar emotional pattern, with interesting variations. In notes to his fiancée, Dancey exulted in the prowess of his elite corps, with his own company winning special praise. At one point in the 1776 Battle of Long Island they took on four hundred riflemen in the woods. Contrary to their reputation for deadly accuracy, the Americans fired at ten yards and missed everyone. He ordered his men to take shelter behind trees, and they killed a rebel captain with their first volley.

A confident Dancey mocked American marksmanship. "No people can shoot black ducks better than they can but ducks carrying firelocks and bayonets are a different matter."

During the winter of 1776–77, Dancey too took part in the heavy skirmishing in New Jersey. There he found "a day of Yankee hunting no worse than a day of foxhunting." He survived a close call when an American jumped from behind a tree with his gun leveled. Dancey "knocked him over" with his fuzee (a light musket carried by officers). In another fight in the woods, firing from behind trees was hot on both sides until Dancey shouted: "By god soldiers they run! Have at them my brave boys!" The Americans took to their heels as the British charged with their bayonets leveled.

Dancey too sailed to Pennsylvania in Howe's army. There, he told his mother he didn't expect to change his clothes until "this side of

Christmas." But the constant marching and Howe's inability to decisively defeat Washington began to take a toll. After the battle of Germantown, in which the light infantry broke and ran, Dancey thanked his mother for her prayers. He could not imagine what else kept him alive.

The captain began to take the war seriously. "Fighting was fun when all the killed and wounded were on the side of the enemy. It was better than a fox chase. I like[d] it prodigiously." But when the dead and wounded belonged to your side, war induced somber thoughts. Dancey's best sergeant, who functioned as the company's paymaster, had been killed at Germantown, with three other good sergeants, leaving him to deal with all sorts of company business for which he had no enthusiasm. "The glory of this war is over," Dancey glumly declared.

The British had defeated the Americans in two pitched battles, but the rebels were still out there, ready to fight another one. Here, from the testimony of this young officer, was evidence of the hidden power of General Washington's army at Valley Forge.

Soon Captain Dancey was talking about going home. He decided honor would not permit him to quit the army in time of war. However, he wondered if he should angle for "a snug berth"—someplace where bullets did not whine. There was "nothing to be gained but hard knocks and broken bones in the light infantry. If it were not for the self-satisfaction it would be all a farce." Promotions had nothing to do with merit. They were all "by favor." Soon Captain Dancey had morosely concluded: "We are only tools for the higherups to work with."[21]

XII

In the midst of this psychological attrition, the Americans supplied the British with something else they did not need: embarrassment. On January 5, 1778, several Philadelphians noticed a large box floating in the Delaware. They rowed out to it, hoping there was something inside it they could sell. As they struggled to get it into their boat, it exploded with a tremendous thunderclap, killing them and shattering the boat into splinters.

Startled sentries on the waterfront and lookouts on the men-of-war and transports clustered off the Philadelphia shore saw more of these floating boxes—or "kegs," as they were soon called. They scampered to arouse their officers, who were equally baffled by their nature and purpose. But the wisps of smoke drifting about the shattered rowboat made it clear that they were lethal. The army rushed light artillery to the shore, and sailors aboard the men-of-war manned their guns. Soon broadsides were hurling cannonballs at these silent intruders.

The Artist was at work. The explosive kegs that were drifting down the Delaware were a variation on the underwater mine David Bushnell had devised for his submarine, the *Turtle*. Instead of a timing device, the kegs had a contact mechanism which triggered the explosion.

Upriver, where he had labored for months to construct the mines, the Artist was an extremely frustrated man. He had gone down the Delaware the previous night in a ship loaded with the mines and a guide who supposedly knew the river. But in the darkness, they had released the kegs in the wrong place, and instead of floating directly into their targets, the British warships and transports, the kegs were seized by the Delaware's tricky currents and swept far off course.

The Artist's (and his backers') only consolation was the consternation their secret weapon stirred in the British navy and army. Francis Hopkinson, the member of the American naval board who had been Bushnell's most enthusiastic supporter, decided satire was the best way to recoup their failure and dashed off a fifteen-stanza poem, "The Battle of the Kegs."

> *Gallants, attend, and hear a friend*
> *Trill forth an harmonious ditty*
> *Strange things I'll tell, which late befell*
> *In Philadelphia city.*
>
> *'Twas early day, as poets say*
> *Just when the sun was rising*
> *A soldier stood on a log of wood*
> *And saw a thing surprising.*

The next stanzas tell how sentries and lookouts decided American troops were packed into the boxes and sounded the alarm. The uproar soon reached General Howe's headquarters, where

Sir William he, snug as a flea
    Lay all this time a-snoring
Nor dreamed of harm, as he lay warm
    In bed with Mrs. [Loring]

Now in a fright, he starts upright
    Awaked by such a clatter
He rubs his eyes and boldly cries
    "For God's sake, what's the matter?"

The next stanzas described one of Howe's generals, Sir William Erskine, hopping around on one boot, the other one in his hand, shouting that the rebels "without a boat are all afloat and ranged before the city." Soon the entire British army was arrayed on the shore, ready to repel an American invasion, while cannon roared and muskets barked at the bobbing kegs.

From morn till night, these men of might
    Displayed amazing courage;
And when the sun was fairly down,
    Retired to sup their porridge.

An hundred men, with each a pen
    Or more upon my word sir
It is most true, would be too few
    Their valor to record sir.

Such feats did they perform that day
    Against those wicked kegs, sir
That years to come, if they get home
    They'll make their boasts and brags, sir.[22]

"The Battle of the Kegs" was a sensational hit. Newspapers from Boston to Savannah reprinted it, and rebel readers, no doubt including the shivering hut builders of Valley Forge, enjoyed a hearty, badly needed horselaugh. Unfortunately, it was the Artist's last appearance on history's stage. He gave up explosions for medicine and died an obscure physician in Georgia.

XIII

After the fleet's cannon and the army's artillery blasted the Americans out of the Delaware River forts in late November 1777, food and merchandise flowed into Philadelphia in an extremely welcome wave. The British and German rank and file began dining on a daily ration of three-quarters of a pound of beef and a pound of the best wheat flour for bread. Rice, peas, and vinegar were also issued during the week. For those with money in their pockets, markets full of fresh food from the countryside were also available, though prices were high.

The people who enjoyed this newly bountiful Phildelphia the most were the German troops. Mercenaries all, they were comparatively well paid by their royal masters. Private Johann Conrad Doehla informed his diary that "everything here is also cheap, because many provisions are being brought into the city from the nearby villages." Captain Ewald remarked in his journal that an officer could support the family he left at home and still live well in Philadelphia. Not a few of the company commanders and staff officers even increased their capital. "Booty money," a term Ewald used without the least sign of a troubled conscience, played a role in this development.[23]

For Ewald and his compatriots, war was a business and loot was a kind of bonus. They could barely wait to go into action in pursuit of it. When a group of loyalists captured 150 cattle being herded to Valley Forge and triumphantly rode into Philadelphia with these luscious prizes to sell, Ewald and his men sent a protest to the high command, asking why they had been "forgotten." General Howe jovially replied that he was only letting them "rest up."[24]

This interest in profits did not prevent these mercenaries from having sentimental feelings for civilians caught between the clashing armies. Most of their officers were assigned rooms in the German-speaking section of Philadelphia. Soon after Ewald settled into the comfortable quarters provided by a former resident of Strassburg, he learned from his landlord the harsh fate of the Reverend Caspar Dietrich Weyberg, pastor of the First Reformed Church of Philadelphia.

The seventy-year-old Weyberg had been a passionate advocate of the Revolution and had repeatedly heaped scorn on George III and on the loyalists and Quakers who supported him. One of the first requests the loyal Philadelphians made to Sir William Howe was for a writ that deposited Weyberg in a prison cell. His church was shut down, and his family was soon in danger of starvation.

Captain Ewald was a member of the Reformed faith. He visited Weyberg in prison and was touched by the old man's suffering. He decided to get the pastor out, relying on the reputation that he and his men had won in combat with the Americans. They were part of the Hessian jaeger (the word means "huntsman") battalion. Armed with short-barreled rifles, these green-uniformed soldiers had proved themselves invaluable in protecting the British army's flanks.

When Howe's second in command, Lord Charles Cornwallis, went back to England on leave, he wrote a personal letter to Ewald, thanking him for his "distinguished merit and ability." Captain Ewald took advantage of this and other encomiums to approach Sir William Howe on Pastor Weyberg's behalf. He soon persuaded the commander in chief to release Weyberg, on the promise that the old man would not call George III any more incendiary names.[25]

XIV

Although plenty of food was flowing into Philadelphia for the British and German soldiers in Howe's army, life for the city's civilians remained grim. About twenty-one thousand people, some of them loyalists but most the citizens Rebecca Franks called "the lower sort," lacked the money or the means to flee the conquerors. They depended on food from the surrounding countryside to stay alive. The royal army was not inclined to share their provisions with them.

For a few weeks, Washington, a humane man, matched Lord Howe's subsistence fishing policy by permitting the country people to bring food to a special market for these needy civilians. But pressure from the government of Pennsylvania and evidence that some of the food was going into the mouths of British soldiers or their dependents forced him to discontinue the policy and begin an all-out effort to make feeding the city as difficult as possible for General Howe.

The chief victims of this hard-line policy were the very poor. The British had turned them out of the poorhouse (called "the Bettering House") and taken it over for a barracks. After the battle of Germantown it became a hospital. The poor were shoved into the Fourth Street Quaker Meeting House and Carpenters' Hall, large buildings but never intended to accomodate several hundred inhabitants on a permanent basis. The poor were "very much necessitated," Robert Morton mournfully noted.[26]

XV

Trying to create a semblance of normal life, General Howe set up a civilian government of sorts. At its head he placed portly, humorless Joseph Galloway, once Benjamin Franklin's close friend and ally in the turbulent politics of Pennsylvania. Galloway had been elected to the First Continental Congress but quit in a sulk when his "plan of union"—an attempt to create a political structure that would give Americans semi-independence within the empire—narrowly failed to win a majority. Alarmed independence men soon expunged it from the Continental Congress's records, and their allies in Pennsylvania declared Galloway an enemy of the American cause.

After menaces and threats of imprisonment from the government of Pennsylvania, Galloway had fled to New York late in 1776. There he had played no small part in the chorus that had persuaded the Howes to attack Philadelphia. Galloway had gained access to the Howes by becoming friendly with Ambrose Serle, Lord Richard Howe's secretary, a hard-liner who had been ordered to America by Lord George Germain to make sure the brothers did not get too sentimental about their American friends.

Howe designated Galloway "Superintendent of the Police in the City and its Environs & Superintendent of Exports to and From Philadelphia." Behind this imposing title, Galloway had little power. Policing as we understand the term remained the army's job. Galloway's task was to issue regulations that would make the city run as smoothly as possible in a difficult time. He set prices on certain foods to combat rampant inflation and issued licenses to do business. He encouraged newspaper editors who had stayed in the city to resume publishing. His goal was to create an aura of normal, orderly city life—a forlorn hope.

Backed by a proclamation from General Howe urging loyalists to respond to the King's call, Galloway spent much of his time trying to prove that the city and its environs were crowded with men who detested the rebel government and were ready to fight. He set out to raise several regiments, financing one troop of cavalry out of his own pocket. It soon became apparent that his predictions of loyalist strength were wildly overstated. It did not improve Galloway's standing with Sir William Howe, who knew his senior officers were muttering behind his back: *For this we abandoned Burgoyne?*

The problem, Galloway soon realized, was the continued presence of the Continental Army at Valley Forge. He began telling General Howe that he had to disperse Washington's half-naked, starving battalions, whose unhappiness was painted in often lurid terms by Galloway's numerous loyalist spies. Surely Howe's well-fed, well-clothed royal army could manage this feat in a fortnight. Then volunteers eager to defend British liberty and its patriot king, George III, would emerge from the towns and villages of Pennsylvania in huge numbers.

Sir William was not inclined to take Galloway's advice. A winter campaign meant a week, perhaps a month, away from the pleasures of Philadelphia and the charms of Mrs. Loring. Valley Forge was a good defensive position, not easily attacked. He might end up throwing away the lives of hundreds of his soldiers. Soon relations between Superintendent Galloway and the British commander in chief were on the chilly side.[27]

XVI

Another matter that occasionally disturbed General Howe's revels was the plight of American prisoners in Philadelphia. The royal army had captured hundreds of soldiers during the autumn campaign. Under the prevailing rules of war, the British had no obligation to keep these captives alive. It was up to the Americans to feed these men. Soon Philadelphia swirled with reports of rampant starvation among the prisoners.

The Continental Congress complicated the problem by passing two contentious resolutions on December 19, 1777, the day the Americans marched to Valley Forge. The politicians decreed that the British would have to pay in gold or silver for the upkeep of their prisoners in American hands. Simultaneously the solons insisted that food for American prisoners in British hands must and would be purchased with Continental paper currency. A second resolution declared that any loyalist captured in a British uniform would be considered a traitor and shipped to his home state for prosecution.

This legislation brought all hope of an early exchange of prisoners to an abrupt, ruinous stop. Congress may have been motivated by a report that the British attitude toward American paper money was laced with mockery and contempt. At one point, under a flag of truce, the king's men sent out an entire wagonload of paper currency to pay for the subsistence of British prisoners. It was an obvious attempt at mockery. The Americans had ordered the money wagon back to Philadelphia, on the justifiable suspicion that the bills were counterfeit.

Also in the motivational mix was an attempt to force the British to recognize American independence. Congress insisted that any exchange of prisoners had to be "general." That meant the British would have to admit Congress spoke for an entire nation, rather than a collection of colonies that held prisoners at various places on the continent. The British would agree only to a "partial" exchange, although General Howe made it clear that he was ready to repeat this partial act until all the captives were swapped.

The Americans continued to feed the prisoners in their hands. In Philadelphia, General Howe let American captives starve and freeze. Over five hundred men were jammed into a huge stone prison built in 1775 called the New Jail. It was on Walnut Street, only a block from the Pennsylvania statehouse, where the Declaration of Independence had been issued. As winter advanced, the place became a gigantic refrigerator. Most of the prisoners had no blankets. They began dying by the dozen.

Among the few persons who tried to help them was a sympathetic black woman, who brought them food for a few weeks. But the inflated prices in the city's markets made it difficult for individuals to offer more than occasional charity.

The man in charge of trying to help the captives was Elias Boudinot, the wealthy New Jerseyan who had offered a sensible plan to solve the shoe shortage. A deeply compassionate man, Boudinot hurled himself into the struggle to feed the prisoners. It was a losing battle. He was competing for food with commissaries who were scouring the landscape to feed Washington's army. He wrote to Commissary General of Purchases William Buchanan in York to arrange for shipments of food to the prisoners. Buchanan ignored him as he ignored everyone else, including General Washington. Boudinot asked for help from the state of Pennsylvania and was icily informed that it was General Washington's responsibility to feed captives—a nasty example of the state's hostility to the Continental Army. Boudinot tried to get wood to the men to relieve the subzero temperatures inside the prison. With the British chopping down every tree in sight to keep their men warm, that too was a struggle against insuperable odds. Boudinot soon concluded that all his efforts were "without effect, or at best a scanty one."[28]

In despair, Boudinot went to General Washington and said he was going to resign. The general's eyes filled with tears. He told Boudinot the starving prisoners haunted him day and night. He seized Boudinot's hand and begged him to stay on the job. "I must be general, quartermaster, commissary—I can't do everything."[29]

Washington wrote an angry letter to General Howe, enclosing testimony from two civilians who had been seized and thrust into the New Jail with the captured soldiers. They reported that they frequently did not receive a morsel to eat for five days at a time. They were kept alive only by the visits of one man's wife, who brought them food. After one five-day starvation period, a soldier jailed near them was issued some meat, which he ate raw, and died in a half hour.[30]

Worsening the situation was the personality of Joshua Loring's right-hand man, Provost William Cunningham, a sadist who enjoyed inflicting pain and humiliation. Cunningham had come to America in 1774 and sided with the king. In New York, he had been mobbed and beaten by the Sons of Liberty, a group that often brawled with soldiers from the British garrison and others they deemed enemies of the Revolution. Cunningham never forgot or forgave his injuries. Often, according to one witness, he would bring broth to a cell in the New Jail where a half dozen men were starving and dump it on the floor. The desperate men would lap it off the filthy stones while Cunningham chortled at the "rebel scum."[31]

Sixty captured American officers confined in the Pennsylvania statehouse were not faring much better than the enlisted men. They were forbidden to see their families or friends, or to communicate with them by letter. A clever captain named Plunkett managed to escape by impersonating a British officer and talking his way past five sentries. On the run he borrowed a set of clothes from a patriot woman and strolled unchallenged past the numerous British pickets guarding the outskirts of the city. But he was an exception. The statehouse was almost as cold as the New Jail, and the British refused to allow sick officers to move to warmer quarters. One man who unsuccessfully attempted to feed the captives smuggled a letter out of the city begging "any officer of General Washington's army" to forward it to the commander in chief in the hope that he could do something to ease the prisoners' plight.[32]

XVII

Reading these horror stories, one wonders: where were the Quakers? About one-seventh of Philadelphia were members of that peace-loving faith. But their traditional compassion for the poor, the sick, and the suffering was short-circuited by the uncompromising position their leaders had taken toward the Revolution.

From the beginning of the difficulties with England, the Presbyterians in Pennsylvania (and New Jersey, among other colonies) had taken the lead in ratcheting up the opposition. In Pennsylvania, relations between the two faiths had always been tense, as both struggled for political control of the colony. At first the Quakers thought the growing acrimony with the mother country emanated from the same Presbyterian hunger for power.

This antagonism led to an almost formal alienation from the Revolutionary movement. By the time bloodshed occurred in Massachusetts in 1775, the Quakers in their Yearly Meetings, which sent epistles to their members, had taken the position that the king had been the true protector of their liberties since Pennsylvania's founding, and he deserved their loyalty and gratitude. The Revolution was not a war for liberty but an attempt by Presbyterians and other radicals to establish "tyranny" in America.

In January 1775, the Yearly Meeting announced it would discipline those who supported any and all aspects of the Revolutionary movement. The Meeting for Sufferings, which dealt with more specific problems, issued a public denunciation of the Continental Congress and its tendency to foment "insurrections, conspiracies and illegal assemblies." That soon led the Yearly Meeting to publicly disown Quakers who supported independence.

As the Revolution became an all-out war, and the rebel government of Pennsylvania called for universal militia service, Quaker resistance stiffened. So did the hostility of the rebels, who opened a ferocious attack on the Quakers' wealth—and their refusal to contribute a cent to the government of Pennsylvania, while the independence men were risking death on the gallows for rebelling against the king.

The ultimate Quaker response was to ban all their members from voting or holding any office under the rebel government. They also refused to pay taxes or take oaths of allegiance. Out of this impasse rose a conviction on the side of the independence men that the Quakers were very close to being traitors who behind their piously proclaimed neutrality were subverting the cause of liberty.

Among the Quakers spread a grim resolution that contact with the war in any shape or form violated the instructions of their Yearly Meetings. So the American prisoners in the New Jail and the statehouse froze and starved while Philadelphia's most pious—and wealthiest—citizens went complacently—even self-righteously—about their business only a few blocks away.[33]

XVIII

Just outside the city limits, at the Southwark Theater on Cedar (now South) Street, comedy, not tragedy, was the order of the day. Until the Revolution began, the Southwark had been something of an institution in Philadelphia. Painted bright red, it had no pretensions to architectural grace. It was essentially a large barn with seats for 660 playgoers. The first American play, *The Prince of Parthia*, a blank-verse tragedy by Thomas Godfrey, was presented at the Southwark in 1767, the year the theater opened.

The Quakers made playgoing a contentious business in Philadelphia. They published essays in the newspapers condemning the Southwark as a source of worldly corruption. They were not alone in this opinion. Plays were banned in Boston and other New England cities where the descendants of the Puritans prevailed. Nevertheless, British theater companies regularly appeared at the Southwark, putting on Shakespeare and the latest London plays. By the 1770s, the theater was often sold out on holidays and weekends.

In 1774, laughter at the London comedies and tears at the death of Hamlet or King Lear came to an abrupt halt. The First Continental Congress arrived in Philadelphia, and one of their earliest pieces of business was a resolution that announced their intention to "discountenance every species of extravagance and dissipation" to guarantee that the Revolution would end in the triumph of a virtuous America. Along with horse racing, cockfighting, and gambling, the "exhibition of shows, plays and other expensive diversions" was denounced. The British company that was performing at the Southwark soon departed for the more relaxed atmosphere of Jamaica, and the theater went permanently (so it seemed) dark.[34]

On December 24, 1777, a notice appeared in the *Pennsylvania Ledger*, one of several newspapers still being published in occupied Philadelphia, announcing that the Southwark would soon be back in business. Other announcements sought stagehands, carpenters, and a manager. But there were no calls for actors. These necessary accomplices were already in the ranks of the British army. In the evenings at the Southwark they would become "Howe's Strolling Players."

Soon the proprietor of the City Tavern was handling the receipts and attending to the business of putting up as many as a thousand posters around the city. Meanwhile, Captains John André and American-born Oliver DeLancey were designing scenery and selecting costumes. Still other officers were scouring the city for books containing the scripts of the plays they had in mind. This proved to be one of the most difficult tasks. With playgoing officially banned, most booksellers had thrown away the few copies they had stocked.

These and other difficulties were overcome, and rehearsals were soon in progress. The concept of a director was largely unknown in those days. Whoever had seen a production of a play or had strong ideas on how to stage it took charge. There was no trouble recruiting actors. The British had staged plays in occupied Boston, and New York's John Street Theater was currently operating with soldier actors.

Actresses were another matter. No respectable Philadelphia woman would venture onto the stage. Actresses in 1778 were synonymous with women of easy virtue. The solution: the officers volunteered their mistresses—and in a few cases, their wives. No one was troubled in the least by the mistresses. With Sir William Howe seated in a box decorated with his coat of arms and Mrs. Loring beside him, who could object?

On January 19, 1778, the Southwark opened for business with two lively farces about soldiers seeking to find love with difficult women. One eyewitness recalled the "six o'clock exodus from the city" as a "gay and splendid sight." The wealthy rode in their carriages. Those without such expensive transportation picked their way along a boardwalk laid to protect the ladies' slippers and their escorts' white stockings from the mud. Since four o'clock, servants had been holding their seats for them.

Unlike moderns, who go to the theater in casual clothes, the women all wore their best hoop-skirted gowns and had spent the early part of the day at the hairdresser. Elizbeth Drinker described the mode in hair as "dressed very high." This meant a two-foot tower "with a great quantity of different colored feathers."

In *The Inconstant*, one of the thirteen plays Howe's Strolling Players produced, a character summed up the pleasures of the theater in what might have passed as a description of the Southwark on January 19. He called playhouses "the Region of Beauty." He thought the ladies "had a more inspiring triumphant air" in the boxes than anywhere else. They wore their "best looks, shining jewels, the treasure of the world in a ring. . . . I could wish my whole life long were the first night of a new play." [35]

For the semiloyalist Quakers, the Southwark was the final blow in their fading romance with George III. They called it "the Devil's Schoolhouse" and began composing letters of protest to Sir William Howe. But some of their sect, known as "wet" Quakers, who saw nothing wrong with the theater and similar amusements, were among the crowd who filled the seats.

In a prologue written by the loyalist poet Jonathan Odell, the thespians announced that the proceeds were to go to the widows and children of dead soldiers. They also made some mocking comments on naive American audiences.

Once more ambitious of theatric glory
Howe's strolling company appear before ye
O'er hill and dale and bogs and wind and weather

With many a hairbreadth 'scape we've scrambled thither . . .
Now beats the Yankee busom at our drum
Hark Jonathan, zounds here the strollers come
Spruced up with top-knots & their Sunday dress
With eager looks the maidens round express
"Jemima see—a'nt this a charming sight?
"Look Tabitha—Oh Lord, I wish 'twas night."

These latter shafts seemed to be aimed at New Englanders, often called Brother Jonathans. Some American theater historians have concluded from the selection of plays that Howe's players wanted to mock moralistic Americans. In *The Duke and No Duke* the main character was a pimp. *The Minor,* by Samuel Foote, one of London's most popular playwrights, savagely attacked pious Methodists and their leader, George Whitefield, a preacher who drew huge crowds when he visited America. But it can equally be argued that the program reflected the tone and temper of the London stage of the era.

Captain John Peebles of the Forty-second Regiment (the Black Watch) complacently noted in his diary that another play was "full of bawdy sentiments indelicate to a modest ear, but most women can bear a little either very publicly or very privately." The Philadelphia loyalists in the audience heartily agreed with Captain Peebles. They knew that the sarcastic language of the prologue and the off-color dialogue of the plays were not aimed at them. They were sophisticates, joining their English cousins in laughing at the bumpkins who had brought on this annoying revolution.[36]

XIX

While the playgoers laughed and the American prisoners starved, and Sir William and his officers enjoyed their mistresses, elsewhere in and around occupied Philadelphia the war ground on. In each of the redoubts ringing the city, fifty men were on duty day and night, ready to meet an attack with cannon fire and musketry. A small guardhouse inside each redoubt had a stove where the soldiers could take turns warming themselves.

Farther out, picket guards checked every person coming in and out of the city. One day they stopped two very pregnant women and discovered beneath the first one's bulging dress a dozen or so pounds of salt, a commodity made scarce by the British blockade. Beneath the second woman's dress were numerous calfskins—enough, one witness claimed, to make shoes for an entire regiment. The British decided to post some soldiers' wives with the pickets, who were often reluctant to search women.

Along the nine capital roads that worried General Washington as well as on bypaths and lanes, farmers continued to carry foodstuffs into the city. Some were undoubtedly loyalists, but most were attracted by the clink of British guineas. The sound had far more appeal than the rustle of the Continental Congress's depreciating dollars.

Sullen Pennsylvania militiamen, who had been drafted to patrol the roads, began brutally punishing those they caught. One smuggler was shot dead as he sat on his wagon. Several others were tied to the tails of their horses and dragged along the road until they died. For several days, the number of contraband carriers dwindled. But in a week or so, they were just as numerous as ever in pursuit of those clinking golden guineas.[37]

Could Joseph Galloway find a way to convert this enthusiasm for the king's hard money into fervor for the royal cause? Pennsylvania, with its thousands of passive Quakers and even more thousands of half-hearted revolutionists with no enthusiasm for militia duty, seemed ripe with possibilities for a revival of loyalty to the empire that had brought riches to so many Philadelphians and affluence to the farmers in the city's commercial arc. If General Howe could be persuaded to strike a blow, or if the American army simply collapsed from starvation and disease, or if General Washington was displaced by the critics whose disillusioned voices reached Philadelphia through many clandestine channels, the clink of those golden guineas might yet become hosannas to "God Save the King."

THREE

IDEOLOGUES FRONT AND CENTER

I F WASHINGTON'S SOLDIERS were melancholy in the snowy hills of Valley Forge, the Continental Congress was even more out of sorts in their new headquarters, the tiny town of York, Pennsylvania, eighty-eight miles by the most direct road from Philadelphia.[1] After enjoying the luxuries and sophistication of America's largest city for two and a half years, the congressmen found little or nothing that pleased them in this rural outpost. York's population barely totaled 1,700, the food was mediocre and expensive, the accommodations in country taverns were abominable, and very few people spoke English; German was the prevailing tongue in this part of Pennsylvania.

Worst of all was the pathetic size of the national legislature: a mere nine men confronted the dismayed president, John Hancock, when Congress resumed its deliberations on the second floor of York's redbrick county courthouse. (Over the next few weeks the number rose to eighteen, a minor improvement at best.) The contrast between the confident body of fifty-six delegates from the thirteen states that had voted for independence fourteen months earlier and this band of disgruntled refugees was painful to contemplate.

For Hancock, the pain led directly to plans for an early resignation and a return to his native Boston, where his wife, Dolly, and his wealth guaranteed him a level of comfort infinitely beyond the resources of York.

II

Shortly after the battle of Germantown, a woman named Elizabeth Ferguson, from a distinguished Philadelphia family, had visited General Washington and given him a long letter from the Reverend Jacob Duche. He had been chaplain of the Continental Congress in 1776 and saluted the Declaration of Independence with a moving prayer. Now Duche had a different message, exclusively for Washington. The Revolution had degenerated into "a little low faction." Washington should seize the opportunity to call for a negotiated peace. The best evidence for this was Congress. "These are not the men you engaged to serve. These are not the men that America . . . chose to represent her," Duche wrote.[2]

The clergyman's gibe was perilously close to the mark. Of the political leaders of 1776 who voted for independence, only six remained in the present Congress. Most of the delegates had never met George Washington. To them he was only a name Washington was equally unacquainted with the new men in power—and there was little in their conduct that inspired respect.

The retreat to York was the second time in two years that the congressmen had been reduced to ignominious flight. The first time, in the dark days of December 1776, when the British army advanced to the banks of the Delaware River, Congress had retreated to Baltimore, which they disliked almost as much as York. Rhode Island delegate William Ellery called it "the dirtiest place . . . [they] ever saw." Benjamin Harrison of Virginia called it "a damned hole."[3]

When Washington's Christmas night victory at Trenton made their flight superfluous, there was not a little jeering among both loyalists and patriots at the haste with which the bold sponsors of the Declaration of Independence had put more than a hundred miles between them and the

British. Pennsylvania merchant Robert Morris, one of the few congressmen who stayed in Philadelphia, told President John Hancock that people were saying Congress had been "too precipitate." There was no love lost between Morris, who had doubts about declaring independence, and those who called themselves the "party of the Revolution."[4]

When the British fleet and army appeared in Chesapeake Bay and began landing men and guns only fifty miles from Philadelphia on August 25, 1777, the politicians resolved to tough it out. Short, stout Eliphalet Dyer of Connecticut told one friend: "We are now very sulky and determined not to move for [Howe] if we can help it." This bravado lasted little more than a week. On September 11, the king's men defeated the Continentals in a major battle at Brandywine Creek. Although Washington's soldiers were reportedly undiscouraged and eager for another contest, as the two armies maneuvered on opposite sides of the Schuylkill River many members of Congress decided they might be safer elsewhere. There was not much doubt that they were prime targets for a charge of treason if the British laid hands on them. Loyalists in New York had dubbed 1777 "the Year of the Hangman," a tribute to the three 7s' resemblance to a row of gallows from which they hoped to see numerous rebels dangling.

On September 18, Henry Laurens of South Carolina deplored the way fright had already "driven some great men" to inglorious retreat. If he had to flee, the wealthy South Carolinian was determined to do it with dignity. But Laurens did not think it would be necessary. "I am really in a comfortable state of confidence that General Washington will be victorious in the next engagement, which will probably happen this evening or tomorrow," he told one correspondent.[5]

III

Shortly after midnight on September 19, President John Hancock received an excited scrawl from Lieutenant Colonel Alexander Hamilton, one of Washington's aides, warning him: "If Congress have not left Philadelphia, they ought to do it immediately without fail." The British had seized boats on the Schuylkill and controlled a ford only a few miles from Philadelphia. They were in a position to "throw a party" into the city when and if they pleased. There was nothing between the enemy and the capital but a handful of Pennsylvania militia.[6]

Hancock took Hamilton at his word and began notifying members of Congress, who in turn spread the alarm among their friends and neighbors. Soon a panicky mass exodus was under way, more or less led by the legislators. One congressman, Nathaniel Folsom of New Hampshire, rode into the night without bothering to find a saddle. Few Philadelphians who had distinguished themselves as advocates of the Revolution wanted to stay and greet the grim-eyed British battalions.[7]

Congressman James Lovell of Massachusetts first roused Samuel Adams and later John Adams, two Bay State legislators the British would have especially liked to seize. They lived a block apart not far from the Pennsylvania statehouse. The Adamses (they were distant cousins) were the men who had persuaded Congress to vote for independence in 1776. Since that time, a coolness had grown between them. Potbelllied, balding John, who had just turned forty, had grown weary of playing right-hand man to gray-haired, fifty-three-year-old Sam. Though he was as lean and opinionated as he was on the day he graduated from Harvard, Sam utterly lacked John's oratorical gifts. He seldom spoke in Congress, and when he took the floor a tremor in his hands, which sometimes extended to his head, distracted listeners.

Although Thomas Jefferson called John a "colossus" in the often ferocious debates on independence, everyone in Congress knew that Sam Adams was the father of the movement. It was no accident that the British and loyalists called Sam "the Grand Incendiary." (His friends called him "the father of America.") Early in the contest, General Thomas Gage had offered an amnesty to Boston agitators but he specifically excluded Sam, which made him, to John's chagrin, world famous.[8]

John could not match Sam when it came to stoking what Sam fondly called "the spirit of resentment." Nor could John come close to Sam's skill at leading a legislature from backstage. Virtually every step on the circuitous road to Congress's vote for nationhood on July 2, 1776, was decided in advance by Sam in caucus with his fellow radicals. Thereafter, Sam and his mostly New England followers formed a bloc in Congress that caused one Virginian to exclaim during their sojourn in Baltimore, "The Yankees . . . rule as absolutely as the Grand Turk in his dominions."[9]

Both Adamses had a low opinion of Philadelphia and Pennsylvanians. On September 18, John Adams had confided to his diary: "We are still in Philadelphia, that mass of cowardice and Toryism." Sam Adams aimed his verbal ammunition at the city's principal citizens, the Quakers. The true religion of Quakers, Sam said, was making money and sleeping in a whole skin. These opinions were widely shared by the rest of New England's congressmen.[10]

When James Lovell announced that the British might be in Philadelphia before morning and "they had not a moment to lose," the Adamses and most of the other congressmen headed north to Bristol, Pennsylvania, where they crossed the Delaware and continued up the east bank to Trenton. Two days later, they began a roundabout trek to York, crossing the Delaware again at Easton, Pennsylvania. John Adams dolefully informed his wife, Abigail, that they had traveled 180 miles to make sure the British did not seize the papers of Congress, which followed them in several wagons. Neither "Honest John," as he liked to call himself, nor anyone else noticed something was missing from their archives: the printed copies of the journals of Congress.[11]

IV

Hot-tempered Thomas Burke of North Carolina was especially reluctant to "retreat with precipitation." When one of his servants awoke him about 2 a.m. on September 19, Burke dismissed Hamilton's letter as a false alarm. The congressman had been on the Brandywine battlefield as an uninvited observer, and had viewed the American performance with dismay and outrage. He had written a ferocious letter to George Washington, demanding the heads of some American generals, notably New Hampshire's military hero, Major General John Sullivan. It was a sample of the way most congressmen considered it their prerogative to criticize the army and its commanders.

In the morning, perhaps recalling Brandywine, Congressman Burke crossed the Delaware and retreated to Burlington, New Jersey, to await "the issue of a battle." Like Henry Laurens, he was convinced that Washington should and would fight to the last man to keep the British out of Philadelphia. Burke had only the foggiest idea of the strategy with which Washington was fighting the war: to avoid at all costs the risk of a winner-take-all battle.

V

The seemingly coolest of the legislators was James Lovell. He too crossed the Delaware to New Jersey on September 19 but soon returned to Philadelphia. Hamilton's letter was a premature rather than a false alarm. Before crossing the Schuylkill, the British paused to destroy the American division commanded by Brigadier General Wayne at Paoli. That eliminated the possibility of an assault on their rear guard as they forded the river. Next General Howe feinted a march on the American supply depot at Reading, forcing Washington to retreat in that direction to protect precious ammunition and powder stored there. Whereupon the British seized the Schuylkill's lower fords and crossed the river unopposed. They advanced on the city in two columns, making its fall a certainty.

On September 25, Lovell wrote to his friend Major General Horatio Gates, who was confronting another British army in northern New York, reporting he had just left Philadelphia, having waited until the British were within a mile of the city before he "slipt into the Jersies." Next came a curious remark for a former teacher at the Boston Latin School and father of eight children: "It was lucky I had a young lady to gallant thither [in New Jersey]." Four American officers who had lingered in the city were captured by British dragoons as they departed.

Lovell omitted a great deal in this account of his departures and returns to Philadelphia. Never a highly organized body, Congress had obviously been more than a little distracted by the oncoming British army. Those who declined to depart did almost nothing about transporting to safety the papers of Congress, which would have been enormously interesting to the British for propaganda purposes—and as evidence in the numerous trials for treason they planned to stage when they won the war.

Only in the frantic small hours of September 19 did various people get to work. Thomas Paine, the already famous author of *Common Sense*, the pamphlet that had galvanized the independence movement, was the secretary of the Committee on Foreign Affairs. He transported their vital diplomatic correspondence with France, Spain, and other nations to Trenton in a sloop. The deputy secretary of Congress, William C. Houston, departed with some unidentified papers in casks. An assistant auditor carried the Treasury books, papers, and money to Bristol. That left James Lovell with the printed journals of Congress.

What did he do with them? Not until December 31—three and a half months later—did Lovell get around to explaining to anyone in an official way. On that day he wrote a convoluted letter to General Washington, in which he reported that he had acquired some wagons to help the printer, Robert Aitken, get the journals out of the city. But Aitken apparently decided to stay in Philadelphia. So Lovell entrusted them to a papermaker who did business with Congress, one Frederick Bicking, whom Lovell described as "an honest timorous man." Bicking, apparently shaking with fright, had persuaded John Roberts, a prosperous miller, to carry the journals to his farm, ten miles outside Philadelphia, where he buried them.

There was one small glitch in this tale of non-derring-do. John Roberts, the mortified Lovell admitted, was a loyalist. The congressman wondered if General Washington could ask some "active Pennsylvania officer" who knew Roberts's neighborhood to dig up the journals and return them to Congress. "They would be a valuable acquisition at this time," Lovell wrote, in a masterpiece of understatement. The British would have paid ten thousand pounds to get their hands on them. But the supposed Tory Roberts was also a Quaker and apparently felt a moral obligation to keep the secret of the volumes' location.

Washington, recognizing their importance, immediately found a

Pennsylvania officer familiar with John Roberts's locale. The officer brought along some enlisted men, who dug up the journals and transported them to Valley Forge. Washington assigned an entire Continental regiment to escort them to York.[12]

There was a lot of irony in this exchange. Congressman Lovell was one of the most relentless denigrators of General Washington among his fellow legislators. A malicious man could have ruined him by spreading far and wide his incredible (and incredibly oblique) confession that in a panic he had given the precious journals of Congress to a loyalist.

Compounding Lovell's case was the way Washington had worked hard to extricate him from British hands in 1776. The British had arrested Lovell and taken him with them when they evacuated Boston in March of that year. When Lovell was released, Washington told the Massachusetts legislature how pleased he was to free a citizen of their state from "tedious confinement." Lovell, one of Sam Adams's most devoted followers, apparently did not feel an iota of gratitude to the army's commander in chief. He regularly lumped Washington and his officers in a contemptuous phrase, "the gentleman of the blade." In this, of course, he was only echoing Adams, who called a standing army "the shoeblacks of society."[13]

VI

In York, Congress displayed their sour mood when President John Hancock resigned and announced his intention to make a farewell speech. Samuel Adams had long since grown irritated with the way Hancock had kept the president's job for two and a half years, and added numerous trappings of office, such as a coach and four when he traveled around Philadelphia. Sam disliked even more the way Hancock gave elaborate dinner parties for men of wealth from other colonies, such as merchant Robert Morris, planter Benjamin Harrison of Virginia, and lawyer James Duane of New York. For over a year Adams had barely spoken to Hancock, and had used his influence in Boston to drive from the Massachusetts delegation anyone who supported him.

Sam Adams and virtually everyone else in the New England delegation complained loudly that no one else had made a speech when he left the national legislature. Hancock ignored them and made the speech. Things got even nastier when someone proposed that the thanks of Congress be tendered to the departing president. The New Englanders, once more led by Sam Adams and his Massachusetts phalanx, objected, resolving that it was "improper to thank any president for the discharge of the duties of that office." Duty, in the credo of these virtuous descendants of the Puritans, was something a man performed without any expectation of reward.

Every member of the Massachusetts delegation supported this resolution, but it failed to win a majority. Next came the vote on the motion to thank the departing president. Once more Sam Adams's and his fellow Yankees' opinion of Hancock was starkly visible. All the New England states except Connecticut voted against the motion; the naysayers were joined by Pennsylvania. Fortunately for Hancock's ego, six states voted yea, and the pleased ex-president, guarded by fifteen Continental Army dragoons, on the theory that Hancock was at the top of General Howe's most-wanted list, headed back to Boston.[14]

The contretemps is worth remembering, not for any impact it had on Hancock's career—Congress operated in secret and no one heard about it—but for what it revealed about the moral and political attitudes that prevailed among the nation's first legislators. Sam Adams and his fellow descendants of the Puritans did not like businessmen, especially wealthy businessmen. They viewed them with a sullen mixture of scorn and suspicion.

Some people thought this attitude had something to do with Sam's egregious lack of ability as a businessman. After graduating from Harvard, Adams had toiled for a few months in the office of a leading Boston merchant, who fired him with the comment that he thought he was training a businessman, not a politician. Adams's father gave him a thousand pounds to go into business for himself, and Sam loaned most of the money to a friend, who promptly lost it. After his father's death, Sam's management of the family's brewery ended in bankruptcy. By 1760 he was reduced to living on the tiny salary of a local tax collector. He did so poorly in that job that his accounts were soon eight thousand pounds in arrears. Making a virtue of necessity, Sam gloried in his poverty and compared himself to one of the "Old Romans" who despised money and devoted themselves to their country's welfare.[15]

In the opinion of Sam Adams and his righteous followers, John Hancock's penchant for expensive coaches, showy clothes, and fine wines set a bad example for the people of Massachusetts in particular and for Americans in general. Such ostentation threatened a fundamental component of their formula for revolutionary victory. Independence would be wrested from the corrupt British because the Americans were superior in public virtue. We have seen this idea recurring sporadically in the letters and remarks of Washington's soldiers. In the Continental Congress, among the New England men and their followers in other colonies, it amounted to an obsession. Their goal was to transform America into a Christian Sparta that would be immune to the temptations and luxuries of amoral, corrupt England.

Another reason for the radicals' refusal to thank President Hancock was their equally obsessive fear of power. They had constructed the office of president to give its holder as little power as possible. A president was barely permitted to say a word while Congress was in session, except to recognize the order in which congressmen might speak during a debate. He could not even answer a letter addressed to him in his official capacity. He could only hand it on to the proper committee.

This fear of power led Sam Adams and his radical followers to look with suspicion and even dislike on General Washington's Continental Army. Sam was fond of saying, "The sins of America may be punished by a standing army." He was perpetually on his guard to make sure the army showed a proper respect for Congress and the great principle of civilian control of the military. General Washington had repeatedly demonstrated he too revered this principle. But that did nothing to alter Sam Adams's dark suspicions that the army had too many "idle, cowardly . . . drunken generals."[16]

To replace President Hancock, Congress chose Henry Laurens. A

South Carolina merchant who had made a fortune in the slave trade, he seemed at first glance to share the views of the Adams radicals who controlled Congress. At one point, Laurens said: "How hard it is for a rich or covetous man to enter heartily into the kingdom of patriotism." But Laurens was rescued from this extremism by his intimate link with General George Washington. Laurens's son, John, the general's aide, sent him a stream of confidential letters from Valley Forge, telling the president what the commander in chief thought and felt about the Continental Army's multiple problems.[17]

VII

It was not an accident that Pennsylvania joined the New Englanders in refusing to give John Hancock a vote of thanks. In this pivotal state there had been an internal revolution far more radical than the revolt against royal authority that united the other twelve ex-colonies. The state's sophisticated economy had created a wealthy upper class that fancied expensive coaches, luxurious homes, stylish clothes, and a presumption that they were more or less in charge of the government. Not surprisingly, a hefty percentage of these people were wary about declaring independence and risking their comfortable lives and substantial fortunes.

Out of the revolutionary ferment of 1775–76 had risen a group of discontented, less successful Pennsylvanians who used the push for independence to overthrow the state government and send delegates to Congress who voted for independence. Typical of these rebels was Timothy Matlack, son of a bankrupt father who in turn went bankrupt and was rescued from debtors' prison by Quakers who pitied his distressed family. When Matlack told a Quaker acquaintance he was joining the Revolution to fight for his property and his liberty, the Quaker replied, "As for thy property, thou hast none—and as for thy liberty, thou owest that to the clemency of thy creditors, me amongst them."[18]

Matlack associate James Cannon had been a teacher of mathematics at the College of Philadelphia for the previous eleven years, more and more embittered by struggling to survive in affluent Philadelphia on a minimal salary. Cannon found his revolutionary vehicle in the Committee of Privates, an organization that supposedly spoke for the average man in the city's militia. He was not above suggesting that the privates were ready to use their guns to win true equality from the supposedly domineering rich.

Also in the mix was former druggist Christopher Marshall, who was always ready to record the latest criticism of Washington in his diary. This personal record reveals that these opponents of the rich had no compunction about enjoying the good life. While the Pennsylvania Assembly was passing its remonstrance deploring General Washington's decision to go into winter quarters and calling for an attack on Philadelphia, Marshall was describing in his diary a Christmas feast he and his friends enjoyed in Lancaster, complete with roast turkey and all the traditional fixings. Washington's blast against legislators who knew (and apparently cared) nothing about his half-naked, starving soldiers was demonstrably on the mark when it came to the druggist and his circle.

Marshall's diary also provides a good glimpse of the radicals' attitude toward the American army. In his entry for December 28, he wrote: "Our affairs wear a very gloomy aspect." He went on to describe the British in Philadelphia "revelling in balls attended with every degree of luxury and excess." He added to this painful thought the image of the British foraging in an arc of twenty miles around the city, "plundering men and women . . . deflowering virgins." He called the British a "handful of banditti to the amount of six or seven thousand men" and lamented that they were pillaging and raping in full view of the American generals and their army, who were more interested in "consulting where they shall go to spend the winter in jollity, gaming and carousing." Marshall closed this jeremiad with a cry: "O Americans, where is now your virtue? O Washington, where is your courage?" [19]

VIII

Another enthusiastic proponent of Pennsylvania's revolt within the larger Revolution was Thomas Paine. Having failed at virtually every job he ever tackled in England, including tax collector, he too loathed the rich. With Sam Adams and other independence men covertly supporting them, Paine and Pennsyslvania's radicals had staged a convention which wrote a new constitution for the state in the summer of 1776. It called for a single-chamber legislature, a ruling council, and annual elections, lest anyone accumulate too much power.

In the ensuing election, the radicals insisted on a test oath, declaring a man's support of this constitution, before anyone was permitted to vote. An estimated four-fifths of Pennsylvania's voters despised the document and were barred from the polls. The Supreme Executive Council and General Assembly were chosen by a mere six thousand voters, about 10 percent of the electorate. The rest of the state's voters seethed with animosity against this power play.

The rhetoric of the election was the language of class war. Matlack boasted that he did not own a "chariot." By that he meant a coach and four, the ultimate sign of wealth in eighteenth-century America. There were eighty-four of these expensive vehicles in Philadelphia. If the Revolution against England was on behalf of the people, Matlack intoned, it was time to let ordinary farmers and mechanics run the government. A man worth fifty pounds was finally going to be entitled to "all the privileges of the first nabob in the country."

James Cannon, in one of his letters on behalf of the Committee of Privates, declared: "There is no rank above that of freeman." The mathematician wrote a bill of rights that included the principle that "an enormous proportion of property vested in a few individuals is dangerous to the rights and destructive of the common happiness of mankind." Therefore the state should have the right to "discourage" the possession of too much property. This was too blatant even for the other radicals running the constitutional convention, and that particular "right" was scrapped. But it remained a signpost on the road to the radicals' view of the future.[20]

IX

Tom Paine later declared that the 1776 constitution was so beloved by the people of Pennsylvania that everyone kept a copy of it handy so he could reread it for sheer pleasure, or to settle a point of law. "Scarcely a family was without it," Paine wrote in *The Rights of Man*, a book he published in 1791. In most Pennsylvania families in 1776 and 1777, if a copy of the constitution was kept around, it was to hurl curses at it. Pennsylvania was in the hands of radical theorists whom the majority hated only slightly less than they hated the British.[21]

Throughout the winter that tried the Continental Army's soul, Tom Paine visited Valley Forge only once, in December. In a later letter he described the soldiers as resembling a family of beavers, building their huts. "The whole was raised in a few days," he reported—which suggests Tom's stay was extremely brief. It was February before the troops finished the last of their log shelters.

To his credit, Paine seems to have ignored a letter from Timothy Matlack on behalf of the Pennsylvania government, which urged him to become a semiofficial "observer" attached to the Continental Army, so he could give the radicals in Lancaster "more regular and constant intelligence." There was (and is) another name for this job: spying. Paine undoubtedly knew the low opinion of General Washington prevailing among the so-called Constitutionalists.

Instead, Paine retreated to cozy quarters in the homes of wealthy friends, first in Bordentown, New Jersey, and then in Lancaster, where he whiled away his days, eating huge dinners and drinking large amounts of liquor in convivial evening gabfests. Not until April did he get around to publishing *Crisis No. 5*. It bore no resemblance to the famous *Crisis No. 1*, written in the dark days of 1776, with its unforgettable lines: "These are the times that try men's souls. The summer soldier and the sunshine patriot will, in this crisis, shrink from the service of their country."

Crisis No. 5 was a rambling diatribe aimed mostly at General Howe,

2. Here is the George Washington who held the army together at Valley Forge, outmaneuvered his political enemies, and rescued the Revolution from extremism. Note the self-assured mouth and unillusioned eyes. This is a man who had thought about war and politics and drawn his own conclusions.

3. Irish-born French army Colonel Thomas Conway persuaded Congress to make him a brigadier general in the Continental Army. Egotistic and ambitious, he became George Washington's most outspoken critic after the British captured Philadelphia.

4. The leader of Massachusetts delegation, Samuel Adams was a power behind the scenes in the Continental Congress. He let his followers criticize Washington and later claimed he never opposed him. But the Boston town meeting denounced Adams for trying to undermine the commander in chief.

5. Elias Boudinot was a wealthy New Jerseyan who became the Continental Army's Commissary of Prisoners. He tried, mostly in vain, to feed and keep warm the hundreds of American soldiers the British held in Philadelphia's freezing prisons.

6. British born General Horatio Gates was the victor in the 1777 battle of Saratoga. A born intriguer, he welcomed the flattery of the congressmen and army officers who thought he should supplant Washington as commander in chief of the Continental Army.

7. General Nathanael Greene of Rhode Island became General Washington's closest adviser in the opening years of the Revolution. This led to savage attacks on Greene's character by Washington's critics. Undeterred, Washington chose him to become the army's new quartermaster general.

8. Handsome, intensely idealistic John Laurens was an aide to General Washington. He kept his powerful father informed about Washington's response to the plot to replace him.

9. South Carolinian Henry Laurens succeeded John Hancock as president of the Continental Congress. At first Laurens was inclined to criticize Washington. But he soon became a vital ally. He was convinced that the plotters were trying to conceal widespread fraud in the quartermaster and commissary departments.

10. Delegate Gouverneur Morris of New York was a masterful debater who sided with Washington and helped him change the congressional policies that contributed to the American army's near collapse at Valley Forge.

11. Dr. Benjamin Rush was a quintessential "true whig" extremist. He despised regular armies, worshipped the militia, and believed patriotic virtue would be the decisive factor in winning the war. This man of lofty principles was not above writing unsigned letters to politicians, smearing George Washington and the Continental Army.

12. This relatively unknown miniature is one of the few portraits of Martha Washington in her middle age. She added a badly needed woman's touch to General Washington's spartan headquarters at Valley Forge.

13. One of the richest men in France, Marquis de Lafayette became a major general in the Continental Army at the age of nineteen. The rank was a tribute to his powerful relatives in the court of Louis XVI. Lafayette played a key role in defeating Washington's enemies during the Valley Forge winter.

14. Many people thought Quartermaster General Thomas Mifflin
of Pennsylvania was the "pivot" of the plot to force General
Washington to resign. He quit his vital job in disgust after the
British captured Philadelphia. President Henry Laurens blamed
him for the deaths of thousands of soldiers at Valley Forge.

15. This painting of the march to Valley Forge is typical of the exaggerated depictions of the American Army's suffering. There were only a few snowstorms. Most of the time the temperature stayed well above the freezing mark.

16. Here we see enlisted men huddling around campfires while others drag logs to build huts during the first wintry days at Valley Forge. It took seven weeks to build the 1,000 huts. Thereafter the army was reasonably warm.

17. In this highly imaginary painting, Washington gives the five-man committee sent by Congress a look at his ragged, hungry men. Actually, Washington stunned the congressmen with a detailed report on the army's problems, which converted them from critics to allies.

18. When the British captured Philadelphia, Congress fled to this small courthouse in York, Pennsylvania. The politicians met on the second floor for nine months. There were seldom more than twenty-five delegates in attendance.

19. Before the Revolution, Philadelphia was the largest and wealthiest city in America. From its wharves flowed thousands of tons of wheat, salted meat, bar iron, lumber, and other products to Europe and the West Indies.

20. German-born General Friedrich von Steuben is seen here training a company of Continental Army soldiers. He not only inculcated new discipline and tactics; he gave officers a sense of responsibility for the well-being of their men.

21. Did General Washington pray at Valley Forge? This painting portrays one of the winter camp's most enduring legends. Recently discovered evidence of Washington's religious faith makes the moment of prayer more plausible.

THE BATTLE OF THE KEGS.

22. In early 1778, the Americans tried to destroy British warships off
Philadelphia by floating contact mines into them from the upper Delaware
River. Currents carried the mines off course and the British destroyed
them with gunfire from ships and shore. Poet Francis Hopkinson satirized
the enemy's consternation in his poem, "The Battle of the Kegs."

23. The Battle of Monmouth was a crucial test of Washington's generalship and the tactical reforms Baron von Steuben initiated in the
Continental Army at Valley Forge. Confounding Washington's critics, the
Americans proved they could stand their ground against the best troops in
the British army.

24. These reconstructed huts at present-day Valley Forge give visitors a good idea of how the soldiers lived at the winter camp. There were twelve men assigned to each hut. Officers had similar huts, with fewer tenants. Each hut had a fireplace.

25. Washington's headquarters is the centerpiece of contemporary Valley Forge National Historical Park. The general lived and worked in this modest stone building, along with numerous aides. Several subordinate generals lived in more spacious houses.

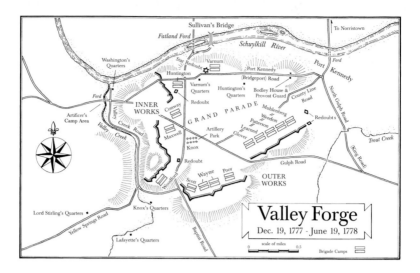

Valley Forge
Dec. 19, 1777 - June 19, 1778

26. Not many people are aware of the numerous well-planned fortifications at Valley Forge. The winter camp was a stronghold which the British never found the courage to attack.

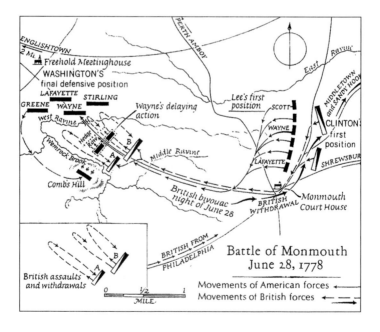

Battle of Monmouth
June 28, 1778

Movements of American forces
Movements of British forces

27. Here is a virtually blow-by-blow diagram of the battle of Monmouth Court House, from the first encounter with the British Army through the American retreat to the position where Washington took charge and repulsed the British attack.

whom Paine called "a military pig" among other nasty names. It was a disjointed rant which barely mentioned General Washington and never said a word about Valley Forge and its suffering soldiers. Maybe Paine was just burned out. Or perhaps what he heard from the angry ideologues in York and Lancaster made him tongue-tied.[22]

X

The trouble with creating a state government that scorned the rich and imposed test oaths that eliminated four-fifths of the voters was the way such tactics resulted in excluding the best brains and talents in Pennsylvania from the government's ranks. Numerous experienced soldiers refused to accept commissions in the militia, because they had to take the test oath pledging their loyalty to the constitution. Former congressman John Dickinson, probably the ablest legislator in the state, was elected to the assembly but refused to serve when the lawmakers ignored his call for a new constitutional convention. In many parts of the state there were no constables or justices of the peace because they too had to take the test oath, and most available candidates refused.

In October 1777, in spite of the British capture of Philadelphia, annual elections were held for new assemblymen. These contests were an even bigger farce than the elections of 1776. Wealthy James Allen, who was hostile to both American independence and the state government, claimed that in the whole province, barely 150 people voted. This was an exaggeration, though not a large one. There is no doubt that Allen was right when he said the polls were in the hands of "private zealots" who often put their own names on the ballot.[23]

Matlack, Cannon, and the other defenders of the state government repeatedly admitted it was not perfect. The whole thing was an "experiment," they maintained. It was giving the average man a chance to prove he could run a government. Those with common sense all but screamed in response that America was fighting a war for survival as a free country— hardly the time to conduct political experiments.

XI

What the Constitutionalists wrought was vividly illustrated in their creation of a new militia law, arguably the most important legislation they undertook. They ordered the enumeration of all white males between the ages of eighteen and fifty-three and divided each county into militia districts. In each district the militiamen were subdivided into eight "classes." These were called out in rotation for two months' service.

Each county was assured that it would not be required to send more men than any other county, in proportion to its population. To assure a truly democratic system, the militia were entitled to elect their own officers, up to and including the rank of colonel. Supervising things in each county was a county lieutenant appointed by the assembly.

As soon as the law began to operate in the spring of 1777, one of the weaknesses of an annually elected legislature became apparent. No one had the courage to decide how many men should be called out. They knew militia duty was unpopular and feared the voters would take their revenge at the ballot box. The Supreme Executive Council asked the Continental Congress to undertake this sticky task. Displaying their own ignorance of military matters, the solons suggested three thousand as a nice round number.

There were more than seventy thousand men on the state's militia rolls. But there was little success in raising the three thousand requested by Congress. York County failed to turn out a man, because the militia declined to meet and elect their officers. When the county lieutenant tried to appoint some officers, they promptly resigned. The virtuous citizens of York threatened the lives of those who accepted.

In Lancaster County, where the county lieutenant was especially vigorous, six militia battalions were organized. But when the lieutenant ordered four hundred men to Chester, where they might be helpful in defending Philadelphia, men from other classes used threats and curses to prevent them from marching, because they feared their class would be the next to be called out. The distraught county lieutenant had to hire substitutes, at a cost of two hundred dollars a man—a year's wages for a laborer in 1776–77.

Those who refused to serve faced fines to compensate the state for the cost of substitutes. But armed groups threatened the life of any constable who tried to collect these fines. They killed one law enforcer in June 1777, and the militia already on duty had to be recalled to suppress this local rebellion. Pennsylvania's internal revolution had given everyone heady ideas about their rights—and barely mentioned their responsibilities.

The militia and the state's officials behaved in similar fashion during the struggle to defend Philadelphia. When the British fleet with Howe's army aboard sailed from New York and remained at sea for eight weeks, the Supreme Executive Council persuaded Congress to let them dismiss most of the militia on duty. On August 23, when the fleet was sighted in the Chesapeake, Congress sent the council a frantic message, urging the men's immediate recall. The council took eight days to get around to issuing the order. Most of the men who showed up were next to useless because, in the words of the lieutenant of Lancaster County, "they have neither arms, accoutrements, camp-kittles etc." The Constitutionalists had done little to remedy these deficiencies during their year in power.[24]

After the capture of Philadelphia, the state's part-time soldiers became even more undependable. General John Armstrong reported "a very infamous falling off of the militia, which may with great justice be called desertion." The Supreme Executive Council and the General Assembly tacitly abandoned the job and created a Council of Safety with virtually absolute power to compel militiamen to serve. County lieutenants were told to stop worrying about calling them out by classes. Alas, the Council of Safety did not have much more success than the elected legislators. In October 1777, Washington told the Pennsylvania lawmakers that it was "a matter of astonishment in every part of the Continent" that Pennsylvania had only 1,200 militiamen on active duty.

In December 1777, a discouraged General Armstrong told the president of the Supreme Executive Council, Thomas Wharton, that "many, too many of the militia are a scandal to the military profession, a nuisance to the service and a dead weight on the publick [*sic*]." A Continental Army general put it even more bluntly: these amateurs were "absolutely good for nothing."[25]

Nevertheless, the radicals clung to their ideological conviction that the militia were preferable to the Continental Army. The widespread use of paid substitutes was fatal to recruiting drives for the Continentals. Being a militia substitute became a sort of trade for many able-bodied men in Pennsylvania. Why would anyone join the Continentals for three years or the duration of the war? All he got for his patriotism was a $45 bounty (eventually raised to $100) and pay of 6 2/3 dollars a month thereafter. Congress and the commanding officers of the depleted Continental regiments begged the assembly to abandon the substitute payments. The radicals sullenly refused.[26]

To excuse the state's failure to fill the army's battalions, the radicals reversed their standard denounce-the-rich-as-too-powerful rhetoric. In a bleating letter to General Washington, they claimed that "in this state, where property is in general very equally divided," they did not see how they could persuade farmers "to enlist their neighbors' children in the service." They did not even think farmers would enlist their laborers, "which they feel themselves in great want of." They suggested that Washington dispatch recruiting officers from the Pennsylvania battalions at Valley Forge to try to fill the gaping holes in the state's Continental brigades.[27]

Washington reluctantly agreed to send the recruiters, which deprived their regiments of valuable officers. The reception they met was totally hostile. One officer came close to being murdered when he ventured into a local tavern. A two-officer team returned from one county with four recruits and said there was not even the faintest hope of finding more. Another officer wasted five weeks touring Chester County (in which Valley Forge was located) and returned without a single man.[28]

The ultimate example of the Pennsylvania radicals' militia worship surfaced at the end of December 1777, when two citizens of Lancaster, Jedediah Snowden and Benjamin Harbeson, began circulating a petition requesting the Pennsylvania Assembly to call out the entire militia of the state. That would create an army of seventy thousand men who would end the war with an all-out assault on General Howe's army in Philadelphia.

General Washington was barely able to feed his ten-thousand rank and file at Valley Forge. How anyone short of a savior who multiplied loaves and fishes could hope to feed seventy thousand men even for a week seems never to have occurred to these small "d" democrats. The petition was presented to the Pennsylvania Assembly on December 31. Nowhere in the proposal was there a mention of General Washington and his Continental Army. These militia worshippers apparently thought they could win the war without them.[29]

XII

While the ideologues of Pennsylvania were perpetrating legislative and military disaster in their state, their counterparts in Congress were busy concocting their own catastrophe: the reform of the commissary and quartermaster departments. "A rage for reformation," said Richard Henry Lee of Virginia, began pervading Congress in early 1777, when the representatives returned to Philadelphia from their ignominious flight to Baltimore. It coincided with the realization that it was going to be a long war.

From 1775 through most of 1776, Congress had pursued a strategy that assumed a short war. It would be won in a single huge battle (called a "general action" in the eighteenth century) in which American numbers would overwhelm the small army that the British would ship to America. The British confounded this premise by shipping an army almost twice as big as Washington's Continentals. In a blunt letter to John Hancock, Washington abandoned the one-big-battle strategy in September 1776. "We should on all occasions avoid a general action or put anything to the risque, unless compelled by a necessity, into which we ought never to be drawn."[30]

This shift from a short war to a protracted conflict meant Congress would have to govern the nation as well as supervise the prosecution of the war. The reign of virtue and republican simplicity would have to be imposed on America in the midst of battles and casualties. The army's commissary department became the first target of this moral-purification campaign.

Throughout the first two years of the war, reports had reached congressional ears about profiteering by numerous commissaries. They received a small percentage of what they spent to buy food for the troops, a custom inherited from the British army. This policy was denounced in Congress as an invitation to corruption. It made commissaries careless about the prices they paid and encouraged collusion between sellers and buyers.

What was the best way to keep things honest? First, Congress decided to divide the commissary department in half, creating a commissary general of purchases and a commissary general of issues. These two men would "check" each other's tendency to aggrandize power, that constant congressional bugaboo. The lawmakers also refused to allow either man to appoint his deputies, who did the real work in the field. Congress decided to name its own men for these myriad jobs, relying on advice from fellow solons and state governors. This decentralized the authority of the top men, further reducing the awful possibility that one or both would acquire too much power. Its real effect was to render them more or less powerless.

Simultaneously, Congress decided to abandon the custom of allowing commissaries a percentage of their expenditures. Henceforth, everyone, including the commissary general, would draw a reasonable salary, decided by Congress, of course. To make sure these public servants were accountable for the money they spent, Congress printed up forms and issued instructions for every imaginable transaction. The orders from on high filled no fewer than fifteen pages in the journals of Congress. They required specific descriptions of every item purchased, the size, the quantity, the quality. The commissary general of purchases was told to give his deputies a book with ten column pages in which to keep their records. Finally, Congress required deputy commissaries to post a five-thousand-dollar bond by way of further guaranteeing their honesty. What was the result of this exercise in legislative righteousness? As one historian wryly concluded, it can be summed up in two words: Valley Forge.[31]

The man who had been supplying the army with food to the satisfaction of the troops and officers, Commissary General Joseph Trumbull of Connecticut, was the son of the state's governor and a merchant of wide experience, especially in New England. Trumbull vehemently protested these changes and finally quit in disgust. Many of his deputies also resigned, complaining that the salaries were too low and the mania for record keeping made the job an exhausting nightmare. Numerous deputies pointed out that a certain amount of wastage was inevitable when dealing with perishables such as vegetables, flour, and meat. Such accidental losses now had to be proven under oath or the money came out of the commissary's pocket. Another problem was the soldiers' cavalier attitude toward the commissaries and their purchases. Supplies were often "embezzled by the soldiery," one angry commissary wrote. How could Congress expect a man to risk his reputation and his own money obeying such a ridiculous set of rules?

As resignations multiplied, Congress found it next to impossible to find replacements. Experienced businessmen insisted on a commission for their labors. Others flatly refused to post a bond for good performance in the midst of a war. Few of the men Congress found willing to serve had the kind of experience that enabled them to perform well. One deputy quartermaster wryly remarked that "the whole race of commissaries" look at each other "like cats in a strange garret. . . . Not one of them knows what he is about. Such are the happy effects of shifting hands in the midst of a campaign." [32]

XIII

The army's quartermaster department was not in much better shape—which added to the commissaries' woes. Quartermasters were responsible for procuring the wagons that transported much of the army's food to camp. They also supposedly supplied the army with tents, tools, and above all, firewood. Here the problem was a lack of leadership that had overtones of treachery. The quartermaster general for most of 1777 was Major General

Thomas Mifflin, a wealthy Pennsylvanian whose rousing speeches to the Philadelphia militia had turned out men General Washington needed for his suprise attacks on Trenton and Princeton in 1776.

Mifflin fancied himself a military thinker as well as a political leader. He had advised Washington to position his army between the British and Philadelphia and fight a last-ditch battle to save the city. When Washington refused to risk the Continental Army in such a winner-take-all gamble, Mifflin had announced his health was failing and withdrawn to his country estate, Angelica, outside Reading, leaving the quartermaster department to run itself.

On October 10, not long after the British captured Philadelphia, Mifflin expressed his disgust with Washington by quitting as quartermaster general—and never bothering to inform Washington of his departure. The commander in chief was reduced to writing a harried letter to Congress, asking if rumors about Mifflin's resignation were true.

The Anglica estate became a gathering place for army officers and congressmen who were no longer enthused by George Washington's leadership. A frequent guest was General Thomas Conway, already on several records as a vocal critic of the commander in chief. Jacob Hiltzheimer, sometimes called the Samuel Pepys of the Revolution, noted in his gossipy diary that he dined with Mifflin and Conway and "other officers of the army" on November 25, 1777.

Lieutenant Colonel James Wilkinson, General Horatio Gates's aide, was invited to tea by General Mifflin when he reached Reading on his way to York with Gates's dispatches reporting the victory at Saratoga. Wilkinson found two New England members of Congress visiting Mifflin. The three men "minutely questioned" him on the Saratoga campaign and "severely strictured" General Washington's "misfortunes" in Pennsylvania. They also discussed General Conway's criticisms of the Continental Army. General Mifflin, Wilkinson noted, seemed "extremely depressed" and talked of the need for insurance on homes and business buildings in Reading against "the depredations of the enemy," whom he apparently thought capable of roaming at will through Pennsylvania, leaving a swath of destruction behind them.[33]

XIV

Once, Washington seemed to have no stronger admirer than Thomas Mifflin. In 1775, when the newly appointed commander in chief was leaving Philadelphia to take charge of the mostly New England army besieging the British in Boston, he began to mount his horse and was startled to find the smiling thirty-one-year-old Mifflin kneeling beside him, holding the stirrup. People cheered this grandstanding gesture, which was superfluous in several ways. Washington, sometimes called the finest horseman of his age, needed no help to mount a horse. He also disliked displays that suggested he was an exalted figure. Modesty was his prevailing style. He had told Congress that he feared he was unequal to the task they had given him.[34]

The stirrup holding reveals almost as much about Mifflin's character as his portrait by John Singleton Copley. There is a crafty arrogance to the sitter's smile and an equally large dose of self-satisfaction. Even more interesting is the way the painter left the right side of Mifflin's face in shadow, as if there were secrets about the man he preferred not to explore.

Born into the Philadelphia upper class, Mifflin liked power and pursued it aggressively. In 1775, he had gone out of his way to befriend John and Samuel Adams, leaders of the New England delegation in Congress.

Washington had already asked Mifflin to be his aide, and he joined the general for the trip to Boston. There he immediately began angling to become quartermaster general. A bare month after their arrival, Mifflin had the job, which would enable him to make quite a lot of money while serving his country. At that time, the quartermaster general got a percentage of the cash he laid out for wagons, horses, and the paraphernalia of war.

Mifflin soon realized that a quartermaster was not going to acquire any military glory. He switched to the fighting side of the Revolution with the greatest of ease, thanks to the backing of the Adamses and other congressional friends. Soon he was a brigadier and then a major general. But as the war expanded, Washington asked him to become quartermaster again. The commander in chief saw no one on the horizon who could handle the job "upon the present large plan."

Mifflin acquiesced, but he still saw himself as a military genius and constantly offered Washington advice. Alas, the commander in chief preferred the counsel of another major general, thirty-five-year-old Nathanael Greene of Rhode Island. Soon a sullen Mifflin was telling his friends that Greene "exclusively possessed" Washington's ear, and that meant more of the military disasters that had almost destroyed the army in 1776. He pointed to the failed campaign to defend Philadelphia as the proof of this messy pudding.[35]

XV

Other officers echoed Mifflin's line. Colonel Daniel Brodhead, commander of a Pennsylvania regiment and a Mifflin close friend, wrote to General Gates from Reading: "Since you left us our divisions have suffered greatly and chiefly by the conduct of Gen'l W——n. Most of the officers are unhappy under his command."[36]

One officer who opted out of this negative chorus was Baron de Kalb. Although he still disapproved of Valley Forge as a winter camp, watching Washington grapple with the problem of feeding his men and somehow sustaining their morale, the German volunteer changed his mind about the commander in chief's leadership. In a letter to Henry Laurens, de Kalb said the Virginian was the "only proper person" to command the army. "He does more every day than could be expected from any general in the world, under the circumstances."[37]

Meanwhile, with no one in charge, the quartermaster department disintegrated. Wagons lay abandoned everywhere, while commissaries begged for them and purchased food spoiled. Hospitals went without wood to keep sick men warm. One diarist reported hundreds of barrels of flour abandoned on the banks of the Susquehanna River.

Congress's perpetual fear that businessmen were making too much money also played a part in the wagon shortage. The lawmakers fixed the price of hiring a wagon at six dollars a day, while private contractors were paying three times that much. Screams of protest failed to penetrate

congressional ears. The righteous men from New England and their followers seemed ready to lose the war if they could not force public virtue
down American throats.[38]

XVI

Thanks to one politician's penchant for writing letters, we have an almost
laboratory specimen of the ideology that was dominating Congress.
Thirty-one-year-old Dr. Benjamin Rush was on his way to becoming a
prominent physician, probably the most prominent in America. But in
1777, he was deeply involved in revolutionary politics. A slender man of average height, Rush had "an uncommonly large head" which some thought
"bespoke strength and activity of intellect." On the other hand, John
Witherspoon, president of the College of New Jersey (later Princeton)
and an occasional congressman, said Rush's addiction to "strong and superlative expressions" made him uneasy.[39]

Rush was, among other things, a hero-worshipper, and he soon affixed
himself to John Adams when the Continental Congress began meeting in
Philadelphia in 1774. Here, Rush swiftly concluded, was not a mere power-
hungry politician but a man who was animated by "disinterested love to
mankind." The two men had much in common. As a young lawyer, Adams
had to struggle for a living against the entrenched leaders of the Boston
bar. As a result, one observer said, Honest John "could not look with complacency upon any man who was in possession of more wealth, more honors, more knowledge than himself."[40]

Rush never forgot or forgave his early experience as a young doctor
in Philadelphia. With a degree from prestigious Edinburgh University, he
thought there would be a demand for his services. Instead, as he endlessly
complained, not "one of my brethren ever sent a patient to me." Rush was
so angry to find himself "neglected and unknown" by "the persons who
called themselves great in the city" that he joined Matlack, Cannon, and
company in overthrowing the government of Pennsylvania in the summer
of 1776 and swinging the state into the independence movement.

When the radicals seized power, they made Rush a delegate to Congress, where he became a late signer of the Declaration of Independence. There, further association with John Adams, a keen student of the theory of government, persuaded the doctor that the radical constitution, with its one-house legislature and virtually no executive authority, was a mistake. But that change of mind did not alter other aspects of Rush's ideological fervor.[41]

The key word in Rush's political vocabulary was "whig." Inherited from England, where whigs (liberals) traditionally opposed tories (conservatives), whig was one of the war cries of the American Revolution. Everyone claimed to be a whig, from George Washington to John Hancock. But for the discriminating ideologue, and Rush was one from his fingertips to his toes, the key phrase was "true whig."

In a letter to John Adams, Rush divided American whigs into five classes: "1st, the whig from the love of power; 2nd, the whig from resentment; 3rd the whig from interest; 4th the whig from a love of the military life; and lastly the whig from the love of liberty." Rush grandly assured Adams that he had his eye on men who belonged to each of these classes and he had decided that most of the "misfortunes" that were afflicting the Revolution came from "entrusting our councils or our arms to any but to the last class of whigs"—the lovers of liberty for its own sake. These wonderful beings scorned self-interest and delighted in sacrificing it for their country.

Rush ended his letter with a remark that was pregnant with trouble for George Washington. "I rejoice to find General Gates appointed to take command in the northern department—he belongs to the fifth class of whigs."[42]

XVII

Rush's next letter to Adams reflected the doctor's growing disillusion with George Washington. He wrote it after a visit to the British army's camp to attend American wounded after the battle of Brandywine. He returned deeply impressed by the order and discipline he saw all around him.

Rush contrasted his visit to the British camp with what he found when he returned to the American camp. "I saw soldiers straggling from our lines in every direction . . . exposed every moment to being picked up by the enemy's light horse." Disorder was equally rampant in American hospitals. In contrast to the British hospitals, where numerous guards kept order, the American sick were unsupervised. In one hospital, Rush saw more than a hundred inmates drunk. He blamed it all on George Washington. "A general should see everything with his own eyes and hear everything with his own ears. He should understand and even practice at times all the duties of the soldier, the officer, the quartermaster, the commissary and the adjutant general. He should . . . despise ease and . . . always sleep in his boots . . . ready for a flight or a pursuit."

Rush concluded that America was "on the brink of ruin." Only one thing could save it: "new measures and new men." The army had to be reformed forthwith. "Let our generals be chosen annually." Here he proclaimed one of the prime articles of the true whig faith. Congressman James Lovell, who called John and Sam Adams his mentors, went him one better. Lovell told Sam Adams he favored "an annual choice of *all* officers."[43]

Approve this annual turnover of generals, Rush insisted, and there would be no need to sign up men for three years or the duration of the war. The American spirit rebelled against such an idea. "Good generals would make an army of six months men an army of heroes." Exactly how or why choosing new generals every year would produce good ones Rush did not say. Anyone with common sense would consider it a recipe for military disaster.

Growing more frenzied with every sentence, Rush continued: "The militia began and I sincerely hope the militia will end the present war. I should despair of our cause if our country contained 60,000 men abandoned enough to enlist for 3 years or during the war."[44]

Rush was a walking, talking paradigm of true whig extremism. It was bad enough when it was applied to constructing a government, as in Pennsylvania. The ideology was close to idiocy when these politicians attempted to apply it to the army.

XVIII

Rush's disillusion with Washington and his army multiplied after the battle of Germantown on October 4, 1777. More than half the British army were camped in and around this village when Washington attacked them at dawn. For a while it looked like the Continentals were achieving a rout. But a heavy fog confused some of the attacking columns, who fired on each other; some brigades got lost and never made it into the battle at all. Militia who were supposed to harry the British flanks also remained nonparticipants. Part of a British regiment holed up in the Chew mansion in the American rear had distracted other attacking echelons. When redcoated reinforcements arrived from Philadelphia, Washington, sticking grimly to his strategy of avoiding a winner-take-all battle, withdrew.

This flirtation with victory and glum acceptance of defeat was followed two weeks later by news that true whig General Horatio Gates had triumphed over the British army in the battles of Saratoga. The two events unglued Benjamin Rush. In his previous letters he had only hinted at Washington's incompetence. Now he abandoned all and every restraint.

> I have heard several officers who have served under General Gates compare his army to a well-regulated family. The same gentlemen have compared General Washington's imitation of an army to an unformed mob. Look at the characters of both! The one on the pinnacle of military glory, exulting in schemes planned with wisdom and executed with vigor and bravery. . . . See the other outgeneraled and twice beated [sic] obliged to witness the march of a body of men only half their number through 140 miles of thick settled country, forced to give up a city the capital of a state. . . . If our Congress can witness these things with composure and suffer them to pass without an inquiry, I shall think we have not shook off monarchical prejudices and that like the Israelites of old we worship the work of our own hands.

Here this supposedly intelligent man was repeating the canard that General Washington had twice as many men as Howe and permitted himself to be outwitted and outfought. The phrase "the work of our own hands" evokes another way of denigrating Washington. He had been a nobody outside Virginia until John and Samuel Adams chose him as commander in chief.[45]

In another letter to Adams, Dr. Rush found another hero who might yet save Washington's army: Brigadier General Thomas Conway. The Irishman obviously had given Rush a long lecture on the battle of Germantown. "General Conway wept for joy when he saw the ardor with which our troops pushed the enemy from hill to hill, and pronounced our country free from that auspicious sight," Rush wrote. "But when he saw an officer low in command give counterorders to the commander in chief and the commander in chief passive under the circumstances, his distress and resentment exceeded all bounds."

Here Rush was referring to the decision to delay the advance to attack the British regiment holed up in the Chew mansion. The decision was unquestionably a mistake, made by General Henry Knox. The fuming Rush declared Conway was "entitled to most of the glory our arms acquired" at Germantown. He urged Adams to make Conway a major general. Not only was he brave and skillful, he was "an enthusiast in our cause."

Rush dismissed the hostility that the condescending, loose-lipped Conway was generating inside the American army. "Some people blame him for calling some of our generals fools, cowards and drunkards in public company." Rush insisted these remarks were "proofs of his integrity and should raise him in the opinion of every friend of America." In fact, Conway's superior attitude had made him the most disliked general in the American army. He was fond of asking officers who served in his brigade: "Did Congress see you before they appointed you?"[46]

There is no record of John Adams replying to Rush with a defense of Washington. It was soon apparent that both Adamses and many other members of the Continental Congress shared the doctor's low opinion of the American commander in chief.

XIX

Another ideologue in this growing conflict was Richard Henry Lee of Virginia. A power in Congress thanks to his early enthusiasm for independence, Lee was a lean, humorless southern puritan who found far more congenial the company of Samuel and John Adams and other members of the New England delegations than the relaxed conviviality of wealthy Virginia planters such as Carter Braxton and Richard Harrison. Lee shared the Adamses' stern views of what constituted a true whig and their suspicion of profit-seeking merchants like John Hancock and Robert Morris. In Paris, Lee's brother, Arthur, was even more maniacal on the subject. He wrote Congress a stream of letters slandering his fellow American diplomats, Silas Deane and Benjamin Franklin, as thieves and potential traitors.

The Lees were one of the most powerful families in Virginia, far surpassing the Washingtons in wealth and prestige. They lived in Stratford Hall, one of the most splendid mansions in America, with sculpted gardens and a magnificent view of the Potomac River. In his boyhood, George Washington had been an occasional visitor. He and Lee were the same age, and they became friends. In later years, when they both served in the House of Burgesses, Virginia's legislature, the friendship deepened.

When Washington took command of the Continental Army in the summer of 1775, he shared some early thoughts about the New England troops with Congressman Lee. There was "an unaccountable kind of stupidity in the lower class of these people which, believe me, [also] prevails too generally among [the officers of] the Massachusetts part of the army, who are nearly of the same kidney as the privates." There were other remarks in a similar vein. The new general was reflecting the widespread dislike of Yankee ways in the rest of America.[47]

Friends in Philadelphia warned Washington that the letters were being leaked, and he resolved never again to say a negative word about any of his soldiers based on their geographic origins. But the damage was done. Lee had mentioned these remarks to the Adamses and other New Englanders, triggering a cooling process that eventually produced something very close to hostility when Washington's battlefield reputation began to slide.

Neither Adams needed much encouragement to distrust Washington. They had long since decided that Virginians and almost everyone outside New England were morally inferior to high-minded, Harvard-educated descendants of the Puritans. In 1775, not long after Washington took command of the army, John Adams persuaded him to appoint Adams's law clerk, William Tudor, as an aide. Adams promptly ordered Tudor to inform him about "the name character and behavior of every stranger [i.e., non–New Englander] that shall be put into any place in the army."[48]

Richard Henry Lee was so clubby with the Adamses, and voted so regularly with them, that congressmen from the middle and southern states began talking about the "Lee-Adams junto" and the high-handed way they controlled Congress. This generalization was based largely on Lee's oratorical sympathy with the New Englanders. He never won enough support to control the Virginia delegation's vote the way Sam Adams dominated Massachusetts and the other New England delegations.

Nevertheless, Lee's pro-Yankee tilt led some people to suggest that he was involved in a plot to remove Washington as commander in chief. In early 1777, the rumors grew so strong that Lee's name was dropped from the list of Virginia's delegates to Congress. Lee rushed back to Virginia and in a fervent speech to the legislature denied he was in any way, shape, or form an opponent of General Washington. The legislature reinstated him and issued a formal apology and a vote of thanks for Lee's faithful service.

Lee's opponents remained unconvinced. A Maryland critic described him as "dark, subtle and designing, he never will openly appear in any point which he wishes to carry, it is impossible to detect him in the prosecution of his schemes." One New York congressman remarked: "I suppose he will return [to Congress] more riveted than ever to his eastern [New England] friends." The New Yorker was largely correct, but the flank attack by Washington's Virginia backers henceforth made Lee extremely circumspect about going public with his doubts about the commander in chief.[49]

XX

Congressman James Lovell had no such inhibitions. He began flattering Horatio Gates at Washington's expense even before General Burgoyne surrendered. On October 5 he told Gates his army was being favorably contrasted with Washington's. He slyly suggested that if Gates captured Burgoyne, who fancied himself a playwright, perhaps the British general could furnish Congress with an evening's entertainment by penning a farce at the expense of General Washington.[50]

In November Lovell told delegate William Whipple of New Hampshire that "the spirit of Enterprise is a stranger in the main army. You may expect as long as the war continues 3 times more men will be lost by marching and countermarching over hills and thro rivers than in *battles*." To Samuel Adams he wrote in December that he had little to say about our *grand* army. "'Tis a subject very sickening to even a strong stomach."

Like his cousin John, Sam did not correct or otherwise disagree with this denigration. In another letter to John Adams, Lovell referred to the suffering army at Valley Forge as "men of leisure on the banks of the Schuylkill."[51]

Former Congressman John Dickinson Sergeant of New Jersey was more blunt about his disenchantment with George Washington. "We want a general," he wrote to Lovell. "Thousands of lives and millions of property are yearly sacrificed to the insufficiency of our commander in chief. Two battles he has lost for us by two such blunders as would have disgraced a soldier of three months standing—and yet [we] are so attached to the man that I fear we shall rather sink under him than throw him off our shoulders."

With unrestrained savagery, Sergeant added that he agreed with his fellow New Jerseyan, Congressman Abraham Clark, a self-styled "people's lawyer," who, like Sergeant, voted with New England. "We may talk of the enemy's cruelty as we will," Clark said. "But we have no greater cruelty to complain of than the management of our army."[52]

John Adams, who declared in mid-1777 that things would not

improve until "we shoot a general," cried out in his diary: "Oh heaven! Grant us one great soul! One leading mind would extricate the best cause from that ruin which seems to await it, from the want of it. . . . One active, masterly capacity would bring order out of this confusion and save this country." Obviously, in Adams's opinion, General Washington was not this great soul.[53]

When Adams heard about Horatio Gates's triumph at Saratoga, he exulted, not only because it was a badly needed victory, but because it was *not* won by General Washington. Honest John was convinced that there was serious danger of Washington becoming a demigod, who would transmute into a dictator who would destroy the liberties of America. "Now we can allow a certain citizen to be wise, virtuous and good, without thinking him a deity or savior," he told his wife, Abigail.[54]

XXI

Behind the scenes, General Mifflin presided over this negative chorus with growing satisfaction. The tenor of his thinking was vividly visible in a letter he wrote to General Gates on November 17. He told the Saratoga victor that he had "saved our Northern hemisphere." Then he went to work on Washington. "We have had a noble army melted down by ill-judged marches—marches that disgrace their authors & directors—& which have occasioned the severest & most just sarcasm & contempt by our enemies." He blamed the army's poor performance on the loss of good officers who "would not worship the Image & pay an undeserved tribute of praise and flattery" to Washington. Their reward was "repeated slights and unjustifiable arrogance" that drove them from the army.

Now, however, Mifflin thought indignation over Washington's performance was beginning to rise. Soon it would swell into a "mighty torrent of public clamor & public vengeance." There was only one thing to do: Gates must come to Pennsylvania and "collect the virtuous band who wish to fight under your banner." Otherwise the army would be "totally lost." With the confidence of a man who knew how many congressmen he had behind him, Mifflin told Gates to "prepare yourself for a jaunt to this place—Congress must send for you—I have ten thousand things to tell."[55]

XXII

Even before he became president of Congress, Henry Laurens revealed to his son John his anxiety about this rising cacophony of criticism. Laurens assured John that he knew the "cruelty of tongues speaking the feelings of designing hearts." But he confessed that he feared there was "some ground for some of these remarks." The South Carolinian wondered if the problem was Washington's reluctance to make hard decisions. "A good heart may be too diffident, too apprehensive" of seeming to wield arbitrary power.[56]

Other people, especially those with "designing hearts," like Thomas Mifflin, saw Washington's supposed deficiencies differently. They repeatedly maintained that he was a puppet in the hands of General Nathanael Greene. They derided Greene's miliitary inexperience and implicated him in decisions that led to defeats in 1776 and 1777. Laurens inadvertently reflected this opinion when he remarked to his son in another letter that Washington tended to accept "the opinion of some who have no superior claim."

Brigadier General Anthony Wayne expressed a similar opinion to Horatio Gates: "I don't yet despair . . . if our worthy general will but follow his own good judgment without listening too much to some counsel." General de Kalb likewise deplored Washington's tendency to make decisions on the advice of "Councils." De Kalb meant councils of war. Having come late to the Revolution, he apparently did not know that Congress had ordered Washington to confer with his generals before making a decision. The politicians took seriously his 1775 confession that he did not feel he was equal to the role of commander in chief. The policy also diluted his power, something all true whigs would approve.[57]

Mifflin leveled even more nasty gibes at General Greene. He was "neither the most wise, the most brave nor the most patriotic of counsellors." This oblique attack enabled the ex–quartermaster general to praise Washington and still claim to be a disinterested friend to his country. He was only speaking his "sentiments on public matters with decency and firmness."

To anyone who understood the dynamics of power, this was, of course, nonsense. To claim Washington was a good general and simultaneously accuse him of taking ruinous advice from a stupid, cowardly, unpatriotic subordinate was a palpable contradiction in terms.[58]

Nevertheless, to those who wanted to replace Washington, the supposed Mifflin-Greene feud was a gift from on high. A delighted Congressman James Lovell told Horatio Gates: "By the winter the middle Army [Washington's army] will be divided into Greenites and Mifflineans, if things do not take a great turn from our present situation."[59]

Lovell's mentor, Samuel Adams, soon chimed in along the same line in a letter to Richard Henry Lee: "Our military affairs in the middle department are in such a situation as to afford us too much reason to be chagrinned. . . . To what are we to attribute it? I believe to a miserable set of general officers. . . . Is there not reason to fear our commander in chief may one day suffer in his own character by means of these miserable creatures?"[60]

XXIII

With this evidence of the growing disillusion with Washington in Congress and at the summit of the American army, it is not hard to imagine the reaction at Valley Forge when the January 14, 1778, edition of *Dunlap's Pennsylvania Packet, or, The General Advertiser* reached the half-finished American winter camp. The newspaper was published by John Dunlap, a close friend of Benjamin Rush. Dunlap met all the idealistic doctor's true whig tests. In the heady days of July 1776, the Irish-born printer had been entrusted with publishing the first copies of the Declaration of Independence. He had fled Philadelphia with the radical Pennsylvania Assembly and set up his press in their substitute capital, Lancaster, where enthusiasm for General George Washington, the man who lost Philadelphia, ranged from minimal to nonexistent.

On the *Packet's* front page was a letter from a "French gentleman" who had been in America for two years and had met "the first characters on the continent." He was, in short, an insider.

Dated "Fish Kill in the state of New York, November 20, 1777," the letter began by noting that twelve out of the thirteen states concurred in the decision to appoint General Gates commander of the northern army. This proved that "the clamours of the people, who govern their rulers in this country, could not be resisted, and private prejudices were made to yield to the general safety and honor of America."

Next the French gentleman described "the joy of the Northern army upon General Gates's arrival among them." The troops adored him because he was a "zealous republican" (a true whig) and "his only object in taking part with them in the present war were liberty and independence." The letter told how swiftly Gates achieved his first goal: "to put his army in order." This was done in a few weeks.

How did Gates achieve this miracle? "His general orders were short but they were implicitly obeyed. He saw everything with his own eyes and heard everything with his own ears. He slept but little and was seldom absent from the morning and evening parade of his troops. He understood every part of the duty of an officer and soldier, as well as of a general, for he had served the King of Great Britain during the greatest part of the two last wars against France, under some of the ablest generals Great Britain had ever sent into the field."

Readers of Benjamin Rush's assaults on Washington will note interesting similarities here to the doctor's description of an ideal general. This rare being knew everything that was happening in his army, twenty-four hours a day.

The writer admitted that Gates's temper tended to be "hasty." That sometimes led him to use "passionate expressions in reproving his officers." But he was loved by all his men, nonetheless. "I have been told that he never had a single personal enemy under his command," the French gentleman averred. In fact General Gates and General Benedict Arnold had become violent enemies by the time the battles of Saratoga ended in victory.

Next came a paean of praise to the soldiers of the northern army, which was "composed chiefly of the farmers and farmers' sons of the Eastern states." Every man among these paragons "felt an enthusiastic attachment to liberty and the lowest sentinel fought alike with his general for all that was dear to them." This was not entirely unexpected, because "the inhabitants of New England are trained up from their infancy, to civil, ecclesiastical and domestic subordination. The transition from these to military subordination is short and natural."

Along with a readiness to obey orders, New Englanders were a moral race. "Drunkenness is not known among them. And since the beginning of the war, there has been but one instance of a New England man deserting to the British army. He was caught and condemned to die, but was afterwards pardoned upon discovering proofs that he was a lunatic."

The French gentleman did not dwell on the particulars of the two battles of Saratoga, which had been reported in the newspapers. He only noted that "every detail" of the two historic encounters left him wondering "what eulogiums can equal the merit of General Gates?" Recovering his courage, the French gentleman essayed a paragraph of eulogiums:

> His successes are almost without a precedent in history. His glory is as yet unrivalled in the annals of America. . . . He has destroyed one half the power of Britain in America. He has humbled the pride of the haughtiest nation in the world. He has given the people or America a confidence in their courage and resources, which can never be taken away by any future misfortune. . . . He has shewed the folly and danger of standing armies in time of peace by conquering a body of veterans with the militia of the country.

Here was another whopper. Gates won the battles of Saratoga almost exclusively with Continentals. Only when Burgoyne was reeling toward defeat did the New England militia show up in large numbers.

A man of Horatio Gates's gigantic accomplishments undoubtedly deserved a reward, the French gentleman continued, even though like a true whig he was not fighting for one. "The Congress are not insensible of the important services of their general. They have voted him their thanks and a gold medal. But no reward can equal his merit. The gratitude of posterity alone will be able to do justice to him."[61]

XXIV

Was that true whig General Horatio Gates about to take charge of the American Revolution, backed by the bayonets of his inherently superior New England soldiers? It must have looked that way to many newspaper readers in Valley Forge and the rest of Pennsylvania—not the least of whom was General George Washington.

FOUR

PLAYING THE INSULT CARD

GENERAL WASHINGTON'S STAFF officers were keenly aware of the rising tide of Gates worship and Washington denigration. John Laurens was already corresponding with his father about it. Another active letter writer was aide Tench Tilghman, who had deep roots in the middle states. His father, James, was a wealthy Philadelphia lawyer, and other members of the family were prominent in Maryland. Before the war, Washington was an occasional guest in James Tilghman's house and several times offered him similar hospitality at Mount Vernon.

Thirty-two-year-old Tench (a family name on his mother's side) had been a successful merchant in Philadelphia for ten years before the war. Older than most of the other aides, he was Washington's friend and adviser as well as an assistant. Tilghman had a personal problem that might have troubled their relationship, if Washington had been a narrow-minded man: Tench's father had sided with the original protests against heavy-handed British rule but could not accept independence. Although he took no action against the Revolution, the elder Tilghman was considered a loyalist and had been banished from Philadelphia by the radical Pennsylvania government. He was now living in Maryland.

Gratitude for the general's understanding of the way the Revolution had divided families played a part in Tench's growing devotion to Washington. With his numerous family and business contacts in Pennsylvania, Tilghman was in an ideal position to find out who was saying what behind the scenes, and to rally support for the general.

In mid-January, Tilghman enlisted his old friend, pugnacious Pennsylvania militia general John Cadwalader, in this secret war. The general was a Washington admirer who had participated in the 1776 victories at Trenton and Princeton. He and Tilghman also happened to have been fellow students at the College of Pennsylvania.

"Great pains are taking to swell the character of the Northern hero and to depreciate that of our worthy general," Tilghman wrote. "Who is at the bottom of this I dare say you will easily guess. . . . It is a gentleman who resigned important offices at a critical time [Thomas Mifflin]. Several letters have already made their appearance in the [news]papers all tending to extol G———[Gates] as the first soldier of the world, giving him the credit of all the Northern successes. . . . The letters are well wrote, but the cloven hoof is too plain."

Tilghman denounced "this damned faction" in sulfurous terms. It was "founded solely upon the ambition of one man, for G———s is but a puppet." It was so "fraught with mischief," Tilghman maintained, that "every honest man ought upon the first discovery to give the alarm, as he would upon the discovery of a fire" in a valuable arsenal. He urged Cadwalader "to speak when there is occasion" in defense of Washington. Tilghman ended this explosive letter with a sly "I have said enough to set you on fire [his obvious intention] but be moderate." Knowing the hot-tempered Cadwalader well, Tilghman undoubtedly hoped the opposite would be the case.[1]

Congressman Charles Carroll of Maryland, by some accounts the wealthiest man in America, gave Tilghman credit for revealing this conspiracy to destroy General Washington and elevate General Gates. Washington was so "straightforward and earnest, he never suspected treachery," Carroll later wrote. "Tilghman was alert, always watchful, and the most wise of them [the plotters] could not circumvent him."[2]

As we shall soon see, this view of the commander in chief as a well-intentioned innocent—or worse, numskull—was wildly wrong.

Nevertheless, it has remained part of the Washington public image for centuries, and is very much alive today in some quarters. We can be reasonably certain that if Tilghman knew this much about Washington's antagonists, the commander in chief knew it too.

Misnamed the Conway Cabal by many historians, this conspiracy has been debated and discussed for decades, with some calling it a myth, others dismissively designating it "the Mifflin Maneuver," still others deploring Washington's supersensitivity to remarks and legislative proposals which supposedly came from the best (i.e., patriotic) intentions. Few if any of these writers have explored the full range of the anti-Washington maneuvers—or grasped the energy and political shrewdness with which the commander in chief fought back.[3]

II

General Washington had been watching Horatio Gates in action for over two years and by this time had no illusions about his deviousness and hunger for power. Older than most of the American generals (he would celebrate his fiftieth birthday in April 1778), Gates looked his age. His hair was gray, and he wore spectacles, which frequently slipped down his aquiline nose. General Burgoyne, after surrendering to him at Saratoga, said his victorious opponent looked more like an "old midwife" than a general. Gates's troops called him "Granny," not only because of his looks, but also because of his mild demeanor.

Perhaps in an effort to counter his unsoldierly appearance, Gates spiced his table talk with oaths and obscenities—a habit that must have troubled some of his more devout New England backers. He was equally foulmouthed about sex. Congressman Lovell, readers will recall, shared the news of his New Jersey girlfriend with Gates while reporting Congress's flight from Philadelphia. This conversational style was not uncommon in the British army. But Gates took it to extremes. He wrote to his British-born confrere, General Charles Lee, boasting that his son Robert had recently acquired a venereal disease and fought a duel. Lee, whose off-color vocabulary and indifference to sexual morality were legendary, replied: "Upon my soul [Bob] is a fine boy—a clap and a duel in the same year for one of his age indicate a great man."[4]

Gates was the son of a housekeeper in the household of the Duke of Leeds. Horace Walpole, son of the most powerful prime minister of the early eighteenth century, was his godfather—a fact that has made more than one historian suspect Gates had a father several notches higher in the social scale than his legal father, whose occupation was journeyman tailor. It was not unusual in eighteenth-century England for aristocrats to provide for their out-of-wedlock offspring, and Gates's career fit this scenario.

At the age of twenty-one, Horatio suddenly became a lieutenant in the British army. His half brother also won a commission, and his father became customs collector at Greenwich. Thereafter Gates repeatedly enjoyed the favor of commanding officers such as Colonel Edward Cornwallis, uncle of the earl who was playing a large role on the British side in the American Revolution. When a captaincy became available, Colonel Cornwallis urged Gates's father to put up the four-hundred-pound price, adding that if the money were not available, he would be happy to advance it out of his own pocket.

Captain Gates became the commander of an independent company, stationed in New York. There he grew friendly with many Americans who prided themselves on their whiggish views of the British establishment, in particular William Livingston, future governor of revolutionary New Jersey. In the French and Indian War, Captain Gates and his company served briefly with George Washington on the 1755 expedition into western Pennsylvania led by General Edward Braddock. Gates received a "slight wound" in the ambush that destroyed Braddock's army and was assisted from the battlefield by a soldier whom he later described as his "savior."

Except for a few spates of Indian fighting, this was Gates's only combat experience. He spent the rest of his twenty years in the British army, during which he reached the rank of major, as a staff officer. This experience not only gave him an inside look at how generals frequently warred with each other as well as the enemy; it made him adept at military politics.

In 1772, Major Gates, irked by his inability to win another promotion, retired from the British army and moved to America with his wife and son, Robert. He bought a farm in the lower Shenandoah Valley in western Virginia. He had sought George Washington's advice before buying it and enjoyed the company of Washington's friend Adam Stephen, who had also served in the French and Indian War, and headed west in search of land and affluence.

They were joined by Colonel Charles Lee, a far more mercurial man who had also failed to win promotion to the rank he felt he deserved in the British army. Gates and Lee emphatically agreed that the British ministry's plans to tax Americans and generally establish stronger control over the colonies should be resisted at all costs. "I am prepared to risque my life to preserve the liberty of the western world," Gates declared.[5]

In 1775, the Continental Congress made Gates a brigadier general, and Washington, eager to systematize the raw army he commanded outside Boston, made the ex-major his adjutant general. Gates rendered important service in organizing and administering what became the Continental Army. He also met and grew friendly with Thomas Mifflin, who was Washington's aide, and with John and Samuel Adams. The two Bostonians were delighted by Gates's outspoken and early support for a declaration of independence, an idea that gave violent tremors to a majority of the delegates to the Continental Congress in 1775.

Horatio Gates's friendship with John and Samuel Adams—and the discovery that they were among the most powerful delegates in Congress—stirred the ambitious side of Gates's personality. He soon convinced himself that he had no desire to spend the war as an adjutant general. Like many staff officers, he had a high opinion of his military talents. Envy of his fellow Briton Charles Lee was another influence. Lee's boasts about his combat exploits had persuaded the Adamses to make him a major general and Washington's second in command.

The first glimpse of Gates's ambition appeared in mid-1776, when he asked Washington to appoint him military commander of the city of Boston. Washington demurred, saying he did not think the British had any further interest in the city. Gates immediately fired off a letter to Samuel Adams, saying he had "positive" intelligence that the British intended to attack Massachusetts. He sneered at Washington's confidence in predicting the future; it was "too mighty for my judgment." Flatly stating that his opinion was as good as Washington's, Gates declared that they "could not have too many armies employed" to save America.

Events proved Washington right: the British never attacked Boston; their fleet and army headed for New York. In this imbroglio, Gates revealed his determination to wangle an independent command—and his skill at saying what his political backers wanted to hear. Reading his letter, Samuel Adams could not fail to be stirred by this true whig's concern for the safety of his beloved Boston.[6]

In June 1776, Gates was given command of the American army in Canada. Unfortunately, it was retreating from that colony as fast as it could transport its multitude of sick and wounded back to northern New York. British reinforcements had shattered the force Congress had sent into the northernmost colony the previous year.

By the time Gates arrived in Albany, there was no army in Canada. Major General Philip Schuyler, the commander of the northern department, suggested they work as a team, with Gates in charge of the fighting army while Schuyler pacified the Indians, shipped him supplies, and kept northern New York's numerous loyalists under control.

Gates would have none of it. He insisted he had orders from Congress to command the army, independent of Schuyler, and began appointing subordinate officers without consulting the northern commander. Schuyler asked Washington to settle the dispute. Washington forwarded the request to Congress, who confirmed Schuyler as the overall commander.

Gates assured President John Hancock of his "intire [sic] satisfaction and acquiescence in the resolve of Congress." He assured Schuyler of his "inalienable resolution" to obey his orders. Simultaneously, he was writing to John Adams, reporting: "I have been deceived and disappointed in being removed from a place where I might have done the publick service."

Soon Gates was being assured by another Massachusetts delegate, Elbridge Gerry, that Congress "want very much to see you in the sole command of the northern department" and the New Englanders were only waiting for "a favorable opportunity" to give him the job.[7]

The opportunity took almost a year to materialize. During that time, General Gates labored to rehabilitate the northern army after the traumatic retreat from Canada. He and Generals Benedict Arnold and Schuyler worked more or less harmoniously to beat off a British attempt to invade northern New York in the fall of 1776.

In and around New York City, meanwhile, General Washington reeled from defeat to defeat and was forced to retreat across New Jersey to the west bank of the Delaware with only a remnant of his army. He ordered General Gates to bring eight regiments from the northern army to reinforce him. After a grueling march through deep snow and icy rain, Gates reached Washington's camp on the Delaware in time to join a council of war on the army's next move.

Along the way Gates received a savage letter from General Charles Lee deploring Washington's leadership in the struggle for New York. "A certain great man is damnably deficient," Lee wrote. There is no record of Gates's reply. But events would soon demonstrate that he shared Lee's low estimate of General Washington.

At the council of war, Washington proposed a strike across the Delaware to attack the isolated German garrison at Trenton. Gates demurred. He told the commander in chief his army was too demoralized to attack anyone. The only hope was to retreat beyond the Susquehanna River into western Pennsylvania, reorganize and reequip the army, and wait for a better opportunity to renew the war.

Washington and his generals were staggered by Gates's defeatism. He was proposing to give up Philadelphia and the prosperous surrounding counties to the enemy without a fight. The commander in chief demurred in turn and renewed his determination to attack Trenton. Gates, in a response that historians still debate, said he was too ill to participate and departed for Baltimore, to which Congress had fled. Washington went ahead with his attack on Trenton, which rescued the Revolution from collapse.[8]

Gates's sympathizers among the historical fraternity argue that the gray-haired general probably was ill. He had been working long and hard in northern New York. More suspicious types, including this writer, point out that the general was not too sick to travel a hundred miles to

Baltimore in midwinter. True, when he arrived there, Gates immediately struck the posture of a very sick man. President John Hancock wrote to General Schuyler lamenting Horatio's poor state of health. Several other congressmen made similar remarks.

Let us not forget General Mifflin's equally convenient illness which enabled him to abandon General Washington and the quartermaster department after the fall of Philadelphia. Like Mifflin, Gates was not too sick to talk politics with his New England backers and display a surprisingly healthy eagerness to take the field. Within two weeks, Samuel Adams was writing to his cousin John, "General Gates is here. . . . How shall we make him head of the northern army?"[9]

These words from the most powerful politician in Congress were the source of Gates's rise to power and glory. The French gentleman's claim in the *Pennsylvania Packet* that "the clamours of the people" were responsible was hot air.

Before the struggle ended, there were ugly scenes in the northern army and on the floor of Congress. General Schuyler did not quietly accept dismissal from his post. The dispute was intensified by the long-standing alienation between New England and New York. The descendants of the Puritans regarded New Yorkers as morally and socially corrupt because they enjoyed the theater, tolerated numerous religions and ethnic groups in their midst, including Jews, and saw no conflict between patriotism and making money.

New Yorkers regarded New Englanders as hypocrites who talked piety and righteousness but were always ready to grab a quick dollar. Temperamentally, George Washington, who enjoyed the theater and a game of cards, sided with New York. Washington and Schuyler had also become warm personal friends during the first sessions of the Continental Congress.[10]

On June 18, 1777, Gates, infuriated by his backers' failure to get rid of Schuyler, invaded the floor of Congress and launched a ferocious personal attack on James Duane, the leader of the New York delegation. Completely losing his self-control, Gates ranted about his background and experience in the British army and the sacrifices he had made to join the

American cause. Various congressmen began telling Gates to withdraw, and soon angry shouts drowned out his harangue.

Undeterred by this performance, his New England backers clung to Gates. When the British army under General Burgoyne appeared before Fort Ticonderoga, General Schuyler's second in command, Major General Arthur St. Clair, decided retreat was the only option to preserve his comparative handful of trained regulars. This decision, which subsequent events would prove to be wise and even courageous, stunned Congress and many others, including General Washington. The New England delegates clamorously demanded that Generals Schuyler and St. Clair be court-martialed. Crying "I told you so" in the faces of the discomfited New Yorkers, the Adams-Lee junto won Horatio Gates's appointment to the command of the northern department by a vote of twelve states to none.

New England's hero proceeded to justify the Yankees' faith in him beyond their most extravagant hopes. Under General Gates's command the northern army defeated General Burgoyne's invasion and forced his army to surrender. Even in victory Gates's first thoughts were political. In an exultant letter to his wife, he wrote: "The voice of fame, ere this reaches you, will tell you how greatly fortunate we have been in this department. Burgoyne and his great army have laid down their arms . . . to me and my Yankees." [11]

III

After his victory at Saratoga, Gates's conduct became a mixture of veiled hostility to Washington and ostensible cooperation. Instead of notifying the commander in chief of Burgoyne's surrender, as one might expect a subordinate general to do, Gates sent a report to Congress via his aide, Lieutenant Colonel James Wilkinson, with not even a copy to Washington. There was some rationale for this discourtesy—Congress, not Washington, had appointed him to the command. But Washington never thought or even intimated that he was abdicating his role as commander in chief.

An angry letter from General Washington to Richard Henry Lee made this very clear. "I cannot help complaining of General Gates's neglect in not giving me the earliest authentic notice" of his victory, Washington wrote. "An affair of that magnitude might . . . give an important turn to our operations in this quarter." The commander in chief described his puzzlement and irritation at being forced to depend on unconfirmed rumors until he "began to doubt the truth of it." Writing almost a month after Burgoyne's surrender, Washington noted that "to this moment" he had not received a single word from Gates about the "important transaction." [12]

When Washington sent his aide Alexander Hamilton to Albany with a request to rush most of the northern army to Pennsylvania to join him in attacking Howe and perhaps ending the war, Gates was difficult. He insisted he needed men to dislodge the British from Fort Ticonderoga and keep the loyalists and Indians under control. An exasperated Hamilton finally wrote him a peremptory letter, demanding the men without further delay. Gates complied, but the impression his footdragging made on General Washington was far from positive.

In this tense atmosphere, a letter from Major General Lord Stirling added another dimension to Gates's equivocal conduct. Still recuperating from a 1776 leg wound, the New Jersey general was resting in Reading. There he encountered Lieutenant Colonel Wilkinson, who was, as earlier noted, en route to Congress in York with Gates's report of the victory over Burgoyne. Wilkinson was fond of liquor—as was Stirling—and they spent a convivial evening together, no doubt discussing the Saratoga victory, among other things.

Toward the end of a night of hard drinking, Stirling went to bed, leaving his aide, Major William McWilliams, to enjoy a final glass with Wilkinson. The well-liquored Wilkinson talked gleefully about the congratulatory letters Gates was receiving from congressmen and fellow generals. McWilliams asked him if there was any truth to the story that General Conway had told the Saratoga victor: "Heaven has been determined to save your country; or a weak general and bad counsellors would have ruined it."

The quotation had been circulating around York, Lancaster, and

Reading for several weeks. Its apparent source was the garrulous General Conway. Wilkinson cheerfully confirmed its authenticity. The next day McWilliams reported the confirmation to Stirling, who was infuriated. He carefully wrote down Conway's insult and enclosed it in his letter to Washington. "I shall always think it my duty to detect such wicked duplicity of conduct," Stirling added.[13]

On November 5, Washington wrote a terse letter to General Conway:

> Sir: A letter which I received last night contained the following paragraph.
>
> In a letter from Genl Conway to Genl Gates, he says—Heaven has been determined to save your country, or a weak general and bad counsellors would have ruined it. I am sir, Yr Hble servant.[14]

Here, once more, we see General Washington doing the unexpected—seizing the initiative in this secret war with his enemies. The careless way General Conway had advertised the contents of his letter to all and sundry suggests that they expected a passive Washington would do no more than bleat to his sycophants, Generals Greene and Lafayette, and to his aides, who were even greater sycophants. The plotters and their friends in Congress were about to learn that behind his formal demeanor, there was a political Washington who could play a very rough game.

An agitated Conway replied to the general's letter the same day. In convoluted prose, the Irishman admitted writing a congratulatory letter to Gates but denied that the quotation sent by Stirling was in it. However, he admitted that he may have alluded to his opinion of Washington as a general: He was "a brave man, an honest man, a patriot and a man of great sense." But his "modesty" permitted men "not equal to you in experience, knowledge or judgment" to influence him. Conway added that he had expressed such sentiments to General Mifflin, in the company of one of Washington's closest Virginia friends, Dr. James Craik. Conway was inadvertently validating the by now tried and true Mifflin tactic—denigrating the commander in chief by attacking his subordinates.

Doubling back, Conway denied using the phrase "weak general" and added that if it had "slipped from my pen" it was only another way of saying that Washington's modesty permitted inferior men to push him around. With a coolness that some would call effrontery, Conway proceeded to lecture Washington: in "all army's" such candid correspondence between general officers was encouraged, in the hope that "something useful" would emerge from an "intercourse of ideas."

Then came a cutting observation that an "inquisition" about such letters was seldom practiced, even in "despotic and tyrannical governments." Nevertheless, to clear his name, General Conway would permit General Gates to send Washington his original letter. It would prove that he had "never said anything but what I could mention to yourself."

The letter ended with a thinly veiled threat. General Conway was obligated to "give an account of my conduct in France." He was planning to write a report of the losing struggle to defend Philadelphia. He pledged his word as a gentleman and an officer that it would contain nothing that he would not tell Washington to his face. The implication was clear: Conway could do the opposite, and perhaps the French would make replacing George Washington a condition of an alliance.[15]

Behind the scenes Conway immediately sent word of the leaked letter to General Mifflin. That devious gentleman was soon warning General Gates that "an extract of General Conway's letter to you has been procured and sent to headquarters." The extract, Mifflin declared, was a "collection of just sentiments," but such a letter should never have been shown to anyone. General Conway had declined to apologize for the "freedom of [his] sentiment," and "no satisfaction" was given Washington. Mifflin closed by urging Gates to be more careful with his correspondence, lest it be used to injure "some of your best friends."[16]

This was, it hardly needs to be added, the language of conspiracy. The assurance that Conway had not apologized, meaning he more or less defied Washington, revealed the schemers' tactics and goal. Washington was to be treated with disrespect and even with contempt by Gates, Mifflin, Conway, and their circle and by Congress. What they hoped to accomplish was carefully concealed from everyone but those who could be trusted to deny the dirty game they were playing.

IV

Meanwhile, General Gates was reacting to the controversy swirling through the army about the leak of General Conway's letter to him. His first instinct was to throw the responsibility for the uproar on Washington. In an agitated letter, Gates declared that as a private gentleman, he of course deplored allowing confidential letters to become "exposed to public inspection." But as a public officer, he assumed that General Washington would give him all the assistance in his power to discover the person or persons who "stealingly copied" his private correspondence and "put extracts from General Conway's letters to me into your hands."

Gates could not "fix the suspicion" on a single officer among his aides. He feared he would lose "the worthiest of men" if he let his uneasiness run wild and began accusing people. That was why it was so important to detect the "wretch" who committed this crime and might commit worse offenses if he was not swiftly exposed. For the moment, he did not know whether General Washington had obtained Conway's letter from a member of Congress, an officer of the army, or a wandering civilian. Because "the safety of the [United] states" was involved, Gates was sending a copy of his letter to Congress. Crimes of "such magnitude" should not remain unpunished.[17]

General Washington decided to take his time about answering this letter. It would be interesting to see what happened while Horatio stewed in his own juice for a while. Meanwhile, there were larger worries to confront.

V

A few days before General Mifflin wrote his warning letter to General Gates, the ex–quartermaster general had agreed to serve on a new version of an old entity, the Board of War. Congress had created this administrative device to free itself from dealing with the myriad details of the Continental Army's day-to-day business. But their absorption with the army had remained intense, and the board had never amounted to more than a paper entity. Now the solons in York had apparently decided it was time to give it blood and a little iron. The new board would consist of five army officers.

Richard Henry Lee, that questionable friend of Washington, informed the commander in chief of this development and almost offhandedly added that Congress was planning to requisition two of the general's staff for the board, Adjutant General Timothy Pickering and Washington's secretary, Robert Hanson Harrison, presuming they were willing to serve. The tenor of the message was subtly hostile. Congress was telling Washington that it was losing its deference to "His Excellency," the victor at Trenton and Princeton. The congressmen felt free to draft these two key men to serve elsewhere, without even asking his permission.

This new, as yet incomplete Board of War soon became a player in the dispute with General Conway. The brigadier had submitted his resignation to Congress soon after his exchange of letters with Washington about his correspondence with General Gates. His ostensible complaint was the politicians' promotion of Johann de Kalb to major general. In France, Conway had outranked the portly German. In a concurrent letter to Washington, Conway informed him of the resignation and asked for a leave of absence to prepare for his return to France. No doubt with a sigh of relief, Washington signed a letter saying he had no objection to Conway's departure.

Strange things happened to Conway's resignation when it was considered by Congress. It was referred to the Board of War, on which General Mifflin had become far and away the most influential member. At the end of November, as Washington's army began its withdrawal toward Valley Forge, Congress filled out the rest of the board: Former commissary general Joseph Trumbull (who declined to serve); Richard Peters, who had been secretary to the "old" board; and General Horatio Gates, who would be president.

The congressional resolution stated that Major General Gates would "officiate at the Board, or in the field, as occasion may require." One wonders where this left General Washington, the army's supposed commander in chief. The wording suggests that he was on his way to becoming a spectator once General Gates took charge of things.[18]

Gates's transfer to York and this delicious swath of power had been percolating for quite a while. Late in November, Richard Henry Lee wrote a letter to Samuel Adams that revealed how deeply this quondam friend was involved in the eliminate-Washington game. (Adams was in Boston recuperating from his labors in Congress.) "General Mifflin has been here [in York]," Lee wrote. "He urges strongly the necessity of having Gen. Gates to be president of the new Board of War. He thinks the military knowledge and the authority of Gates necessary to procure the indispensable changes in our army. I believe he is right."[19]

As for Conway's resignation, it was apparently forgotten. Instead, various members of Congress began talking about the army's need for an inspector general, who would teach the soldiers discipline and improved tactics. The source of this idea was General Washington. He first heard it from a French volunteer, the Baron d'Arendt. After consulting with his generals in late October and obtaining their agreement, the commander in chief had sent the proposal to Henry Laurens, who had submitted it to Congress.

The solons referred the idea to the Board of War, which soon adopted a plan prepared by none other than General Conway. It called for an inspector general who would be independent of Washington and report directly to the Board of War. That entity dispatched a perfunctory letter to Washington, asking him if such an officer would be useful. Without waiting for Washington's reply, Congress created the office of inspector general, outlined his duties, and chose Conway for the job, with the rank of major general. Could there be a stronger signal than this appointment of General Washington's most outspoken critic that Congress was no longer inclined to treat "His Excellency" with deference, much less respect?[20]

These new arrangements were a power shift of major proportions. There were no public announcements, but the message was clear. As president of the Board of War, General Gates was under no obligation to consult the commander in chief about anything. If he deemed it necessary, he could appoint himself or another general to command the northern army or an army in the South without asking General Washington's permission. He also had the power to supervise the commissary and quartermaster departments, propose reforms, and issue reports, some of which might well be critical of the Continental Army and its commander. Meanwhile, Inspector General Conway would be in Valley Forge telling Washington what was wrong with the way he ran the army—and issuing hostile reports to the Board of War, which would pass them on to Congress.

VI

Washington fought back in an angry letter to Congress. He told the politicians that "General Conway's merit . . . as an officer, and his importance in this army, exists more in his imagination than in reality." He warned that elevating Conway would trigger resignations among the army's twenty-three brigadier generals, all of whom held commissions that were senior to Conway's. If his brigadiers starting quitting, the army might dissolve into chaos. "I have been a slave to the service," the general wrote. "I have undergone more than most men are aware of, to harmonize so many discordant parts; but it will be impossible for me to be of any further service, if . . . insuperable obstacles are placed in my way." This unmistakable threat to resign was ominous evidence that Washington was vulnerable to the Mifflin-managed disrespect and insult campaign.[21]

Behind the scenes, John Laurens wrote to his father, Henry, that "the promotion of Genl Conway has given almost universal disgust" in the army. It had also "given a deep wound to the line of brigadiers." They regarded it as an insult to their honor, exactly as General Washington had warned. "It is said that the influence of a certain general officer at Reading is productive of great mischief," John added, obviously certain that the president of Congress would have no difficulty identifying the mischief maker as General Mifflin.[22]

VII

The mood of the new power brokers was more than indicated by the letter that Horatio Gates wrote to Henry Laurens. The Saratoga hero enclosed the letter he had written to General Washington, demanding to know the identity of the man who had purloined his private correspondence. Gates's letter to Laurens vibrated with more of the same outsized indignation and fulminations against "the wretch" who had betrayed him. He saw military secrets being leaked by this same "traitor."

Then came a reminder that Gates had influence in Congress. "I cannot believe that the traitorous thief will long escape detection after the patriotism of the delegates shall have been alarmed." Gates seemed to be suggesting that General Washington, the recipient of the leaked letter, might somehow be involved in the treacherous business and ought to be investigated by the righteous true whigs in Congress.[23]

VIII

Simultaneously, Inspector General Conway visited Valley Forge, where General Washington was frigidly polite to him. The commander in chief told Conway he had not received from Congress the resolution describing his powers and responsibilities. For the time being, the new IG could not begin his duties. An irked Conway took the offensive in a letter to Washington, informing him that he had been "directed by the Board of War" to prepare a set of instructions for maneuvering the troops. "You have not a moments [sic] time to lose," he lectured Washington. "The enemy . . . will probably be powerfully reinforced, your army is melting by sickness."

In his usual confrontational style, Conway made it clear that he knew Washington had objected to his promotion to major general. "I begg [sic] leave to observe to you, sir, that in our European armies all inspectors have ranks of major general and some of lt. [lieutenant] general," he wrote, implying that Washington, the American tyro, knew nothing about military matters in the big (European) leagues. There was "nothing extraordinary" in his promotion—except that the office of inspector general was "not thought of sooner." Now "the honorable congress" had taken a "dispassionate view of the matter" and appointed him, without any "art or interest" on his part to "steal" the appointment.

As for the resentment of his fellow brigadiers and Washington's concern for their delicate feelings, Conway pointed out that the gift of genuine military talent was rare among soldiers. Only a few "men of merit" had been acknowledged to possess it—"the great Frederick" in Europe and the "great Washington" on this continent. The underlined words, the mocking comparison to Frederick the Great of Prussia, considered the most brilliant soldier of his era, typified Conway's snide style at its nastiest. The Irishman claimed "no superiority in personal qualities" to his fellow brigadiers—but he had been soldiering before many of them were born, and "you sir, and the great Frederick know perfectly well that this trade is not learned in a few months." [24]

Again, the implication was clear. If Washington hoped to play in Frederick the Great's league, he had better listen to General Conway, whether he liked it or not. Without bothering to answer it, Washington forwarded Conway's letter to President Henry Laurens with a request that it be submitted to Congress. He noted Conway's complaint about his "cool reception" at Valley Forge. If by that he meant that Washington did not receive him "in the language of a warm and cordial friend," the commander in chief "readily confess[ed] the charge." He was not capable of "the arts of dissimulation" and in fact despised them. "My feelings will not permit me to make professions of friendship to the man I deem my enemy." [25]

IX

The next day, an infuriated John Laurens wrote to his father from Valley Forge. "By this day's courier you will be informed of the base insult offered to the commander in chief which will raise your indignation." He paused to tell the story of Conway's letter to General Gates, calling Washington a weak general, and Conway's evasive reply to Washington's inquiry, which "expos[ed] his guilt." This latest Conway letter went far beyond a negative comment to a third party. It was an insolent attempt at what the French call persiflage—humoring a man in a condescending, insulting tone.

"It affects the Gen'l very sensibly," Laurens wrote. "It is such an affront as Conway would never have dared to offer if the General's situation had not assured him of the impossibility of its being revenged in a private way." The young lieutenant colonel meant a challenge to a duel. That is why Washington had decided to lay the matter before Congress, who would have to decide "whether Gen'l W. is to be sacrificed for Gen'l C." There was no other alternative, because Washington had decided never to conduct any military business with a man from whom he had received "such unpardonable insults." [26]

In this secret war within the public war, Washington was using every weapon at his disposal. The link between President Laurens and his son was what today's diplomats would call a "back channel" of surpassing value. Washington was using it here to make another threat to resign, but it was through a third party, carefully muting its potential danger.

After reading Conway's letter to Washington, the elder Laurens agreed with his son. "The taunts and sarcasm . . . are unpardonable." The president of Congress cast aside his doubts about Washington's leadership and became an ally in the struggle. For some time, Laurens told his son, he had suspected the formation of a "party" in Congress. It was an event which he "dreaded" and it was now "coming to maturity." He was not entirely sure, but he believed John had identified the "pivot" of this anti-Washington faction: Thomas Mifflin.

But the opposition was much larger than the former quartermaster general. Many other people were involved, some of them ostensible friends of Washington. These men were not active plotters but they "want[ed] [lacked] the honor" to defend the commander in chief." In all such "junctoes" [juntos], Laurens observed, "there are prompters and actors, accommodators, candle snuffers, shifters of scenes and mutes." [27]

The president was convinced that behind the attack on Washington's generalship was a desire to conceal a great deal of corruption in the administration of the army's departments. He was "well informed" that some had already acquired "vast paper money estates." The "pivot," General Mifflin, was one of these men. It was a game at the public expense that "cannot be successfully played without knowledge & the aid of a circle." To "break the combination" was not going to be easy. But henceforth, he would "attend to all their movements."

To illustrate the difficulty, Laurens told his son what had happened in Congress when he had read Washington's letter defending his cool treatment of General Conway. The commander in chief had suggested Baron d'Arendt as an alternative inspector general. When the baron was mentioned, one congressman shouted: "As great a rascal as any in the army!" Laurens called this "ill-manners and breach of order" striking evidence of "party-affection and prejudice." It unquestionably demonstrated that some in Congress were not at all hesitant to publicly sneer at General Washington's advice.

President Laurens began this letter to his son on January 8. He wrote it after long, exhausting sessions in Congress on many matters. A day later, at 10 p.m., he apologized to John for this "patch work." It was his sixth attempt to complete the letter. After more discussion of the faction, Laurens again vowed to watch the plotters closely. But he told John that the best way to defeat them lay in General Washington's hands—to stay calm and continue to do his job. The president of Congress simply did not believe any "rooted enemy" or combination of enemies could "degrade" Washington without his cooperation (Laurens used "consent")—by yielding to angry outbursts or, worst of all, a resignation.[28]

The letter closed with more ominous news, written late in the evening of January 10. The president had just returned from a large party, where he had heard a discussion of appointing a new quartermaster. General Washington had suggested a New Englander, Udney Hay, who had been a deputy under General Mifflin. The commander in chief 's recommendation "and his opinions" were treated with "such indecent freedom and levity" that it "affected me exceedingly," Laurens wrote. He was again convinced there was a faction behind this "baneful influence."

He advised John (and General Washington) to have "a little more patience" until they found proof there was "a system" whose aim was "to overturn & rule." Perhaps there was an even more sinister goal: to throw everything into confusion and "bring in the ancient rule." He meant George III. With the British army ensconced in Philadelphia and four-fifths of Pennsylvania disgusted with the radical state government in Lancaster, the idea was by no means implausible.[29]

X

A week after Washington wrote to President Laurens, strenuously defending his cool reception of General Conway, the commander in chief received a letter from Portsmouth, New Hampshire. The writer enclosed a letter from Benjamin Franklin and Silas Deane, the diplomats who were representing the United States in Paris.

> The gentleman who will have the honor of waiting upon you with this letter is the Baron Steuben, Lieut. Genl in the King of Prussia's service, whom he attended in all his campaigns, being his Aid de Camp, quartermaster genl etc. He goes to America with a true zeal for our cause and a view of engaging in it and rendering it all the service in his power. He is recommended to us by two of the best judges of military merit in this country, Mr. Le Comte de Vergennes and Mr. Le Comte de St. Germain, who have long been personally acquainted with him.[30]

The Comte de Vergennes was France's foreign minister. The Comte de St. Germain was the minister of war, and a famous general in his own right. It would be difficult to imagine more superlative recommendations. Washington quickly read the rest of the letter. The former lieutenant general said he was so eager to assist the United States of America that if "the distinguished ranks" which he had attained in Europe were an obstacle to giving him similar rank in the American army, he was ready to serve as a volunteer rather than be "an object of discontent" to General Washington's officers. He hoped that "the respectable Congress" would accept this offer.

Steuben added that General Washington was the only officer, other than his former commander, the King of Prussia (Frederick the Great), under whom he wished to practice the military arts.

For a man who had just been insultingly compared to Frederick the Great by General Conway, this letter must have had a special impact. General Washington could not help thinking that here was a foreign officer whose European rank vastly exceeded Conway's; he had been a mere colonel in the French army. Moreover, the Baron seemed to be miraculously aware of how touchy American officers had become about foreigners, and was asking neither rank nor pay. He was almost too good to be true.

General Washington wrote a cautious reply, telling Steuben it would be up to Congress to decide where and how he could best serve the American army. But Washington would be "glad" to see him at Valley Forge.[31]

The commander in chief had no idea that he was corresponding with a man who would soon be an invaluable partner in his struggle to rescue the Continental Army.

FIVE

ENTER THE COMMITTEE IN CAMP

IN MID-JANUARY 1778, more than half the troops at Valley Forge were still living in tents. The shortage of tools had slowed the efforts of the hut builders to a standstill in some brigades. Even completed huts left a good deal to be desired. One lieutenant noted in his diary that when it rained, his hut's leaky roof guaranteed them "water over their shoetops."

The weather was as inconsistent as the workmanship of the hut builders. Contrary to the traditional impression, the winter camp was not perpetually snowbound and whipped by subzero winds. One diarist reported January 11 was an "exceeding snowy day." The same man called January 30 the pleasantest he had ever known for that time of year. Bluebirds were chirping in the trees.[1]

Other diarists confirm that overall temperatures at Valley Forge added up to a relatively mild winter—more or less typical weather for southeastern Pennsylvania. More than half the time the mercury was above the freezing mark. Only twice did the temperature drop into the single digits.[2]

The National Park Service recently conducted an experiment in one of the reconstructed huts at contemporary Valley Forge. Ranger Mark Brier and several volunteers spent from January 27 to February 1 in a hut with a brisk fire blazing in the fireplace. With the temperature 31 degrees outside, the temperatures in the hut ranged from 70 degrees in front of the fire to 47 at the other end, by the door. In 1778, with 12 men in each hut, there was hardly room for everyone in front of the fire. We are not talking about comfort here—but no one was in danger of freezing to death or suffering frostbite.[3]

Another building project on which General Washington placed high priority was a bridge across the Schuylkill River to provide the army with a quick retreat, if the British attacked and the battle went badly. The commander in chief put General John Sullivan in charge of this task. The New Hampshire soldier was soon lamenting his slow progress. Tools to deal with large timber were nonexistent, and many of the axes he received were worthless. Again and again, men detailed to do the work simply failed to show up—a silent protest against their miserable living conditions.

The army's food shortage remained at the head of the list of General Washington's many worries. Alarmed letters from Colonel Ephraim Blaine, deputy commissary general of purchases for the middle department, and his harassed aide, John Chaloner, made this dolorously clear. The thirty-six-year-old Blaine, the son of Irish immigrants, had been a successful merchant in Carlisle, Pennsylvania, where he owned several gristmills and sawmills. He had also served a term as sheriff of Cumberland County, testifying to his political smarts. Stationed at Valley Forge, he was the man directly responsible for feeding the Continental Army. He and his network of assistants were supposed to be buying the food they needed from the farmers of the middle states, nearest to the winter camp.[4]

On December 28, Blaine wrote to Chaloner from Carlisle, where he had been searching for beef and flour. Blaine described himself as "one of the most miserable creatures living" since Chaloner had told him about the supply crisis at Valley Forge. On the way to Carlisle, Blaine had stopped at York to talk to William Buchanan, the do-nothing commissary general of purchases. "Though the army are in the greatest distress for want of the necessarys of life, yet Mr. Buchanan will not be convinced but there is great plenty in the country and holds to the old prices," Blaine wrote. The feckless Buchanan operated out of a single room, with no clerks, no records worth mentioning, and no talent for the job.[5]

There was a veritable cargo of coming woe in Buchanan's smug assertion of the status quo, based on totally imaginary evidence of vast quantities of wheat and cattle waiting to be purchased in Pennsylvania. The commissary general was reflecting the attitude of his congressional masters, who refused to admit that the depreciation of the Continental dollar was making it harder and harder to buy from Pennsylvania farmers at the rock-bottom prices Congress had set in the spring of 1777. Since that time, the value of the paper money had depreciated 75 percent. When told that the farmers were refusing to sell at the old prices, the Adams-Lee true whigs in control of Congress preferred to lament the lack of public virtue in Pennsylvania rather than deal with the threat of the Continental Army's collapse.

From Valley Forge, Chaloner tried to awaken Commissary General of Purchases Buchanan from his lethargy with a letter that quoted General Washington's increasingly angry view of the situation: "Dammit, what is the reason Mr. Buchanan is not here, does he think to indulge himself at home whilst we are distressed and suffering for want of provision?" Chaloner added that this was the sort of language "His Excellency is by no means accustom'd to use."

The latter was hardly the case. When Washington lost his temper he used language far stronger than "Dammit." Chaloner may well have invented the quote to convey evidence of the general's rising wrath.

Chaloner told the commissary general of purchases that the attempt to procure food from the vicinity of the camp had produced something less than a third of one day's allowance. Moreover, "the crys petitions and complaints of the inhabitants" were "beyond description." Another factor that Buchanan refused to recognize was the widespread dislike of the Revolution in Pennsylvania. Although some parts of the state "abound[ed]" in flour, "the disaffection of the people is such that they will not spare it at a reasonable compensation tho they have to detain it or withhold it [unto] destruction."

Chaloner added another sarcastic comment from Washington: that it was "damn'd hard that flour could not be brought on from the Susquehannah," a reference to a favorite Buchanan excuse—the quartermaster department was failing to supply wagons to transport his purchases. Lecturing Buchanan as if he (Chaloner) were the commissary general, the deputy told him to obtain a "positive resolve of Congress" to give his commissaries power to obtain wagons and teams. Unless Buchanan did this immediately, "your reputation & every person under you will be ruin'd and undone."

The fate of his reputation was not the only thing that was worrying Chaloner. He was morally certain that if nothing was done "I shall fall prey to the prejudiced and starved soldiery." Although he had a sardonic sense of humor, the English-born Chaloner, formerly a successful Philadelphia merchant, was not joking. Meat from one drove of recently arrived cattle was so lean, the troops threatened several issuing commissaries with bayonets.[6]

Before many more weeks passed, an issuing brigade commissary was murdered by his infuriated clients. The widespread belief, propagated by the true whigs in Congress, that the commissaries were a swarm of thieves feeding at the public trough did not make for warm relationships with the troops, even in ordinary circumstances.

II

Snow and wintry winds continued to batter the camp. On January 5, Lieutenant Colonel John Brooks of the Eighth Massachusetts Regiment told a friend that for the previous week the weather had been "as cold . . . as I ever knew at home." It pained him to see "our poor brave fellows" still living in tents, "bare footed, bare leg'd." Brooks went on to discuss an even more explosive problem, "the unequal distribution and scanty allowance of provisions."

Brooks blamed the "cursed Quakers and other inhabitants" of Pennsylvania for the shortages and the commissaries for the unequal distribution, implying they were often bribed. Also on his list of complaints was a shortage of money. The soldiers had been paid only twice in the last twelve months. In spite of all these difficulties, Brooks was still able to say: "No men ever show more spirit . . . than ours. In my opinion, nothing but virtue has kept our army together thro this campaign."

Brooks's attribution of virtue to the army was not a new idea in the ideology of the Revolution. But to politicians like Benjamin Rush and Sam Adams, a regular army's virtue lacked the nobility displayed by civilians and militiamen, who were voluntarily virtuous. The army's virtue was enforced by military regulations and strict supervision. A standing army was a sullen beast, which had to be watched constantly. True whig-style disinterested virtue was mainly expected from the officers.

Valley Forge was changing Brooks's mind about that idea. The only principle that sustained both him and his men, Brooks continued, was "love of country . . . and that only." What else could have motivated the soldiers, without food, clothing, or money from their so-called government? It was a convincing argument, as Brooks saw it.

Then Brooks added ominous words. Love of country would not last indefinitely. "Some other motives must cooperate with this" to keep an army together for any length of time. "The private interest" of the officers must also be taken into account. Officers with families to support, with business careers abandoned or suspended, could not be expected to stay in the service for years. "I know of no reason why one part of the community should sacrifice their all for the good of it while the rest are filling their coffers."[7]

This frank view of the Revolution by an undoubted patriot has seldom appeared in standard textbooks. It presaged a clash between the army and Congress that threatened the future of the embryo republic.

Worsening the problem was the attitude toward the army among civilians. The Pennsylvanians were not the only ones who imagined the men at Valley Forge doing little or nothing for their pay. Colonel Brooks's wrath was directed at this mind-set as much as at the unfairness of the officers' lot.

Sergeant Ichabod Crane of Connecticut was also concerned about "the uneasiness there seems to be at hum [home] concerning the soldiers." He gathered that the civilians wondered why "we have not kill'd all the enemy [and] what we are about [at] 40 shillings [eight dollars] a munth [sic] and nothing to do." Crane was sure that there would be no grumbling at soldiers if the critics were forced to undergo "half so much as one of us have this winter." Their pay, when they got it, did not go very far. A small bread pie (bought from a peddler) cost two dollars. The sergeant summed up his opinion in a blunt sentence that made it clear he too sensed a growing gap between civilians and soldiers: "It is trublesum times for us all but wors for soldiers."[8]

III

Colonel Brooks thought the army's food troubles were almost over. "Large supplies of provision from N England" were coming into camp. Alas, this was a myth. John Chaloner was getting letters from Boston commissaries telling him they had to feed Burgoyne's captured army and garrisons at Albany, Providence, and elsewhere and would have little left to send to Valley Forge. The frantic Chaloner lamented on January 4 that he was faced by an army that required thirty thousand pounds of bread and an equal amount of meat per day and he had been "deserted and deceived by almost every assistant purchasing commissary" in the country.[9]

The purchasing commissaries were not entirely to blame. They had a problem even more basic than the widespread civilian reluctance to sell at the prices set by Congress: no money. In mid-January Chaloner told Blaine, who was still on the road: "You must look for no supplies until you send cash" to the commissaries in the field so they could pay for cattle and hogs already purchased. One assistant commissary told Chaloner that he was planning to stay in camp until Blaine arrived, hopefully with money. He owed so much that he "dared not go home."[10]

Even worse, as Chaloner saw it, was a recent decision by the Pennsylvania Assembly to send "commissioners" into the countryside to purchase supplies for the army. If Blaine thought he could rely on these reinforcements, he was dreaming. "If you cannot supply the army with assistants appointed by yourself," he asked, how could he hope to do it with strangers over whom he had no real authority?[11]

Beef and flour were not the only absent staples. At least as important to the troops was whiskey. They were supposed to get a gill (four ounces) a day. Here the problem was competition from the civilian economy. "The damned forestallers," as Blaine called them at one point, were buying up all the whiskey in sight, hoping to sell it to the troops at exorbitant prices through the numerous sutlers who swarmed around the army. These thoroughly corrupt hustlers were ready to trade whiskey for clothing, blankets, even muskets.

Two other badly needed items were soap and candles. Chaloner told Blaine there were no candles on hand, "not a candle to write by, even for his Excellency [Washington] if wanted." Soap was critical for the health of the troops. Unable to bathe or wash their clothes, they became infested with lice, which produced the often fatal "camp fever"— typhus.

Less fatal but horribly tormenting was another offshoot of the soap shortage, scabies, which the soldiers called "the itch." This malady began as small sacs between the fingers. A man scratched them and the fluid that oozed out soon spread the disease over the rest of his body. When a scabies sac was broken, it acquired a crust. If not treated, it could become an ulcer that burrowed into the skin. Meanwhile, the soldier was tormented day and night by incessant itching, which incapacitated him for duty.

On January 8, Washington realized scabies had become epidemic and ordered infected men isolated in separate huts, where doctors covered their afflicted bodies with sulfur in hog's lard. Some soldiers tried their own remedies. One covered his body with mercury ointment. He died the next day. Another man, who guzzled six gills (a pint and a half) of rum, also died.[12]

Whiskey in more reasonable quantities was part of the treatment. Private Joseph Plumb Martin of Connecticut told of being so tormented with the itch that he could scarcely lift his hands to his head. Ordered on an overnight foraging party, he and other sufferers in his company borrowed some sulfur from the artillerymen, mixed it with brimstone and tallow, and added a supply of "hot whiskey toddy." They applied these remedies to each other's "outsides and insides."

By the time they finished, they were all so drunk, they did not notice as they staggered back to their quarters that two of the patients had passed out and "all night lay naked in the field." Nevertheless, they hailed their "decisive victory" over the itch. It was, Martin remarked wryly, "the only one we had achieved lately." [13]

IV

An increasingly troubled Washington demanded from John Chaloner a comprehensive report of the purchasing commissary department's plans to feed the army. Living from day to day, hoping against hope for the sight of a drove or two of cattle, the desperate Chaloner could only plead that Colonel Blaine would soon arrive and give the general a full account. Poor Chaloner had lost all confidence in their collapsing system. He told one correspondent that he had assured Washington they could depend on a seventy-nine-day supply of beef, but when he was called to headquarters to ask how many cattle were on hand at the moment, "poor me answered two days [supply]." Two days later, he was summoned again and had to confess there was "not a beast alive" in the camp. [14]

"I am thoroughly tired of the frowns of His Excellency and all ranks of people in and out of the army," Chaloner told Blaine. "For God's sake come to camp [and] relieve me or I must quit altogether." [15]

Blaine's reply was not reassuring. The deputy commissary for the middle department told of the resistance he was encountering "purchasing and seizing cattle and whiskey." The emphasis was clearly on seizing. He frequently had to "break open stable doors and windows." Unfortunately he could not speak German, which made the business "very disagreeable." The locals often stole the cattle he seized within twenty-four hours, and Blaine was forced to import soldiers from Lancaster to guard his four-legged captives. [16]

V

The cold weather, the minimal rations, and the lack of warm clothes and soap began to have dire effects on the enlisted men. Scarcely a day passed without a man dying silently during the night. Rhode Island Colonel

Israel Angell's diary became a lament on this subject. On January 18, he wrote:"Died last night. Dan Philipps of my regiment. A civil honest young man who drove my waggon." On January 23: "buried two of our soldiers, viz Oliver Greene and William Foster." On January 24:"Three more of my Regt died last night and this day were deacently [sic] buried. . . . It is a very alarming time amongst us the troops are very sickly and die fast."

On January 25, Angell wrote: "This morning was exceeding pleasant but I was no sooner up and drest [sic] before I was called upon to give one more mellencully [sic] order, viz, a coffin for one of my men who departed this life last night. . . . What an alarm this must be to us, a small handfull of poor naked soles [sic] destitute of money and every necessity of life, to see how we are struck off on the list of time, one two and three in the space of twenty four hours." On February 4, Angell returned from picket duty at Radnor, fifteen miles from Philadelphia, to find a corporal and a private added to the list of the dead.[17]

If conditions in Valley Forge were unhealthy, the situation in the army's hospitals can only be described as catastrophic. Many of the men who died in their huts probably concealed their sicknesses because it had become common knowledge in the army that going to a hospital was too often a one-way trip.

Some brigadiers sent officers to visit their men in the hospitals to make sure they were not being neglected. Colonel Angell drew this duty in late December. The report he brought back was grim. Medicines were seldom available, the food was abominable, and many of the men had no blankets. Visiting the hospital in Princeton, he wrote: "Two of the poore soldiers in the hospital belonging to the state of Virginia froze to death last night owing in the negligance [sic] of the quartermaster not providing wood."[18]

VI

In February, Angell returned from another trip to New Jersey and informed his diary that he had found "all the officers well but the soldiers very sickly they was buring [sic] two when I arriv'd in camp." Here the colonel offhandedly recorded a little-discussed aspect of Valley Forge. The officers survived the hardships of the winter far more comfortably than the enlisted men. It seems never to have occurred to Angell or his subordinate officers to visit their men's huts to find out who might need medical help. Their contact with the rank and file was minimal at best.

Lieutenant James McMichael of the Thirteenth Pennsylvania Regiment seemingly had only one thing on his mind at Valley Forge: his new bride, Susanna, who was living with her parents in Stony Brook, New Jersey. Three days after the army reached the winter camp the lieutenant applied for a furlough. While his men were starving, he and Susanna and her friends passed their time "in jollitry."

On January 8, McMichael returned to Valley Forge and helped fellow officers build a hut for their winter quarters. On January 14, their colonel, Walter Stewart, invited all the officers of the regiment to dine with him at his quarters, and Lieutenant McMichael informed his diary that they "passed the day in civil jollitry." Not a word about starving soldiers or men dying of camp fever or tormented by the itch.[19]

When he was not in pursuit of "jollitry," Lieutenant McMichael wrote poems to his Susanna. In February, when he was laid low by camp fever, he offered her the following testament:

> Dear Creature I must from you go
> But yet my heart is filled with woe
> I wish you in my absence may
> Have all the bliss love can display
> Your Jamey must stay in the wars
> And try the labors of bold Mars.[20]

Lieutenant Samuel Armstrong of the Seventh Massachusetts Regiment, who had turned up a dozen fowls while the army was starving in the Gulph, continued to improvise solutions to the food shortages. When the regiment reached Valley Forge on December 19, Armstrong and his fellow officers were appalled that there was nothing to eat. They immediately put their "Boy" to work baking bread, which they ate like "insatiate monsters." Their Boy then concocted a pudding which they ate "till our guts began to ake."[21]

On December 20, when the commissary issued a half pound of salt meat per man, and officers drew the same unpalatable ration, Lieutenant Armstrong observed that the men "never bore up with such bad usage before, with so little mutiny, for I believe it gratified them in a great measure to think the officers endured the same and indeed there was more mutiny among the officers than among the men." Obviously, the officers seldom dined on the same food as the men.[22]

On December 23, Lieutenant Armstrong and a detachment from his regiment were ordered to stand picket duty at Springfield, on the outskirts of Philadelphia. They were "within a mile and a half of the enemy," he nervously noted. The commissary had no meat to issue when they left Valley Forge. Both officers and men were issued only flour, which they baked into cakes. Later in the day, Armstrong reported they killed some sheep and broiled them over coals. There was no mention of sharing this meat with the enlisted men, who apparently subsisted on their "fire cakes," as they were called.

To relieve the tedium of the winter camp, Armstrong and his friends developed a habit of crossing the Schuylkill River and not returning until the next evening. They spent the time there "frolicing and dancing." Often each officer would buy a bottle of wine from the sutlers who camped on the east bank of the river. That added to the enjoyment. So did the camp followers who did duty as dancing partners.[23]

When not frolicking, not a few of these young gentlemen resorted to dueling to pass the time. Washington repeatedly banned the practice but to little avail. Often these deadly encounters occurred between friends. The cause might be a rough jest that offended the recipient's honor. If both men survived, they would shake hands and resume their friendship as if nothing had happened. Not all duelists were so lucky. Lieutenant McMichael recorded the death of a fellow lieutenant from General Greene's division, "a gentleman of amiable disposition." Virtually all the officers in the division went to his funeral. He was interred with "the honors of war" as if he had died on a battlefield.[24]

Not all the officers spent their time in jollity or dueling. Those in the higher ranks, such as Colonel John Cropper of Virginia, had a broader view of the army's desperate condition. Cropper struggled with a strong sense of responsibility that clashed with his equally strong desire to see his wife, Peggy, who was furious at him for his long absence. She was alone in Accomac County with their baby daughter and extremely unhappy.

In the middle of March Cropper wrote her a long letter, explaining how often he had tried to get a few weeks' leave, but each time General Washington said he could not spare him, because so many other officers in the Virginia brigade had resigned or taken furloughs. Cropper urged her to share his feelings for their "distressed country, tottering at this time on the brink of ruin." He was sure she would understand that his honor was at stake. Just in case, he told her that he was planning to bring some fine presents when he came home in a month, at the most.[25]

VII

We know a good deal more about the enlisted men who endured Valley Forge than the early writers on the winter camp. These historians portrayed them as more or less faceless but patriotic yeoman farmers, not essentially different from the men who fought at Lexington and Concord. More recent historians have described the enlisted ranks at Valley Forge as largely landless men who joined the army because it offered a steady wage, plus food, whiskey, and clothes paid for by the government. They were, in the words of one historian, "surplus population." In this analysis, patriotism was the last thing they thought about.[26]

This writer believes there is a middle ground between these extremes. There is no doubt that the new research has exploded the myth of the yeoman farmer who left his plow and family to defend his liberty à la the volunteers of 1775. Almost all the soldiers at Valley Forge were in their teens or early twenties, unmarried, and poor. A study of 710 New Jersey Continental soldiers concluded that almost all came from the lower economic classes of the population. Only a tiny percentage listed a skill or profession.

The predominance of the poor in the ranks is not as surprising as some historians seem to think. The armies who have fought in all America's wars have been mostly poor and young. But this does not mean that the soldiers at Valley Forge saw themselves as hapless cannon fodder. Many hoped an independent America would give men like themselves a brighter future. At the very least they sought a sense of self worth from testing their courage on a battlefield.[27]

Perhaps the most surprising thing about the soldiers was the number of foreign-born men in the ranks. By far the highest percentage of these newcomers were Irish. More than three hundred thousand Irish men and women, mostly Presbyterians but with a goodly sprinkling of Catholics, had come to America before the Revolution. All of them bore bitter memories of British oppression in their home country, and they often led the way in issuing calls for independence.

In New England regiments, 10 to 20 percent of the men had Irish surnames. In the middle states, to which most of the Irish had emigrated, the percentages were much higher, with Pennsylvania winning the prize for the most Celts in its regiments. The First Pennsylvania reported 315 of 660 rank and file were Irish. Another 215 men simply listed "America" as their place of birth, making one historian suspect they were sons of immigrants trying to disguise their country of origin.[28]

It was no accident that one memoirist of the Revolution called the Pennsylvania brigade "the line of Ireland." Although the records are fragmentary, the muster rolls of Continental units from Maryland, New Jersey, and Delaware frequently were 45 percent Irish. There were times when the whole Revolution seemed "nothing more than a Mac-ocracy," commented one Continental Army general.[29]

Small wonder that St. Patrick's Day was celebrated with vigor at Valley Forge. When some non-Irish troops tried to make fun of the saint by hoisting a scarecrow-like "stuffed paddy" on a pole, a riot nearly ensued, until General Washington arrived to calm the outraged Celts. The commander in chief declared himself "a great admirer of St. Patrick" and issued an extra ration of rum to smooth things over.[30]

While the Irish filled a hefty percentage of the Valley Forge army's ranks, the Germans were not far behind. They were the largest ethnic group in America in 1775, with most of them settled in New York and Pennsylvania. By far the greatest number of the Continental Army's German recruits came from the latter state. They composed between 10 and 20 percent of the soldiers at Valley Forge. Another study found 12 percent of the rank and file with Germanic surnames.[31]

African Americans were also numerous at Valley Forge. They were in almost every regiment. They numbered 117 of the 1,065 troops of the Connecticut brigade. Thirteen percent of the troops in one Virginia brigade were black. A return by the adjutant general, taken not long after the army left Valley Forge, identified 755 men as blacks—almost 10 percent of Washington's total manpower at that time.[32]

Many of these men enlisted voluntarily. A good example was thirty-two-year-old, aptly named Shadrack Battles of Virginia. Described as "a free man of color," he joined the Tenth Virginia Regiment on December 3, 1776. He fought at Brandywine and Germantown and endured the winter at Valley Forge.[33]

Another volunteer was Windsor Fry of Rhode Island, also a free man of color. He first joined the army at fifteen, in March of 1775, apparently for a brief enlistment. In 1777, he signed up for three years or the duration of the war in the First Rhode Island Regiment, and he was listed as "sick present" in the early winter at Valley Forge. By the time he was discharged in 1783, Fry had served almost six years.[34]

This length of service was not unusual for black soldiers. Far more than whites, they seemed to have found a home in the army. It was mournful testimony to the precarious life free blacks led in a mostly slave society.

Thirty-six-year-old Salem Poor of Massachusetts was another free black who joined the war early, after purchasing his freedom from his master, John Poor, in 1769. Salem fought at Bunker Hill and distinguished himself so remarkably that six officers signed a petition asking the state legislature to cite him as "a brave and gallant soldier." This testimony had not a little to do with changing George Washington's mind about enlisting blacks in the Continental Army. Eventually, Poor joined the Thirteenth

Massachusetts Regiment and fought at Saratoga, before marching with his fellow Yankees to Valley Forge. He too served until the end of the war.[35]

Many other black soldiers at Valley Forge were slaves who accepted an offer from their masters to serve in the army on the promise that they would be free men when the war ended. Patriotism was seldom the master's motive. As white volunteers dwindled, the states began drafting men from the militia. The slave was often a substitute for his drafted master. Samuel Sutphen was one of these involuntary volunteers in the New Jersey Brigade. He too served until the end of the war, when he had the unenviable experience of being reinslaved by his double-crossing master. It took Sutphen another twenty years to purchase his freedom.[36]

We know little more about these black soldiers beyond these minimal facts. They apparently were accepted by their fellow infantrymen as "brother soldiers," the preferred term when enlisted men spoke to or about each other. So thoroughly did they blend into the white majority that when they died in the night, their deaths were mentioned by their officers in the same almost casual way. On December 25, 1777, Surgeon's Mate Jonathan Todd of Connecticut wrote to his father: "Jethro, a Negro from Guilford . . . died in his tent, the first man that hath died in camp belonging to our regt."[37]

VIII

This survey of the composition of Valley Forge's soldiers would be incomplete without including another large contingent of army personnel who drew rations and marched with the troops and shivered in the freezing tents and the not much warmer huts: the more than four hundred women who belonged to the army. The term "camp follower" has given them an unfortunate reputation. Some were members of the oldest profession; early in the winter one diarist reported that a woman was drummed out of camp for infecting numerous men with venereal disease. Washington sometimes ordered the regimental surgeons to examine suspected women for VD. But most of the Continental Army's camp followers were wives of soldiers, who went to war with them because there was little hope of surviving in their home communities without a man's support.[38]

Washington insisted that the women had to earn their rations by working in some capacity. Many chose cooking for the men; still more chose washing. There are numerous references in letters and orderly books describing a woman as a "washerwoman for a company." In Valley Forge, with the shortage of soap, not much washing was done for the first three months. But women were sometimes pressed into service as seamstresses, when cloth or cast-off clothes arrived to outfit the almost naked soldiers.

A handful of women followed their husbands into battle. At Valley Forge the best known was Anna Maria Lane, who wore a uniform and posed as a brother or cousin of her husband, John. She was adventurous enough to see action at Germantown, where she was wounded. In the hospital startled surgeons discovered she was a woman. When Anna Maria recovered, she put on a dress and joined her husband at Valley Forge, where she was considered a camp follower more than entitled to her daily ration.[39]

Only a few camp followers served as nurses. Army hospitals were so disease-ridden and chaotic that only a woman with a strong sense of mission, a strong personality, or both could tolerate such duty. Most hospitals were a good distance from Valley Forge, which meant the woman and her soldier husband were separated, making the duty doubly hard.

IX

While Colonel Israel Angell was making his troubling tour of the hospitals, on George Washington's desk was an explosive letter from Dr. Benjamin Rush, director of the hospital in Princeton. Rush said he had been waiting to hear from the director general of the army's hospitals, Dr. William Shippen, but had given up hope of any response from him. Dr. Shippen was supposed to keep Washington informed about the hospitals, but, Rush implied, he must have failed to do so, because the commander in chief would never tolerate the conditions that confronted the doctors and their patients.

According to Rush, there were no fewer than five thousand patients in the army's hospitals. The number was staggering, but the lack of care was even more appalling. A great majority of these patients were likely to die from diseases caught in the hospitals after they arrived. In the hospital at Princeton, which had five hundred sick, men were dying at the rate of four or five a day. Why? As many as twenty men with "fevers and fluxes" (dysentery) were crowded into rooms barely large enough for six or eight.

Even worse was the shortage of shirts, sheets, and blankets. "Nothing but a miracle can save the life of a soldier who lies in a shirt and blanket which he has worn for four or five months before he came to the hospital." The shirt and blanket were almost certain to be crawling with lice, bearers of that fatal fever, typhus.

On top of this neglect was a wild disorder. There were no guards or officers to command the hospitals. This meant no discipline. The patients went out in the freezing weather and caught colds. They were selling their guns, blankets, and clothes to buy rum and food. The ambulatory sick frequently plundered and insulted local civilians. Inside the hospital, they fought with one another, disobeyed their surgeons, and frustrated the doctors' "salutary plans" to help them recover.

Far better, Rush averred, would be a policy that put as many sick men as possible into local farmhouses, where "the air and diet" would speed their recovery. If this was done, Rush prophesied Washington's army would have an additional three thousand fully recovered soldiers in the spring. "If Your Excellency will only recommend it, I am sure it will *immediately* take place," Rush added.

Washington waited over two weeks to answer this letter. Perhaps he already knew that Dr. Rush was not his friend, much less an admirer. There was a tinge of sarcasm in Rush's underlined "immediately," hinting that by failing to exercise his power, Washington would be derelict and responsible for the hospitals' death rates. Dr. Rush was already on record to his fellow true whig, John Adams, that a general should know everything that was happening throughout his army and by implication was responsible for every and any defect in all its departments.[40]

On January 12, 1778, Washington told Rush he had forwarded his letter to Congress, along with a similar denunciation from William Livingston, governor of New Jersey. The general remarked that "it was to be regretted" that a department on which Congress had lavished so much money should be "inadequate." If the present medical establishment was, as Rush claimed, a bad one, "no time ought to be lost" in fixing it. As for discipline, he was about to order a "discreet field officer" to visit the hospitals and enforce a better military system.

Washington did not mention Rush's wildly impractical idea of finding three thousand farmers willing to take in diseased soldiers. But he assured the doctor that he was ready to do "all in my power" to improve the system. It was a cool, nonconfrontational way of letting Rush know that he was not responsible for the malfunctioning army's hospitals—any more than he was for the commissary or quartermaster departments. They all operated under the direct authority of Congress, with their appointees chosen by the politicians.[41]

X

On the same January day that Washington wrote this letter, Dr. Rush was in York, writing a letter to Governor Patrick Henry of Virginia that revealed how little honesty mattered to true whigs when ideology inflamed their brains. Rush had become friendly with Henry during his days in the Continental Congress in 1775–76, when the Virginian had been a fierce independence man, famous for his cry, "Give me liberty or give me death!" Now Henry was chief executive of the largest state in the union, which made him one of the most influential public officials in America. He could be a key figure in the evolving agitation to get rid of General Washington. If Virginia—his own state—turned against him, the commander in chief would almost certainly resign.

Rush opened his letter with a veritable fusillade of flattery. He gave Henry credit for being the first to teach Americans "to shake off our idolatrous attachment to royalty." He recalled how he had listened with near rapture to Henry's "conversation and eloquence."

But those wondrous days under Henry's inspired leadership had only given the Americans, God's newly chosen people, a passage over the revolutionary Red Sea. The Americans now confronted a dreary wilderness and were in desperate need of a Moses or a Joshua to help them reach the promised land. Congress was a disaster, dwindled to a mere twenty-two members. The army was even worse. Rush had recently heard a major general (probably General Conway) call it not an army but a mob. Discipline was unknown. The commissary and quartermaster departments were "filled with idleness and ignorance and peculation." The hospitals were jammed with six thousand sick (a gain of one thousand since his letter to Washington). More men were dying in them in a single month than had been lost in the field during the entire last campaign.

"But is our case desperate? By no means," Rush avowed. "We have wisdom, virtue and strength *enough* to save us if they could be called into action. The northern army has shown us what Americans are capable of doing with a GENERAL at their head. The spirit of the southern army is by no means inferior to the spirit of the northern."

Where could they find these superlative generals? Rush had three in mind. A Gates, a Lee (Charles Lee), or a Conway would in a few weeks transform Washington's army into "an irresistible body of men." At first, Rush seemed to think Major General Conway was the best hope. Congress had appointed him inspector general with a mandate to "reform abuses." But reforming the defects that the careless, incompetent General Washington had allowed to creep into the army was at best "a palliative." What they needed was one of those capital-letter GENERALs—and there was only one extant, since General Charles Lee had allowed himself to be captured in 1776. In a recent letter to General Gates, General Conway had remarked: "A great and good God hath decreed America to be free, or the _____ [commander in chief] and weak counsels would have ruined her long ago."

Coyly refusing to sign this treacherous demolition of a man he ostensibly admired, Rush mailed it off to Williamsburg, Virginia. He urged Governor Henry to throw the letter on the fire after he read it—especially if he recognized the handwriting. The letter took more than a month to arrive, and the overworked governor, who could not identify Rush's scrawl, sent it to General Washington. He apologized for troubling him with a letter from someone who might be "too insignificant to deserve any notice." But Rush's rant made him suspect there was "a scheme or party" forming against Washington. This troubled Henry, who added that he believed Washington's "personal welfare and the happiness of America are intimately connected."[42]

XI

In Valley Forge, Washington decided early in January that it was time to answer General Gates's outraged letter about the traitor or traitors who had purloined his correspondence and revealed General Conway's nasty remarks about the commander in chief. Washington coolly identified Gates's aide, Lieutenant Colonel Wilkinson, as the source of the leak and described how Lord Stirling had forwarded the gist of General Conway's gibes to headquarters. Washington had sent the remarks to Conway "to show that gentleman I was not unapprized of his intrigueing [sic] disposition."

Washington assured General Gates that no one in the army had been told about the letter except the Marquis de Lafayette, who had read it "under injunctions of secrecy." As befitted his position, Washington had done everything in his power to protect "the tranquility of this army." He had no desire to give the enemy "a gleam of hope" by revealing dissensions among the general officers.

Neatly turning Gates's imputation of treason on the victor of Saratoga, Washington claimed that he never for a moment thought the "safety of the states" could be affected by the leak of Conway's letter, or that he should be called upon "in such solemn terms" to reveal the leaker. He thought Gates had sent him the information via Wilkinson "with a friendly view to forewarn . . . me against a secret enemy." Alas, "in this and other matters of late, I have found myself mistaken."

It was a delicious demonstration of how well Washington could manage the cuts and thrusts of the political game. The closing sentence implied that he now thought Gates's towering indignation suggested a strange desire to protect General Conway.[43]

The day after Washington wrote this letter, he received a note from the Marquis de Lafayette, written just after he came from his division's daily parade. Washington had shown the quotation from Conway's letter to Lafayette because the Marquis, dazzled by Conway's military vocabulary, seemed to be falling under his influence. An indignant Lafayette now told Washington that a French officer who had recently returned from Lancaster reported that all the politicians "speack [sic] of Conway as a man sent by heaven for the liberty and happiness of America. He [Conway] told so [sic] to them and they are fools enough to believe it." [44]

Next came a letter from Colonel Ephraim Blaine addressed to Robert Hanson Harrison, Washington's secretary. While roaming the countryside in search of beef and flour, Blaine had encountered an innkeeper, John Jones, who owned a tavern near Windsor Forge, not far from York. His manner still reflecting shock, the innkeeper told Blaine that a certain "general officer" had been in the tavern a few days earlier, standing at the bar with a captain in a Pennsylvania regiment and his brother and another civilian. Jones said that the general officer had held forth on the deficiencies of General Washington. He was by no means a great general; in fact he was much closer to "an old woman." If necessary, Blaine offered to get the insults "wrote down" by those who had heard them. [45]

A few days later, Washington heard from one of his oldest and closest friends, Dr. James Craik. He had served with Washington in the French and Indian War and been his family's physician for over two decades. The two men liked and admired each other. Writing from his home in Maryland, where his wife was seriously ill, Craik told Washington what he had learned while serving in the hospitals attached to Valley Forge. At work in Pennsylvania and elsewhere were "secret enemies" who were doing their best to "lessen you in the minds of the people" by "underhanded methods to traduce your character."

The morning that Craik left camp, a man who was a "true freind" [sic] of Washington told the doctor that "a strong faction was forming against you in the new Board of War and in Congress." The man urged Craik to warn Washington immediately, but Craik decided to wait until he got home on the chance that he might learn more about the plot on his journey. In Bethlehem and Lancaster, people talked freely to him about the faction, and he heard more "all the way down" to Maryland. Though no one was willing to name names, hints strongly suggested that one of the plotters was Richard Henry Lee. Stronger evidence pointed to General Mifflin, and Craik urged Washington to treat this deceptive gentleman with special care. "He is plausible, sensible, popular and ambitious, takes great pains to draw over every officer he meets with to his way of thinking and is very engageing [sic]."

Craik now got to the heart of the matter. "The method they are taking is by holding up General G——s [Gates] to the people and making believe you have had three or four times the number of the enemy, and have done nothing, that Philadelphia was given up by your mismanagement and that you have missed many opportunities of defeating the enemy, and many other things as ungenerous and unjust—these are the low artifices they are making use of."

Washington's prestige and popularity were still large. Therefore, Craik wrote, "they dare not appear openly as your enemy." But the new Board of War "will throw such obstecles [sic] and difficulties in your way as to make you resign," Craik reiterated that he had heard all this from "such authority as I cannot doubt it."

Here was confirmation of everything that Washington and his aides had suspected, with names named—and a description of the plotters' game plan. "May God of His infinite mercy protect & defend you against all your secret and open enemies," Craik wrote in the final lines of this remarkable letter. It was also clearly up to Washington to take care of himself by fighting this secret war within the bigger war with determination and skill.[46]

XII

From Boston came two letters that revealed how far the rumors (and hopes) of Washington's resignation were floating. The writer was the Reverend William Gordon, a self-appointed historian of the war, who was already gathering materials for a book. In his first letter, he wondered if there was any truth to the story that in late 1776, before the victories at Trenton and Princeton, Congress had been abuzz with a plan to replace Washington with General Charles Lee. "It was first projected," Gordon wrote, "by a Virginian." He did not have to name anyone. They both knew he was talking about Richard Henry Lee.[47]

In the second letter, Gordon reported that John Hancock, no less, had recently told him that Washington was about to resign. "I should dread your doing it," Gordon told Washington. "The cause would suffer amazingly." He could not envision another man around whom the revolutionists could unite. However, he knew Hancock's enormous ego all too well. Gordon suspected the former president of Congress would "propagate such a report on the slightest foundation," hoping he would replace the commander in chief.[48]

Washington replied that he had never bothered to find out whether anyone in Congress had thought of replacing him with General Lee. But he had been told "a scheme of this kind is now on foot by some on behalf of another gentleman." He was, of course, referring to Horatio Gates. As for resigning, the general assured the would-be historian that "no person [had] ever heard me drop an expression that had a tendency to resignation." This rumor was being spread by those who "hope to bring it to pass." If the public wanted to get rid of him, he would go gladly. But it was only the public's voice, not that of a "faction," that could produce his departure. He authorized Gordon to say this, but cautioned him that it should be "nothing formal"—an oblique way of warning him to keep it out of the newspapers. The commander in chief added that he was growing more and more confident that "things will come right again."[49]

XIII

Another side of the controversy emerged in a letter from John Clark Jr. to Nathanael Greene. The spymaster had quit his exhausting duty on the outskirts of Philadelphia, and Greene had helped him obtain an appointment as an auditor in the army paymaster's office in York, supposedly to recuperate from his dangerous labors. One suspects more than benevolence in this transfer. Clark was soon writing Greene inside news about the doings of Congress.

Clark reported that the solons were having second thoughts about their recent promotion of General Gates's courier, talkative Lieutenant Colonel Wilkinson. Their infatuation with Gates had prompted them to make Wilkinson an instant brigadier general, even though he had dallied along his route to see his girlfriend and drain bottles with acquaintances such as Lord Stirling before delivering Gates's dispatches about Saratoga. The Continental Army's colonels had deluged Congress with protests over this unwarranted elevation. The delegates, Clark reported, had "rescinded their late resolve" and hoped to salve Wilkinson's disappointment by making him secretary of the Board of War, where he would work as a top aide to General Gates.

The lawmakers were also debating "in and out of doors" General Conway's promotion to major general. Not a little ire was expressed in these debates at the tone of a protest from the army's brigadier generals, who were extremely exercised by Conway's elevation. Clark also reported on the attacks on Washington and Greene in York and claimed with not a little satisfaction that he had warned some of the detractors that they were flirting with a duel. "The gentleman [officers] of the army" were not likely to let abuse of Washington pass without "calling the persons to account." Henceforth, Clark predicted, "they will sing small." If not, "a few oz. of gunpowder will answer a good purpose." [50]

With any commander in chief other than Washington, this letter would have had ominous overtones of an impending clash between the Continental Army and Congress that might have sent the American Revolution careening off on a very different course. A march on York and the banishment of the inept politicians that currently constituted Congress loomed as a possibility. The memory of Oliver Cromwell's dismissal of Parliament in the English revolution of the previous century was well known to every officer in the army.

Colonel Daniel Morgan gave a good demonstration of what Clark meant when he arrived in York on his way home to Virginia for a furlough. The Old Wagoner encountered Richard Peters, the secretary of the Board of War. Morgan began upbraiding him about the outrageous plot to ruin

Washington's reputation. Peters was no warrior, and he became more and more upset as Morgan bellowed insults in his face. When Peters denied any such plot existed, Morgan grew only more infuriated and asked if he was calling him a liar. The terrified Peters realized this was the prelude to a challenge to a duel. Peters managed to avoid this "last extremity," but two days later, he was still shaking when he described the encounter to a friend.[51]

XIV

On January 19, the Reverend George Neisser, pastor of the Moravian Church in York, recorded in his diary: "This afternoon, Gen. Horatio Gates, who has been appointed president on the council of war, arrived in town and was received with demonstrations of joy."

Five days later, the new president of the Board of War, having settled into quarters in a local tavern, wrote to Washington about the much discussed letter from General Conway. He began by reporting that Washington's letter to him on January 4, stating he assumed the nasty lines in the letter had been sent by Gates to warn him against Conway, had "relieved him from unspeakable uneasiness." Now, Gates all but chortled, he had discovered the offending paragraph was "spurious."

Gates launched into a lengthy discussion of Conway's letter. It contained "very judicious remarks" upon the army's lack of discipline, which had deprived them of crucial victories. But there was no mention in the letter of the "weakness" of any general, nor the influence of "bad councsellors [sic]." Conway's comments were those of a "candid observer"—the sort of thing "officers in every service write to each other." General Conway focused on "particular actions," and no persons were blamed for what went wrong. The letter was "perfectly harmless." But now that publicity had blown it out of all proportion, Gates did not think it should be published or submitted to the solemn inspection of "even those who stand most high in the public esteem" (including Washington, one presumes). It was liable to excite anxiety and jealousy in the minds of too many "respectable officers." Honor and patriotism bade him to return the letter to General

Conway. But General Gates solemnly reaffirmed that the offending paragraph that was sent to Washington was "a wicked forgery."

Gates closed the letter by hinting that he suspected Lieutenant Colonel Wilkinson might be the wicked forger. He reported that Wilkinson had tried to blame the leak on another Gates aide, Robert Troup, or on Alexander Hamilton, when he rushed to Albany to pry some troops out of Gates's grasp after Burgoyne surrendered. But the general abruptly dropped this line of thought and returned to General Conway. As far as Gates knew, he was "a firm and constant friend to America." But he (Gates) had never had "any sort of intimacy" or the "smallest acquaintance with him" until he met him a few days ago in York.[52]

This letter suggests that Gates the intriguing military politician was still at work. Not only did the Saratoga hero's letter echo the obnoxious letter Conway sent to Washington, with its condescending assurance that "every officer in every army" exchanged nasty opinions about fellow officers by mail. Gates seemed to assume that Washington had no evidence of Conway's disloyalty besides the offending letter, which Gates refused to show the commander in chief.

Did Gates think Washington would show the letter to his general officers? Or publish it in the newspapers? The commander in chief had already told him he was determined not to publicize the army's internal dissensions. Gates's pontificating about "honor" forbidding him to show the letter, and "patriotism" forcing him to return it to Conway, was patent nonsense. Such posturing could only make Washington suspect all over again that he was dealing with a slippery character who was deep in Thomas Mifflin's conspiracy to force him out of command of the army.

Meanwhile Gates was displaying to the Continental Congress a less admirable side of his personality than the true whig version that was trumpeted in the newspaper article by the so-called French gentleman. At the close of his first two weeks in York, Gates wrote a ferocious letter to President Henry Laurens declaring that he had expected to find decent quarters provided for him in the little country town.

Instead, the victorious general was living in a "most disagreeable tavern" where it was costing him nearly one hundred dollars a day to feed his military family, horses, and servants. For the "honor of the United States,"

Gates thought he deserved quarters where he could entertain "strangers and persons of distinction who come among us." At the very least, he did not think Congress expected him to be "ruin'd in my private fortune" while serving the United States. These were hardly the sentiments of a disinterested patriot who sought only his country's betterment and was ready to sacrifice everything and anything to that end. To be fair to the general, he was probably goaded to this diatribe by his snobbish wife, Elizabeth. One of Gates's close friends described her as "a Medusa who governs with a rod of scorpions." [53]

XV

General Conway, meanwhile, was not idle. He began showing a copy of his letter to Gates to various members of Congress to prove that Washington was creating an uproar about nothing. To be sure, the members were carefully chosen; all of them were known to be hostile to Washington. His goal was not a wide dissemination of the letter but the recruitment of a chorus who would say with a straight face that the offending lines Washington had received from Lord Stirling were not in the letter, thus making the commander in chief a dupe at best and a slanderer at worst.

At the same time, Conway conferred with Henry Laurens, striking the posture of a much-wronged man. He said Washington had been "deceived and imposed on"—and he asked Laurens what he thought of going public with the text of the letter. But he "did not offer to shew [show] it to me," Laurens told a South Carolina friend. The president of Congress strongly objected to printing the letter. Like General Washington, he did not want to reveal dissension in the American army to the watchful British.

President Laurens was soon aware that Conway was showing the letter to many members of Congress, but there was nothing he could do about it. The minimal powers of his office left him a hapless spectator. Finally, Daniel Roberdeau, a true whig delegate from Pennsylvania, agreed to let Laurens scan the letter, to prove the offending sentences were not in it. After Roberdeau left, Laurens wrote out one passage from memory: "What a pity there is but one Gates. But the more I see of this army the less I think it fit for action under its actual chief and actual discipline . . . & wish I could serve under you." The president told a friend: "The whole letter contains charges against Mr. Washington of a very high nature. . . . Gen'l Conway was guilty of gross hypocrisy or gross and unpardonable insult when he wrote [this] letter."[54]

XVI

In the third week of January, a hitherto unknown Virginia cavalryman named Henry Lee—whose son Robert would achieve fame in another war—pulled off an unlikely coup that momentarily distracted everyone from the nasty politics and semistarvation prevailing at Valley Forge. Captain Lee had already distinguished himself as a daring cavalry leader. Roaming the roads around Philadelphia with a force of about twenty-five dragoons, he had captured 124 German and British prisoners, including four officers, with the loss of only a single horse. His mobility enabled him to move swiftly from road to road, frequently discouraging loyalist farmers who were trying to bring food to Philadelphia. He also took over Major Clark's espionage operations and was soon sending Washington a stream of good intelligence.

General Sir William Erskine, the British cavalry commander, decided to put a stop to Lee's bold patrols. Probably with the help of loyalist informers, Erskine learned that Lee was posted about six miles from Valley Forge at the Spread Eagle Tavern. Erskine marshaled a seemingly irresistible force of about 130 dragoons and ordered them to demolish Lee. The British rode twenty miles along byroads in the darkness and came thundering down on the captain and his men in a dawn attack.

Four sentries and a sergeant, caught in the open, surrendered after a brief resistance. But Captain Lee, two officers, and five men barricaded themselves inside the stone tavern. Their goal was not only their own survival, but the preservation of their horses in the nearby stable. The British, led by Major Richard Crewe and daredevil Captain Banastre Tarleton, charged. They were met by well-aimed fire that killed three men and wounded five. Tarleton had his helmet shot off, and a blast of buckshot put holes in his coat and his horse.

"Fire away, men! Here comes our infantry. We will have them all!" Lee shouted as the British retreated. More flying lead discouraged any and all attempts to get into the stables and drive off the horses. The rank-and-file dragoons decided they preferred looting and began ransacking nearby buildings. "Comrade, shame on you," Lee shouted to Crewe. "That you don't have your men under better discipline! Come a little closer and we will soon manage it together!"

The British went back to Philadelphia with five prisoners, and Captain Lee remained very much in business. His rescue of a victory from almost certain defeat inspired letter writers at Valley Forge to spread the story of his courage in all directions. General Washington congratulated him on the very day of the skirmish for his "gallant behavior." He also praised him in the general orders the next day. The Americans needed some good news, however small.[55]

XVII

The Continental Congress soon installed their hero General Gates in a two-story Georgian-style town house that satisfied him and his demanding wife. Now that the Saratoga victor and Generals Mifflin and Conway theoretically had the power to humiliate or at least embarrass George Washington, thanks to their control of the Board of War, what were they going to do with it? Washington's public detestation of Inspector General Conway had blocked their plans in that direction. With the brigadier and major generals supporting Washington to a man, Conway was not welcome in Valley Forge. There was no prospect of his strutting about the encampment, lecturing all and sundry about how poorly the Continental Army marched and maneuvered, adding sotto voce comments about Washington's incompetence.

The plotters and their allies in Congress decided on two moves. The first was to seize control of the quartermaster department by announcing a plan to reform it. This would serve two purposes, one defensive, the other offensive. It would block or at least control any investigation of General Mifflin's service as quartermaster, during which, according to President Laurens, the "pivot" had accumulated a mountain of illicit cash. It would also guarantee them leverage over Washington, who could not fight the next campaign without the department's cooperation. The general would have to submit his plans to the Board of War, tacitly giving them a veto by telling him they were impractical or even impossible from the quartermaster's point of view.

The second move, to be selected by that already acclaimed military genius, the new president of the Board of War, was a separate military campaign. General Washington would be informed but not consulted, emphasizing his secondary status. A substantial victory would be tantamount to proving that General Gates, not the weak, old-womanish taker of advice from General Nathanael Greene, was the leader America needed to win the war.

Where was the greatest likelihood of a quick, easy victory? The word "Canada" soon reposed on the plotters' table like a succulent side of beef. It had multitudinous appeals. Canada had been the first attempt by Congress to play general. In 1775 the Americans had lost more than ten thousand men trying to bring the "fourteenth colony" into the Union. These volunteers had been, it should be added, the elite of America's Revolutionary warriors, patriots who had rushed to their country's call in 1775.

On paper Canada had looked like an easy conquest. Most of the Canadians were French Catholics, who had no great love for George III. Many Anglo-Canadians had been outspokenly eager to embrace the American cause. But the French Canadians had turned out to be equally unenthusiastic about the American Protestants, who had made no secret of their detestation of the pope and other aspects of the Catholic religion. Rebel Anglo-Canadians proved to be not nearly as numerous as Congress had thought.

Now, however, Canada looked like easy pickings for the victor of Saratoga. There was only a handful of British regulars left in the colony, and the French Canadians were now reportedly eager to switch to the winning side. The province could be seized by 2,500 to 3,000 determined, well-armed men. Best of all, Gates, Mifflin, and Conway had a leader for the expedition who would all but guarantee the French Canadians' support: the Marquis de Lafayette.[56]

This was a political card that trumped everything and everyone else in the deck—including General Washington. Conway, having spent time with Lafayette, knew how acute was his thirst for glory. What better triumph to offer him than the reconquest of Canada, the French province that the arrogant British had captured in the Seven Years' War and refused to return in the peace negotiations? King Louis XVI would shower praise and rewards on such a victor. Lafayette in turn would be extravagantly grateful to the men who had given him this opportunity for fame. No more would the Marquis' effusive praise of Washington be heard in the court of Louis XVI. The Great Man could be discarded without any fear of international repercussions.

To bolster the expedition, the Board of War had some ready-made shock troops. Many Anglo-Canadians had retreated to rebel territory with the survivors of the 1775–76 invasion. Several hundred of them formed a regiment in the American army, under the leadership of Colonel Moses Hazen, a former New Hampshire man who had fought in the famed guerrilla regiment, Rogers's Rangers, during the French and Indian War and had settled in Canada. Hazen and his men had forfeited valuable property in Canada when they embraced the American cause. They would fight hard to regain it.

Best of all, waiting for them in the northern department was Brigadier General John Stark, the hero who had won the August 1777 battle of Bennington, a clash that had destroyed a third of the German troops in General Burgoyne's army. Moreover, Stark had worked this miracle with the militia of New Hampshire, which made him a double hero to the true whigs in Congress. These same rough-hewn warriors would respond to the call of their "rustic Achilles," as Stark was sometimes called, and turn out in overwhelming numbers to conquer Canada.

On paper the plan looked foolproof. It combined daring and valor. The troops would be transported in sleds across the frozen surface of

Lake Champlain to the Canadian border. With an assist from General Stark, General Gates could demonstrate his fabled appeal to New England militiamen, further enshrining him in the hearts of true whigs everywhere. There must have been more than one toast drunk to Canada and to the Marquis de Lafayette at the dinner table in the Gates house in York and at General Mifflin's Angelica estate outside Reading.

XVIII

At Valley Forge, by the end of January almost all the soldiers were in huts. New Englanders and not a few middle state soldiers had modified Washington's specifications, thanks to their experience in coping with a harsh winter. They dug pits three or four feet deep and put roofs over them to obtain more protection from the cold winds. Southern troops, especially the North Carolina brigade, built their huts aboveground, condemning them to a winter of shivers and chills.

In spite of these variations, the more than one thousand huts now resembled an orderly village. But bringing order to the inhabitants of this military community was another matter. With mounting exasperation, Washington issued warnings in his general orders against men who failed to use the "vaults" (latrines) to relieve themselves. With so many men half naked and the temperature frequently near freezing, it was a difficult regulation to enforce. Finally, Washington issued orders to flog the disobedient if they were caught. The health of the army was at stake.

The food supply remained precarious. The same remained true of the clothing supply. A few states, notably Connecticut, had rounded up used clothes and shipped them to their regiments at Valley Forge, but most members of the supposedly united American confederation did nothing. Worst of all was Pennsylvania. General Anthony Wayne spent much of his time writing raging letters to the state government in Lancaster, excoriating them for failing his men in this department. He reiterated that nothing made a soldier feel more military than a good uniform. Leave him in rags, and he will begin acting like a resentful outcast.[57]

What Wayne meant was soon visible in the daily reports on Washington's desk. Men began deserting by the dozen for the comparative comfort and security of the British army in Philadelphia. Although Valley Forge was ringed by sentries, and Captain Lee and other cavalrymen patrolled the roads to Philadelphia day and night, catching deserters was mostly luck. There were plenty of woods in which a man could hide, and not a few of the local farmers were loyalists who were more than willing to conceal a deserter until the roads looked clear. On January 30, Colonel Israel Angell glumly recorded in his diary the pursuit of nine deserters by forty officers and men. The Americans were not more than a hundred yards behind the runaways when they reached the safety of the British redoubts ringing Philadelphia.

A singular example of how much help was available to deserters is the story of Johann von Krafft. This former Hessian officer came to America to join the Continental Army. Arriving at Valley Forge in February, he was offended when Washington was too busy to see him and the highest rank offered to him was first lieutenant. The German decided he could get a better offer (and better pay) from the British. Pretending to return to Europe, he obtained a pass from Washington's headquarters that got him past the encampment's pickets. Thereafter he was fed and protected by various German farmers. One of them was an officer in the Pennsylvania militia, but he confided to von Krafft that he hated the "Wiecks" (whigs). In Philadelphia, the fugitive procured interviews with General Howe and General von Knyphausen, the German commander, and was soon a lieutenant in a Hessian regiment, in which he fought for the rest of the war.[58]

XIX

Another form of desertion, even more troubling to Washington, also multiplied daily. In one week, more than fifty officers in General Greene's division resigned their commissions. Dozens of other resignations cascaded into headquarters from other divisions. There was little the general could do about this escalating abandonment of the cause. Almost all the would-be departees had seemingly legitimate—even touching—excuses.

One officer told Washington his fiancée was so lovesick for his company, he feared she would die. Washington assured him that women "don't die of such things." But it was harder to answer an officer whose mother was unable to cope with the family farm since the death of her husband. Even more troubling were officers' wives and children who faced starvation as the value of their husbands' salaries dwindled with the depreciation of the Continental Congress's money. The true whig theory of war assumed that the "virtue" of the patriots in a wife's hometown would prompt them to step forward to make sure she was not in want while her husband risked his life in defense of American liberty. Letters from distressed wives made it clear that this idealistic expectation was a fantasy. Officers' wives and children were living on gruel while their neighbors prospered.

One officer wrote in his diary: "The present circumstances of the soldier is better by far than the officers." This may seem an odd observation in the light of the sufferings and death of so many enlisted men. But the diarist, Surgeon's Mate Albigence Waldo, was disturbed by a little-known fact about the Continental Army: an officer's pay was only about a third of his British counterpart's. An American enlisted man, on the other hand, was paid far more than the rank and file in the British army, and in theory had rations, clothing, and equipment given to him at public expense. That Congress delivered few and often none of these necessities was beside the point. An officer had to pay these expenses out of his own pocket. For those without private incomes, Congress's depreciating paper dollars did not go very far.[59]

What was behind this situation? The true whigs in Congress were trying to use the army to introduce their version of equality in the new republic. In the eighteenth century this tactic was called "leveling." As we have seen, the true whigs who were running Pennsylvania were inclined to inflict the idea on the entire state.

This policy only made more acute the question that Colonel John Brooks asked not long after the army reached Valley Forge. Why should an officer have empty pockets and watch his family suffer while everyone else was making money from the booming wartime economy, especially when the officer was called upon to risk his life on the battlefield?

For General Washington there was only one answer to this ominous problem. The officers had to be convinced to stay in the army by making their commissions valuable to them. In the British army, a captain's commission in a good regiment could be sold for as much as 2,200 pounds. Washington had proposed this idea to Congress in rather tentative fashion in several letters. Now, faced with a veritable deluge of resignations, he decided it was essential to the Continental Army's survival.[60]

The commander in chief knew that the proposal was sure to infuriate the true whigs in Congress. It was bad enough that businessmen tried to make money out of the war. But the idea that officers and gentlemen, from whom the purest, most disinterested patriotism was to be expected, should profit from their noble struggle in defense of liberty was unthinkable. Nevertheless, Washington was determined to make Congress think about it, with the help of some new allies. Congress had finally sent to Valley Forge the committee to confer on reforming the army for which Washington had pleaded on Christmas Day.

Arriving on January 24, 1778, the five solons could not have come at a more crucial time. But a large question remained unanswered: would they do anything? They were by no means the first committee to visit the army; most previous delegations had accomplished nothing. Their reports "lay on the table" while Congress debated other matters. Would this be more of the same? Complicating everything was the secret political war that was swirling through York and spreading its evil fumes throughout the shaky American union.

For a while, the anti-Washington faction in Congress had talked of sending General Gates and General Mifflin from the Board of War along with three congressmen to confer with the commander in chief. The anti-Washingtonians liked the idea of the Great Man forced to plead with and cajole his enemies for help—and accept their judgment on final decisions. But these two worthies, after thinking about the frosty reception General Conway had received, lost their nerve and decided they could more profitably spend their time planning the invasion of Canada.

Even without Mifflin and Gates, the committee was not at first glance pro-Washington. The chairman, Harvard-educated lawyer Francis Dana of Massachusetts, was a thin-lipped quintessential Puritan, usually allied with the Adamses. He also happened to be James Lovell's Harvard roommate. Nathaniel Folsom of New Hampshire was another member of the "eastern [New England] party" that regularly said nasty things about Washington.

A third member, handsome, astute Joseph Reed of Pennsylvania, had served as Washington's top aide in 1775–76—until the commander in chief found him corresponding with General Charles Lee about Washington's "indecisive mind . . . one of the greatest misfortunes that can befall an army."[61] Fourth on the list was bulky Gouverneur Morris of New York; he was only twenty-six years old, and had just arrived in Congress. Washington considered him a friend, but not a few New Yorkers had become partial to General Gates, who had saved them from conquest by General Burgoyne.

Morris had a reputation as a roué. One of his New York mentors, Hudson Valley landowner Robert Livingston, wrote him a stern letter around this time, urging him to behave. Morris coolly told him not to worry. "There are no pretty women in York."

Only wealthy John Harvie could be depended upon to support General Washington, his fellow Virginian. It was not hard to imagine votes on crucial issues going the wrong way by a 3–2 and even a 4–1 margin. In York, one of Washington's nastier critics, James Lovell, wrote his mentor Samuel Adams that Congress was more than ready to "rap a Demi G—— [demigod] over the knuckles." It was time to put a stop to the "Gentleman of the Blade's" notion that "no citizen shall dare even to talk about . . . one great man."[62]

General Washington, with that instinct for seizing the initiative, decided not to worry about how the committee's votes would go. He welcomed the visitors with his usual politeness and made sure they were installed in comfortable rooms in Moore Hall, a large stone house about three miles west of Valley Forge, where the army's quartermasters lived and worked.

Simultaneously, the commander in chief prepared to present the politicians, not with pathetic complaints about do-nothing commissaries and quartermasters, and whines about desertions and resignations, but with a series of positive proposals, well researched and closely argued, to bring them around to his way of seeing the situation. In a letter to Henry Laurens, Washington explained why he had not answered any of his mail for two weeks: the press of "preparing and digesting matters" for the committee had been too great.[63]

At headquarters, Lieutenant Colonel Alexander Hamilton, the most talented writer on the general's staff, sharpened his quills, filled his inkpot, and went to work on a document that was aimed not only at rescuing the army but also at defeating the men who were trying to destroy George Washington.

"CONGRESS DOES NOT TRUST ME"

For the moment, the initiative lay with Generals Mifflin and Gates on the Board of War, in York. They began by proposing a reorganization of the quartermaster department along two possible lines. One would be the appointment of a powerful figure who would run both the quartermaster and commissary departments—an idea they knew would almost certainly fail to win support in Congress, where the mere word "power" gave everyone hives. Mifflin and Gates did not favor it either. A too powerful quartermaster might be able to talk to them as equals.

The other alternative was to create a quartermaster with almost no power, a kind of supervisor who would oversee a department chopped into four semi-independent parts. Taking advantage of their proximity to the congressmen in the little country town, Gates and Mifflin began to push this second solution at dinner parties and other get-togethers outside of Congress. The Board of War would have the final say on who should run these smaller entities and how they should operate. Neither they nor their allies in Congress seemed concerned that this solution was virtually guaranteed to increase the chaos afflicting the department.

For the moment, the quartermaster proposals were mere politics and paperwork. The heart of their program to elevate General Gates above

General Washington was the invasion of Canada, led by the Marquis de Lafayette. To guarantee Washington's humiliation from the start of this venture, General Gates wrote a flattering letter to Lafayette offering him the command of the expedition and enclosed it with other paperwork from the Board of War to Washington.

This was a deft way of letting Washington know he was now commander in chief in name only—and simultaneously converting him into a postman. Gates added a polite note remarking that if Washington found "any steps wanting or any directions omitted" in the invasion plan, they would be happy to receive his "directions and advice."[1]

In his letter to Lafayette, General Gates expressed his admiration for the Marquis' "ardent desire to signalize yourself " in the struggle for America's liberty. The Board of War had therefore chosen him to lead the expedition, and Congress had approved the appointment "in compliance" with the board's wishes (a nice way of telling the Marquis who was in charge of the war). Lafayette was encouraged to take with him as many "gallant French officers" on duty at Valley Forge as he wanted.

Time was of the essence, General Gates continued, and the board wanted Lafayette to leave immediately for Albany. There he would meet General Conway, who would give him the "particular instructions . . . and principles" on which the expedition was based as well as the board's advice on how to execute them. Gates added that the board assumed the officers "appointed by Congress" to cooperate with him would be acceptable to Lafayette (another way of saying General Conway had the lawmakers' political backing). Colonel Moses Hazen, who would serve as the expedition's quartermaster, had also been given instructions that he would communicate at Albany.[2]

The letter made a mockery of Gates's request for General Washington's advice. The expedition's "instructions and principles" were in General Conway's hands, and he was on his way to Albany. The commander in chief, maintaining the veneer of politeness with which Gates was trying to coat their relationship, replied three days later, coolly noting that the president of the Board of War had told him (and Lafayette) nothing about the purpose of the expedition or other salient details, such as the number of troops involved and the route they would take to invade Canada. All he could do was wish everyone, especially Lafayette, for whom he had "particular esteem and regard," success in the venture.[3]

II

Things started going wrong with this scheme even before Lafayette read General Gates's clever letter, which presumed he was so hungry for glory that he would leap at the chance to conquer Canada, even if there was little more than a hint of how this victory would be achieved. Gates also assumed the Marquis would ignore the rather obvious fact that he would be a figurehead, with General Conway the real commander of the expedition.

The same day (January 24) that Gates wrote his letter, Henry Laurens wrote to Lafayette from York. In his missive the president of Congress noted that the Board of War had appointed the Marquis to a command—and added owlishly "to which I shall add no opinions of my own." The next day, Laurens, in another letter to Lafayette about a Frenchman seeking a commission, remarked with studied innocence that General Conway had been appointed second in command of the expedition.[4]

The president of Congress had a courier who made far better time than Gates's letter carrier. On January 26, Lafayette was replying to Laurens in extremely agitated terms. He regarded the assignment as a "precious mark of confidence" from Congress and vowed that he would spend "the last drop of my blood" to prove his gratitude.

But there were problems, not the least of them that he had not heard a word from Congress or the Board of War about the assignment. Moreover, he wanted the expedition to contribute to the success and glory of "our respectable friend" (Washington) and therefore wished it to be made clear that he was commanding only a "detachment of General Washington's army" and was "an officer under his immediate command." That in turn made it impossible for him to accept General Conway as his second in command. He was a man who would "sacrifice honor, truth and everything respectable to his own ambition and desire of making a fortune."

What made him especially detestable to Lafayette was the way he had pretended to be "submist" [submissive] and humble in Lafayette's company.[5]

Here was a state of mind that Generals Gates and Mifflin had not come close to anticipating. Gates's letter, which arrived on January 27, did little to alter Lafayette's opinion. Nor did a letter from General Conway in which he claimed to be happier serving under Lafayette than he would be as commander in chief of the expedition. Conway vowed he was prepared to exert all his strength "to contribute some things to my reputation," as Lafayette translated it. The Marquis' mood was not improved by another letter from Laurens in which the president told him he had warned Conway (and presumably Gates) that Lafayette should be consulted about the expedition's second in command. "But the thing had not only been preconcerted but apparently predetermined," Laurens wrote, hinting how totally Congress was under the influence of the Board of War.[6]

There was not much doubt whose side Laurens was on, though he still piously claimed to steer clear of party disputes. He told Lafayette that he had no trouble discerning "on which side virtue and honor predominate as well as that where craft and design are lurking." He added that "by some contrivance I was deprived . . . of the honour of informing you of the appointments." (So the news could come from General Gates and the Board of War.)[7]

III

On this same day, January 27, Washington received a message from Henry Laurens that added new intensity to the sense of plot and counterplot coursing through Valley Forge. The previous day, the South Carolinian was in the president's chair in Congress when a member came in and handed him a sealed manuscript that he claimed to have found on the stairs. Laurens broke it open and read the title: "Thoughts of a Freeman." A cursory glance through the contents revealed a series of propositions, several pages long, all relentlessly denouncing George Washington. Typical of them were:

"That if the Army is not better managed than heretofore numbers will avail nothing . . .

"That the head cannot be sound when the whole body is disordered . . .

"That the people of America have been guilty of idolatry in making a man their God."

Looking up, Laurens realized that "the House" (Congress) was watching him expectantly. With five men in Valley Forge as the committee in camp, there were only thirteen members present (another reason for General Mifflin's large influence). Did some of them—or all of them—expect the president to lay this message before them, as he was required to present letters and other documents addressed to him? That could have led to an explosive debate about how many of these strictures were true and, possibly, a resolution approving some of them; perhaps even an order to send the results of the debate to General Washington.

Laurens coolly stuffed the pages into his pocket and remarked that it was "an anonymous production" of the sort he got as part of the "perquisites of office." The fireplace, he added, was the "proper disposition for such records." Whereupon he secretly dispatched the screed by courier to General Washington.[8]

The commander in chief took "Thoughts of a Freeman" seriously. He told Laurens he was "not unaware that a malignant faction" was trying to ruin him. The fact gave him "some pain on a personal account," but he was more concerned about the damage revealing such dissensions might do to the "common cause." No doubt to Laurens's amazement, Washington said he wanted the president to submit "Thoughts of a Freeman" to Congress. He feared that concealing it might embarrass Laurens. Who knew how many people were aware of its contents? Let the politicians debate these "serious charges" and decide whether there was any merit to them.

His enemies, Washington again noted, were taking advantage of the need for secrecy about the army's numbers and condition, which made it impossible to answer their "insidious attacks." He never imagined he would be "exempt from censure" in his job. Far more talented men had endured such sniping. His only consolation was the assurance of "my heart" that he had tried to do his best. He added that Laurens's attempt to protect him meant a great deal personally. He was deeply grateful for the president's support.

Laurens, keenly aware of the unfavorable disposition Congress currently entertained toward General Washington, did not take his advice. "Thoughts of a Freeman" was never submitted to the politicians for debate.[9]

IV

Meanwhile, Lafayette sought advice on what to do about the Canadian invasion. He was passionately, even desperately eager to accept the command. As he remarked to President Laurens, the thought of driving the British from Canada and persuading the French Canadians to join the United States and enjoy the blessings of liberty had immense appeal to him. He also knew it would win him enormous fame and glory in France.[10]

The Marquis talked the proposal over with the members of the congressional committee, in particular Gouverneur Morris, who was close to his age. No doubt Lafayette discussed it with General Washington, too. All agreed it would be best if he went to York and learned the details of the expedition from General Gates firsthand.

Lafayette undertook the fifty-mile slog to York, which involved crossing the broad Susquehanna River, no small task in winter. It was, he later recalled, choked with "enormous ice floes." In the tiny temporary capital, the young Frenchman was quickly directed to General Gates's house, where he was welcomed with surprise and hastily concocted good cheer. Gates was in the midst of dinner with the Board of War and several congressmen. The general urged Lafayette to join them. The Marquis explained his desire for more details about the invasion, and Gates smoothly assured him that they would be forthcoming.

At the end of dinner, there were toasts to Lafayette, to Congress, and to the United States. As everyone began to rise from the table, Lafayette said: "Gentlemen—you seem to have forgotten to drink to the health of General Washington."

The stunned diners refilled their glasses and toasted Washington "but not with much exuberance of feeling," Lafayette recalled in his memoirs. The Marquis proceeded to tell General Gates that if he accepted command of the expedition, he would not correspond directly with the Board of War. He would "only send them copies of letters addressed . . . to General Washington," whom he would continue to consider his commander in chief. All orders to him from the Board of War would also have to pass through Washington's hands. The flabbergasted Gates could do nothing but mutter his assent.

This was only a warm-up for Lafayette's performance in York. In letters to Henry Laurens, who was happy to cooperate with him, the Marquis pressed his demands on Congress. Instead of General Conway, he wanted General Alexander McDougall of New York or the Baron de Kalb as his second in command. He insisted on ample funds to finance the expedition—at least $2 million in paper currency and $200,000 in gold or silver, plus commissions for a half dozen French officers. He also extracted a promise from General Mifflin that there would be "ammunition, stores, provisions and as many carriages [wagons] as may be requisite."[11]

Lafayette won everything he demanded by issuing an ultimatum that sent tremors through Congress. "If my going [on these terms] is not agreed upon immediately," he told Laurens, "I'll resign . . . and the other French officers will send their resignations in two days." This image of a mass French departure might mean farewell to hopes of an alliance with France. The politicians capitulated instantly. General Alexander McDougall, who was currently recuperating from a severe illness in New Jersey, would be his second in command. If he was unable to march, Baron de Kalb would substitute for him.

Meanwhile, President Henry Laurens was writing to his friend John Rutledge, the governor of South Carolina: "I count it a misfortune that I do not approve of this Canada expedition because I am almost single in [my] opinion." Here was a glimpse of how thoroughly Gates and Mifflin had sold the idea to Congress.[12]

Back in Valley Forge, Lafayette collected the French officers he had demanded. As he departed from the camp on February 7, he wrote another letter which must have made General Gates even more uneasy. Taking a cue from Washington's policy of surface politeness, he said he would be deeply troubled by the immensity of the task confronting him if he did not have confidence in Gates's friendship. Then he added words that were a thinly veiled threat. "The project is yours, sir, you must make it succeed. If I had not depended on you, I would not have undertaken this operation." [13]

Five days later, the congressional committee in camp wrote Congress a letter which must have given Generals Mifflin and Gates additional sleepless nights. The committee expressed its "deep concern" about the Canadian expedition proposed by the Board of War. They feared it would involve "the most serious consequences" if the expedition failed.

Among these consequences were "desertion among the troops . . . disgrace to our arms and all its consequences upon our money, upon our people, upon our friends in Europe and upon the enemies [loyalists] we have in our own bowels." They added a brief survey of previous generals— Richard Montgomery, the American commander in 1775, and John Burgoyne, the British commander in 1777—who had discovered the folly of "distant expeditions across [the] inhospitable wilderness" of northern New York and Canada.

"Is not the very season against us?" the committee asked. The troops lacked wool uniforms, coats, fur-lined shoes, and mittens against the "rigors" of the Canadian winter. Worse, by the time they reached Canada on the frozen surface of Lake Champlain, the ice might have begun to melt, leaving them with no way to retreat if things went wrong. Worst of all, "our troops cannot be fed." Even if they won "laurels" in Canada, they would "undoubtedly starve." [14]

In York, there was no doubt in anyone's mind that this prediction of catastrophe did not originate with these five politicians. They were undoubtedly reporting the opinions of General Washington. The fact that the congressmen were delivering it as their own opinion was bad news for Generals Gates and Mifflin and their backers in Congress. It meant that the committee in camp was becoming an ally of the Continental Army's embattled commander in chief.

V

There were several factors in this enormously significant transformation. One was the mere sight of the army at Valley Forge. On February 2, 1778, a shocked Gouverneur Morris wrote to his friend John Jay that they were confronted by "the skeleton of an army . . . in a naked starving condition, out of health, out of spirits." The wealthy, conservative New Yorker instinctively despised the ideology-driven Lee-Adams junto that was running Congress, and had already become Washington's most vocal advocate on the committee.[15]

Another factor was the representatives of the commissary department whom the committee interviewed in their first days at Valley Forge. The congressmen found no evidence of peculation or gross corruption in the department's well-kept books. That exploded one of their strongest preconceptions—that the department was a veritable worm's nest of fraud. From these interviews also emerged another shock: the staggering quantities of food the army consumed. When Ephraim Blaine said the soldiers ate a million pounds of meat and a million pounds of bread a month, the politicians sat there goggle-eyed. From would-be villains, the commissaries (at least the ones stationed at Valley Forge) became something close to victims of the malfunctioning system.

Another vital factor in changing the committee members' minds was meeting George Washington. The man was physically impressive, towering over everyone in sight. Equally impressive was his demeanor. He emanated self-control and calm decision. There was no trace of the indecisive advice-taker regularly described in York by Thomas Mifflin, James Lovell, and other sneerers and deriders.

Most unexpected of all was the man's talent for politics. Chairman Francis Dana was the first and most important committee member to discover this political Washington. One night, early in Dana's visit to Valley Forge, the commander in chief invited the Massachusetts congressman to dinner at headquarters, where he was given a thorough description of the army's problems.

The hour became late and Dana was invited to stay the night. Before going to bed, he decided to get some fresh air. Descending to the first floor, he stepped out the front door and became aware of a large cloaked figure pacing up and down in the darkness: Washington. Dana hesitated for several moments and finally made the general aware of his presence.

Abruptly Washington turned to him and said: "Mr. Dana—Congress does not trust me. I cannot continue thus." Profoundly touched, Dana assured him that a majority of Congress had not lost faith in him. Soon the Massachusetts lawyer was a Washington ally.[16]

Washington handled John Harvie, who was already on his side, in a less confrontational way. Like the others, Harvie was appalled by the half-naked, sickly soldiers. When he was alone with Washington, the Virginia congressman all but cried out: "My dear General, if you had given some explanation [to Congress], all these rumors would have been silenced a long time ago."

"How could I exculpate myself," Washington asked him, "without doing harm to the public cause?" His choice of the word "exculpate" implied volumes. Aside from the danger of revealing the army's weakness to the British in Philadelphia, Washington was telling Harvie how distasteful he found the idea of using his men's suffering as an answer to the accusations emanating from York and Lancaster.[17]

VI

The final factor in the capture of the committee was the immensely impressive report that Washington presented to the five congressmen on January 29, 1778. In the latest edition of the *Papers of George Washington*, it fills twenty-eight closely printed pages—more than sixteen thousand words. Most of the manuscript is in the handwriting of aide Alexander Hamilton, which has prompted some of his biographers to give the gifted young West Indian all the credit for it. But interior examination of the document and a study of Washington's recent correspondence make it clear that the contributors included a number of general officers from whom Washington solicited advice. Probably the most important was a long, trenchant letter on the army's ills from Major General Nathanael Greene. Like staff officers before and since, Hamilton put all these opinions and proposals into serviceable prose.

One effective touch in the report's composition again revealed the political Washington: the entire account was in the form of a letter that ended with his signature, adding a powerful personal dimension. Again and again, the general stated his opinions or recommendations in the first person, creating a steadily increasing impression of urgency and authority.

The overriding theme was struck in the first paragraph: "Something must be done—important alterations must be made." Otherwise they were faced with the possible "dissolution of the army" or its continued operations as a "feeble, languid, ineffectual" force.[18]

At the top of Washington's list of changes was half pay after the war for officers. Here the commander in chief did not need any advice. He was expressing one of his strongest personal beliefs. He attacked head-on the Adams-Lee-Rush true whig view of human nature, with its unreasonable insistence on virtue as the only acceptable motivation for a republican revolutionary. "Motives of public virtue may for a time actuate men," Washington conceded. But it was fanciful to think that such motives would endure for more than several months. "Few men are capable of making a continued sacrifice of all views of private interest . . . to the common good," he insisted. "It is in vain to exclaim against the depravity of human nature on this account—the fact is so."

Not many historians have grasped the all but earthshaking dimensions of those words. Washington was revising the basic philosophy of the American Revolution, as articulated by college-educated would-be philosophers such as Richard Henry Lee, John Adams, and Samuel Adams and their worshipful followers such as Benjamin Rush. It was a remarkable performance for a man with only three or four years of formal schooling. Washington did it by arguing that it required only a "small knowledge of human nature" to see the wisdom of what he was saying. "The experience of every age and nation has proved it" and it would require changing "the constitution of human nature" to make it otherwise.

Without reservations, he insisted: "No institution not built on the . . . truth of these maxims can succeed."[19]

He used the American army as an example of what he meant. Officers were resigning in droves. Those who remained were growing more disenchanted every day. It explained the "apathy, inattention and neglect of duty" which pervaded all ranks. An officer who was "impoverished by his commission" began to think he was doing the government a favor and became impossible to discipline. Threats of dismissal meant little. As for the cost of providing half pay for life, it would be far less than the cost of a longer war.[20]

Next Washington turned to remodeling the army. It had regiments of all sizes because anyone who offered to recruit one and raised a decent number of men was accepted by Congress. There were no fewer than ninety-seven regiments in the army, many ridiculously small. North Carolina had nine regiments, which totaled only 572 men fit for duty. He recommended consolidating these Tar Heels into one regiment. It was time to insist on a uniform size for a regiment and limit the number of officers in each one.

As for enlisting rank-and-file recruits, Washington was, again, grimly realistic, no matter what the true whigs thought. He saw no point in paying extravagant bounties or making oratorical appeals to patriotism. The country was "pretty well drained" of the men who were temperamentally inclined to go to war. The best solution was to draft men from the militia of each state to serve one year in the Continental Army, with no exceptions and no bounties.

Next Washington assailed the helter-skelter way Congress had given commissaries and quartermasters military ranks, which infuriated the army, and the politicians' habit of promoting men like James Wilkinson to exalted ranks for no good reason. All promotions, he urged, should be "from the line" (the fighting men) and should be made in consultation with the army's high command.

Next he dealt with clothing the army, stressing its crucial importance. Where and how should clothing be obtained? From France, from the individual states? He more or less left the decision to Congress, but he ended this section with another dig at the true whigs, this time their aversion to profits. He urged Congress to let the clothier general contract for large quantities of shoes and stockings to be made in the United States. He even suggested "a Mr. Henry of Lancaster" who was ready to make one or two hundred thousand pairs of shoes a year, if they would supply him with the hides of the hundreds of cattle slaughtered each month at Valley Forge. Henry may have been one of the men Commissary General of Prisoners Elias Boudinot had recommended in vain.[21]

Next Washington turned to the quartermaster department. Here his language grew unsparing. He called the quartermaster general a position of "great trust and magnitude." On it all the operations of the army "essentially depend." The person who filled the job ought to be "a military character," a man of "abilities, business and activity." In a dig at General Mifflin, who had spent as little time as possible with the army, Washington said a quartermaster should be "almost constantly with the army."

Next came the commissary department, which elicited even more unsparing language. It was a department which "all along" has been very defective and in the recent past has been in "a very deplorable situation." Washington urged a complete overhaul, from the top down, diplomatically saying that it was "not for me to decide" the changes needed.[22] The hospitals and the artillery and engineering departments received similar analyses and recommendations.

In a final section, Washington made some random suggestions. One of the best was to recruit two or three hundred Indians to serve with the army as scouts. Given the extravagant cost of hiring wagoners, he wondered if it might be possible to hire free blacks from Maryland, Virginia, and the Carolinas. He ruled out slaves because they were likely to take themselves and their wagons to the British to "obtain their liberty."

The commander in chief closed by hoping the congressmen were impressed "by the defects in our military system" and the need for quick action. He knew the wants and sufferings of the soldiers and the discontents among the officers made for "a disagreeable picture." But it was all true, and in equal parts "melancholy and important." If remedies were not applied "without loss of time," the consequences were certain to be "ruinous."[23]

The report was nothing less than America's first great state paper. Unfortunately, Washington's insistence on half pay for officers and his blunt assault on the true whig preconceptions of the New Englanders and their allies made it all too possible that this document would end up lying on the table in Congress, contemptuously neglected by the ruling ideologues. But a new ingredient was abruptly thrust into the purview of the five politicians at Moore Hall. The Continental Army began to starve in a new, more demoralizing way.

VII

The crisis began with a January 31 letter from George Washington to Deputy Commissary of Purchases Ephraim Blaine, who was on the road as usual, searching for provisions. Washington told him that Thomas Jones, Valley Forge's deputy commissary of issues, had just reported there were only ninety head of cattle and 560 barrels of flour in camp and Jones "knows not of any supplies coming on." [24]

Coincidentally, at this point the Board of War decided to flex its authoritative muscles and take charge of supplying the army. They persuaded Congress to empower them to appoint "superintendents" for districts in Pennsylvania and western New Jersey with the authority to supersede commissaries such as Colonel Blaine. They also superseded commissioners appointed by the Pennsylvania state government to buy food for the army on the somewhat dubious premise that they could do a better job of persuading their fellow Pennsylvanians to sell their wheat and cattle at the low prices Congress insisted on paying. The result was chaos. With three organizations bidding for the same food, canny Pennsylvania farmers tried to play them off against one another to get better prices. It did not help matters that most of the men appointed by Generals Gates and Mifflin were hostile to the radicals running the state government. [25]

Ephraim Blaine took a dark view of this chaos. He suspected Generals Mifflin and Gates were deliberately creating it to embarrass Washington and the commissary department. He told one correspondent that a "certain gen'l now a member of the Board of War" had been "studying [plotting] our fall in the purchasing department." Thomas Jones, the issuing commissary at Valley Forge, harbored similar thoughts. A more probable goal of the Mifflin-Gates move was an expansion of their power base. Unfortunately, in their warm, comfortable houses in York and Reading, they—and Congress—had no idea of the horrific conditions developing at Valley Forge and how their power play was worsening them.[26]

Aggravating the sense of chaos was the death of dozens of horses for want of forage. Each horse consumed twelve pounds of hay and eight pounds of grain a day. They suffered in silence until starvation toppled them to the ground. Soon their numbers multiplied into the hundreds (eventually seven hundred would die), and their decaying bodies lay everywhere, mute witnesses to the Congress's inability to feed its faithful servants. These deaths placed an even greater burden on the hungry soldiers. Congressman Joseph Reed of Pennsylvania felt especially guilty, knowing how many horses were in his home state, when he saw soldiers hauling wood and water in small handmade sleds or carrying it on their backs. Reed's conclusion was grim: the army was on the point of dissolution.[27]

Other congressmen on the committee drew similar conclusions. On February 7, Chairman Francis Dana heard that an entire Massachusetts regiment, commanded by Colonel William Brewer, had marched to the quarters of their immediate commander, Brigadier General John Paterson, and announced they were going to quit the army and go home. Paterson did his best to calm the infuriated men. But he finally had to agree to let them leave camp and purchase meat from nearby farmers with their own money. When their cash ran out, they could give the owners of the cattle they seized government certificates, and Paterson promised to pay them out of his own pocket.

Obviously this stopgap solution was not the answer to the crisis. Dana mounted his horse and rode through the camp, talking with officers he knew in various New England brigades. He concluded that the men were not literally starving. They had been receiving rations of flour. But they had been "destitute of fish or flesh for four days." On the previous Saturday they had received about a half pound of salt pork per man, barely half one day's allowance. They had not seen an ounce of meat since that time, and their brigade commissaries told them there was no prospect of any flesh in the foreseeable future. "The want of it will infallibly bring on a mutiny," Dana morosely warned in a letter to a friend.[28]

Commissary of Issues Thomas Jones was soon reduced to raw terror. He and Blaine were dragged before an array of cursing generals and exasperated congressmen to explain in vain that they were doing their best in an impossible situation. Jones and his assistants were afraid to sit down to dinner lest "a whole brigade of the starv'd soldiers will come to our quarters and lay violent hands on us." It was too much for flesh and blood to endure, and Jones announced that he did not intend to stay "one hour longer" in his job than the first of March. In the meantime, out of fear for their lives, Jones and John Chaloner moved across the Schuylkill River to a house owned by a man named Pawlings. There, with the presumed help of a few sentries, they were at least able to get a night's sleep.[29]

Deputy Purchasing Commissary Ephraim Blaine told Purchasing Commissary General Buchanan on February 18 that he was "the most unhappy man living." General Washington summoned him to headquarters "three and four times a day" to explain the near famine. There were "hourly appearances of mutiny" in two brigades. The disheartened commissary sent his resignation to Congress.

Exacerbating matters was a blizzard that began on February 7 and continued for two days, burying the camp and the surrounding countryside in several feet of snow. Without horses, it was almost impossible to transport wood for fires, much less food if any showed up. The magazines from which food was distributed to the brigade commissaries were a good distance from camp, to reduce the possibility of theft by hungry soldiers. Brigade commissaries were supposed to pick up their quotas there and distribute them to the men in the huts.[30]

Although the weather warmed briefly, on February 11 it rained hard, and the next day the temperature plunged, creating sheets of ice everywhere. One diarist reported that the roads were impassable. The congressional committee advised Washington that "the travelling is so bad," they could get along without him at Moore Hall for a day or two. The general came anyway and told them that numerous enlisted men were coming to headquarters to respectfully inform him that they had seen no meat for four days. God only knew how long they would continue to speak softly—but for the moment their moderate tone was an index of the men's respect and trust in Washington's leadership.[31]

Those who saw Washington speak to these enlisted men reported that more than once his eyes swam with tears. "Naked and starving as they are," he told one correspondent, "we can not enough admire the incomparable patience and fidelity of the soldiery." We can be sure the members of the committee in camp witnessed some of this same emotion when the commander in chief told them about the men's visits.[32]

In this atmosphere of starvation and impending mutiny and collapse, the committee underwent a change that was little less than a conversion. They switched from being critics to comrades of General Washington in the army's struggle to survive. No one was more totally converted than Francis Dana.

We hear an echo of his transformation in Henry Laurens's response to a letter Dana wrote in the third week in February. "Your description of the miseries of the Army affected me beyond common feeling, altho' I thought myself prepared by having perused it at home," the president of Congress wrote. Laurens found he "could not go through . . . reading your letter to Congress" without losing his composure. "Deep sympathy for the poor suffering soldiers blended with as deep indignation against the infamous delinquents who have been the authors of their distress."

Those latter words reveal Laurens the politician at work, in spite of his undoubtedly genuine emotion. The politician also wrote the next paragraph. Even "from his slight acquaintance" with Dana, the president was confident that he had the "fortitude and integrity" to tell his countrymen "in the presence of their representatives" the origins of the "evils" that were threatening to destroy the army. Laurens was sure that Dana would be neither "flattered nor affrighted" by any man in Congress who might think otherwise. The president was telling the New Englander it was time to defy Samuel Adams (represented for the moment by James Lovell—Adams was still resting in Boston) and stand boldly with General Washington against Generals Mifflin and Gates.

By this time, Laurens was firmly convinced that General Mifflin, at least, was one of the "infamous delinquents" responsible for the army's crisis. General Gates, by joining him on the Board of War and offering him the protection of his fame, shared the responsibility.[33]

VIII

In the midst of the army's miseries, General Washington somehow found time to deal with his ongoing argument with Horatio Gates about General Conway and his by now famous letter. On February 9, the commander in chief wrote the president of the Board of War a long letter, which began by puncturing Gates's gleeful assertion that the offending quote was not in the letter that General Conway wrote to him, and Conway was therefore exonerated and remained a loyal friend of the American cause. Washington bluntly informed Gates that "the discovery" he had mentioned in his previous letter "was not so satisfactory and conclusive as you seem to think it."

Washington was having "no small difficulty" reconciling General Gates's statements about Conway's letter. It was probable that Conway had warned Gates of the supposed extract that Washington had sent him. Wouldn't Conway want Gates to return the letter so he could find out if the extract was accurate? If he did not notify Gates, that made Washington think Conway thought the extract was substantially accurate, give or take some minor differences in wording.

If Conway had notified Gates, that left Washington puzzled over Gates's first letter from Albany, which did not challenge the authenticity of the extract, but only fulminated over having his papers rifled. Again and again in that letter the accuracy of the extract was more or less conceded. Then came Gates's triumphant letter, proclaiming the extract "in words as well as substance a wicked forgery." Washington was forced to conclude there was *something* in Conway's letter that contained or resembled the offensive passage. If not, why didn't Gates show the letter to him and prove his case?

This point had become particularly vexing when Washington learned Conway was showing the letter to members of Congress. How was it that

Gates found no fault with communicating its contents in this fashion, but did not think it was proper to show it to Washington or his officers—after all, it contained criticism of "the army under my command?" Washington was willing to admit that the faults of his officers and himself were "not improper topics" to be shown to members of Congress. But why did this "adept in military science" (Conway) never mention these criticisms in the course of the last campaign? The commander in chief conjectured perhaps Conway was better at criticisms after the fact than in the exercise of the foresight to avoid mistakes while the battles raged.

In spite of these contradictions, why did Gates continue to insist that Conway was a trustworthy friend of America? Washington disagreed politely but firmly. He thought he was entitled to pass judgment on the qualities of Conway's heart, having been a victim of his backstabbing and sarcastic letters. He predicted that if Gates continued to associate with him, he would find Conway capable of "all the malignity of detraction and all the meannesses of intrigue" to satisfy his disappointed vanity and his thwarted ambition—and simultaneously "to promote the interests of faction."

This was a letter that can best be compared to artillery fire in a drawing room. It did not give General Gates much room to maneuver.[34]

IX

The day after Washington wrote this letter, another important event occurred at Valley Forge. Martha Washington arrived from Mount Vernon to spend the rest of the winter and spring with "the general," as she often called him. Not enough historians have recognized the importance of this portly, affable woman in George Washington's life. One scribe has speculated that if her name had been more romantic—Kitty or Sally or Nancy—and she had somehow avoided too many portraits in her later life wearing a large old lady's cap, Americans might have a very different view of Martha Washington.

Usually forgotten is the story of Martha's youth: marriage at sixteen to a man twice her age, widowed after eight years, then marriage to a man her own age, the most famous soldier in Virginia. She was very rich, but there is little evidence that money was the chief motive or that the marriage was a plodding round of dull convenience. In an early portrait of Martha, with her sleek dark hair and glowing eyes, one historian has found "cold fire" and a readiness to be awakened by a man like George Washington, who emanated masculinity.

That seems to be what happened. When Washington accepted the command of the army in 1775, he and Martha had been married sixteen years. He wrote to "my dearest" and spoke of "an unalterable affection that neither time nor distance can change." Martha preserved the white gloves she had worn at her wedding until the day of her death. One of the more astute observers among the army's women, Nathanael Greene's wife, Catherine, told a friend: "Mrs. Washington is extremely fond of the general and he of her; they are very happy in each other." [35]

Every winter of the war, Martha made the long journey from the comforts of Mount Vernon to the unpredictable arrangements of a winter camp, braving ice-choked rivers and swamped roads. With all he had on his mind, Washington planned and supervised every mile of her trips. It was clear that he wanted her by his side.

No other winter was quite as grim as the one at Valley Forge. Martha found a half-naked army on the verge of mutiny and a camp buried in snow. But she brought with her an indefatigable good cheer and news from Mount Vernon. Soon she was visiting sick soldiers in their huts, braving camp fever and the odors of decaying horses and open latrines. She took charge of the meals at headquarters, transforming the bachelor's hall atmosphere into at least a semblance of gentility.

X

Washington was not privy to any of the reports that the committee in camp wrote daily to Congress, summarizing the members' interviews with various members of the army's departments. The congressmen did not express their shift to his side of the secret war between him and Gates and Mifflin in backslapping terms. All of them, especially Chairman Dana, were conscious of the need to maintain a facade of independence from the army and to reassert firmly and frequently that they were spokesmen for the army's rulers, Congress.

Meanwhile, General Washington did his utmost to cope with the food crisis. On February 12, he permitted the soldiers to move beyond the borders of the camp and take whatever edibles they could find in the neighboring countryside. The decision contradicted his repeated refusal to use military power to seize civilian property. But the crisis was too grave to worry about consistency.

Also on February 12 the commander in chief ordered General Nathanael Greene to take two thousand men and scour the region between the Delaware and Schuylkill rivers in search of food and forage. The expedition was conducted with grim ruthlessness. On the day Greene departed, General Varnum had warned him: "The army must soon dissolve."

Three days later, Greene wrote the commander in chief: "The inhabitants cry out and beset me from all quarters, but like Pharoah I harden my heart." When the civilians hid their cattle and horses and wagons in nearby woods, and his men were lucky enough to find them, Greene seized them as the spoils of war and refused to pay a cent for them. Soon Greene was shipping fifty head of cattle to Valley Forge, apologizing for his inability to find more. But fifty was enough to forestall the oncoming mutiny.[36]

Washington's aide Tench Tilghman conducted a smaller, more impromptu expedition in Trenton, New Jersey, when he went there on army business and discovered cattle and grain within easy reach. General Anthony Wayne invaded the Garden State with five hundred men farther south along the Delaware. Wayne's foragers found some 150 cattle, but General Howe made things uncomfortable by dispatching four thousand men to annihilate him.

Wayne lived up to his nickname, Mad Anthony, by attacking this force with the help of fifty dragoons commanded by the Polish volunteer Count Casimir Pulaski. The British commander thought he was being assaulted by thousands of enraged rebels and retreated to Philadelphia. Wayne was able to get his cattle across the Delaware north of the city and delivered them to Valley Forge.[37]

Simultaneously General Washington bombarded the state governors of Pennsylvania, Maryland, New Jersey, and New York with desperate pleas for help. It must have pained this proud man to be forced to play the beggar on his starving soldiers' behalf. Perhaps he sensed that the letters might make people wonder why the commander in chief had let his army stumble into such a pit of woe. He was well aware that politicians in York and Lancaster were ready to blame the situation on him.

XI

All the foraging parties, General Greene's in particular, reported to Washington that they were finding wheat for the men and forage for horses, but there were no wagons to transport them. It became more and more obvious that the breakdown of the quartermaster department was at least as serious as the disarray in the commissary department. Responding to frantic pleas from all directions, the Pennsylvania state government drafted wagons and drivers wholesale, ignoring the protests of the dismayed civilians. During the last week in February, this led to a tragedy at Valley Forge.

Two brigades of wagons—twenty-four wagons and ninety-six horses—were drafted in Northampton County. To make the drivers more amenable, the state-appointed wagonmaster told them they would have to serve only eight days. This was a promise that he was not authorized to make. When the men reached Valley Forge with their loads of grain on February 25, they were told to get some sleep and prepare to depart the next morning to the Head of Elk on Chesapeake Bay, thirty miles away, to transport flour and wheat that Commissary Blaine had stored there.

During the night, the angry men conferred around their campfire and decided to desert. The wagonmaster, a neighbor and fellow farmer, agreed to go with them. Hitching up their horses, they headed for Fatlands Ford on the Schuylkill. The night was moonless and cold; the river was swollen and full of floating ice. Plunging into the swift freezing stream, they realized too late that in the darkness they had missed the ford and were in deep water.

Thrashing horses screamed in terror as the icy water congealed their flesh. First one, then two, three, four wagons tilted crazily into the black depths, drowning horses and drivers. The rest struggled back to the Valley Forge shore. After severe chastisement and threats of punishment, the survivors departed for the Head of Elk in the morning. No one in starvation-racked Valley Forge was in the mood to sympathize with them.[38]

XII

In the midst of this turmoil, the secret war with Gates and Mifflin again intruded its ugly head. Washington received a letter from one of his aides, Lieutenant Colonel John Fitzgerald, who passed through York on his way to Virginia on leave. He told of paying a call on President Laurens, who asked him if Washington had ever seen a copy of the letter General Conway had written to General Gates. Fitzgerald said it had never been seen in Valley Forge. Laurens told him of Conway's showing it to members of Congress, and said it was now in the hands of Daniel Roberdeau, the Pennsylvania congressional delegate who had allowed the president of Congress a brief glance at it. Roberdeau was showing the letter to other members of Congress to prove the offending paragraph that had begun the uproar was not in it. Fitzgerald immediately accosted Roberdeau and asked to see the letter so he could make a copy and send it to General Washington.

Roberdeau, known for his piety (he regularly spent entire Sundays in church) said he no longer had the letter. He had given it to a "French gentleman" at Conway's order, as he left for Albany. Roberdeau vowed he had shown the letter to only two members of Congress and said he had the greatest esteem for both General Gates and General Washington.

Fitzgerald returned to Henry Laurens, who opined that Roberdeau, "in spite of his acknowledged piety," was lying. The president of Congress gave Fitzgerald the passage from the letter that he had copied from memory, which began, "What a pity there is but one Gates!" Fitzgerald sent it on to Washington, adding that he understood (thanks to Laurens) that the whole letter "was couched in terms of the most bitter invective, of which this is a small sample."[39]

A few days later, Governor Patrick Henry's letter enclosing Benjamin Rush's unsigned blast at Washington arrived in Valley Forge. Washington's familiarity with Rush's handwriting led him to suspect the paragon of true whig virtue, which made the letter an especially low blow.[40]

General Washington did not know whether Rush was working in concert with Gates and Mifflin. Was the hypocritical physician also the author of "Thoughts of a Freeman," the assault on Washington which some congressmen were eager to debate until President Laurens short circuited that ploy? The ranting tone of both documents and some similar phrasing in "Thoughts" made this conclusion more than plausible. At the very least, Rush reflected the dissatisfaction with the commander in chief that permeated York and Lancaster. The wordy doctor was intimate with many politicians in both towns.

XIII

During these nightmarish February weeks, Isaac Potts, the owner of the house Washington was using as his headquarters, visited Valley Forge. As he passed his former home, he saw Washington emerge and go into some nearby woods. A curious Potts followed him at a discreet distance and saw the general on his knees in the snow. Potts later told a friend that the sight had changed his mind about the war. As a Quaker he had been opposed to it. From that day he became a revolutionary.

Thus was born one of the most debatable legends of Valley Forge. It has been perpetuated in statues and paintings. Historians have attacked it because the story did not emerge until almost a century after Potts supposedly saw the moment of prayer. Others have concluded from analyzing Washington's religion that he was a deist who viewed God as Isaac Newton's impersonal clockmaker, presiding over a world where everything was foreordained and there was nothing the divinity could do about it even if he wanted to change things on behalf of this or that human's hard fate.

We also know that in his later years, Washington made it fairly clear that he was not a practicing Christian. He attended divine service in the Episcopal church but seldom knelt when others did, as part of the ritual. Although Martha regularly received communion, Washington never did, an apparent rejection of Jesus Christ's divinity. When Washington was president, the priest at Christ Church in Philadelphia became so exasperated by this noncompliance that he preached a sermon suggesting that prominent men should set a good example. Washington switched to another Episcopal church. Based on such evidence, this historian has long been one of the strongest skeptics of the prayer in the snow at Valley Forge.[41]

But recent research has revealed a surprising depth to Washington's faith in the divinity he called "Providence." The evidence surfaced in a book that focused on the general's comments about a passage from a projected postwar biography by a former aide, David Humphreys, about Washington's experience in the French and Indian War. The general discussed four episodes in which he had narrowly escaped death in battle. The last incident, in which Washington and his men came under friendly fire in a twilight skirmish, "involved the life of G.W. in as much jeopardy as it had ever been before or since," Washington wrote in the third person.

How deeply these experiences affected Washington's faith in providence can be glimpsed in a letter to his wife, Martha, shortly after he accepted command of the Continental Army. He told her he would rely "confidently on that Providence which has heretofore preserved and been bountiful to me." A year later, as he was preparing to fight the British in New York, he wrote to his French and Indian War comrade Adam Stephen. Referring to two of the battles in which they had narrowly escaped death, he said he could not let their anniversaries go unmentioned. "The same Provedence which protected us on these occasions will, I hope, continue his mercies."[42]

These sentiments come close to the conventional Christian's attitude toward a loving God. There is ample evidence in Washington's writings that he turned to this mysterious but merciful being repeatedly throughout

the Revolution. In October 1777, writing to his Virginia friend Landon
Carter after losing two major battles at Brandywine and Germantown, and
surrendering Philadelphia to the British, he wrote: "I flatter myself that a
superintending Providence is ordering everything for the best, and in due
time it will end well."[43]

On March 1, 1778, Washington wrote in a similar vein to his close friend
and Mount Vernon neighbor Bryan Fairfax, who had rejected independence
and become a neutral. "The determinations of Providence are always
wise . . . and tho' its decrees appear to bear hard upon us at times, is, nevertheless meant for gracious purposes—"[44]

In the agony of those two mid-February weeks, with his army dissolving into mutiny, with Generals Mifflin and Gates doing their utmost to
ruin him, and with Lafayette about to invade Canada with unforeseeable
but potentially ruinous consequences to Washington's prestige, could this
man, alone in the wintry woods, have sunk to his knees (or one knee, as
some artists imagine)? Perhaps. If he prayed, he probably was not seeking
some sort of divine intervention. He was trying to regain his inner certainty that together he and America were somehow destined to achieve a
glorious future. The alternative was a mire of petty jealousies (Mifflin) and
egocentric arrogance (Gates) and fanatic ideology (the Adamses, Lovell, et
al.) that would ultimately destroy the Revolution. These were thoughts
that might bring the strongest man to his knees.

XIV

Washington's spirits may have been raised by a small gesture from the
army's artillerymen on Sunday, February 22. There is no evidence that he
or his family ever made a fuss about celebrating his birthday. There are no
letters of congratulation or best wishes from President Henry Laurens or
anyone else in his files. He seems to have devoted this natal day, his forty-
sixth, to work, even though it was Sunday. In lengthy general orders, he
approved the findings of several courts-martial for disciplinary offenses
and wrote letters to the governors of Delaware and New Jersey.

Toward the end of the day, the artillery band of fifers and drummers marched to the snowy field before the Potts house and serenaded the general. It was the first public celebration of Washington's birthday. The artillerymen may have been acting under the orders of their commander, General Henry Knox, though he was home in Boston on furlough. Knox was well aware that Washington was under attack, and this musical salute was his way of demonstrating his support. As Knox well knew, the gesture had larger implications. Already, some private correspondents and at least one newspaper had called the commander in chief "the father of his country." By hailing Washington, the musicians were endorsing this title, which had previously belonged to George III. In England, the king's birthday was celebrated with music and merriment.[45]

Washington wisely declined to pay any attention to this gesture. If the true whigs in Congress heard about it, they would read dark portents of a Cromwellian grab for ultimate power in America's future. But something had to be done to express the general's appreciation to the shivering musicians. Martha Washington emerged to thank them on her husband's behalf, claiming he was getting ready for bed. She distributed a generous tip in hard money—about two hundred dollars in twenty-first-century cash—and the band went back to their huts the happiest campers in Valley Forge.

XV

Throughout this food crisis that brought the army to the brink of collapse, Lafayette's invasion of Canada was never far from Washington's thoughts. With that calm realism that pervaded so much of his thinking, the general foresaw that a triumph could radically alter the Marquis' attitude toward Horatio Gates and Thomas Mifflin. The young general could soothe his twinging conscience by remaining hostile to General Conway, the man who had unmistakably insulted Washington. Gates and Mifflin were far more artful politicians.

The ex-quartermaster was still telling everyone that he was an admirer of the commander in chief. It was Nathanael Greene who had to be jetti-soned. Gates would deny he ever had a hostile thought about Washington until Conway's letter disrupted their relationship. For them, Lafayette was only a means to an end: harassing and embarrassing Washington into re-signing his command. Think of what Dr. Rush's warm friend John Dun-lap, editor of the *Pennsylvania Packet and General Advertiser*, would do for Gates as the conqueror of Canada! The hero of Saratoga would grow from fifty to a hundred feet tall.

In Albany, Colonel Moses Hazen was already hard at work assem-bling men, sleds, wagons, and supplies. The governor of the embryo state of Vermont, which was not part of the American confederation, promised him three hundred men. Hazen got permission from the governments of New York and Massachusetts to seize wagons wherever he found them. Unfortunately, the Bay State only sent enough winter clothing to outfit Hazen's regiment. That was a worry, but Hazen remained optimistic about finding more warm shirts and breeches in and around Albany.[46]

Meanwhile, Lafayette was slogging toward Albany in awful winter weather, which left him, he told Washington on February 9, "sometimes pierced by rain, sometimes covered with snow, and not thinking very hand-some thoughts about . . . Canada."[47] He reached Albany on February 17 and immediately contacted the three ranking officers in the vicinity, Generals Philip Schuyler, Benedict Arnold, and Benjamin Lincoln.

Arnold and Lincoln were both recovering from wounds suffered at Saratoga, but they immediately sent couriers, telling Lafayette the expedi-tion was madness. Arnold added that Horatio Gates was "the greatest poltroon in the world" and anyone who served under him needed his head examined. Lincoln was more temperate about Gates but was equally neg-ative about the expedition. As for Philip Schuyler, he apparently managed to conceal his detestation of Gates. However, as the man who had tried to supply the 1775–76 invasion, he spoke with great authority on the impossi-bility of feeding 2,500 men in the subzero climate of northern New York and Canada.[48]

From lesser officers the Marquis soon learned that there were nowhere near 2,500 Continentals ready to march—the number was closer to 1,200, and they were all in sour moods because they had not been paid in months. Worse, a majority of them had no winter clothing.

Most dismaying of all was a letter from Brigadier General John Stark, the hero of the battle of Bennington. Gates had assured Lafayette that Stark would have swarms of militia waiting for him. Instead, Stark wanted answers to such basic questions as how many men he was expected to raise and where they were supposed to rendezvous; his knowledge of the expedition was close to zero. Meanwhile the clock was ticking remorselessly toward the day that the ice on Lake Champlain would start to melt.

A stunned Lafayette wrote Colonel Hazen a frantic letter, asking what was going on. He got back a chirpy missive, assuring the Marquis that it was "next to impossible" that he (Hazen) would fail to raise the eight hundred sleds they needed to cross Lake Champlain, although he had only about fifty so far. "The only difficulties," Hazen continued, were the "want" of the expected number of men for the expedition and the lack of winter clothing if more soldiers turned up.[49]

Lafayette wrote a similar letter to General Conway, who had arrived in Albany two days earlier, asking him to explain the situation. Conway had already reported to Gates that the number of men was "infinitely short of what was expected by the Board of War." He sent the same bad news to Lafayette but claimed he was ready to march if Lafayette issued the orders.[50]

Conway's letter was an impersonal report. Lieutenant Colonel Robert Troup, Gates's chief aide since talkative Lieutenant Colonel James Wilkinson had fallen into disfavor, also wrote to the president of the Board of War. In one letter he reported that virtually every living soul in Albany said the Canadian expedition was madness.

The second letter was far more personal and gives an interesting glimpse into what General Gates and his circle thought of Lafayette and Washington. Troup blamed "bitter, vindictive" Benedict Arnold for prejudicing people (possibly including John Stark) against the Canadian expedition by accusing Gates and Hazen of being "ignorant designing men." Most people dismissed Arnold's spleen, but some accepted it—notably Lafayette. "He cannot believe how you came to be so little acquainted with

the situation of affairs in this department," Troup wrote. "I have had several skirmishes with him" (defending Gates).

The question now was: "What [do] you intend to do with him?" Troup
suggested it might be best if Lafayette returned to his division in the
"southern army." (This was the designation General Gates and his supporters had taken to using for Washington's force, suggesting the two
armies were more or less equal in power and importance.) "There," Troup
sneered, "the blunders of his youth & inexperience will pass as manoeuvres
[sic] in the sublime art of war."[51]

As Lafayette saw it, the mistakes were all the property of Horatio
Gates. The Marquis fired off an all but incoherent letter to President
Henry Laurens to let him know "which hell of blunders, madness and deception I am involved in." He denounced General Stark's inaction, but he
reserved his nastiest line for Gates: "You will be . . . surprised that Gal
[General] Gates seems not so well acquainted with the Northern Department as myself, who has been here . . . two days."

The twenty-year-old would-be hero revealed his fear that the collapse
of the expedition made him look ridiculous. He asked the president of
Congress "how schall [sic] I do to get of[f] from a precipice where I embarked myself out of love for your country?" He was beginning to wish "to
have never put the foot in America." Everyone in the United States knew
about the expedition, and at Congress's urging Lafayette had written numerous letters to Paris on the assumption that Louis XVI and his ministers would be pleased to learn about the plan to conquer France's former
colony.

The Marquis was sure he was now in danger of becoming the laughingstock of both countries. Rather than let his reputation be ruined,
Lafayette vowed to "publish the whole history." He would ruin the honor
of "twenty Gates and twenty boards of war" rather than let his own reputation be "hurted" this way.[52]

The same day, Lafayette wrote to Washington in a very different
voice. "Why am I so far from you, and what business had that board of
war to hurry me through the ice and snow without knowing what I
schould [sic] do or what they were doing themselves?" He proceeded to

tell the commander in chief the story of his "fine and glorious campaign." The 1,200 men he found fit for duty were mostly "naked even for a summer campaign." In a separate memorandum, he noted that they were mostly boys and old men of sixty. Worse, a deserter from the British army in Canada brought information that the king's forces were much stronger than the Americans had thought.

Almost piteously, Lafayette begged Washington to help him rescue his reputation. He wondered if he should resign as major general and reduce himself to a mere volunteer on Washington's staff. Was an attack on New York City, led by Lafayette and Benedict Arnold, feasible in the spring? Grimly the Marquis vowed he would never ask Congress for the assignment. He would trust in Washington, who understood "the only thing I am ambitious of: Glory."[53]

While Washington undoubtedly sympathized with Lafayette's emotional anguish, his letter had another, far more important meaning for the commander in chief. It signaled the collapse of the Mifflin–Gates–Board of War plan to seize power over the Continental Army and humiliate Washington into resigning. Instead of a bold irruption into the defenseless fourteenth colony, the victor at Saratoga had perpetrated a fiasco, which made him and his backers in Congress look like fools.

General Gates had embarrassed and enraged Lafayette, whom many regarded as the linchpin of the hoped-for French alliance, and made the Americans look idiotic to King Louis XVI and his generals in Paris. The letter from the committee in camp warning that the expedition was a disaster in the making acquired new weight in the eyes of their fellow congressmen. So did the undoubted source of that letter: General George Washington. The stage was set for some power plays from Valley Forge.

XVI

The Board of War had already suffered two minor defeats in their push for power. Complaints had poured into Congress about the high-handed way in which the board's commissary superintendents were doing business.

They had been supposed to supersede the army's purchasing commissaries and the state of Pennsylvania's commissioners. Congress, rattled by reports from the committee in camp about the army's starvation and threats of mutiny, ordered the superintendents to cease their operations. At the same time the solons, probably with some behind-the-scenes lobbying by President Laurens, grew more and more reluctant to implement the Board of War's plan to chop the quartermaster department into four pieces, even though they had approved it in a voice vote—another loss of face for Mifflin and Gates.

Early in February, Henry Laurens had told General Washington that Congress hoped he would make some suggestions for men who could head the quartermaster department. Asking Washington's advice was a subtle slap at Mifflin, the supposed authority on the subject, whom many in Congress regarded as the quasi owner of the franchise, even though he had resigned five months before. Washington, with a presumably straight face, observing all the politesse and submissiveness that Congress expected of the army, persuaded the committee in camp to send to York his first suggestion: Philip Schuyler.

If the general had mounted his horse, ridden to York, and tossed a mortar shell with a sputtering fuse into this band of harried politicians on the second floor of the York County Courthouse, the shock could not have been more stunning. Schuyler was not only a back of the hand to Mifflin, it was a veritable explosion of contempt in the face of Major General Horatio Gates. The Saratoga hero must have all but choked when he heard the name. Schuyler! The man he had denounced on the floor of Congress, whom he had routed in the struggle for command of the northern army, thanks to the support of his New England congressional allies. Those worthies could have been only slightly less undone by the suggestion. Schuyler, the rich New Yorker whom every Yankee east of the Hudson River supposedly hated, the man whom his moneyed New York friends had defended with dislike for New England's oozing in every syllable of their oratory. Schuyler!

Worst of all, their fellow congressmen in the committee in camp were not only emphatically backing Schuyler for quartermaster; they informed

Congress that in their opinion the Board of War's plan to dismember the department was a terrible idea. Two months earlier, when Benjamin Rush was penning his apostrophes to true whiggery, and James Lovell could not wait to rap a demigod over the knuckles, the air in the York County Courthouse would have been purple with superheated oratory, denouncing the arrogance of "a certain great man's" suggestion, along with dark warnings about the army's attempt to defy the wishes of Congress. Now the flabbergasted solons in York could think of only one reply: they let Philip Schuyler's name lie upon the table, and said nothing.

It is hard to believe that General Washington really expected Schuyler to be approved. Suggesting him served several purposes, even if he was rejected. It cemented Washington's alliance with this powerful man and his friends, whose influence in New York remained strong. It stated in unmistakable terms where Washington stood in the secret war between the true whig ideologues and the realists in Congress. Most important, the name became a kind of bargaining chip, a threat that the commander in chief and the committee in camp might insist on cramming Schuyler down the ideologues' throats.

As the rest of February unfolded, with its nightmare weeks of starvation and imminent mutiny, and the collapse of the expedition to Canada, Washington began preparing the committee in camp for the man he really wanted as quartermaster general: Major General Nathanael Greene. He made sure the committee heard about Greene's successful foraging expedition, which had not a little to do with holding the army together during the worst of the meat shortage. Simultaneously, he was conferring with Greene, who was unenthused by the prospect of abandoning his major generalship to become a staff officer.

In many ways, Greene was as eager for glory as Lafayette. "Nobody has ever heard of a quartermaster in history," he told Washington. But the general soon convinced him that only someone with his experience could save the army from more disasters like the starving time of mid-February. More important, Washington assured him that they were going to jettison the rigid system of price controls and staff officers appointed by Congress which the politicians had devised in 1777. Greene would have the power to appoint every man in his department. Henceforth, officials in both the commissary and quartermaster departments would be permitted to take a percentage of their costs as payment. Once more, Washington the realist was taking on the true whig ideologues, this time with confidence that he was going to win.

Beneath this dickering lay the supremely political context of Greene's appointment. For all his stated reluctance, it is impossible to believe that the Rhode Islander did not see the delicious political side of it. He was about to replace Thomas Mifflin, the man who had spent the previous year vilifying him for his supposedly malign influence on the commander in chief. Greene was not only replacing him, he was becoming a more potent quartermaster than Mifflin dreamed of, even in his most power hungry fantasies.

Crucial in this political power struggle was the congressional committee in camp. Their reports consistently followed Washington's lead. The congressmen stressed that the quartermaster department was "the great wheel in the machine." Everyone agreed that the scarcity of wagons was a major cause of the army's food shortage. Yet the committee found "not an encampment, route of the army or considerable road, but abounds with waggons [sic] at the mercy of the weather and the will of the inhabitants." (This denunciation has a strong resemblance to the angry letter about the quartermaster department's dissarary that General Washington received from his friend, militia General John Armstrong in December.) Meanwhile deputy quartermasters were making fast bucks transporting private property in the army's wagons. In 1777 Congress had "reformed" this department too, creating decentralized semi-independent deputy quartermasters, who were clearly out of control. It was time to select "characters of known and proven abilities" to run the department.[54]

Abandoning Congress's fondness for penny pinching salaries, the committee recommended giving the new quartermaster and his top assistants one percent of all the money handled by the department. A year ago, this would have provoked volcanic wrath from the ideologues of the Lee-Adams junto. Now it was being recommended in unflinching terms by their fellow congressmen, led by New Englander Francis Dana. With a common sense worthy of General Washington (and probably originating from their sessions with him), the committee observed that there was "an infinity of ways" for a dishonest man to cheat the government, and—irony of ironies—the commission system offered the easiest way to detect a fraudulent operator. Better for Congress to put its faith in honest men, not complicated systems. Unspoken was the basic component in the argument: men chosen by General Washington.[55]

Backed by such emphatic support, in his ensuing negotiations with Congress, Greene insisted on two key appointments, his friends Charles Petit and John Cox. Both were Philadelphians; Petit was a lawyer and accountant, Cox a successful merchant. They would keep the books and handle vast amounts of administrative detail, enabling the quartermaster general to operate as policy maker and a partner in planning the army's movements.

The committee applied the same realistic logic to the commissary department. Instead of multiplying deputy and assistant commissaries on tiny salaries, they urged Congress to find "a man of abilities, extensive connections and influence" to handle the job—and proceeded to suggest him: Jeremiah Wadsworth of Connecticut, another Greene friend. At the committee in camp's request, Congress meekly surrendered its previous insistence on appointing all the deputies in the department. Wadsworth was to receive 0.5 percent of all the money he disbursed, and the deputies he chose would have the same remuneration.

The dissaray of the Lee-Adams ideologues was almost amusing. One of them, wordy Eliphalet Dyer of Connecticut, glumly summed up Congress's reversal of its supposedly fundamental true whig principles: "They wish to have the army supplied at any rate."[56]

XVII

A triumphant letter from Henry Laurens, Washington's sub-rosa ally in Congress, to Francis Dana summed up these stunning political victories over Mifflin and Gates. Referring to a letter Dana had written on February

25, Laurens explained that the messenger had apparently made a long halt at a popular tavern. Otherwise, the president would already have obtained Congress's approval for the committee's recommendations for the quartermaster general's job. Now he would have to wait until the coming Tuesday. But there was no doubt of the approval.

Laurens's tone abruptly shifted from pleasant to irascible. He seized on Dana's remark that most of the evils that were engulfing Valley Forge stemmed from "gross neglect and abuse" in the quartermaster department. The president was inclined to agree and demanded to know why everyone was so "courtly and mincing" about naming names. Were they going to allow the "peculator . . . whose neglect of duty has brought thousands to misery and death" to get away unscathed? He wanted to see the offender "dragged forth" and the people told "this is the man!" [57]

Unquestionably Laurens was writing about Thomas Mifflin. Dana never responded to the president's demand, and Mifflin's many supporters in Congress closed ranks to protect him from an inquiry that might have led to the kind of condemnation Laurens wanted to see. That did not mean General Mifflin and his friend Horatio Gates had anything to smile about. On March 2, after more vitriolic letters from the Marquis de Lafayette, Congress officially canceled the expedition to Canada.

Around the same time, General Washington wrote to his aide John Fitzgerald to thank him for obtaining the new information about Conway's letter from Henry Laurens, and added some comments which show his growing confidence that the Board of War's grab for power was rapidly coming to an inglorious close. "Matters have, & will, turn out very different to what that party expected. G——s has involved himself in his letters to me in the most absurd contradictions. M. has gotten himself into a scrape he does not know how to get out of, & C——is sent upon an expedition which all the world knew & the event has proved, was not practicable. In a word, I have good reason to believe that the machinations of this junto will recoil upon their own heads." [58]

XVIII

In York, General Gates was drawing a similar conclusion. He conferred with President Henry Laurens, asking if he could help heal the breach between himself and General Washington. Laurens wrote to his son John, reporting the gesture of peace, and was told that Washington considered Gates "only the instrument of more dangerous . . . personages."[59]

On February 19, Gates wrote a labored letter to Washington in which he disowned General Conway and the true whigs in Congress. He reiterated that Conway was not only not a friend, but was "responsible" for the entire messy controversy. As for promoting dissension in Congress or anywhere else, Gates denied all. "I solemnly declare I am of no faction." The victor of Saratoga added a whopper to this catalog of lies: "I heartily dislike controversy, even on my own account." This was rich indeed coming from the man who had waded onto the floor of Congress to scream insults in the faces of the men who supported Philip Schuyler in 1777. Gates closed with the hope that Washington would not allow "his own suspicions or the prejudices of others" to prolong the quarrel.[60]

In Valley Forge, General Washington recognized surrender when he saw it. There was no longer any point in torturing General Gates about his inconsistencies. But he could not resist a farewell dig at Gates's hint that the imbroglio was begun by the commander in chief's hypersensitivity or the influence of his jealous staff. He told Gates he was "as averse to controversy as any man." If he had not been "forced into it," Gates would never have had reason to "impute to him even the shadow of a disposition toward it."

However, Gates's denial of any and all offensive views made Washington willing to join the president of the Board of War in burying the controversy "in silence, and as far as future events will permit, in oblivion." The latter part of that line carried an unmistakable warning: *I'm still watching you, Horatio.*[61]

XIX

While this elaborate peace process was in progress, General Gates, having revealed his strategic shortcomings in the expedition to Canada, was making a fool of himself in a subsidiary quarrel with his aide James Wilkinson. This pompous young man was in a fury because forty-seven colonels in the Continental Army had protested his promotion to brigadier general, which Gates had recommended. It was not unusual for bearers of good news to be given a promotion; Gates had been upped from captain to major for bringing the news of a victory in the Caribbean to London during the Seven Years' War. But the promotion of an aide, whose rank of lieutenant colonel was purely honorary, to brigadier general was off the charts and could be explained only by Gates's Saratoga-swelled head or bad judgment or both.

Wilkinson had accepted Congress's offer to make him secretary of the Board of War, but he soon discovered that his relationship with General Gates was barely civil. The ex-aide wrote Gates a blustering letter, accusing him of using "the grossest language" when he talked about him in private and public. Gates replied the next day with an extract from Washington's letter, stating that Wilkinson was the source of the leak of Conway's letter. He also rebuked "Wilky" for attempting to cast the blame for the leak on his fellow aide, Robert Troup. Wilkinson's reply was a challenge to a duel.

There was no necessity for General Gates to take this challenge seriously. Wilkinson was barely twenty-one: Gates was a victorious general of fifty. No one would have called him a coward if he had dismissed the challenge with contempt. Moreover, Congress had barred dueling in the Continental Army. Whatever his motivation—resentment at the frequently repeated gibe that he had let Benedict Arnold and Daniel Morgan do the fighting at Saratoga; distress at the unraveling of his invasion of Canada; a determination to prove that his nickname, "Granny Gates," was a misnomer—General Gates accepted the challenge.

On the morning of February 25, Gates was preparing to meet Wilkinson in a field outside York when a mutual friend urged him to talk things over with his ex-aide, who still "loved" him. Gates agreed to meet with Wilkinson, and they took a long walk together, discussing their differences. According to Wilkinson's memoirs, Gates finally burst into tears and sobbed: "I injure you? It is impossible. I would as soon think of injuring my child."

Many historians suspect Wilkinson fabricated these words. But Gates's acceptance of the duel is incontrovertible. The letter from the peacemaker, Benjamin Stoddert, is in Gates's papers at the New-York Historical Society. Whether he broke down and cried is almost irrelevant. His acceptance was enough to convict him of behavior unbecoming a serious general. The story was soon all over York—and traveled swiftly to Valley Forge.[62]

XX

The collapse of General Gates's hopes of superseding General Washington, followed by this descent from high drama to low comedy, produced an amusing sidelight. Anti-Washington congressmen rushed to deny to their friends and constituents that they had ever harbored a negative thought about that great and good man, George Washington.

Jonathan Bayard Smith of Pennsylvania told Joseph Reed that if Congress had ever passed a resolution favoring an enemy of Washington, it was accidental. "The Generals conduct" had convinced Smith that he "prefers the good of his country to any personal considerations." But he admitted that after so much abusive talk in York and Lancaster, "something should be done" to prevent the people of Pennsylvania from losing confidence in the commander in chief.[63]

James Lovell, the primary congressional character assassin, tried to dismiss the whole imbroglio in a letter to John Adams. Lovell called it "foolish bickerings which had been raised out of Conway's indiscretion."[64]

Perhaps the most effusive reversal came from Eliphalet Dyer of Connecticut, who voted with the Lee-Adams junto on almost everything and had claimed the appointment of General Gates to the Board of War had met with "universal applause." On March 10, the fifty-six-year-old Dyer, who had been in politics in the State of Steady Habits for decades, chose his friend William Williams, a former delegate and signer of the Declaration of Independence, as the man to spread his innocence far and wide. "Be assured," Dyer piously claimed, "there is not the most distant thought of removing Genll Washington nor ever an expression in Congress looking that way."[65]

Missing from this chorus was Samuel Adams. Aware of Washington's popularity among the people, this adroit gentleman avoided putting any obviously hostile remarks on the record. He let his follower James Lovell and others do the negative talking and letter writing. Adams went so far as to carefully obliterate the signature on the vituperative anti-Washington letter from Jonathan Dickinson Sergeant that Lovell had forwarded to him. Not until the twentieth century did scholars identify Sergeant's handwriting.[66]

The man Sam Adams had made his avowed enemy, John Hancock, did his best to make the former Grand Incendiary uncomfortable about his backstage role in the anti-Washington game. Hancock used his wealth and popularity in Boston to build a formidable political machine. In the spring of 1778, the Boston Town Meeting produced a denunciation of Sam for his attempts to undermine General Washington. In York, Sam frigidly assured a correspondent that he considered the accusation beneath his notice.[67]

There years later, Sam admitted the barb was still under his skin. In a letter to his wife, he declared: "I never wished for the removal of General Washington." Sam blamed the canard on John Hancock, and added a significant sentence. Even if he (Sam) had tried to remove the general, it would have been evidence only of bad political judgment, but "it could not be evidence that I was his enemy." Like many politicians, Sam liked to parse his sentences so he could have things both ways.[68]

SEVEN

DISCIPLINE FROM A BARON

WITH GENERAL CONWAY wandering morosely around Albany and General Gates in a state of capitulation in York, the stage was set for the arrival of former Lieutenant General Baron Friedrich Wilhelm von Steuben at Valley Forge. The timing of this distinguished soldier was so impeccable, one is almost tempted to believe in the old Puritan idea of "remarkable providences" arranged by the same mysterious Providence to whom General Washington may have prayed.

The former lieutenant general's trip from Portsmouth, New Hampshire, to York, Pennsylvania, to obtain the approval of Congress was close to a royal progress. In Boston, John Hancock gave him a dinner and loaned him money. At other towns along the way leading citizens turned out to greet him. At Manheim, beyond Reading on the road to York, he had conferred with Robert Morris, the premier merchant of America, for an update on the political situation in Congress. Morris had immediately written to Henry Laurens telling how deeply impressed he was by this volunteer, who had served "upwards of twenty years under so great a master as the King of Prussia."[1]

At York the Baron was treated as an important personage. Richard Peters of the Board of War said he received "more particular attention" than any previous foreign soldier. General Gates invited him to be his guest, but Robert Morris, a staunch supporter of General Washington, had advised the Baron to avoid any hint of an alliance with the Saratoga hero. Steuben's inability to speak a word of English did not trouble anyone. Lafayette and other volunteers had been almost as inarticulate when they arrived. The Baron and his four-man staff settled into a fine house formerly occupied by John Hancock during his presidency.

A committee from Congress soon called on the Baron, and with the help of his English-speaking secretary, a seventeen-year-old French nobleman named Peter Stephen Duponceau, he reiterated his willingness to serve without rank or pay. However, Steuben told the committee that he had surrendered a substantial revenue derived from "places and posts of honor" in Germany by coming to America. He hoped that if America won the war, he would be recompensed for his losses. The committee was awed by the generosity of this offer, in their eyes a win-win wager for America.

No one asked the Baron to specify the places and posts of honor he had abandoned or how much he had made from them. The committee's report to Congress verged on the ecstatic, and Congress was equally enthused. At a reception in his honor, President Henry Laurens told Steuben that Congress wanted him to join the army at Valley Forge without a moment's delay.

II

The Baron and his entourage, which included a large Russian wolfhound named Azor, set out for Valley Forge, armed with a warm letter to General Washington from President Laurens and another one to his son, John, urging him to do everything in his power to assist this large-hearted volunteer. On his way the Baron stopped at Lancaster, Pennsylvania, where the citizens gave a ball in his honor. On such occasions he wore on his chest a splendid jeweled star, which everyone presumed had been bestowed on him by Frederick the Great.

Here is how the Baron described his reception at Valley Forge to one of his European friends.

"Upon my arrival at camp, I was again the subject of more honors. . . . General Washington came several miles to meet me on the road, and accompanied me to my quarters, where I found an officer with twenty five men as a guard of honor. When I declined this, saying that I wished to be regarded merely as a volunteer, the general answered me . . . that the whole army would be gratified to stand sentinel for such a volunteer. . . . On the same day my name was given as a watchword. The following day the army was mustered and General Washington accompanied me to review it. . . . If Prince Ferdinand of Brunswick or the greatest field marshal of Europe had been in my place, he could not have been received with greater marks of honor."[2]

There is no evidence of any such events taking place at Valley Forge. The Baron's letter was one more piece of theater in the greatest public deception ever perpetrated in a good cause. The author of the play was that master of the newspaper hoax, Benjamin Franklin, with some assistance from his diplomat confrere, Silas Deane, and from their chief French collaborator, Caron de Beaumarchais, author of the controversial drama *The Marriage of Figaro*. The latter had been shipping tons of arms and ammunition to the Americans for the previous year through his dummy company, Hortalez et Cie, with money provided by the French government. The lively imagination of the chief actor, who thoroughly enjoyed the role they designed for him, also played no small part in the play's success.

There was a kernel of truth in the drama. Friedrich von Steuben was a Prussian officer who had served with distinction in the Seven Years' War and had become an aide-de-camp to Frederick the Great. But he had never advanced beyond the rank of captain. Discharged from the army after the war, he had made a precarious living as chief minister at the court of Hohenzollern-Hechingen, one of the many small principalities into which Germany was divided at the time.

This ministate in the Black Forest region was presided over by a relative of Frederick the Great, Prince Joseph Frederick William Hohenzollern-Hechingen, whose royal expenses constantly outran his annual revenue. Steuben's pay seldom exceeded more than four hundred dollars a year. One of his few consolations during these years was his nomination to an elite order of knighthood, which carried with it the right to wear the Star of the Order of Fidelity on his breast.

This order was bestowed through the favor of Princess Frederica, niece of Frederick the Great. She was married to the prince of the neighboring principality, Baden-Durlach. Frederica was extremely fond of the ex-captain and hated her abusive husband. It was through her intervention that Steuben had obtained his post at Hohenzollern-Hechingen. There are some grounds for speculating that they had been lovers. Her influence may also have played a part in persuading the prince of Hohenzollern-Hechingen to bestow the title of baron on his faithful chief minister.[3]

The finances of Hohenzollern-Hechingen more or less collapsed in 1777, and Steuben wandered around Europe, seeking appointments in the Spanish army and the French army. One old friend tried to rescue him by introducing him to a rich widow. With a trail of IOUs behind him, the Baron came to Paris, where Franklin's agile imagination concocted his imaginary career and the idea of offering his services as a volunteer. Congress had sternly warned they wanted no more foreigners arriving in America with contracts for brigadier and major generalships in their trunks.

The canny Deane added another masterful touch: after Steuben sailed, he wrote to Robert Morris that in the hurry of his departure, the Baron had left behind the proofs of his long service in the King of Prussia's armies, but there was no need to be concerned. He (Deane) and Franklin had examined them and they were entirely convincing. Beaumarchais added a final fillip to the story with a letter to Morris, asking him to advance the Baron money and assuring him that he had "discussed the merits of this officer with the greatest generals that we have."[4]

III

General Washington's actual reception of Baron von Steuben was so low-key, it was barely perceptible. Four days after he arrived, the commander in chief mentioned him in the middle of a long letter to Henry Laurens about several pressing matters, such as a resolution of Congress demanding that he court-martial General Philip Schuyler for his conduct as commander of the Northern Department before General Gates took over. This was obviously a backlash from Washington's congressional enemies expressing their frustration over the collapse of the Mifflin-Conway-Gates power play. The commander in chief coolly explained to Laurens that it would be impossible to court-martial Schuyler without knowing what instructions he had received from Congress during his tenure. The same problem applied to General St. Clair, Schuyler's subordinate, who was also on Congress's court-martial list.

Almost offhandedly, Washington next wrote: "Baron Steuben has arrived at camp. He appears to be much of a gentleman, and as far as I have had an opportunity of judging, a man of military knowledge and acquainted with the world." He went on to other things, such as General Putnam's desperate need for money to pay and feed his troops in the Hudson Highlands.[5]

Fortunately, we have John Laurens's letters to his father to give us a better appreciation of the Baron's progress. On March 9, two weeks after his arrival, John wrote: "The Baron Steuben has had the fortune to please uncommonly for a stranger at first sight. All the general officers who have met him are prepossessed in his favor and conceive highly of his abilities. . . . The General [Washington] seems to have a very good opinion of him and thinks he might be usefully employed in the office of inspector general."

For the moment, Laurens reported, Washington was "cautious" about recommending Steuben for the job. He did not want to look like he was "implacably pursuing" General Conway, who still held the title. This sidestep was further evidence of Washington's political astuteness. He was well aware that James Lovell and his friends would welcome a chance to rush to Conway's defense.

Next young Laurens undertook what contemporary politicians would call damage control. He told his father that Congress had "mistaken" Baron Steuben's rank in Prussia. He was never more than a colonel in Frederick the Great's service. The title of lieutenant general was acquired when he commanded the troops of the principality of Baden. The Baron was hoping to win the rank and pay of major general in the American army, but he preferred to waive the question of an actual command until he was better known and his English improved.[6]

This revision of the Baron's biography probably occurred to him when he discovered how many knowledgeable French officers were in the American army. An old soldier such as Baron de Kalb was likely to have a working knowledge of the past and present lieutenant generals in the Prussian army and might start asking questions. De Kalb would be far less likely to know the names of all the Prussian colonels, and a lieutenant general from Baden would be totally unknown to him—and scarcely worthy of comment. The Baden "army" probably amounted to no more than a regiment.

The Baron also had to cope with another problem. Henry Laurens wondered if a Prussian lieutenant general would accept a reduction in rank to major general in the Continental Army. The Baron smoothly assured the president of the misunderstanding about where he had achieved his lofty rank—in the "Circle of Suabia," which would not interfere with becoming an American major general. The Circle of Swabia was another German ministate. The Baron seems to have forgotten that a few days earlier, conversing with John Laurens, he had placed himself at the head of the armed forces of Baden. In either case, there was no such rank in their army, but few kept track of the inner workings of these tiny states, where grandiose titles were not at all uncommon.

At any rate, Henry Laurens got the message and soon began describing Steuben as a "lieutenant general in foreign service." Neither the president nor Congress ever specifically repudiated the Prussian title, which continued to be accepted by most Americans without a smidgen of doubt.

IV

Washington soon devised a solution to the problem of offending the surly congressional aficionados of General Conway. While that gentleman was sojourning in the wintry winds of Albany, Baron von Steuben would become the army's "acting" inspector general. Steuben, by this time thoroughly acquainted with the political problem, accepted the offer with alacrity. He understood that Washington's motives were both political and practical. The commander in chief wanted to see what Steuben could accomplish before he gave him more than tentative backing.[7]

Meanwhile, the Baron had already gone to work. He toured Valley Forge, talking to officers and enlisted men. To his reputation as a military expert nonpareil, Steuben added the charm of his rough-and-ready personality. There was little of the legendary Prussian harshness and formality in his style. Letters from friends in Europe attest to the warmth of his relationships. With the help of interpreter Duponceau, and occasional assists from John Laurens and Alexander Hamilton, who were fluent in French, the Baron's second language, Steuben persuaded everyone to be candid. What he discovered was nothing less than appalling. He was confronting a wrecked army. A less courageous (or less bankrupt) man would have quit on the spot.

In his reminiscences, Steuben described the disorder that pervaded the Continental Army. Thanks to the ebb and flow of short enlistments, there was no such thing as a complete regiment or company. "Sometimes a regiment was stronger than a brigade. . . . [Another] regiment consist[ed] of thirty men and a company of one corporal!" Washington had pointed out this problem to the congressional committee in camp, but Steuben put it in far more vivid terms.

It was also impossible to estimate the size of the Continental Army. A mustermaster general, as in the English system, received monthly reports from the captains of each company, who simply listed those absent and present "to the best of his knowledge and belief." No one checked to find out if the captain was lying or careless. When Steuben asked one colonel how many men were in his regiment, the colonel replied, "Something between two and three hundred." Most captains were equally ignorant of how many men they commanded at any given moment.

Steuben chose a company with twelve men listed as present and asked the whereabouts of each man listed as absent. One soldier was the valet to a commissary general in the northern army, over two hundred miles away. Four others were in different hospitals. Two were drivers of wagons. Others were bakers, blacksmiths, carpenters, employed elsewhere. "The soldiers were scattered about in every direction," Steuben concluded. "The army was looked upon as a nursery for servants." Commissaries, quartermasters, and officers from the rank of captain to general thought they were entitled to a servant—sometimes several servants. If the army had to go into action on short notice, Steuben opined, Washington would be lucky to find a third of the men he had on paper.[8]

Equally appalling was the state of the army's weapons. Neither captains nor colonels were required to report on the condition of their men's guns or clothing. Steuben found muskets "covered with rust, half of them without bayonets." The ammunition pouches were as decrepit as the guns. Some were made of tin, virtually guaranteed to rust. Other men had cow horns. Worse, many companies had a mixture of muskets, rifles, carbines, and ancient fowling pieces, making a usable ammunition supply impossible.

As for the army's uniforms, many of the enlisted men were literally naked. Officers had coats "of every color and make." The astonished Steuben saw one officer mounting guard wearing "a dressing gown, made of an old blanket or woolen bedcover." Consistent organization was nowhere to be seen. Regiments ranged from three platoons to twenty-one. Almost every colonel followed a different system of drill.

Worse, there were no regulations to keep order in the camp or to direct how and when to mount guards. Sometimes guards were left on their posts for two and three days at a time. Marching in compact formations was totally unknown. The standard advance was in Indian file columns, which often extended the line of march for miles, and made for fatal delays in deploying men into a battle line.

Steuben blamed much of this disorder on the Continental Army's imitation of the English system. An officer had little sense of responsibility for his men. Sergeants were assigned the task of drilling the men and maintaining a semblance of order in camp. As the officers saw it, their duty consisted of mounting guard and putting themselves at the head of their companies or regiments when the army went into action. Steuben, trained in the exacting school of Frederick the Great, had a vastly larger vision of the officer's job.[9]

There may be some exaggeration in Steuben's description of the Continental Army after two and one-half months in Valley Forge. But there was more truth than fiction, as a report on the army's numbers dated February 29, 1778, makes clear. There was a grand total of 22,283 men under Washington's command. Present and fit for duty at Valley Forge were a dismaying 7,556. No fewer than 3,201 were listed as sick present, 3,680 were sick absent, and 3,558 were "on command and extra service," many of the latter no doubt the servants that Steuben deplored. Another 1,256 were on furlough, and a staggering 3,558 lacked clothes, in spite of Washington's repeated pleas to Congress and the states.[10]

In a letter to Henry Laurens a few days after this report, which probably reflects Steuben's desire to get an exact accounting of the Continentals' strength, John Laurens confirmed the army's harrowing condition. The nakedness of the men and the number in hospitals had prevented them from a task as basic as fortifying the camp. Several generals had resisted assigning their half-starved men the heavy work of building redoubts. General Duportail, the chief engineer, had been reduced to digging trenches, which could easily be overrun by the British army's favorite tactic, a bayonet charge. With the worst of winter over, the likelihood of a British assault increased with every passing day. "It is a very bad principle to trust to the usual sluggishness and inactivity of the enemy," the younger Laurens nervously observed.[11]

Baron von Steuben's reforms were not only a struggle against mounting chaos; they were a race against time.

V

By the first weeks of March, when the Baron was getting to work on reforming the army, the starving time of mid-February had subsided into a precarious balance between supply and demand. The foraging efforts of Greene, Wayne, and Tilghman had brought some relief to the hard-pressed commissaries, but they were still only three or four days ahead of another famine. Suddenly, with a profusion that could only be called miraculous, the Schuylkill River was swarming with fish. The shad were making their annual migration upstream to spawn.

The hungry Continentals could not believe their eyes. The river was "almost boiling with the struggling fish." Shouting with joy, some men leaped into the freezing water at Fatlands Ford and began flinging them onto the banks. Pennsylvanians in the crowd, used to this annual visitation, said there was a better way to catch them. They advised the cavalry to ride into the river while other soldiers rushed upstream to Pawling's Ford, and stretched nets from bank to bank. Over a hundred cavalrymen went to work, beating the water with bushes, tree boughs, and sticks, shouting like madmen to further terrify the fish.

At Pawling's Ford, the catch was stupendous. With each haul, thousands of "tasty rich shad" were dragged ashore. Day after day, from dawn to dusk, the soldiers and the horsemen stayed on the job, until the whole Continental Army was "stuffed with fish" and hundreds of barrels were filled with surplus shad, which was salted for future consumption. "The lavish fish feast was a dramatic close to a long period of starvation," wrote the original teller of the tale, historian Harry Emerson Wildes. Since he published his book on Valley Forge in 1938, it has become part of the story of the encampment, repeated in at least a half dozen other books.

Alas, not so much as a single shad appeared in the Schuylkill River in March 1778. The story is as bogus as Baron von Steuben's lieutenant generalship. There are reams of evidence to support this rueful conclusion. In early March, Commissary General of Purchases William Buchanan roused himself from his usual torpor to write a letter reporting the existence of three hundred thousand pounds of dried fish at Baltimore. The committee in camp issued orders around the same time to buy ten thousand barrels of fish as an alternative to the dwindling meat supply.

Deputy Commissary John Chaloner, frantic as usual, was calling for the capture and salting of every available shad in the Delaware River. The Board of War, in a letter signed by no less than General Gates, deplored the absence of shad in the American camp. The fish was "much preferred" to pickled herring, Gates wrote. It was also preferred by General Washington, whose expense account records several purchases of shad for his headquarters table. Such an outlay would hardly seem necessary if the Schuylkill had been boiling with shad that spring.

Another problem with the story is the use of cavalry to drive the shad upstream. There were no cavalry at Valley Forge. They had all been sent to Trenton, where it was easier to procure forage for their horses. Far from undergoing an invasion of swarming shad in 1778, the Schuylkill was apparently devoid of the fish. Local diaries record that the price of shad skyrocketed because of the scarcity.

Is there an explanation for this mystery within the larger fable? The answer emerges from a letter written by Sir Charles Blagden, a physician with the British army. In April he wrote: "We have passed a seine across the Schuylkill to prevent the fish from getting up that river." Dr. Blagden was a fellow of the Royal Society, Britain's premier scientific group, and he added that he planned to "take some pains to find out how far this precaution is found effectual."

From the evidence of the desperate search for shad by the American commissary, the seine was very effectual. As Joseph Lee Boyle, former librarian at Valley Forge National Historical Park, has wryly concluded, "the miracle of the shad run at Valley Forge is just another fish story."[12]

VI

On the other hand, there was nothing fishy about acting Inspector General Baron von Steuben's overhaul of the Continental Army. Accompanied by his interpreter, Peter Stephen Duponceau, Steuben made frequent visits to Washington's headquarters, where he confided his dismaying discoveries to the commander in chief. It soon became clear that there was no hope of one man doing the job. To back up the Baron, Washington selected fourteen inspectors—one for each infantry brigade—from among the most talented and intelligent majors in the army. They would be Steuben's assistants. But the big question remained: where to begin?

Steuben decided the key to reviving the army was a manual that would enable the troops, with sufficient practice and instruction, to march and maneuver with precision and confidence on a drill field and on a battlefield. No such manual existed, and Steuben decided he would write one specifically for the American army in its present situation. Thus began a new ingredient in the race against time and other formidable difficulties.

Steuben still knew only a few English words. He had to write the chapters of his manual in French, which was translated by Duponceau into rudimentary English. In the late hours of the night, after a laborious day at headquarters, aides Alexander Hamilton and John Laurens added military terminology that was beyond Duponceau's knowledge.

As soon as chapter 1 was finished, Steuben had it distributed to the entire army, in itself no small task. There was no printing press at Valley Forge to speed the distribution. Copies had to be made in longhand. Here the brigade inspectors began playing a crucial role. They saw to it that additional copies were written and distributed throughout each brigade.

Reading the manual was only a first step. It would have been difficult enough to start a new form of drill by describing it to an army full of trained drillmasters. Such beings did not exist in the American army. Moreover, there was no hope of overcoming with a mere announcement the fixed opinion that officers did not descend to drilling their troops, even if the decree was backed by General Washington.

Steuben decided there was only one way to achieve this transformation. He would set the example by personally drilling a model company. He would show these self-satisfied lieutenants and captains and majors that it was not beneath the dignity of a lieutenant general from the King of Prussia's army to issue such commands—and the results would, he hoped, convince them that maybe there was something to be said for this portly foreigner's bizarre ideas.

The Baron quickly obtained General Washington's agreement, and an order was issued from headquarters, calling for one hundred men to be added to the commander in chief's guard. These soldiers became Steuben's model company.

So began a drama of large historical importance that now and then degenerated into comedy. The Baron's English remained rudimentary. None of his pupils spoke a word of his two principal languages, French and German. Nor did any of the brigade inspectors. His only interpreter was Duponceau, who still had zero grasp of military terminology. Aides Laurens and Hamilton could not help. They were needed at headquarters to handle General Washington's enormous correspondence.

March 19 was D (for Drill) day. The Baron arose at 3 a.m. and spent some time trying to memorize the English words for the first lesson. On Valley Forge's grand parade, his one hundred men, carefully selected from all fourteen brigades, were waiting for him, along with the fourteen brigade inspectors. Steuben ordered a dozen men to form a squad and began with a fundamental: how a soldier stood and carried himself. Here are the exact words from Steuben's manual: "He is to stand straight and firm upon his legs, with his head turned to the right so far as to bring his left eye over the waistcoat buttons; the heels two inches apart; the toes turned out; the belly drawn in a little, but without constraint; the breast a little projected; the shoulders square to the front and kept back; and the hands hanging down the sides, close to the thighs."[13]

Visit West Point or Annapolis or the Air Force Academy today and you will see cadets standing and walking in this basic posture, exactly as Friedrich von Steuben taught it on March 19, 1778, at Valley Forge.

The Baron's memorized English was soon exhausted, and he resorted to pantomime as he taught the rest of the first day's lesson: how a soldier came to attention, how he went to parade rest, how he "dressed" to the left and right with precise motions of his head. Next, with the Baron still performing, the squad learned to face to the left and right, and how to turn at the command "right about face." In each of these maneuvers, they were told exactly where to place their feet and hands.

Next came a lesson in marching in both the traditional 75 steps a minute and the "quick step" of 120 a minute. Steuben taught all these things to each soldier in his squad individually and then placed three men in a rank and reissued all the orders in the stentorian tones of the drillmaster he had been in his lieutenant's days in the Lestwitz Regiment of the King of Prussia's army.

Soon the ex–lieutenant general created by Ben Franklin's imagination had his entire squad dressing right and left and facing about and marching by files—another important lesson, in which each man had to maintain an exact distance from his file leader. They also learned the important battle-field maneuver of marching obliquely to the right and left, again with exact instructions on how the feet and shoulders were placed, so no one got bumped and threw the whole squad into confusion.

Finally, Steuben bellowed: "Squad—halt!" and went back to individual instruction to teach each man the position of the soldier under arms. Here the manual was lengthy and exact, specifying the precise height of the "fire-lock" (gun), the location of the fingers on the butt, and the need to keep the barrel "almost perpendicular" on the left shoulder.

The brigade inspectors and the rest of the model company had been watching all this with intense interest. For them, Steuben was a celebrity. With his Star of Fidelity on his breast and his soldierly bearing, he looked and acted like a lieutenant general from the army of Frederick the Great. Here he was, drilling a squad of soldiers with passion and even ferocity, something they had never seen even a lieutenant do in the American army.

Steuben now broke up the rest of the model company into squads and ordered the brigade inspectors to take over teaching them the manual's first lesson. The Baron walked from squad to squad, adjusting a musket here, demonstrating the footwork of facing about there. Meanwhile, on the edge of the Grand Parade, a crowd was gathering that included officers and enlisted men. They too found the spectacle of the lieutenant general doing a drill sergeant's work an irresistible sight. At the end of the day, Steuben collected the squads into the entire company and they performed all the evolutions with an élan that left the spectators virtually speechless.[14]

VII

On succeeding days, Steuben taught his model company how to wheel to the left and right. Next came a simplified version of the manual of arms and the art of firing the musket and reloading swiftly for another round.

Then came the equally difficult art of charging with the bayonet, a primary eighteenth-century tactic. The butt of the gun had to be under the right arm and the rest of the piece firmly gripped by the left hand, while the butt was pressed by the right arm against the soldier's side.

Perhaps the most important of the later lessons was the art of marching in a compact column, instead of the Indian files to which the Continentals had become addicted. Steuben's manual provided instructions as well as illustrations of how a regiment assembled when it was ordered to form a column.[15]

Even in these first lessons, Steuben was teaching something far more important than the mechanics of drilling and marching and handling a gun. He was showing these men and the spectators that doing these things right made a soldier proud of himself. Marching in exact formations gave him a sense of confidence in himself and his brothers in arms. Here and in future lessons in his manual the Baron was inculcating the idea that being a soldier required far more hard work and attention to detail than civilians imagined.

To perform courageously on a battlefield, a soldier had to prepare for that ultimate test by acquiring pride and a readiness to obey orders instantly. He had to keep his weapons in pristine condition. His uniform must also be neat and well fitting; when he looked in a mirror, he should see a *soldier*, a special being radically different from the civilian he had once been.

VIII

The Baron was not satisfied with transforming the drill and marching procedures of the Continental Army. He wanted to see a psychological, even a spiritual change in the relationships between the officers and men. He wrote succinct summaries of the duties of each officer in a regiment, from the colonel to the lieutenants. Perhaps the most important were the instructions to the captain. The opening lines are worth reading because they remain the cornerstone of the U.S. Army's philosophy of leadership today.

A captain cannot be too careful of the company the state has committed to his care. . . . His first object should be, to gain the love of his men, by treating them with all possible kindness and humanity. . . . He should know every man of his company by name and character. He should often visit those who are sick, speak tenderly to them, see that the public provision, whether of medicine or diet, is duly administered and procure them besides such comforts and conveniences as are in his power. The attachment that arises from this kind of attention to the sick and wounded, is almost inconceivable.[16]

IX

Steuben realized, of course, that the army would not achieve these practical and spiritual transformations instantaneously. Even his model company did not always perform up to his expectations. When it failed, the troops got a glimpse of another side of the ex–lieutenant general: his volcanic temper. He showered his pupils with oaths in French and German, adding to this choice collection the only English curse he had acquired, "Goddamn!"

During one of these blowups, caused when the model company misunderstood some complicated command, perhaps "to the rear march!" and one half collided with the other half, the Baron's temper rose to stratospheric heights. Duponceau was frantic at his inability to communicate Steuben's orders. The men stumbled around, trying to sort themselves back into orderly ranks.

Out of the spectators on the edge of the parade ground stepped a New York captain named Benjamin Walker, who asked in perfect French if he could help the great lieutenant general communicate with his pupils. "If I had seen an angel from heaven," Steuben later said, "I could not have been more rejoiced." Captain Walker instantly became his aide-de-camp, and in a few minutes the company performed the maneuver perfectly.[17]

As other companies and regiments began doing the Baron's exercises, they too were sometimes treated to a barrage of multilingual Steuben curses. It did not bother the soldiers in the least; the language they spoke inside their huts was not exactly drawing-room English. If anything, the curses contributed to Steuben's reputation as an exotic character who was good for a laugh now and then.

Soon there was a genuine affection between this odd but famous German general and the men in the ranks. They told stories of how he occasionally cursed the slow learners until he was exhausted and then turned to Walker for help: "Viens, Walker, mon ami, mon bon ami! Sacré! Goddamn de gaucheries of dese badauts. Je ne plus. I can curse dem no more."[18]

The Baron's long years as a bachelor also made him the right man in the right place when it came to making Valley Forge a more hospitable place, in spite of the ragged uniforms and bare feet of the troops. He had a dread of dining alone. Whenever possible he had guests to dinner. One of his first parties mocked the army's lack of decent clothing with a soldierly bravado that delighted the guests. No one was admitted to the feast unless he showed up in a torn pair of breeches.

As Duponceau recalled in his memoir, the guests all "clubbed" their rations, and Steuben's German manservant saw to the cooking. "We dined sumptuously on tough beefsteak and potatoes, with hickory nuts for dessert," the young Frenchman wrote. Instead of wine, they procured some cheap whiskey from one of the camp's sutlers and made "salamanders"—a potion that required the drinkers to set the liquid on fire and gulp it down, flames and all.

"Such a set of ragged, and at the same time merry fellows was never brought together," Duponceau concluded. The story sent the Baron's popularity soaring to new heights.[19]

X

While Steuben drilled and cursed and drilled an ever larger number of Continentals, another form of national salvation, this one engineered by General Washington, was taking shape in Nathanael Greene's hut, where the new quartermaster was hard at work. From his first orders, the Rhode Islander emphatically took command of the disorganized department.

To Deputy Quartermaster General James Abeel, who worked at Moore Hall, Greene wrote: "I wish you to minute down every place where you find publick [sic] stores, what they are and in whose hands. There has been great losses sustained for want of attention." To General William Smallwood in Wilmington he opined: "It appears to me more and more probable that this dispute will terminate in a war of funds." That meant it was absolutely necessary to stop wasting millions of dollars in the style of the old quarter-master department. Greene told Colonel Clement Biddle, the army's forage-master, that "we have been looking over your plan for the foragemaster general's department. . . . You will give us an account of your former condi-tions of serving, who were paid by the month, who received a commission, what it was and on what it arose. Give us a full history of the latter." [20]

This was the voice of authority speaking. Greene was no less blunt in discussing his department with President Henry Laurens. He pointed out how short the time was before the next campaign was likely to open. That meant he would have to pay the highest prices for every-thing and needed "a large and immediate supply of cash." He expected Congress to support him without quibbles or harassment. He had heard nothing from General Mifflin (he never would) and had no idea of the size of the mess he was inheriting. But he had already learned that the depart-ment owed huge sums to many people. They would have to be paid as soon as possible.

Rather than let Congress into the picture, Greene wanted the author-ity to appoint a board to settle the accounts. With brutal realism he re-minded the president that their money was depreciating faster and faster. He added, almost as an aside, the wry comment, "Nothing can correct this evil but a large tax," assuming both he and Laurens knew no such measure would ever pass Congress, which was still determined to rely on public virtue to force its currency to be accepted.

Wagoners were "not to be got" for under ten pounds a month, which Greene admitted was "a most extravagant demand." But "necessity" would oblige the department to pay it. Hundreds of horses were lost each year because of the carelessness of underpaid drivers. Saving even one good horse would equal the pay of a wagoner for a whole year.[21]

Greene not only could be hardheaded, he could think big. To Clement Biddle went a mind-boggling letter on March 25, urging him to begin setting up a chain of magazines to create a reserve food supply that the army could use on the march. Greene wanted the foragemaster to collect as many as two hundred thousand bushels of grain in each magazine, which were to be located in both Pennsylvania and New Jersey. "You cannot get about this too soon," Greene wrote.[22]

The general also published in Dunlap's *Pennsylvania Packet, or, The General Advertiser* an open letter to the "Inhabitants of the United States" which demonstrated he had a talent for what we would call public relations. Greene announced that he was giving his deputy quartermasters certificates drawn upon the credit of the United States which they could use in lieu of the depreciating currency to pay for their purchases. He frankly admitted that the previous regime had been responsible for the employment of "improper persons" who perpetrated numerous "irregularities" in seizing grain, hay, and cattle belonging to "the good people of the country." He promised an end to these practices by hiring new personnel who would behave more decently and pay fairer prices. The certificates would be redeemed as swiftly as possible after they were issued.

General Greene hoped these reassurances would win the "cheerful aid and assistance" of all those who were ready to promote "the common cause of American freedom and the rights of mankind."[23]

XI

Reforming the quartermaster department was not the only problem on General Greene's mind. His wife, Catherine, had arrived at Valley Forge while he was wrestling with the decision to take the job. Known to most people as Caty, she was a shapely brunette with "high color . . . vivacious expression and a snapping pair of dark eyes." Caty was twelve years younger than Nathanael and had a tendency to flirt with handsome men.

She was, to use current terminology, high-maintenance, and she frequently reminded Nathanael of his tendency to neglect her while trying to win the war.

At Valley Forge, Caty was soon visiting with Mrs. Washington, who found her good company. General Steuben was another conquest; Caty was probably the only woman in the camp who spoke French. This talent soon led to not a little dalliance with the Marquis de Lafayette. Somewhat more serious was her flirtation with swaggering General Anthony Wayne, whose wife, Polly, had told him he was not welcome in his nearby home because of his frequent philandering. Wayne already had two attractive women in the vicinity of the winter camp to whom he paid frequent visits.

Another general's wife, Lucy Knox, spouse of artillery commander Henry Knox, began telling people that "all was not well" between General Greene and his wife. Caty and Lucy, who weighed over three hundred pounds and was unlikely to charm any of Caty's conquests, began a feud that lasted until the end of the war. Nathanael, knowing how much it pleased Caty, often reported on Lucy's latest weight gain.

General Greene refused to worry about Wayne as a romantic rival. The Rhode Islander had been through similar contretemps with Caty before, and there would be many more in the future. Flirting was her way of avoiding boredom; he was fairly certain that she would never be unfaithful to him—nor he to her, although he occasionally used the threat to make her obey him.[24]

Also very much on the scene was the wife of Major General Lord Stirling, Lady Sarah Livingston Stirling, and her attractive daughter, Catherine, known as Lady Kitty. Determined to live like the Scottish nobleman whose title he claimed, Stirling used the wealth left to him by his father to build a mansion on a thousand-acre estate in Basking Ridge, New Jersey. Lady Stirling and Lady Kitty arrived at Valley Forge in an elegant coach accompanied by a swarm of servants.

No one seemed to find incongruous the Stirlings' espousal of upper-class British ways in the midst of a revolution that preached equality. But their high style intimidated many of the officers' wives at Valley Forge, in particular Catherine Greene. She grew convinced that her husband's attentions to Lady Kitty were virtually synonymous with infidelity. All in all, this handful of ranking wives created almost as much emotional furor at the winter camp as General Washington's struggle with Mifflin, Conway, Gates, and their allies in Congress.

XII

In York, General Washington's spokesmen from the committee in camp began arguing with the ideologues of Congress about the commander in chief's demand for half pay for his officers. Leading the charge were none other than Francis Dana and his New Hampshire colleague, Nathaniel Folsom. The sight and sound of these two staunch New Englanders advocating the key proposal of Washington's program must have given James Lovell and his friends instant dyspepsia.

On the eve of the committee's departure for Valley Forge, Lovell had smugly assured Sam Adams that "both my colleagues" (Dana and Folsom) were opposed to half pay. They too were sick of the way the officers talked about "wounded feelings, spirit of the soldier, honor dearer than life" when degrees of rank were the issue. But when money became the topic, honor went out the window. Now, thanks to Washington's persuasive powers, "Brother D. [Dana] differs," Lovell wrote sourly to another New England colleague.[25]

Half pay split Congress into two ferociously quarreling blocs. Dana and Folsom argued on behalf of Washington that not only should the officers have half pay for life, but their widows should have pensions and the officers should have the right to sell their commissions, in the style of the British army. The New Englanders marshaled a solid bloc, led by James Lovell, to contest the idea. The southerners responded with an equally solid bloc, leaving the middle states of Pennsylvania, New York, and New Jersey divided.

At the heart of the argument was the old clash between the true whig ideology of virtue and the voices of realism. The ideologues claimed that half pay was a large step toward a standing army, which would endanger the liberties of the republic. They also argued that Congress lacked the authority to bind future American governments to such a promise. The realists pointed out that Congress was borrowing huge sums of money and promising to pay interest on it, which would require annual outlays long after the war ended.

The two sides regularly indulged in shouting matches and personal vitriol which, fortunately for them, went unreported because most of the time they were in the committee of the whole, a legislative device in which no records were kept. Even in the formal exchanges in Congress, the language was so intemperate that sixteen delegates drew up a "Pledge of Order" in which they agreed to speak no more than ten minutes and never more than twice on any subject, and they would "unite in supporting order & preserving decency and politeness in debate." [26]

Ironically, one of the more violent opponents of half pay was General Washington's strongest supporter in Congress, President Henry Laurens. There was more than a little of the puritan spirit in this descendant of French Huguenots. In the committee of the whole, during which various congressmen held the chair, Laurens waded into the claims of imminent disaster that Washington and his congressional spokesmen made about the vital importance of half pay.

Laurens was equally vehement in his letters. He told James Duane of New York that he found the way the demand for half pay was couched particularly offensive. He simply did not believe that they would lose "all your good officers." Laurens thought there were still "thousands" of potential officers whose hearts "have not bowed the knee to luxury or to mammon and clung to the spirit of the "original compact" —the pure patriotism that launched the Revolution. [27]

Demonstrating their reluctance—and their hostility to the regular army—in the midst of this raging debate Congress produced a resolution empowering General Washington to call up five thousand militia from the states of Maryland, Pennsylvania, and New Jersey. The commander in chief struggled to remain calm in replying to this brainstorm. He thanked Congress for the power but earnestly pointed out that mustering so many militia would take a huge amount of "time, difficulty and expence." The previous year, when Congress had told him to call up a similar number of Pennsylvanians, not more than a thousand could be raised. When they went home after their two months' service, not more than a hundred showed up to replace them.[28]

XIII

To bolster Francis Dana and Nathaniel Folsom, Joseph Reed and Gouverneur Morris rushed to York, where Morris, with his gift for fast answers and, when necessary, invective, swiftly became the leader of the pro–half pay bloc. Soon they had a narrow majority, and it looked as if the ideologues were on the brink of defeat. But the crafty New Englanders pulled another argument from their collective hat: the question was so momentous, it should be submitted to the states for a final decision. This was tantamount to a sentence of death, and everyone knew it. Allowing every legislator in the thirteen states to pontificate on such a contentious subject would reduce it to drivel before summer.

The motion was defeated by a single vote, and a glum James Lovell wrote to Samuel Adams that he had better prepare himself for "a half pay system, on which the existence of the army [during] this campaign is said . . . to depend." Lovell thought a distinction should be made between half pay, which he called "a nuisance," and a military establishment, which was a "curse." In other words, the true whigs reserved the right to abolish the regular army at the first opportunity.[29]

At this point, both sides were exhausted. Neither had the energy to muster its forces for voting on a resolution to make half pay the law of the land. In Valley Forge, this congressional foot-dragging did not go down well with the officer corps. Washington, having done everything in his power for the measure, was reduced to a worried spectator.

XIV

Not all the news from York was bad. In the good-news category was the disintegration of the Board of War. First Horatio Gates decided the make-Washington-resign game was over and requested an assignment to a field command. His friends in Congress sent him back to the Northern Department, where there was little to do. But Horatio had not quite abandoned his fondness for intrigue. On March 24 Henry Laurens wrote Lafayette: "There was lately the appearance of a pretty little attempt to render that command [Gates's] independent of all orders but that of Congress." The arrangement would have made Gates a somewhat murky equal of Washington. But the narrow pro-Washington majority defeated the proposal.[30]

Next General Thomas Mifflin saw the mounting wave of the Washington counterattack—signaled by the rush in Congress to deny that anyone had ever uttered a word against the commander in chief—and started looking for an exit. For a while there was talk of making him commander in chief of the Pennsylvania militia. Board of War member Timothy Pickering, Washington's former adjutant general, supported this idea. "I do not know anybody who would be so likely to rouse the militia as he; and they will need a spur." Since he was referring to the Pennsylvania militia, this came close to the understatement of the century.[31]

Benjamin Rush, who had spent the winter supporting the Lancaster ideologues who wanted to call out every militiaman in Pennsylvania, may have had a hand in this idea. But it apparently did not suit General Mifflin. He decided to join the chorus of those who were denying they had ever entertained so much as a negative thought about George Washington. To the historian (and gossip) William Gordon, who was collecting information about the plot, Mifflin wrote: "I declare to you, with the greatest sincerity and solemnity, that I never formed a plan or a party to injury General Washington's command."

Gates wrote an almost identical letter with the same fervent disavowal. Gordon piously assured them he believed every word of this nonsense. Both men also devoted not a little time to trashing General

Conway as the real author of the supposedly fictitious plot—a tactic their friends in Congress likewise pursued with vigor.[32]

Mifflin had not spent the winter wining and dining congressmen at his Angelica estate in vain. With no warning, Congress passed a resolution to grant General Mifflin leave from the Board of War to rejoin Washington's army. Once more the anti-Washington bloc in Congress was flexing its mostly New England muscle. Quartermaster General Nathanael Greene was outraged. Washington accepted the news with unruffled demeanor, probably because he suspected—or even knew—that President Laurens had an unpleasant surprise up his political sleeve for the "pivot."

In a wry letter to Gouverneur Morris, the general claimed to be "not a little surprized [sic] to find a certain gentleman who some time ago, (when a cloud of darkness hung heavy over us and our affairs looked gloomy) was desirous of resigning, now stepping forward in the line of the army." Washington said he had "nothing *personally* to oppose to it." But he wondered how Mifflin could reconcile his conduct to his status as "an officer and man of honor." This was the sort of letter that Morris could show to selected congressmen, making it clear that General Washington's opinion of Mifflin remained low. In a few weeks, with the anticipated help of President Henry Laurens, the commander in chief would reveal just how low his opinion was.[33]

XV

At Valley Forge, as March ebbed into April, Baron von Steuben was busy spreading his reforms to every brigade and division of the Continental Army. The process began with an order from General Washington on Tuesday, March 24: "At nine o'clock precisely all the brigades will begin their exercises." Steuben had already conferred with his brigade inspectors, and at nine they went to work, dividing each regiment into squads of twenty men, who were drilled on their brigade's parade ground. Steuben, looking like a veritable god of war on a huge horse, rode from one brigade to another, correcting here, praising there.

A glimpse of how hard the men worked at this new regimen comes from Private Joseph Plumb Martin of Connecticut. He and his company had spent the worst of the winter on foraging duty in the countryside, where they guarded what the commissaries purchased and loaded wagons with hay, corn, flour, and other farm products for Valley Forge. Martin slept in a warm farmhouse and never had to worry about where his next meal was coming from. Back in Valley Forge in early April, he went hungry again and spent all his time "in learning the Baron de Steuben's new Prussian exercise." Life, Martin groused, "was a continual drill." [34]

Soon it was time to make a great leap forward. The army would stop drilling by squads and companies and begin learning how to maneuver as battalions. Steuben now had to deal with the appalling disorganization of the American army—companies consisting of a single man, regiments of a handful. He solved the problem by creating his own "provisional" regiments—a nice match for his role as provisional inspector general. He amalgamated all the privates in a brigade into one or two regiments for drill-field purposes. He subdivided these temporary entities into companies and platoons and assigned officers to them. That usually left a surplus of officers, which did not bother Steuben. He ordered them to stand by and watch. Later in the training session, they took charge of the privates and issued the orders they had learned from Steuben's manual. [35]

The army's progress was phenomenal. No one from General Washington to the lowliest lieutenant could believe it. The mails were soon full of praise for the Baron. John Laurens told his father: "I must not omit to inform you that the Baron is making sensible progress with our soldiers. The officers seem to have a high opinion of him and discover [display] a docility from which we may augur the most happy effects." [36]

The new adjutant general, Colonel Alexander Scammell, was even more enthusiastic. "Baron Steuben . . . has undertaken the discipline of the army and shows himself to be a perfect master of it, not only in the grand maneuvers, but in the most minute details." Soon, in the Baron's own words, the army was making maneuvers with ten and twelve battalions (regiments) "with as much precision as the evolution of a single company." [37]

John Laurens told his father that Steuben was "exerting himself like a lieutenant anxious for promotion." It was time to reward the Baron, who made it clear that he expected to be made inspector general with the rank of major general. General Washington still hesitated. He wanted to make sure his brigadiers did not erupt, as they had over Conway's promotion. Even more important, General Conway was still the official inspector general.

Washington had John Laurens canvass the brigadiers, who all praised the Baron's "zeal and abilities" and thought he was "deserving of the grade which he asks for." A few days later, the Conway problem was solved by none other than General Conway. Stewing over the disaster of the aborted Canadian expedition, he grew even more petulant when Congress and General Gates left him in limbo in northern New York. The result was an infuriated letter to Henry Laurens detailing how he had been "box'd about in a most indecent manner" and submitting his resignation as major general and inspector general. The letter was undoubtedly a bluff, like so many other resignations in this narrative. But Henry Laurens did not waste a moment in persuading Congress to accept it. The same day he notified General Washington of this gratifying event.[38]

Two days later, Washington replied to President Laurens, saying he could be "no longer silent about the merits of Baron Steuben." He described the drillmaster's achievement with the army and closed by recommending him as the new inspector general with the rank of major general, which would, he hoped, include the "incidental emoluments"—namely, a major general's salary. It hardly needs to be added that Congress acquiesced, and soon the Baron was telling friends in Europe how he had managed this semimiracle.

To the Prussian ambassador in Paris, Baron von der Goltz, Steuben wrote in his most ebullient style that the task had not been an easy one. The Americans wanted everything in the English manner, the French in their own distinctive *mode*. "When I presented a plate of *sauerkraut* dressed in the Prussian style, they all wanted to throw it out the window." But he persisted and by the "force of Goddamns" proved that his cookery was "the best."[39]

The Baron's most interesting observation revealed that he too had learned a great deal from his experience. To another old Prussian friend he wrote: "The genius of this nation is not in the least to be compared with that of the Prussians, Austrians or French. You say to your soldier 'Do this and he doeth it'; but I am obliged to say: 'This is the reason why you ought to do that: and then he [the American soldier] does it.'"[40]

XVI

Did a well-trained army mean that General Washington had nothing to fear from the British? Far from it. The month of April, when Baron von Steuben's program reached its zenith, General Greene's revitalized quartermaster department began functioning in high gear, and Jeremiah Wadsworth's reorganized commissary department began delivering ample food, was a month of high anxiety at Valley Forge.

EIGHT

FROM ANXIETY TO EXULTATION

THE WORRY THAT fueled anxiety throughout Valley Forge in April was fear of a British offensive. There were persistent rumors that General Howe would soon receive massive reinforcements—as many as twenty thousand men. Meanwhile, all the other reforms General Washington had persuaded the committee in camp to recommend lay on the table in Congress while the politicians debated half pay for officers.

In long letters to President Henry Laurens and Virginia congressman John Bannister, Washington reiterated his support for half pay. To prove his point, he reported that almost ninety officers had resigned from the Virginia Continental line because they were convinced that Congress was going to reject the half-pay proposal. If this opinion spread to officers of other states, it would "shake the existence of the army."

This looming disaster stirred Washington to a searching commentary on patriotism. In his report on the army's needs, he had already criticized the true whig theory that public virtue should be entirely disinterested. Now the commander in chief extended his argument to an emotion that few politicians dared to discuss frankly. "Men may speculate as they will— they may talk of patriotism—they may draw a few examples from ancient story of great achievements performed by its influence. But whoever builds upon it as a sufficient basis for conducting a long and bloody war, will find themselves deceived in the end."

Washington added that he did not mean "to exclude altogether the idea of patriotism. I know it exists, and I know it has done much in the present contest. But . . . it must be aided by a prospect of interest or some reward." [1]

An even bigger worry was the failure of the states to fill the quotas for their Continental regiments. Officers who had just returned from Massachusetts reported there was "not the least prospect" of getting men from there before June—"if then"—and the numbers would be small. The various towns were being asked to supply only the shortfall from last year's quota—with no reference to men who had died or were invalided by wounds or sickness in the interim. This meant that the fifteen Bay State regiments would be short four thousand men. New Hampshire was doing the same sort of halfhearted recruiting. A letter from General Putnam revealed a similar state of lassitude and/or indifference in Connecticut.

Pennsylvania and Maryland, ignoring Washington's advice, resorted to offering bounties for voluntary enlistments, "to little purpose." The Pennsylvanians, continuing their career of contemptuous indifference to the Continental Army, had ignored Washington's "pointed injunctions" and recruited deserters from the British army, who, Washington predicted, would "embrace the first opportunity of escaping with our arms." Virginia was the only state that had taken Washington's advice and drafted men from the militia. But the numbers were inadequate and had since been lowered by desertion. Worse, the wholesale resignation of officers had left the state's regiments in disarray.

The clothier general, James Mease, in spite of his resignation, was still wandering somewhere in the interior of Pennsylvania, instead of joining the army, as Washington had insisted he should in the report to the committee in camp. Adjutant General Alexander Scammell, reported on April 18 that of the 7,489 rank and file fit for duty, 1,183 were unable to stand guard duty or serve in detachments "for want of clothing." It was almost criminal for the army to be shirtless when there was reportedly enough cloth in New England to make uniforms for one hundred thousand men.

This "fatal error," which had contributed to the deaths and desertions of thousands of men, must be corrected, General Washington wrote.

Dolefully, Washington summarized his situation to President Henry Laurens: "My agreement with the 'Comee' [committee] entitled me to expect upwards of forty thousand Continental troops, exclusive of artillery and Horse [cavalry]" for the coming campaign. "Instead of these, what are my prospects?" [2]

II

On April 16, Congressman John Bannister of Virginia wrote sympathetically to Washington that Congress's ignorance of military affairs was appalling. It is worth noting that this frequent correspondent was a political opponent of Richard Henry Lee. He was also one of the few congressmen who combined politics with a military career. Later in 1778, he left Congress to become a lieutenant colonel of cavalry in the Virginia Continental Line. Washington replied in a long, cordial letter that tackled another problem facing the army.

The commander in chief expressed his concern about the hostility— he called it "jealousy"—which some congressmen labored to foment against the army. He thought there was "nothing more injurious or more unjustly founded." This emotion emanated from the "received opinion" that standing armies were dangerous to a state. But this opinion was originally directed at standing armies in time of *peace*. Congress seemed inclined to the bizarre opinion that they were dangerous in time of *war*. The opinion was especially inappropriate to the American army, all of whose members were fellow citizens. With a fervor that bespoke deep conviction, General Washington insisted, "We should all be considered, Congress, the Army &C as one people, embarked in one cause."

Here the commander in chief, without naming names, was again criticizing "the narrow politics" of Samuel Adams, James Lovell, and too many other New England congressmen, with their obsessive conviction that a regular army was a menace. He called their opinions "impolitic" in the extreme and feared they would have an opposite effect. Instead of browbeating the army into submission, they would arouse hostility in its ranks. "Among individuals, the most certain way to make a man your enemy is to tell him you esteem him as such."

As one historian commented, the letter was meant for "more eyes and more minds" in Congress than Mr. Bannister's.[3]

III

Another worry was the continuing American inability to prevent loyalists and profit-hungry Americans from selling food to the British in Philadelphia. The problem was those nine capital roads that General Armstrong, commander of the Pennsylvania militia, bemoaned back in December. The dilemma was compounded by the continuing decline in the militia's enthusiasm to do their share of the job. General Washington had assigned them the task of patrolling the area east of the Schuylkill, and given the west side of the arc around Philadelphia to the Continentals.

The British soon added another ingredient to this more or less insoluble problem. They organized some of the loyalists in Philadelphia and its vicinity into armed bands. One was called the Pennsylvania Volunteers, the other the Independent Dragoons. They served without pay, living on plunder from the rebels. Another combative group lived in a mountainous area called Tulpehocken, between Philadelphia and Lancaster. Loyalists to a man, they formed a corps of horsemen, equipped with rifles and axes. They were all dead shots and were soon terrorizing rebel militiamen and politicians.[4]

More and more militia officers found it dangerous to sleep in their own houses, lest a knock on the door lead to inglorious captivity. In one of their first raids, the Tulpehocken guerrillas brought in fifty prisoners, many of them badly wounded, and the leader of a local rebel committee. The Pennsylvania Volunteers did almost as well, capturing five officers and forty privates. The Independent Dragoons swept into Bucks County and burned a fuling mill and thousands of yards of cloth for Washington's army. They also captured cattle being forwarded to the Continental Army, forcing the escorts to take a more circuitous route to Valley Forge, which markedly reduced the flesh on the animals. This show of force vastly encouraged the farmers who were eager to sell their produce to the British.[5]

An agitated Joseph Reed warned Thomas Wharton, the president of Pennsylvania's Supreme Executive Council, of the impact of these minor defeats. Reed said he was not terribly worried about the British buying food from the locals. With the Delaware open, there was no hope of starving the royal army out of Philadelphia. What concerned him was the way the "minds of the inhabitants" were being "seduced." The more familiar the civilians became with the British and loyalists, the weaker their revolutionary principles became. For twenty miles around Philadelphia, no one accepted America's depreciating currency. The hope of getting hard money for their produce inclined most farmers to hide it from American foragers and deny its existence. In Reed's opinion, this was tantamount to disloyalty, if not treason.[6]

Things were not much better on the west side of the Schuylkill, where the Continentals were patrolling. Here, the problem was the tendency for the soldiers to be sweet-talked by the farmers, once they got to know them. Too many Continental officers imitated Colonel Daniel Morgan, whose regiment of riflemen spent most of their time on this detached duty. The Old Wagoner was a softy when dealing with civilians, especially women. Often, when he caught a man or woman heading to Philadelphia with provisions, he would seize the produce, pay for it, and tell the smuggler to go home. Morgan tended to think of the food sellers as merely misguided. General Washington, on the other hand, grimly warned he would execute one of them to terrify the rest.[7]

Joseph Reed's solution, he told Thomas Wharton, was to give up on the Continentals and turn the whole enforcement of the quarantine of Philadelphia over to the militia on both sides of the Schuylkill. Here the normally astute Reed succumbed to the illusion that significant numbers of Pennsylvanians could be persuaded to fight for the Revolution. He assured Wharton that the more often the militia were summoned to duty, the better soldiers they would become. This would have drawn a guffaw from Daniel Morgan, whose letters were a veritable litany of contempt for the militia, especially their officers.[8]

The commander of the Pennsylvania militia on the east side of the Schuylkill was Brigadier General John Lacey, who was all of twenty-three years old. His letters to Washington are a continual refutation of Reed's optimism, and a confirmation of Morgan's contempt. Reflecting the illusory world in which the Pennsylvania government lived, President Wharton told Washington that General Lacey, though "active," might need advice from time to time. But thanks to their "righteous cause," Wharton was sure they would "surmount their difficulties."

Lacey needed a lot more than advice from General Washington and true whig inspiration from Wharton. Early in March he wrote Washington that he had just received four hundred reinforcements from Cumberland and York counties. But only one hundred of them had guns, and half of these lacked flints, which meant the guns could not be fired. Previous to the arrival of this well-equipped band, he had a grand total of fifty men in his force. That explained why he was unable to do much about loyalist raids on cattle being herded to Valley Forge.

As for people "taken on the road going to market" in Philadelphia, Lacey found it very difficult to get enough evidence to convict them of anything, since they were ready with a plethora of excuses to evade the law.[9]

IV

Another glimpse of the chaos with which Washington was dealing comes from Major John Jameson, who was assigned to the east side of the Schuylkill to supervise the militia. Washington told him to disable all the flour mills in the area, to cut off this popular form of smuggling at its source. Jameson told Washington he was aware of the flow of flour from the mills but could do nothing about it because the militiamen on duty were "the greatest villains I ever heard of." Many of them were accepting bribes from the local inhabitants to let them into Philadelphia. He had caught two of these miscreants, but when he ordered the militia officers to summon all their men to his headquarters to arrest them, the two malefactors, obviously warned, deserted to the British.

Jameson had discovered that two other militiamen were robbing both patriots and loyalists without discrimination, but he was unable to seize them because there were not three men in the entire militia detachment that he would "trust my life with." He was going to wait for a new round of militia to arrive before he took action. When Jameson finally seized several of these perpetrators, including "one Tyson, a notorious villain," and shipped them to Valley Forge, they were tried by court-martial two months later.

Their punishment hardly fit the crimes Jameson so heatedly described. For "supplying the enemy with provisions" they were ordered confined to the Valley Forge guardhouse for a month, and during the day were to work as laborers in the camp. Meanwhile the distraught Jameson reported that in a single week, no fewer than one hundred women were intercepted carrying flour and other provisions into the city. Apparently they were simply ordered to go home, and their bundles were seized.[10]

After a wearisome search, Major Jameson located Brigadier General Lacey, and together they destroyed all the flour mills on creeks that ran into the Schuylkill. In Philadelphia, one of General Howe's aides smugly informed his diary: "This does not hurt us very much because we are always sure of provisions from England, while they ruin their own country by such acts."[11]

Washington did not share this view of the struggle. He agreed with Joseph Reed that the more business the local inhabitants did with the British, the faster their patriotism declined. He prodded Lacey to start court-martialing the violators using militia officers as judges. Soon the young brigadier was reporting that nineteen prisoners were in the dock. Washington told him to send the worst offenders to Lancaster to be put at hard labor for five or six months. Those with good character ought to be released "with an assurance of being hanged" if they were caught again.[12]

V

Pennsylvania was not the only state showing the strain of the lengthening war. In Delaware about 150 loyalists, led by a man known as China Clow, built a fort on the Maryland border, proclaimed the Revolution a fraud, and began plundering nearby patriots. The leader's real name was Cheney Clow; he was born in England, like many loyalists, and knew how to arouse resentment against the rebel government. Caesar Rodney, the president of Delaware, assembled 140 militia and laid siege to the fort. Clow and company panicked and fled. "If they had not been opposed verry [*sic*] suddenly and with spirit," Rodney told Henry Laurens, "they would have become formidable in a little time."

Rodney ordered the fugitives pursued by horsemen, who captured about fifty of them. Twenty of the prisoners were bachelors, and they were forced to enlist in the Delaware Continental regiment—not exactly a sign of the government's ability to raise men for General Washington's army. Supported by the numerous loyalists in Delaware and Maryland, Clow would remain at large until 1782.[13]

In New Jersey, above Philadelphia on the Delaware, another group of loyalists, the West Jersey Volunteers, set up a base at Billingsport and began attacking militia leaders and revolutionary spokesmen and looting farms of food and forage for the British in Philadelphia. The base was too well fortified for the militia to attack, and an ugly civil war was soon ravaging the countryside. The rebels retaliated savagely on anyone they caught. On Easter Sunday, 1778, they flogged one loyalist so badly the man died. This was probably a sign of their weakness and frustration in the face of the well-equipped loyalists.[14]

In the South Carolina backcountry, a group of six hundred loyalists led by a man named Joseph Coffell revolted against the rebel government in Charleston and rampaged across the state, looting, burning, and terrifying patriot farmers. The loyalists soon crossed the Savannah River into Georgia, where they began wreaking similar devastation. The backcountry people begged for support from the Continental soldiers in South

Carolina. There was grave concern that the marauders would join forces with British troops and Indian allies in Florida, and open a new front in the war.[15]

VI

These worries were suddenly reduced to the trivial level by news from England. In mid-April, a visitor to Valley Forge gave General Washington a copy of a handbill reporting two acts passed by the British Parliament, offering the Americans terms on which they might be reconciled to the mother country. On the outskirts of the camp was a cart loaded with additional copies.

The first act surrendered Parliament's right to lay "any duty, tax or assessment" on Americans in all the colonies in North America. The second bill empowered George III to appoint commissioners who were prepared to negotiate with the Continental Congress and other legislative bodies to bring an end to "the disorders" that were agitating some colonies and reassure all and sundry that they had no reason for further concern about their "liberties and rights." The commissioners would also have the power to declare a "cessation of hostilities" if they deemed it appropriate and also to suspend the act of Parliament forbidding British trade with America, as well as grant pardons and appoint governors of colonies if the negotiations ended successfully.[16]

General Washington warned Henry Laurens that General Howe had dispatched "a large cargoe [sic]" of these handbills from Philadelphia. Washington was not sure the news was genuine or "contrived in Philadelphia," but he had no doubt that it was "meant to poison the minds of the people & detach the wavering, at least, from our cause." After eight months in Pennsylvania, where the wavering seemed to be in the majority, it was easy to see why Washington was alarmed. He urged Laurens to push Congress to launch an immediate investigation of the document and expose "the delusion and fraud it contains."[17]

If this peace proposal was authentic, it made Washington only more alarmed about the condition of his army. It struck him as all too logical that the British might launch an offensive to try to inflict a defeat on the Continentals, making Congress and the average citizen more willing to talk reconciliation. His nervousness was not assuaged by news that the British were also pushing these peace proposals in and around New York. They had sent copies to General Alexander McDougall in the Hudson Highlands and to Jonathan Trumbull, the governor of Connecticut.

When the handbill reached President Laurens in York, he too was inclined to suspect "General Howe and his emissaries." He was sure Congress would return it "decently tarred and feathered." Not everyone in Congress agreed with the president. Samuel Chase of Maryland told the governor of his state that "the far greater number" of delegates thought the handbills were authentic. But they too thought the purpose was to disarm American plans for the next campaign. Chase also worried about the "baneful effect it may have upon the weak and credulous" and urged the governor to publish it with a ringing refutation attached. Another Maryland delegate, John Henry, feared it would "prove more dangerous to our cause than ten thousand of their best troops."[18]

Two days later, General Howe forwarded to General Washington a copy of a Philadelphia newspaper, which contained a speech by the British prime minister, Lord North, supporting the two conciliatory bills. John Laurens rushed it to his father. Calling it "Ld North's recantation," the younger Laurens, who frequently reflected Washington's thinking, nervously observed, "The present moment requires . . . uncommon management."[19]

In the body of his letter, John Laurens added news that was almost as startling: "There is no doubt of Genl Howe's being recalled, and that Genl Clinton is to succeed him." Did this mean a new British plan for subduing the Americans if the peace offering was rejected? Was Clinton to be given reinforcements? John Laurens warned his father that he had "many fears relative to our prospects for the ensuing campaign."[20]

His father was equally worried. Along with the unsettled matters of half pay for Washington's officers and the reorganization of the army, there was the appalling condition of the forts defending the Hudson River, which the British had captured and destroyed in the fall of 1777 when they tried to rescue General Burgoyne. The river at present was an open highway into the heart of New York state. If the British seized it, they could cut off communication with New England. "I tremble at every arrival of a messenger from that quarter," President Laurens wrote.[21]

VII

Congress, all doubts about the authenticity of the British conciliatory bills resolved, appointed a committee to draft a reply. The chairman was Gouverneur Morris of New York, which virtually guaranteed the answer would contain the essential principle George Washington wanted: there would be no compromise on independence. Afterward, Morris said his goal was to show "the wickedness and insincerity of the enemy," and he groused that he had to make some compromises to mollify less pugnacious congressmen. But the final result was hardly timorous.

The crucial issue, in the face of this temptation to waver, was the continuance of the union that had enabled the Americans to defend their common rights and privileges. The Morris-composed response from Congress declared that "Any men or body of men" who undertook to reach an agreement with the British commissioners would be "treated as open and avowed enemies of these United States." The United States, meanwhile, would not negotiate with the commissioners unless they first withdrew their fleet and army and recognized American independence. Congress approved the response unanimously.[22]

This blast of defiance did not defuse the anxiety that was swirling through Congress and the army at Valley Forge. Henry Laurens told Washington that the British offer was creating "a most important crisis" which would require "all the wisdom of these states" to resolve. He thought the time would come when Congress would have to appoint a "deputation" to deal with the British commissioners. He had no hope of finding "able men" in the thin ranks of the present Congress. He favored scouring the union in search of them. Washington, whose opinion of Congress was equally low, undoubtedly agreed with him.[23]

All but confirming their worries, Laurens was soon reporting that second thoughts about absolute defiance were beginning to creep through Congress. On the heels of Gouverneur Morris's reply, the politicians began discussing whether they ought to state a willingness to negotiate with the British. Laurens vigorously opposed this idea. "We have made an excellent move on the table," he said, using a metaphor from chess. The next move was now up to the other side.[24]

Congressmen were writing frantically to their native states, asking the governors and legislatures to fill the seats which had been empty at York all winter. Henry Laurens told Rawlins Lowndes, the governor of South Carolina, that Congress now had about twenty-five members. But New Hampshire, Delaware, and North Carolina frequently had nobody, and New Jersey and Rhode Island had one delegate each.

The uncertainty many felt about the reaction to the British proposals was starkly dramatized by a letter from Thomas McKean to Caesar Rodney, the president of Delaware, where loyalists and semiloyalists were rife. McKean, who was attending Congress as a delegate from Delaware and was also serving as chief justice of Pennsylvania (he had property in both states), begged Rodney to send two more delegates. But McKean wanted the new appointees to know before they came to York that he would never give up the independence of the United States "while I have a breath to draw." If the Delaware assembly did not agree, they should remove him immediately. The implication was all too clear: that the new men and the assembly might be willing to compromise on independence.[25]

James Lovell, writing for the Committee on Foreign Affairs, dashed off a letter to the American "commissioners," as the diplomats were called, in Paris. He told them Congress had heard nothing from them since May of 1777. He acknowledged that this silence did not mean dereliction of duty. Two ships, probably carrying dispatches from the diplomats, had been lost at sea, and a third messenger, Captain John Folger, had been hoodwinked into crossing the Atlantic carrying what he thought were dispatches but turned out to be numerous sheets of blank paper, courtesy of the British secret service. The royal spooks had surrounded the diplomats with agents who were doing everything in their power to disrupt their communications—and incidentally read what they were telling Congress.[26]

A fretful Richard Henry Lee told Thomas Jefferson, "We have no news, not a scrip from our commissioners. The gold and sea power of our enemies have prevailed to deprive us of most important dispatches." In a postscript Lee begged Jefferson to use his influence to raise more men for Virginia's depleted Continental Army regiments.[27]

VIII

While congressmen fretted and General Washington worried about the swirling international politics, the war on the outskirts of Philadelphia continued. On April 30, a loyalist spy reported that General John Lacey and his militiamen would be camped at the Crooked Billet Tavern (in what is now Hatboro, Pennsylvania) that night. In his letters to General Washington, Lacey had referred to the Crooked Billet as an advanced post, at which he seldom stayed long, because he knew it was dangerous. It was only seventeen miles from Philadelphia. But he now had six hundred men under his command, and probably thought he was strong enough to beat off the small patrols the British usually sent out to provide security for the farmers carrying food to Philadelphia.

Perhaps sensing Lacey's complacency, the British put together a formidable strike force: fourteen companies of light infantry and Colonel John Simcoe's Queens Rangers, a 430-man loyalist regiment that had been patrolling and fighting in the area all winter. With these infantry were two troops of regular dragoons and the two loyalist dragoon regiments that had also seen a lot of action by now—a total of about 800 men. Marching out in the predawn darkness, they split into two groups. The Queens Rangers were to circle the militia camp and attack from the rear. The rest of the column, led by Lieutenant Colonel Robert Abercrombie, the overall commander, would attack from the front.

Lacey had issued strict orders to have numerous scouts patrolling the roads around the Crooked Billet starting at 2 a.m. But dawn found them still asleep, along with the rest of his little army. A lone lieutenant was on his horse two miles from camp when he saw looming up in the predawn gloom the two troops of British dragoons, gleaming sabers at the ready. A braver man would have fired a shot at them, which would have awakened the American camp. But the panicked lieutenant knew that would probably mean instant death for him. Rather than be "cut to pieces," as he later lamely explained, he ordered one of his scouts to run and warn Lacey and his men. The messenger decided it would be far healthier for him to head for distant pastures.

The dragoons, spotting the fleeing lieutenant, decided to charge. This premature attack prevented the Queens Rangers from getting into Lacey's rear to cut him off. Hearing the hoofbeats and shouts of the cavalrymen, Simcoe's men and the British light infantry joined the assault.

The mortified General Lacey later reported "the alarm was so sudden, I had scarcely time to mount my horse before the enemy was within musket shot of my quarters." His men staggered from their tents, even more bewildered, to be ridden down by the charging dragoons and bayoneted by the oncoming light infantry. A few minutes later, Simcoe's men opened fire from their flanks and rear, completing the militiamen's panic.

They ran in all directions. A few dozen joined Lacey and formed a "little party," which retreated in a fairly compact formation, returning the gunfire that rained on them from all sides. Inside the camp, ugly scenes took place. Some militiamen claimed that when haystacks were set afire by flaming muskets, the British flung a half dozen wounded men into the blazes. Lacey also complained that scarcely one of his dead men was found "without a dozen wounds with bayonets or cutlasses [sabers]." But such excesses were not uncommon in surprise attacks, which often degenerated into savage melees.

Over a hundred militiamen were killed or wounded and about fifty were taken prisoner; the British reported only nine wounded. The attackers also captured over a dozen wagons loaded with provisions and whiskey and returned triumphantly to Philadelphia with this booty. It was a daunting example of what professional soldiers could do when fighting amateurs.[28]

Was this the opening attack in a British offensive? This would have been the first question that occurred to General Washington when the bad news reached Valley Forge later on May 1. But news of a very different sort had arrived at headquarters by courier late the previous day, making the crushing defeat at the Crooked Billet far less threatening.

IX

The courier had come from Bethlehem, Pennsylvania, with a letter from a stranger: Simeon Deane. Washington of course knew that Silas Deane of Connecticut was one of the American commissioners in France. But Simeon Deane was unknown to him. When the general opened the letter, he read the most astonishing imaginable news. The letter writer was en route from Paris to York to deliver to Congress copies of two treaties signed with France, creating an alliance in which King Louis XVI guaranteed the independence of the United States. Simeon, who was Silas Deane's brother, thought General Washington should be among the first to hear this news. The commander in chief rushed a letter to Henry Laurens in York, telling him "no event was ever received with more heart-felt joy." [29]

Washington added that he would await confirmation from Congress before he officially announced the glad tidings to the army. But he could not resist telling his aides and visitors to headquarters, and the next day the news spread through Valley Forge with the speed and impact of a bolt of electricity. Among the first to hear it was the Marquis de Lafayette. As he recalled it in his memoirs, he burst into headquarters, embraced General Washington, and kissed him on both cheeks, *à la française*.

An hour or two later, in a rush of premature optimism, the Marquis wrote to Henry Laurens: "Houra, my good friend, now the affair is over." Losing all control of his English, the Marquis burbled: "Very happy I find myself to see things so well brought to the common glory and satisfaction." More to the point, Lafayette said he also felt "the greatest satisfaction in hearing [presumably from Simeon Deane] what justice and respect is pay'd in Europe to my respectable friend and commander in chief." [30]

May 1 was May Day, a traditional feast that celebrated the end of winter with drinks and songs. In Valley Forge every regiment erected a maypole, and bands of soldiers toured the camp with flowers in their hats, cheering each pole and being rewarded with glasses of rum. Elsewhere various games, such as "base," a forerunner of baseball, and wicket, a version of cricket, were soon in progress.

Some officers, doubly inspired by May Day and the good news from France, spent the afternoon enjoying a bibulous barbecue on the banks of the Schuylkill. A fifer and a drummer played patriotic and sentimental tunes, which the celebrators bellowed into the sunshine. Not a few of them drank more than they could handle and noticed that the two musicians were giving them peculiar looks. One officer, Alexander Graydon of Pennsylvania, called their expressions "sneering."

The music makers were deserters from the British army and apparently retained their superior attitude toward the Americans. When some of the drinkers staggered or slurred their words, the Britons apparently thought this was conduct unbecoming an officer and a gentleman. But the sensational news from France made everyone, drunk or sober, indifferent to British condescension.[31]

Washington's exuberance continued for several days. On May 4, he dined at the artillery park with General Henry Knox. On his way back to headquarters, he found the younger artillery officers organizing a game of wicket, and the commander in chief, in the words of Ensign George Ewing, "did us the honor to play at wicket with us." The image of Washington wielding a cricket bat has an American informality that no British general could ever match. It is another glimpse of the leader who won the affection as well as the admiration of his men.[32]

X

In York, Congress had adjourned on Saturday, May 2, by the time Simeon Deane arrived with the treaties. He showed them to President Laurens, who immediately sent messengers scampering through the little town ordering the members to reconvene for an emergency session. The delegates listened to the glorious news and exchanged joyous congratulations. They adjourned again until Monday to celebrate the Sabbath, but most of them spent Sunday spreading the news to their friends and families and the governors of their states.

Charles Carroll wrote to his father, telling him the treaty with France was "bottomed on principles of the most wise and generous policy." At least as important from the Carrolls' moneyed point of view, British stocks had fallen 10 percent on the news of the treaty. Like Nathanael Greene, they saw the war as an economic as well as a military and political struggle.

Henry Laurens complained to several correspondents that he could get nothing done because so many people visited to congratulate him. He managed to finish two letters to General Washington, telling him that he would send copies of the treaties to him the following day and one hundred copies of a broadside written by his fellow South Carolina delegate, William Henry Drayton, for circulation to the army and civilians in the vicinity of Valley Forge, telling them the news.

On May 5, Washington's general orders announced the alliance, which Congress had ratified unanimously on May 4. "It having pleased the almighty ruler of the universe to defend the cause of the United American-States . . . by raising us up a powerful friend among the princes of the earth to establish our liberty and independence, up[on] lasting foundations, it becomes us to set a day for gratefully acknowledging the divine goodness and celebrating the important event."[33]

XI

There was no time wasted in choosing the celebratory day: May 6. Washington had conferred with Baron von Steuben the day the news arrived at Valley Forge, ordering him to make sure the army would give the best possible performance at this "Grand Review." Steuben passed the word to his brigade and division inspectors to begin preparing the men. By now he had perfect confidence in these officers, and they in him.

At nine o'clock on the great day, a cannon boomed and the men lined up without their muskets to hear their chaplains preach on the various brigade parade grounds, praising God and the King of France for the benevolent alliance. When the chaplains finished, another cannon boomed, and the men rushed to their huts to get their muskets.

General Washington and his staff rode to the center of the grand parade and waited expectantly while brigade inspectors barked orders and the men marched to their assigned battalions. The inspectors strode to the waiting brigadier generals of each brigade and reported: "Sir! The battalions are formed!" The brigadiers ordered colonels to take command of the battalions, and they in turn ordered the men to load their guns.

Another cannon boomed and the army was in motion. Rank by rank, with not a single straying step, the battalions swung past General Washington and deployed into a double line of battle with the ease and swiftness of veterans. There was a long silence. Then came thirteen thundering blasts from the artillery park. Another pause and the climactic moment, for which Steuben had trained the army, began. One by one, the men in the first line raised their muskets and fired. Down the line went the blasts of smoke and sound with rhythmic precision to the last man. An instant later the muskets blazed one by one in the second line. This was the ultimate performance of a well-trained army, the *feu de joie*, which gave every man a sense of individual participation in the celebration.

The first fire was in honor of the King of France. More orders from the brigade commanders. The men reloaded and the cannon again boomed thirteen times. Once more the running fire went down the first line and up the second line without the slightest flaw, honoring the "friendly European states," notably Prussia and Spain, who were expected to support the French alliance. A third round of cannon and running musketry honored the United American States. The whole ceremony, John Laurens later told his father, was "executed to perfection." [34]

Next, the field officers commanding the battalions shouted in unison: "Long live the King of France!" The men responded with a tremendous cheer. "And long live the friendly European states!" Again the response was a huzzah from seven thousand young throats. "To the American states!"

This time the cheers soared over Mount Joy and rebounded off Mount Misery in unforgettable ghostly echoes, as if the voices of the army's dead had joined the triumphant living.

Once more the cannon boomed thirteen times. The men promptly, confidently executed another *feu de joie* and grounded their arms. The field officers shouted crisp commands. The lines wheeled and formed into the original battalions and marched back to their respective brigades, exhilarated and proud. In their brigade streets, they found commissaries waiting to ladle a gill of rum into every man's canteen by order of General Washington.

The commander in chief, as pleased as his soldiers, rode in the opposite direction toward the artillery park. Outside this home of the booming cannon, with wisps of gunpowder still scenting the air, artificers had created a kind of large bower from the marquees of dozens of officers' tents. There were hundreds of tables and benches and a space in the center where General Washington stood with his wife, Martha. To this improvised garden spot, the officers marched from the huts of their brigades in a column, thirteen abreast, their arms linked as a symbol of unity.

A smiling Washington took every officer by the hand and each made his bow to Martha. Soon a merry party was in progress. The wives of other officers, notably Caty Greene and Lady Stirling and her beautiful daughter, Kitty, joined the party along with some civilian exiles from Philadelphia who lived in the neighborhood. Burly Baron de Kalb, who liked his victuals, told one correspondent there was "a profusion of fat meat, strong wine and other liquors." The starving time at Valley Forge was a thing of the past, at least for the moment.

Numerous toasts were offered to Congress, the states, and that new favorite, the King of France. For many in the party, remembering the gloom and rancor of the days of the Board of War's campaign to eliminate General Washington, the greatest pleasure was, in John Laurens's words, "the proofs of the love and attachment of his officers." He was sure they gave the general "the most exquisite feelings."

Before the toasts, Washington summoned Baron von Steuben to his table and announced to the officers that just before the review began, a messenger had arrived from York with the news that Congress had confirmed the Baron's appointment as inspector general of the army, with the rank and pay of major general. The news was greeted with cheers and raised glasses.

No longer would the Baron have to hide behind the slippery title of "a lieutenant general in foreign service." In general orders the following day, Washington presented his "thanks to Baron Steuben and & the gentlemen under him for their indefatigable exertions." [35]

Additional proof of the officers' affection, if it was needed, was their tribute when Washington left the party. There was a veritable storm of applause followed by cheers, which continued until Washington and his aides were a quarter of a mile on their way to headquarters. There the aides turned and shouted a final huzzah, in which Washington cheerfully joined. It was answered by a thousand hats tossed in the air. [36]

XII

Back in headquarters, Washington abandoned his usual caution and told one correspondent there was a good possibility that the war would end soon. "The game, whether ill or well played hitherto," he wrote, "seems now to be verging toward a favorable issue." He would soon discover the game was far from over. Within two months the army that had just performed so beautifully on the grand parade would be fighting for its life—and he would face another challenge to his leadership. [37]

NINE

THE FOLLIES OF SPRING

I N PHILADELPHIA, MOST of the British army was in a funk. Their victory at the Crooked Billet, the loyalist uprisings in Delaware and west Jersey, meant little in the shadow of the parliamentary politics that was engulfing their dreams of glory. London magazines and newspapers flowed into the city, telling them how Burgoyne's defeat had enabled the opposition in Parliament to open a savage attack on George III's ministers, especially Sir William Howe's nemesis, the American secretary, Lord George Germain. The result was a drastic change in the government's policy from conquest to reconciliation, which depressed and infuriated the army.

When copies of Prime Minister Lord North's conciliatory bills and his speech in Parliament were posted on various bulletin boards around Philadelphia in mid-April, not a few were torn down and ripped to shreds by exasperated young officers. Another group burned the prime minister in effigy. They did not want to conciliate the rebels. They wanted to thrash them!

On paper, at least, a military victory did not seem out of reach for the king's men. The British army, according to an official return around the time conciliation became the government's policy, had 14,420 rank and file fit and ready for duty, plus 1,343 loyalist volunteers. During the winter and early spring, Washington had barely 7,500 men fit for duty at Valley Forge.

This secret remained unpenetrated. General Washington made it a point to send double agents into the city with vast exaggerations of his numbers. He even took the trouble to spread the same whoppers among his own troops. When jaeger Captain Johann Ewald captured a rebel rifleman in a skirmish, the prisoner told him that the Continental Army numbered 25,000 men.[1]

In the higher ranks of the British army, after a winter of watching apparent loyalists swarming into Philadelphia to sell flour and fish and beef, the idea of a reconciliation did not seem an impossible dream. Sir William Howe and those around him thought that most Americans were "very generally desirous" of ending the war with harmony between George III and his colonies restored. This was, of course, largely wishful thinking. Reconciliation had been the goal that had brought Howe and his brother Admiral Lord Richard Howe to America and guided their strategy for their first two years of the war. How wonderful it would be if the dream became a reality![2]

A skeptical Captain Johann Ewald, who spoke good English, conducted his own informal poll in Philadelphia to find out what the Americans thought of the reconciliation bills. His conversations with various inhabitants split "half and half." But the rebel sympathizers told him they would never agree to peace without independence. Ewald, having participated frequently in the savage civil war raging around Philadelphia, expressed no surprise.[3]

II

For the moment, mounting a winner-take-all battle seemed doubly unlikely because the same ship that brought the news of the conciliatory proposals carried a letter from Lord George Germain, dourly informing General Howe that his resignation had been accepted and he could prepare to go home. His brother Lord Richard would be unable to join him until a replacement admiral reached America's coasts. But General Howe's replacement was already in America: Sir Henry Clinton, the commander in New York City.

Howe's departure added to the army's gloom. In spite of his lackadaisical approach to making war on the rebellion, he remained extremely popular with the younger officers. Many of them believed Sir William's cautious tactics had kept them off the casualty lists.

III

During the winter months, the City of Brotherly Love had drifted far from its original name. There was now little love between the occupiers and the occupied, except among the wealthy loyalists who participated in the high life personified by General Howe and his blue-eyed mistress, Elizabeth Loring. For them, the balls and dinners and plays and nights at the faro table continued. So did the gossip. One of the favorite topics among the city's women was Mrs. Loring's fondness for extremely low-cut gowns.

The Southwark Theater remained crowded and its repertoire grew more varied. On March 25 and 30, Howe's Strolling Players essayed *Henry IV, Part I*, featuring one of the best comic parts in Shakespeare's canon, Falstaff, the boon drinking companion of Prince Hal, the future Henry V. The old profligate was played by a captain of the British guards. Dr. Hammond Beaumont, a surgeon at the British hospital, starred in another play on the bill, *The Mock Doctor*. He was the favorite "low comedian" of the troupe.

The following week's presentation, *The Wonder, or A Woman Keeps a Secret*, was noteworthy for another reason: the author was a woman, Susan Centlivre, who wrote eighteen plays for the London stage, many of which remained popular for two centuries. She specialized in the comedy of intrigue. As usual, the plot of *The Wonder*, a sort of bedroom farce set in Spain, was improbable, but the audience loved the characters, especially the outspoken Mrs. Ichabod, who maintained "for a female to hold her tongue is a cool act of deliberate fortitude."[4]

The rest of Philadelphia, especially the Quakers, continued to be scandalized by the often racy dramas Captain John André and his chief collaborator, Captain Oliver DeLancey, chose for the Southwark's repertory. They were even more shocked by the British indifference to putting churches to mundane uses. Only a handful of houses of worship, mostly Catholic and Anglican and the city's four Quaker meetinghouses, were spared. The others, from Presbyterian to Baptist to Reform, were converted into riding schools and stables. This was not entirely accidental. Their members, especially the Presbyterians, were heavily identified with the rebellion.[5]

IV

Once the Delaware River blockade was lifted and the British army settled into the city, the local citizens got a look at why the king's men were trying to retain their grip on the American colonies: it was good for business. Flooding into Philadelphia were several hundred merchants from New York, Cork, Antigua, and other ports of call, who began selling a variety of wares not available in the blockaded city since the war began. Soon 121 new shops had opened on the downtown streets. A pleased General Howe issued a statement claiming the British army and navy deserved the credit for providing these amenities.[6]

For the native Philadelphians, the temptation to go on a shopping spree was complicated by a basic problem: the sellers all wanted hard money for their wares. The buyers had nothing but currency printed by the colony of Pennsylvania before that government expired in the summer of 1776. The Philadelphians reasoned that this money should be acceptable if the British were serious about restoring the civil governments of the revolted colonies. It was a nice theory but it did not get them very far with the newly arrived merchants.

The Philadelphians organized a "Loyal Association" and even a "Ladies Association" and petitioned General Howe. They published articles in the local papers attacking the foreign traders. They pointed out that General

Howe had legalized paper currency in New York when he was in command there, and it was still in use, with none of the depreciation that afflicted America's Continental dollars. But the traders stubbornly insisted on gold or silver, and General Howe and his agent, Superintendent Joseph Galloway, did nothing to change their minds. That put a large dent in Galloway's popularity among his fellow Philadelphians.[7]

Some of the briskest business was conducted by auctioneers, suggesting that not a few people of the "better sort" were selling furniture and clothing to acquire hard cash. Another source of salable goods came from the six hundred houses that rebel adherents had abandoned in the city. These were soon thoroughly plundered by British and German soldiers, and the loot was sold at auction for bargain prices.

The prices of food and scarce commodities such as salt were another matter. They skyrocketed, and Superintendent Galloway began trying to set and enforce price controls, in the style of Congress and the rebel government in Lancaster. Philadelphia's capitalist instincts were much too strong to stifle with edicts. Many merchants met food smugglers outside the city or at the wharves and paid far more money than the smugglers could hope to get at the regulated prices in the three public markets Galloway had set up.

Oddly, one of the busiest merchants in town was a native Philadelphian, bookseller Robert Bell. He would have been prosperous no matter what era or continent in which he operated. He ran a popular circulating library and regularly auctioned off slow-selling books at cut-rate prices. The newspapers ran large ads listing his latest titles. In the parlance of the publishing trade, Bell knew how to "move books."

Another local merchant who prospered was Tench Coxe. Barely twenty when the Revolution began, he was already a successful businessman thanks to numerous affluent relatives. Like Joseph Galloway and other Philadelphians, he had balked at the Declaration of Independence, and the radicals who took over the city forced him to flee to British-held New York. There he persuaded many prominent merchants to make him their agent in Philadelphia.

Coxe headed for his native city the moment he heard General Howe had captured it. The genial, self-confident young merchant, now all of twenty-three, developed an understanding with Sir William which may have involved money under the table. He was permitted to import and sell dry goods, all sorts of merchandise, and even one hundred pipes of choice Madeira while the royal navy struggled to clear the Delaware of rebel forts and obstructions. Coxe's New York friends shipped cargoes to him in swift small ships that were able to ascend the Delaware in the darkness.

Coxe's favored position vanished when the foreign merchants flooded into the city. But he managed to stay in business, thanks to his assiduous cultivation of General Howe and his subordinates. Interestingly, he made a point of making sure his wealthy father, William Coxe, a neutral, had nothing to do with his affairs. Coxe told one correspondent that might: be "dangerous" to his fond parent. He also wryly noted in his correspondence the large number of British officials, notably the army's commissary general, who lined their pockets by shipping cargoes from London disguised as government goods and selling them for handsome profits in Philadelphia.[8]

V

Joseph Galloway struggled to do his largely thankless job in spite of numerous discouragements. He raised enough money from voluntary subscriptions to hire a night watch to police the city, with the aid of one hundred soldiers who were prepared to enforce the law with their muskets when necessary. He also raised the cash needed to reignite the city's streetlamps, a rarity at this point in the development of urban life. They were the brainchild of Benjamin Franklin, who had pleaded in vain with Galloway to support the independence movement when Ben returned from England in 1775.

By the end of the winter, Galloway's continuing effort to recruit loyalists had persuaded 750 volunteers to join so-called provincial regiments. He made a special appeal to Philadelpha's Catholics, most of whom were

Irish, and persuaded 180 to join the royal ranks. Considering his handicaps, in particular General Howe's refusal to do anything about the American army at Valley Forge, this was a fairly respectable showing.

Galloway also reopened the city's poorhouse, which had been used as a barracks and then as a hospital by the British, and tried to maintain it with voluntary contributions. But it filled up so rapidly with men and women from the more than one thousand loyalists who had fled to Philadelphia from the hinterlands to escape rebel vengeance that the superintendent had to resort to a lottery to raise funds. That enabled him to keep food in the stomachs of these hapless victims of Pennsylvania's quasi civil war.[9]

In all these activities, Galloway tried to persuade prominent Philadelphians to assist him. He never recruited a single civic leader from the prewar years. Many of these VIPs had, of course, joined the Revolution and fled when the British arrived. But a fair number, such as timorous Edward Shippen, had chosen to stay in the city to protect their houses and families. All too aware that Washington's army was waiting at Valley Forge to renew the war when the winter ended, these men preferred to straddle the question of loyalty for the time being.

Mr. Shippen continued to allow his beautiful daughter Peggy to enjoy parties at the homes of affluent loyalists. He himself was not averse to dining with loyalist friends. But that was as far as he chose to go. Ultimately, from a potential field of perhaps five thousand adult males, Galloway was able to persuade fewer than fifty men to help him run the city's government.[10]

VI

Meanwhile, the prisoners in the New Jail continued to die. The cause was no longer starvation. The Americans had persuaded David Franks, an American merchant who had remained in Philadelphia, to accept responsibility for distributing food to the captives. He was able to procure a fairly steady supply of meat and bread after both armies went into winter quarters. But Franks could not obtain any vegetables, and the prisoners began succumbing to "putrid fever," a common jailhouse disease. The Quakers persisted in turning their collective backs on the prisoners, and General Howe and the Continental Congress remained unable to reach an agreement on an exchange. In February Captain John Peebles of the Black Watch noted in his diary: "No communication allow'd with the Rebel prisoners here now & if any of them are detected in making their escape they are to be put to death—poor devils, they suffer enough and many of them are dying."[11]

The problem of keeping warm during the winter afflicted everyone. Hundreds of British soldiers marched into the countryside every day to chop wood for the army, which consumed six hundred cords a week. Before the winter ended, Penns Woods, to the west of town, had vanished. So had almost every fence in the city. Occasionally an abandoned house was added to the fuel supply. Other deserted houses were stripped of every square inch of wood, and often furniture was added to the barracks stoves.

Volunteer woodchoppers were paid five shillings (a dollar) a cord, very good pay. They often added to it by stealing some of their loads instead of carting them to the army wood yards, and selling the pilfered logs to civilians. Other woodcutters allowed regimental friends to swipe a portion of their loads if no officer was watching.

Inevitably, the price of wood for civilians soared, and a great many Philadelphians relied on layers of wool clothing to survive. Among the prisoners in the stone interior of the New Jail, cold as well as starvation added to their death toll.

Hygiene was as important as warmth for defense against disease. Here the dismaying ignorance of enlisted men proved a recurring problem. General James Pattison, the British artillery commander, issued a scorching reprimand to his men in early February. Most of them were living in the statehouse, which had been converted into a barracks. "Some of the men have been so beastly as to ease themselves on the stairs and lower areas of the house ... during the night." Pattison ordered sentries to "put a stop to such scandalous behavior." It would soon become clear that the sentries paid no attention to the general.

Even worse in some respects were dragoons who cleaned their stables by chopping holes in the floors of churches and other buildings in which the steeds were quartered and shoveled the manure into the cellars. Some soldiers cut holes in the floors of their barracks (often vacant private houses) and evacuated their bowels into the basements. By the end of the winter, Philadelphia had acquired a pervasive stink.[12]

VII

A rumor, never confirmed but deemed more than probable by many, spread through the city that the British had imported, along with a flood of manufactured goods, three hundred prostitutes from New York. The ladies of the evening were tolerated in New York, so why not in Philadelphia, where there were even more military customers? Throughout the winter, there were enough victims of venereal disease to create a separate treatment center for them in the Pennsylvania Hospital.

For those who preferred self-medication, newspapers carried ads for Dr. Yeldall's "Anti-Venereal Essence." It was guaranteed to conceal the disease from the sufferer's "most intimate acquaintance," which suggests unpleasant possibilities. It was also guaranteed to "prevent the infection." The cost of this wonder drug was two dollars a bottle.[13]

Thanks to Superintendent Galloway's night watch and its one-hundred-man armed escort, the city's crime rate remained fairly low. But Howe had to deal with numerous complaints from outraged citizens who claimed they were insulted and harassed on the streets by officers who were undoubtedly drunk. The British commander said he could "scarcely believe" that officers and gentlemen could commit such "horrible outrages." He added dragoons to the military patrols, presumably to intimidate those with Dutch courage and perhaps to capture runaways.

The numerous courts-martial in the course of the winter revealed some lively encounters between soldiers and citizens. Sixteen-year-old Mary Figgis accused Captain Alexander Campbell of trying to use her to send intelligence to the Americans. This was probably a case of a liaison gone awry. The captain was court-martialed and acquitted, and Mary, no doubt under duress, recanted her testimony. Another officer said Campbell was a "victim of the malice and depravity of an abandoned little wretch," which gives us a more than adequate character sketch of Ms. Figgis. Mary was escorted to the outskirts of the city and told to ply her trade elsewhere.[14]

Occasionally civilians intervened in matters of military justice. A corporal named John Fisher was accused of raping a nine-year-old child while minding her (or a younger sibling) for a fellow soldier and his wife. He was sentenced to hang, but Rebecca Franks, in an act of mercy uncharacteristic of her public image, appealed to General Howe for clemency. According to Captain John Peebles's diary, Sir William wrote to Lord George Germain for a royal pardon for Corporal Fisher and it was granted.[15]

VIII

The same day that Corporal Fisher won a reprieve, two other soldiers were hanged for desertion. There was a steady flow of deserters from both armies throughout the winter, with those unfortunate enough to get caught often suffering the ultimate sentence in both Philadelphia and Valley Forge. Thanks to Joseph Galloway's careful records, we know exactly how many Americans deserted as of March 25, 1778: 1,134. The diaries of Captain John Peebles and other British and German soldiers note the daily arrivals of these runaways. At one point Galloway estimated Washington was losing 50 men a day. With the end of winter, these numbers declined steeply. The final count was below 1,500.[16]

The deserters and other evidence of the rebels' problems—especially the depreciation of their currency and deserters' reports about starvation at Valley Forge—prompted Galloway to renew asking General Howe to do something besides go to parties with Mrs. Loring on his arm. Some of Galloway's intelligence was on the mark. He estimated 2,500 Continentals had died during the winter—about the same as Washington's figure.

He also told Howe that all of Washington's horses had died at Valley Forge—again not far from the truth. This was important information. Without horses, there was no way for the Continentals to deploy their artillery in a battle or rescue it if they had to retreat.[17]

Galloway's calls for action may have had some influence on the spurt of vigor the British displayed in April and May. The Hessian jaegers and their dragoons had numerous clashes with American detachments. On April 15, they ambushed men from Daniel Morgan's regiment, killed forty, and captured seventy, many of them wounded. For the next two weeks, the angry riflemen played cat and mouse with the Germans, hoping for revenge. But the shrewd jaegers never went out at the same time or marched the same route. Contact was confined to occasional rifle or musket shots.[18]

A week after the victory at the Crooked Billet, the British launched an ambitious operation to wipe out what was left of the Pennsylvania navy's fleet and assist loyalists around Bordentown, New Jersey. Another inviting target was two Continental Navy frigates. Washington had recommended sinking them. They could easily be raised and pumped out when and if the British departed. But during the winter of discontent, his advice was ignored.[19]

On May 7 a battalion of British light infantry supported by two cannon went up the Delaware on flatboats. They were accompanied by a small fleet of galleys, gunboats, and armed schooners. The unarmed frigates were quickly captured and burned, along with about twenty other small craft in the vicinity. The light infantry went ashore, routed a detachment of New Jersey militia, and captured Bordentown, where they burned warehouses full of army matériel and several houses of local rebel leaders. Cruising down the Delaware, they tried to wreak similar havoc at Trenton but were beaten off by two rebel cannon and a large turnout of New Jersey militia.[20]

IX

This aggressive activity suggests that Howe or subordinate generals in his army were trying to revive or sustain loyalist morale in the vicinity of Philadelphia. Loyalists no doubt walked with a more lively step for a while. But on May 8, these hopes suffered a demoralizing blow. The sloop of war HMS *Porcupine* arrived with the news that France had signed the treaty of alliance with the American rebels and war was now considered virtually inevitable between the two great powers. Also aboard the aptly named *Porcupine* were orders from Lord George Germain for Sir Henry Clinton, the army's new commander. Philadelphia was to be evacuated as soon as possible, and the main British army broken up to defend the king's valuable possessions in the West Indies.

Perhaps it was a testimony to the isolation of the British garrison in Philadelphia, but numerous officers were stunned by the French declaration of war. The same day, Sir Henry Clinton arrived to take command and decided to conceal for the moment the government's decision to abandon Philadelphia.

Three days later, on May 11, Howe turned over the army to Clinton and issued a statement praising the "spirit, alacrity and unanimity" of every officer and soldier in the ranks in spite of campaigns that involved "much fatigue & hardship." But Sir William seemed in no hurry to depart, and the army soon learned why. His devotees in the officer corps, led by Captain John André, were planning a farewell party for him that would be the talk of two continents.[21]

X

The Southwark Theater's repertoire was a mere prelude to the British army's ultimate dramatic presentation. Its chief creator, Captain John André, called it "The Misquianza." The usual spelling these days is *mischianza*, from the Italian meaning "medley" or "mixture." It was a form of entertainment that had become popular in Georgian London, combining regattas, parades, massed bands, gorgeous clothes, and touches of medieval knight errantry. In a long letter that was published in a London magazine, André described the event as "the most splendid entertainment ever given by an army to their general," a testament of nothing less than the army's "love" for General Howe.

The fete was financed by twenty-two high-ranking officers, who each pledged 140 pounds to get things moving. This 3,080 pounds proved only a down payment on the total cost. An English firm on Philadelphia's Second Street sold André and the other organizers hundreds of yards of silk, damask, and velvet, valued at 12,000 pounds. André hired a squadron of tailors to create the costumes, which he designed.

The elaborate invitation was obviously intended to be a piece of memorabilia. At the top was the coat of arms of the Howe family, with the Latin inscription *Vive, Vale* ("Be Happy, Farewell"). Beneath it was a drawing of a setting sun with another Latin inscription, roughly translated as: "He is shining as he sets, but he will rise again in greater splendor." The border was a laurel wreath, the traditional decoration awarded a victor. On the back was the guest's name and directions to assemble at Knight's Wharf, in northern Philadelphia, the following day at 3:30 p.m.

A historical controversy has long raged in Philadelphia about whether Peggy Shippen and her two sisters were among the guests at the Mischianza. In later years, the Shippen family claimed that on the night before the grand event, a deputation of Quakers visited Edward Shippen and persuaded him to refuse to permit his daughters to attend, because of the exotic Turkish costumes they would wear. But other members of the family dismiss this story as a fabrication designed to protect their reputations, after Peggy Shippen married General Benedict Arnold and joined him and John André in the treasonous plot to betray West Point in 1780. One member of the family, a granddaughter of Peggy's sister, Sally, claimed that her grandmother repeatedly and delightedly reminisced about the Mischianza and never mentioned the intrusion of the frowning Quakers.[22]

At 4 p.m. on May 18, the four hundred guests, who included General and Admiral Howe, the army's other principal officers, leading loyalists, and a careful selection of the most beautiful women in the city, including Elizabeth Loring, boarded flatboats lined with green cloth and sheltered by bright awnings.

Pennants and ensigns fluttering, "the gaudy fleet," as André called it, was rowed by British sailors. Bands on three flatboats played festive music. They cruised past Philadelphia's mile-long waterfront, which was jammed with spectators. More onlookers crowded the roofs of buildings, which were trimmed with bunting and flags.

On glided the gaudy fleet until they reached a landing south of the city. On a slight rise above a six-hundred-yard lawn stood Walnut Grove, the mansion of the late Joseph Wharton, one of the city's wealthiest merchants, who had sided with the rebels. The house had been confiscated by the British, which gave André carte blanche to do what he pleased with the interior and the grounds.[23]

Ashore, the guests were greeted by two huge arches decorated with emblems and symbols, one in honor of Admiral Howe, the other dedicated to the guest of honor, General Howe. Soon all the guests were within what André called a carousel—an amphitheater flanked by rows of seats. Prominently displayed in their gauze-turbaned Turkish costumes were the women who had been selected by the fourteen officers impersonating knights.

Once the ladies were seated, the other guests encircled the amphitheater and a medieval tournament began. Watching from a distance were "spectators not to be numbered" who "darkened the plain" around the grounds. A very strong guard "controlled their curiosity" and framed the ground "with martial uniformity and splendour."

Seven white knights and seven black knights participated in the tournament. The whites called themselves the Knights of the Blended Rose and wore costumes from the reign of Henry IV of France which were as elaborate as their ladies' outfits. Each knight had a squire (a candidate for knighthood) who was dressed largely in pink, with a white sash. He carried the knight's lance and shield.

The Knights of the Blended Rose paraded in single file around the amphitheater and drew up in a line. Excitement mounted as a herald, flanked by four trumpeters, stepped forward and announced that the ladies of the Blended Rose "excel in wit, beauty and accomplishment those of the whole world" and the knights were ready to "maintain their assertions" against any knight or knights who dared to dispute it.

The herald's challenge was the signal for the entrance of the seven black knights, whose satin costumes were equally elaborate. They called themselves the Knights of the Burning Mountain, and said they were ready to challenge the Knights of the Blended Rose on behalf of the beauty of *their* ladies. The chief knight of the whites threw down his glove as signal that they were ready to meet this challenge by force of arms.

With a blast of trumpets, the knights charged. "Each knight's spear appear[ed] to be shivered against his antagonist," wrote André. "The charge back again was immediate and . . . a third charge was made." Next the knights assailed each other with their swords and the fighting raged hand to hand until at a signal they withdrew and let the chief white knight engage the chief black knight in single combat. Then the "Judges of the Field" intervened and decreed that the ladies were so fair and the knights so brave, it would have been "impious to decide in favor of either."

The knights now paraded through Admiral Howe's arch in black and white pairs, signaling they were adversaries no longer. They and their squires formed two lines before General Howe's arch, where they were joined by an officer and twenty men from each regiment in the garrison. Led by the young ladies in Turkish costume, the guests passed between this military array into Walnut Hill's blooming flower garden and followed a gravel walk to the steps of the mansion.

In the reception hall, which had been painted in imitation of Siena marble, the guests were served tea, lemonade, and similar cooling drinks and mounted the stairs to a spacious ballroom, where an orchestra was playing. This room too had been redecorated in what André called "a light elegant style of painting" with panels of small gold bead and festoons of flowers. The pleasing effect was multiplied by eighty-five mirrors "decked with rose-pink silk ribbands."

The knights opened the ball by dancing with their ladies, who then danced with the squires. Captain André was one of the white knights, and his lady was Peggy Chew, a sign of his growing attachment. The guests soon joined the dancing, and enjoyment was general for another two hours. At ten o'clock the windows were opened and the revelers were treated to a magnificent display of fireworks. Twenty different combinations filled the sky with color and explosions.

The climax was, in André's words, "an uninterrupted flight of rockets and bursting balloons" that illuminated General Howe's arch, which took on a life of its own. "The military trophies assumed a variety of transparent colors," André wrote. "Fame appeared on top, spangled with stars and from her trumpet streamed the burning words: 'Tes lauriers son immortel'" (Your laurels are immortal).

Most people resumed dancing but not a few responded to the announcement that a faro bank had opened in the adjoining room. At midnight, another set of doors was thrown open and the banquet hall was revealed to the wide-eyed guests. Built as an addition to the mansion by British engineers, the room was 210 feet long and 40 feet wide. The canvas walls, painted a light straw yellow, were covered with painted vines and garlands of flowers and lined with a new fleet of fifty-six mirrors. Waiting to serve the guests were twenty-four blacks wearing blue and white turbans and sashes, silver collars, and ornamental robes. At two tables that ran the length of the room were seats for 430 people. On the tables were 1,200 dishes, plus fifty pyramids of sweetmeats, jellies, and cakes.

An unending flow of wine and other spirits was supplied by the black waiters from alcoves off the main room. In the midst of this revelry, there was a startling sound of distant gunfire, followed by the glow of a fire. A ripple of anxiety swept through the room. What was it? All the guests were aware that well-armed Americans were in the vicinity, and had a fondness for surprise attacks.

The gunfire was not a signal for a Germantown-like major assault. The rebels were only trying to ruin General Howe's love feast. Captain Allan McLane, who had replaced Captain Henry Lee as spymaster on the outskirts of the city, led a troop of dragoons who had dismounted, crept up to the British redoubts, and poured whale oil over the sharpened wooden stakes, called abatis, that guarded the walls, and set them ablaze. The startled guards in the redoubts responded with random gunfire and a drum roll signaling an attack.

No doubt Sir William Howe and others familiar with the drum roll were momentarily alarmed. When nothing else happened, the soldiers told the civilians the noise was just another part of the fireworks, and everyone resumed feasting unperturbed.

At the end of the supper, the Herald of the Blended Rose stood up and signaled his trumpeters, who responded with a peal that got everyone's attention. Raising his glass, he toasted the king's health. A hidden orchestra struck up "God Save the King," which everyone sang with presumed gusto. Many more toasts followed. After the royal family, the Howes were next and won a huge acclamation. André claimed that those sitting near them could see on their faces "a generous emotion" in reply to "the undissembled testimony of our love and admiration."

Finally, after toasts to the army and navy, to the Hessians and other German detachments, the guests cheerfully saluted themselves. By that time, they were no doubt ready to toast anyone, even General Washington. In the ballroom, the orchestra continued to play, and the hardier (or younger) among the revelers danced until dawn.[24]

XI

After the officers returned to their quarters for a few hours' sleep, they arose to hear discomfiting news. Captain McLane's sortie the previous night had not been merely to disrupt the Mischianza. It also enabled seven American officers and forty-nine enlisted men to escape from the city.

The fugitives had dug their way out of the New Jail via a tunnel that emerged outside the walls. In the cellar where the digging began, the British found the bodies of five men concealed under straw. They had been killed in collapses during the course of the tunneling. The casualties had not discouraged the rest of the diggers. Obviously, risking sudden death by suffocation was preferable to death by inches in the New Jail.

For the prisoners not in on the secret, the future was bleak. When the British evacuated Philadelphia, they took them along to New York, where life in such vermin-infested hellholes as the prison ships off the Brooklyn shore exceeded the cruelties they had endured in the City of Brotherly Love.[25]

XII

The Mischianza had undoubted political overtones. Captain André rushed his account of it to London in time for an August publication with the obvious intent of discomfiting Lord George Germain and Howe's other enemies in the British government and press by showing how beloved Sir William was by his troops.

The sheer extravagance of the party undermined most of this probable purpose. The *London Chronicle*, one of the more outspoken antigovernment newspapers, called the spectacle "nauseous." Many others thought it was ridiculous to hail Sir William as a conqueror when Washington's army remained undefeated at Valley Forge. Even Ambrose Serle, Lord Howe's hard-line secretary, was among the critics. "Every man of sense, among ourselves, tho not unwilling to pay a due respect, was ashamed of this mode of doing it."[26]

Also in the mix of motivations was the British sense of cultural superiority to the American yokels—a sentiment that has already been noted in many of the plays at the Southwark Theater. Some speculate the choice of Turkish costumes for the knights' American ladies was a way of labeling them as inferior creatures who could never inhabit the world of British preeminence. Whether or not that is true, from a distance of two hundred years, the Mischianza's mish-mash of faux history and culture and luxury comes off a poor second to the Americans' austerity at Valley Forge. Even those who are wary of historical moralizing find it hard to resist the conclusion that these gaudy guzzlers and gourmands were poor candidates to become America's rulers.

With or without the Mischianza, Sir William Howe must have known that his hope for vindication was at best a long shot. The war with France was a diplomatic disaster that could, without too much effort, be blamed on him. He had squandered the years 1776 and 1777 without crushing the rebellion, convincing the French that the American alliance was a good gamble. If the general could have foreseen that an enraged Joseph Galloway would pursue him back to England and do his utmost to destroy his reputation, he would have been even more morose.[27]

XIII

On the day before the Mischianza, the president of the Continental Congress, Henry Laurens, wrote to his friend Rawlins Lowndes, the governor of South Carolina, surveying the situation as things now stood, with the French in the war and Washington's Steuben-trained army growing more professional every passing day. "When I look back on the precipice on which . . . my country . . . ha[s] been tottering all the past winter, I shudder. Had the British general been a man of enterprise, Congress would have been on ship board [to England] and Sir William Howe in quiet possession of York Town & of Albany. He could not be ignorant of our circumstances but our safety lay in Mrs. Lowry's [Loring's] lap."[28]

For those whose interest in history includes the personal as well as the military and political, this comment raises a pertinent question: did Mrs. Loring accompany Sir William Howe back to England?

The answer is no. Mrs. Loring returned to British-held New York with her husband, Joshua, and eventually retreated to England with thousands of other loyalists when the British lost the war. There the couple had three more children in addition to the two Joshua had fathered in America. In 1782, when Joshua was preparing to join Elizabeth in England, he wrote a letter to his eleven-year-old daughter, another Elizabeth, urging her to take her mother as a model woman and imitate her example in all things. He assured her that this would guarantee her possession of a "treasure of virtue and knowledge."

When Elizabeth Lloyd Loring died in 1835, her surviving children, one of them an Anglican bishop, erected a stone over her grave with the following inscription:

SACRED TO THE MEMORY

OF ELIZABETH

RELICT OF THE LATE JOSHUA LORING ESQ

WHO DIED OCT. 2ND 1835

FULL OF YEARS AND HONOR

AND OF THE FAITH IN THE MERCY OF GOD

THROUGH THE MERITS OF HER REDEEMER

SHE FULFILLED THE DUTIES OF LIFE TO ALL

WITH EXEMPLARY CONSTANCY

ESPECIALLY TO HER CHILDREN

WHO IN GRATEFUL REMEMBRANCE OF HER DEVOTION

TO THEM DURING FORTY SIX YEARS OF WIDOWHOOD

HAVE ERECTED THIS RECORD

OF HER VIRTUE AND THEIR AFFECTION.

How this computes with the Jezebel portrayed in most histories of the American Revolution is more than a mere historian can answer. Only a novelist can probe the mystery of the woman to whom some attribute America's survival. A few fiction writers have attempted it with unconvincing results.[29]

XIV

Sir William Howe apparently enjoyed Captain André's medieval fantasy, but it could only have dismayed Sir Henry Clinton. The new commander had been hoping for a recall to England when he was handed the job of replacing Sir William. He struggled to believe his government knew what it was doing. But he admitted to one correspondent that it was not easy. "My fate is hard," he complained. "Forced to an apparent retreat with such an army is mortifying."[30]

There is no need to pity poor Sir Henry. He had spent much of the previous two years in America skewering General Howe's reputation in letters and visits home and was more or less getting what he deserved—up to a point. A short, pudgy, round-faced man with a fussy mouth and intense, penetrating eyes, Clinton had a general's brains and a drill sergeant's personality, which had enabled Howe (and others) to ignore him most of the time.

At Bunker Hill, Clinton's battle plan would have snuffed out the rebellion before it gained military momentum. He gave Howe the plan that shattered Washington's army in the battle of Long Island—one of the few pieces of advice Howe took from him. He urged Howe not to attack Philadelphia without first securing General Burgoyne's safety in Albany, a what-if that would have altered the course of the war.

So here Sir Henry was in Philadelphia, wallowing in self-pity, his favorite hobby. But he was by no means a pitiful general. Even before Howe departed, Clinton began making hard decisions. When the loyalists learned that Philadelphia would be evacuated, panic reigned. Joseph Galloway went to Howe and asked if they could open negotiations with General Washington to see if they might work out terms that would permit the king's friends to stay in their native city as neutrals.

Howe, no longer in command by this time, asked Sir Henry if he would mind if a delegation led by Galloway went to Valley Forge under a British flag of truce. Clinton's answer was a curt, unconditional no. Perhaps they could approach Washington privately, the easygoing Howe suggested. Sir Henry was even more negative. "It is to be remembered that half the garrison of New York are provincials, who might be certain of getting what terms they pleased by betraying the post," Clinton replied. "Would they not be tempted if they conceived all our hopes in this country to be over, which an accommodation between these people and Washington would give them just reason to suspect?"

Clinton's response was irrefutable, and Sir William went home without further argument. Soon three thousand desperate men and women, many with children, and all with tons of baggage, were beseeching Sir Henry for space on the transports crowding the Delaware to ferry the

British army to New York. Sir Henry was forced to make a difficult decision. Having accepted responsibility for these people, he had to offer them
transportation, which meant there would not be enough room on the
available ships for his soldiers. That meant he would have to march over-
land through New Jersey to New York City.[31]

This may be why Clinton referred to his coming departure as an "apparent" retreat. The word suggested that the new commander in chief was
by no means averse to turning the withdrawal into a decisive battle if General Washington gave him an opportunity. Sir Henry and his frustrated
soldiers had not abandoned all hope of victory.

TEN

GENERAL DOUBLE
TROUBLE

I N VALLEY FORGE, the Continental Army was not only acquiring discipline, it was gaining in numbers as new recruits arrived in response to
General Washington's repeated calls. By the end of May the army was
reporting 10,576 infantry on hand. With commissioned and noncommis-
sioned officers and artillerymen added, the total was 15,061. That number
was a long way from the 40,000 men the committee in camp had promised to push for in Congress. But it made Washington confident that the
army could handle a British offensive if the enemy had such a move in
mind. Just in case, Washington detailed men to improve the camp's fortifications, which had never been completed during the rigors of the winter.[1]

As the weather warmed, the huts of the enlisted men grew fetid and
unhealthy. They had no windows, and twelve men had been living in each of
them for five months. The odors are not hard to imagine. Washington
ordered two windows installed in each hut to let in some fresh air. This
order may not have been widely obeyed. Later in the month he ordered
the mud removed from the chinks in the logs to improve the circulation.
But the inside air remained odoriferous. The outside air was not much
better. The commander in chief ordered cleanup squads to get to work
burying dead animals and the decaying leftovers from butchered cattle.

The commissary and quartermaster departments were beginning to operate smoothly under Nathanael Greene and Jeremiah Wadsworth. The army was eating well. Major Samuel Ward Jr. of Rhode Island gave his prospective bride, Phebe, a summary of his diet: At dinnertime he got "a piece of good beef or pork tho generally of both—and have as good bread as I ever eat." They had tea, coffee, milk, and sugar "in plenty." He added that he had two blankets on his cot and was in danger of becoming a "macaroni" (a dandy). He had his hair powdered every day.

As for the enlisted men in Ward's regiment, they had begun to "grow healthy as the fine season approaches." If recently ordered uniforms arrived, they would also begin to look "decent." Blankets remained in short supply, so he was going to leave his two behind him for "the poor lads" when he left camp to journey to Rhode Island and Phebe's arms. Whenever he had a chance, he tried to "alleviate their sufferings." [2]

This new sense of responsibility for the enlisted men is evidence of the impact of Baron von Steuben's reforms. There were other signs of the changes the Baron had wrought. Steuben told one correspondent that the most satisfying sight he had seen since he came to Valley Forge was a colonel, the commander of a regiment, teaching a new recruit the manual of arms. The Baron all but shouted the eighteenth-century equivalent of "Right on!"

II

Colonel John Cropper of Virginia was still trying to placate his impatient wife, Peggy. On May 10, he dolefully informed her that he would have to stay at least another two weeks, until a replacement arrived to take charge of the brigade he had been commanding in the absence of Brigadier General William Woodford. Colonel Cropper assured Peggy that he was "persevering in the same love I left you with, for I am sure my angel cou'd never doubt my sincerity." In the letter he enclosed a "plain gold ring, an exact fellow to which I have on my finger." [3]

Less than two weeks later, Colonel Cropper wrote another plaintive letter to Peggy, informing her that he would not be home until September, if then, because the campaign of 1778 had begun and he was "desirous to see the end of it." A glimpse of the kind of letters he was getting from Peggy is visible in his confession that he knew he had disappointed her in "my several promises to come home from time to time." He admitted he was not surprised to learn that she had begun to wonder if he planned "never to come."

In a tight corner, Colonel Cropper counterattacked. He reminded Peggy that he had married her over the objections of his mother and father and virtually all his friends. He had been "faithful & constant at a time I might have ruin'd your reputation forever"—words that suggest he and Peggy had become lovers before their marriage. The colonel begged his wife "by the remembrance of the pleasures we have enjoyed together" to be content. In a momentary reversal, Cropper vowed that if she still insisted on his return, he would "resign immediately" on the receipt of her letter and come home. But this offer patently assumed that such a letter would never arrive. The next paragraph was full of requests for "two or three shirts" and other clothes he would need for the campaign. Colonel Cropper went home on furlough later in the year.[4]

III

Thanks to the porous state of the British lines around Philadelphia and the industry of General Washington's secret agents, there is little doubt that American officers at Valley Forge were aware of the dramas that Howe's Strolling Players presented at the Southwark Theater during the winter. The Americans considered themselves officers and gentlemen on a par with their redcoat counterparts, so it is not entirely surprising that they too decided to stage some plays. During the winter, these theatricals were performed for understandably small audiences, since there was little room in any of the structures at Valley Forge for a crowd. From mentions in a few letters and journals, Washington's Strolling Players seem to have performed in the Bakehouse, where the army's bread was made. The plays were so popular, Ensign George Ewing ruefully noted in his journal, that one night he and others with tickets could not find a seat.[5]

The balmy spring weather and the ebullience created by the French alliance combined to produce an interest in staging plays for a larger audience. General Washington, who loved the theater and regularly attended plays in Williamsburg, Virginia, before the war, was more than amenable. In fact, he may well have suggested the first production, *Cato*, the 1713 drama by Joseph Addison, which was his favorite play.

Even if he had not been commander in chief, there would have been no argument from his strolling players. *Cato* was the most popular play in eighteenth-century America. It had been presented at playhouses and on college campuses from Harvard to the College of William and Mary since 1732. The drama had played a crucial role in establishing the commercial theater in America.[6]

Cato was also a shrewd choice from a political point of view. The plot deals with the fate of Marcus Portius Cato the Younger, a Roman aristocrat who opposed the rise of Julius Caesar and tried to rally Rome to its traditional republican virtues. As the play opens, Cato has retreated to Utica, an outpost in North Africa near Carthage, with a forlorn remnant of his army. Caesar's legions are only a few miles away, ready to annihilate the fugitive and his followers.

Cato remains grimly defiant. When the body of his son, Marcus, killed in a fight with traitors who want to surrender, is laid before him, Cato says:

> "Who would not be that youth? What pity is it
> That we can die but once to serve our country."

Captain Nathan Hale remembered those lines when he faced a British hangman in New York in 1776. Hale had probably performed and certainly read *Cato* at Yale. Other lines inspired Patrick Henry early in the revolutionary ferment:

> "It is not now time to talk of aught
> But chains or conquest, liberty or death."[7]

In the end, Cato chooses suicide rather than surrender to Caesar. For a general who had just defeated a conspiracy to replace him because, among other things, he was in danger of becoming a demigod like Caesar, General Washington's choice of *Cato* was a perfect refutation of this slander. There were obvious comparisons between his ordeal at Valley Forge and Cato's in Utica. The commander in chief did not have to waste time in wordy attacks on his enemies in and out of Congress. All he had to do was attend the play.

Cato also stirred powerful personal memories in General Washington. When he was in his twenties, he had performed in the play at the mansion of Mount Vernon's aristocratic neighbors, the Fairfaxes. At twenty-six, forlornly in love with Sally Fairfax, the wife of his close friend William Fairfax, Washington had written her tormented letters during the French and Indian War, wondering if there was a similar love in Sally's heart. At one point, on his way to the war zone in western Virginia, he wrote: "I should think my time more agreeably spent, believe me, in playing a part in Cato with the company you mention, and myself doubly happy in being the Juba to such a Marcia as you make." Juba was a Numidian prince who was in love with Cato's daughter, Marcia.[8]

Late on the sunny afternoon of May 11, did these memories swirl through General Washington's head as he escorted Martha to the open-air theater his engineers had constructed on the banks of the Schuylkill? Perhaps. He could face the memories without guilt. He and Sally had done nothing dishonorable, beyond exchanging an occasional longing look. The general was more than happy with the woman he had married little more than six months after he had written that letter.

IV

At the theater the Washingtons were greeted by General Nathanael Greene and his sultry wife, Caty; General Knox and his rotund spouse, Lucy; and several other generals whose wives had been inspired by the spring weather to pay them a visit. Officers by the dozen were also on hand in their best uniforms. Enlisted men gathered beyond the theater's boundaries to enjoy the spectacle, even if they could not hear the actors.

The officer actors performed superbly, according to letters from witnesses. The play's message rang out in the soft May air, against the background of the thousand fetid huts where the army's commitment to freedom and public virtue had been so harshly tested during the winter. Cato was the model to whom all the male characters aspired. One of his sons says they must "copy out our father's bright example" as a model for their lives. Again, the implication, that Washington was America's Cato, was clear to the officers who had endured with the commander in chief the physical and political ordeal of Valley Forge.

William Bradford, deputy commissary general of musters, was one of the play's enthusiastic spectators. He wrote to a friend: "The camp can now afford you some entertainment." He described the audience for *Cato* as "numerous and splendid," the scenery "in [good] taste," and the performances "admirable." He added that "if the enemy does not retire from Philadelphia soon, our theatrical amusements will continue."[9]

With General Washington's warm approval, two more plays were soon in rehearsal and a third was in the planning stage. But news of the theatricals received a very cool reception in York. No matter how noble the sentiments of *Cato*, Samuel Adams, James Lovell, and company considered plays incompatible with their vision of revolutionary America as a Christian Sparta. The performance only added fuel to their continuing animosity toward the Continental Army and its commander.

V

At headquarters, General Washington was in a sunny mood. General Gates was on his way to semioblivion in the northern department, subject to Washington's orders. General Mifflin had arrived in Valley Forge with the blessing of Congress, and the commander in chief had assigned him a division. At a council of war on May 7, before Gates headed north, the utmost politeness prevailed on both sides as the army's generals discussed the coming campaign.

In a candid letter to his congressional ally Gouverneur Morris, Washington said "it was determined out of respect for Congress" (which had ordered to council) "to treat the new members [Gates and Mifflin] with civility." The language suggests there was a discussion between Washington and the other generals, some of whom were inclined to incivility. We know that Nathanael Greene was outraged by Mifflin's return to the army. Gates reported General Washington's courteous reception to Henry Laurens with obvious relief, which the president of Congress echoed in his reply.[10]

Meanwhile Gouverneur Morris told Washington how he had disposed of General Conway once and for all. When the former inspector general returned to York from Albany and began claiming he had not really resigned, the burly New Yorker immediately saw that Conway's backers in Congress were readying declamations in his behalf. Morris took the floor and expressed in "the very strongest terms" his "satisfaction and joy" at the resignation. "This gave a very different turn to affairs," he continued. "Panegyrick dwindled to apology" and the resignation was accepted. It was a smashing demonstration of Washington's support in Congress.[11]

VI

Vastly increasing the commander in chief's satisfaction was news from York on May 15 that Congress had finally worked out a compromise on the issue of half pay for officers. The righteous true whigs of New England, led by Sam Adams's disciple, James Lovell, refused to condone a pension for life and the right to sell commissions. Washington's supporters, led by Gouverneur Morris, proposed half pay for seven years to officers who stayed in the service until the end of the war. Still the true whigs said no and insisted on submitting the proposition to the states. It swiftly became apparent that Pennsylvania was the swing state, with its delegation split 1–1.

Gouverneur Morris described the dicey situation to Pennsylvania delegate Robert Morris (no relation). Absorbed in running his farflung enterprises, the merchant king seldom attended Congress. "Think one moment and come here the next," the brusque young New Yorker wrote. Another New York delegate, William Duer, scrawled at the bottom of the letter: "Be here by eleven o'clock to Morrow." The merchant king came, and on May 13 half pay for seven years passed, six states to five.[12]

The victors accepted an additional gesture to congressional authority from the true whigs. Only those officers who took a solemn oath of loyalty to the government of the United States would be eligible for this considerably reduced generosity. They also agreed to give enlisted men a bonus of eighty dollars at the end of the war.

Most of the officers were satisfied with the compromise. Half pay for seven years would give a man time to repair his finances after he left the army. Major Samuel Ward told Phebe he now had the pleasure of "feeling myself in some degree independant [sic]." The scion of a wealthy family, Sam did not need the money, but he thought that "commissions will now be valuable and will be sought after by young gentlemen of parts and breeding." He saw a "new ardor for the service" invigorating the army.[13]

Two weeks later, on May 27, Congress passed another reform aimed at soothing the disgruntled officer corps. They raised officers' salaries by a third to keep pace with rising inflation and the depreciating Continental currency. A colonel would now receive $75 a month, a captain $40, and a lieutenant 26\frac{2}{3}$. This was still only about half of what a British officer of the same rank pocketed. But the Americans accepted the idea that their salaries should not be too far beyond the scale of what sergeants ($8) and privates ($6$\frac{2}{3}$) were paid each month. They appreciated the general idea of equality as stated in the Declaration of Independence and did not want to be imitators of the British class system.[14]

For Washington, the half-pay compromise resolved his potentially ruinous argument with Henry Laurens. The president of Congress had written the general several letters, setting out his objections to half pay in often strident terms. At one point he portrayed officers on half pay living on money that had been contributed by "widows and orphans of soldiers who had bled and died by their sides." Laurens pictured the ex-officers "bated [baited] in every House of Assembly as the drones & incumbrances of society, pointed at by boys and girls, there goes a man who robs me every year of part of my pittance."

Considering the importance that Washington attached to the measure, it was almost miraculous that he kept his temper. He never replied to any of Laurens's diatribes in kind. He simply affirmed in the plainest, tersest sentences that after "giving the subject the fairest consideration I am capable of," he still favored it. The happy outcome of the disagreement was a testimony to the mutual respect and affection felt by the two men, even when a vital issue drew them in opposite directions. It was also additional evidence of Washington's talent as a politician.[15]

VII

During this same proverbially merry month of May, General Washington had to deal with the appearance of a potentially troublesome figure: Major General Charles Lee, the second in command of the Continental Army. Lee had finally returned to the Americans after eighteen months in captivity in New York. Congress still placed enormous value on this gentleman. The ideologues of the Benjamin Rush–James Lovell–Samuel Adams persuasion considered him another true whig and a military genius in the bargain.

Like Horatio Gates, Charles Lee had been a passionate advocate for an early declaration of independence, which endeared him to both Adamses. Well read and well educated, he could discourse on military and political history by the hour. He never stopped reminding everyone within range of his voice that he had distinguished himself as a fighting captain in the French and Indian War and later won cavalry battles for the British in Portugal as a lieutenant colonel. After the war, he had acquired a major general's commission in the Polish army when he became an intimate of Poland's king.[16]

Lee constantly dilated on the sacrifices he had made for the American cause—in particular his abandonment of his retired officer's half pay for life and the loss of property he owned in England and the West Indies. He did not accept a commission as a major general in the American army until Congress agreed to compensate him for his losses. Later they advanced him thirty thousand dollars to pay for his estate in Virginia.

Whigs had to admit that Lee was a peculiar character. He traveled everywhere with a pack of dogs, whose company he often said he preferred to humans. He made no attempt to conform to conventional morality and openly consorted with prostitutes he picked up in his travels. If any other general in the Continental Army had committed such public faux pas, Samuel Adams and his followers would have fulminated by the hour about the moral failures of the gentlemen of the blade.

Physically Lee was unprepossessing. He was short and skeletonically thin, with a permanent sneer affixed to his sardonic mouth. His personal appearance was slovenly. He was the worst possible choice for second in command of the Continental Army, which needed leaders who looked and acted like soldiers and could communicate military pride to their men. Lee's one talent was an imperious style. He never displayed the slightest doubt about any tactic or strategy he proposed, and could defend them ferociously. For a while, General Washington and many other Americans, including Nathanael Greene, were impressed by him.[17]

Capping this picture of Lee's unsuitability as an American leader was his typically British contempt for the Irish, who constituted two-fifths of the Continental Army by the time he reached Valley Forge in 1778. He never missed a chance to denigrate the Celts in his conversation and letters. He frequently referred to them as "banditti." In one 1776 letter he told Washington some recent recruits were good men, "some Irish rascals excepted." In another letter he claimed the Irish had "contaminated" native-born soldiers.[18]

VIII

In 1776, General Lee had turned his acerbic tongue on Congress and the American army's high command when the Continental Army lost its struggle to defend New York. At one point he told his friend Horatio

Gates that Congress "stumble[d] every step—I do not mean one or two of the cattle but the whole stable." Lee reserved his nastiest shafts for General Washington. He agreed heartily with Joseph Reed that the commander in chief 's "indecisive mind" was a "curse" that guaranteed "eternal defeat." This conviction gave Lee carte blanche (as he saw it) to ignore Washington's repeated orders to march his four thousand troops into New Jersey to contest the British invasion of the state and defend Philadelphia. Instead, Lee wanted to call out every militiaman in America and put himself at their head with the temporary title of dictator.

At first glance, this idea seems to make Lee a compatriot of Benjamin Rush and his fellow military geniuses who had spent the winter urging the Pennsylvania true whigs to adopt their version of this insane idea. But Lee was a European radical. Temperamentally he was closer to Robespierre and Danton than to Washington and most Americans leaders.

General Lee closed his 1776 performance by separating himself and his staff from his troops in a part of New Jersey where a former cavalryman should have known British dragoons were apt to be roaming. He was captured by a handful of horsemen—a fiasco that would have left most generals so mortified they might have resigned or at least apologized. But Lee's huge ego made him incapable of any such gesture.[19]

IX

The captive arrived at Valley Forge a few days after the British paroled him in April and agreed in principle to swap him for a captured British general. General Washington sent one of his aides, Richard Kidder Meade, to meet Lee on the road with a half dozen dragoons and escort him to headquarters, where he was the guest of honor at a dinner that night. Lee was given a bedroom behind Mrs. Washington's sitting room in the tiny house. The next day he was late for breakfast because he had invited into the house by the back door a British sergeant's wife he had picked up in Philadelphia. Elias Boudinot, the commissary of prisoners, who had grown to dislike Lee intensely during their numerous contacts while the general was in British hands, called her "a dirty shameless hussy."

A few days later Lee headed for York, where he told General Washington he had a "hobby horse" he wanted to lay before Congress: a plan for remodeling the American army. Lee was soon hobnobbing with the New England delegates who still worshipped him. They were in an angry mood because Lee was still a prisoner, albeit on parole, and unable to rejoin the army.

In the course of the dickering that led to Lee's parole, Washington had obtained the exchange of Colonel Ethan Allen of Vermont for a British officer of his rank. Allen had been a captive since 1775. The ideologues accused Washington of violating their instructions to exchange no prisoner before General Lee. They persuaded Congress to write a nasty rebuke to the commander in chief, virtually accusing him of delaying Lee's return to the army.

Numerous pro-Washington delegates objected to the rough language of this resolution. At one point, when it looked as if the majority of delegates present would approve it, Thomas Burke of North Carolina walked out, leaving Congress without a quorum. That led to a separate brawl, in which Burke defended himself against the charge of contempt of Congress. The North Carolinian had long been convinced that the New Englanders never stopped looking for an opportunity to insult General Washington.[20]

The contretemps revealed that hostility toward Washington and the army was still running high in the true whig parts of Congress. Many New Englanders believed that General Greene and others around Washington were jealous of General Lee and would prefer to see him remain a prisoner indefinitely. This idea had its roots in Thomas Mifflin's attacks on Greene during the brawl over Horatio Gates.

A disturbed Henry Laurens told his son John: "I am greatly distressed by circumstances now in agitation respecting your friend. I think I once said 'I hope he will never afford . . . them his own consent [cooperation] to hurt him.'" These words suggest that Laurens feared the paragraph was so insulting, it might give Washington new thoughts of resignation.[21]

Only after more hours of strenuous argument was the offensive paragraph deleted by a vote of five states to three, with two others divided.

There is little doubt that Lee thoroughly enjoyed this blowup, which made it clear he was still the darling of the congressional radicals. This emboldened him to unveil his "hobby horse," which, with characteristic modesty, he promised would lead to "the formation of the American army in the least expensive manner possible." At the same time it would supply them with maneuvers so simple, the enlisted ranks could learn them in a few weeks.[22]

Lee's plan made a mockery of Washington's and Steuben's attempts to professionalize the Continental Army. Lee derided their approach as the "European plan." He insisted Americans would never learn it. They would always make "an awkward figure," Europeans would laugh at them, and they would lose every battle that depended on formal maneuvers. It was "nonsense" to expect Americans, even with superior numbers, to surpass British regulars in discipline and ardor.

Lee's solution was to fight on the defensive, harassing the British wherever they went. Meanwhile, a huge increase in American cavalry would provide a new weapon in this "partisan" (guerrilla) war. In short, Lee saw little use for General Washington's army. Militia could harass the British just as well.[23]

This version of his plan was relatively restrained compared to the proposal Lee had given Elias Boudinot while still a captive. At that time, he had virtually ordered the commissary of prisoners to tell Congress that the American army and the rest of the revolutionary apparatus should retreat to Pittsburgh, where they could regroup and presumably learn from the great General Lee how to fight the war his way. When Lee arrived in Valley Forge, he asked Boudinot what Congress thought of this earlier brainstorm. Boudinot replied he had not thought it was worth mentioning to them.[24]

Both proposals were all too visible evidence of Lee's incredible arrogance—and his defeatism, an interesting paradox. The setbacks of 1776 had destroyed his faith in the American soldier. Here was a man whom Washington had worked hard to liberate presenting Congress with a plan that made the commander in chief a mere figurehead. Worse, Lee had not even discussed it with Washington, except in jocose references to his "hobby horse." Although there is nothing on the record, it is hard to believe the political side of General Washington thought highly of Lee's performance.

X

After several days in York, Lee set off for Virginia to visit his estate. Along the way he sent Henry Laurens a letter suggesting that he be swapped for General Burgoyne. He said it would speed his exchange because Howe had no use for Burgoyne, while "I am well and hope always shall be with General Washington and . . . am persuaded (considering how he is surrounded) that he cannot do without me."

This echo of Mifflin's accusations aimed at Greene and other generals was hardly music to Laurens's ears. Around the same time, Lee sent Washington a copy of his plan, blithely indifferent, so it seems, to the fact that he had first gone to Congress to get backing for it.[25]

In these erratic proceedings, one thing is certain: Lee did not impress President Henry Laurens. Toward the end of his plan to transform the army, Lee added a warning that the British were planning a foray up the Susquehanna River to Lancaster. Laurens told one of his correspondents that he was tempted to add "and be cut off " à la Burgoyne. With equal skepticism, Laurens reported Lee's claim that "British officers of his acquaintance" generally wished for a generous peace and "not a few approve of our opposition."

Along with these loaded remarks, Lee threw in numerous aspersions on Washington's ability as a commander in chief, which left Laurens with a very sour view of the Continental Army's second-ranking general. Out of the loop for eighteen months, Lee apparently had not a clue that Laurens was unshakably pro-Washington.[26]

XI

While Lee was roiling the political waters, General Washington and President Laurens were dealing with the military meaning of the British conciliatory proposals and the news of the French alliance. Analyzing reports from the numerous spies Captain Allan McLane sent into Philadelphia, the commander in chief concluded there was little doubt that General Clinton intended to evacuate the city. However, the possibility of an offensive thrust from this new commander could not be discounted.

Washington decided to commit 2,200 troops to a reconnaissance in force under the Marquis de Lafayette. He ordered the Frenchman to move closer to Philadelphia and choose a position that would enable him to report any sudden movement by the enemy. Lafayette was expected to check such a thrust until the rest of the American army mustered to meet it. If there was a chance to attack the British rear guard as they left Philadelphia, he had orders to inflict maximum damage on them.

It was a risky assignment to give a twenty-year-old major general. But Washington was aware that the Marquis was still disgruntled after the ludicrous failure of his expedition to invade Canada. Although General Washington and President Laurens had assured him that his reputation remained undamaged, the Marquis was not entirely convinced. The news of the French alliance, and the imminent arrival of a French fleet, made Lafayette's state of mind important to the Americans. This new assignment was public proof of the commander in chief's continuing confidence in him.

General Washington all but confessed his uneasiness in the detailed orders he gave the Marquis. He was to observe the utmost caution against a surprise attack. It was "unadvisable" to take a "stationary post," because the enemy had numerous spies who would be quick to report his position. Lafayette's detachment was "very valuable" and its loss would be a "severe blow to this army." Under no circumstances was he to attack "without the greatest prospect" of success. To protect Lafayette personally, the commander in chief added two platoons of his lifeguard to the

expedition. His aide John Laurens volunteered to serve in the same capacity for the Marquis.[27]

As an added precaution against surprise, Washington gave Lafayette
fifty of Daniel Morgan's riflemen as well as Captain Allan McLane and his
troop of cavalrymen to serve as scouts. To these experts at partisan warfare
he added forty-seven Oneida Indians. The Oneidas were a product of the
Marquis' diplomacy during his trip to northern New York. Lafayette had
joined General Philip Schuyler and other Indian commissioners at a
council to try to persuade the Iroquois Confederacy to join the Americans
or at least remain neutral. Only the Oneidas and some Tuscaroras and
Onondagas showed up, but Lafayette's presence proved to be a catalyst to
an agreement.

During the French and Indian War, the Oneidas had been allies of the
French, and they responded with enthusiasm when they were told that
Lafayette represented their ancient "father," the French king. They adopted
him into their tribe and named him Kaywela, after one of their greatest
warriors. Lafayette, who had never seen an Indian before, referred to them
in a letter to Washington as "scalping gentlemen." [28]

After several days of parleying and distributing presents, the Oneidas
and their allies agreed to take up the hatchet for the Americans and promised to send about fifty of their best warriors to Valley Forge to serve
under General Washington. The commander in chief greeted them with
great ceremony. They were escorted to the artillery park, where thirteen
cannon were discharged to welcome them. Washington invited their chief
warrior to dinner at headquarters, along with the French interpreter who
had accompanied them from northern New York, Chevalier Anne-Louis
Tousard.

XII

As the reconnaissance in force prepared to leave Valley Forge, Lafayette
wrote to Captain Allan McLane, telling him price was no object when it
came to obtaining some spies. He was prepared to pay as much as fifteen

guineas per agent out of his own deep pockets.[29] Marching at 10 a.m. on May 18, Lafayette crossed the Schuylkill at one of its many fords and soon reached Barren Hill, a steep-sided ridge some twelve miles from Philadelphia. Here, contrary to Washington's orders, the young general decided to set up a permanent camp. The site was protected by the river on the right, and the Ridge Road, down which he had marched, offered a ready retreat. Nearby was a ruined church and cemetery, which could easily be converted into strong defenses. Another road ran to a nearby Schuylkill ford, which would be handy in an emergency.

The Marquis ordered McLane and his horsemen to patrol the Ridge Road, which ran directly to Philadelphia. The Oneidas and Morgan's men accompanied him with orders to range through the woods and seize anyone who might be reconnoitering the camp. Other roads were to be protected by General Potter and six hundred Pennsylvania militia. One road was especially important. It ran through the town of White Marsh, curved around Barren Hill, and could be used to cut off Lafayette's retreat. The Marquis ordered General Potter to station a strong detachment of his militia in White Marsh to bar access to this route. Why Lafayette gave this vital task to the militia remains a mystery. His two-month absence in northern New York must have led him to forget their unreliability.[30]

Unlike the trumpet blasts and toasts of the Mischianza that preoccupied the British high command in Philadelphia, the night of May 18 was quiet to the point of dullness on and around Barren Hill. There does not seem to be any evidence that Lafayette—or Washington—factored the grand fete into their plans for the expedition. Lafayette's confidence in his choice of a base camp grew stronger. He devoted himself to interviewing prospective spies brought in by Captain McLane.

That daring horseman no doubt told the Marquis about the prodigal tribute to General Howe and the caper he and his men had attempted to disrupt the festivities. The extravaganza may have made Lafayette feel all the more secure. It would take the British high command several days to recover from their hangovers. The gorgeous farewell confirmed rumors that General Howe was going home, and this change of command would logically leave the royal army even more hors de combat.

The journal of Private Joseph Plumb Martin reveals how relaxed the Americans became. To pass the time, the Oneidas began giving a display of their phenomenal marksmanship with the bow and arrow. They were shooting in the vicinity of the ruined church. Private Martin spied a bat high up in the roof and asked one of the Indians to shoot it. He did so, and the single bat turned out to be one of a cluster. In an instant, the whole interior of the church was full of flapping bats. "It was likewise instantly full of Indians and soldiers," Martin recalled. "The poor bats fared hard; it was sport for all hands." [31]

There is an old adage in the art of warfare: Never assume you know what the enemy is going to do. General Howe was indeed going home, but his departure date was a week away. He was still de facto commander in chief, even though he had handed over the army to Henry Clinton. On the morning of May 19, a deserter from Lafayette's force arrived in Philadelphia and told the British where the Americans were camped and who was in command. The traitor had followed the road that ran through White Marsh, which enabled him to bring even more vital news: there was not a trace of General Potter and his militiamen in or near the town. [32]

XIII

The news dispelled any and all alcoholic fumes from the brains of the British high command. Here was a chance to execute what the eighteenth century called a "coup de main." It would be a blow that had exquisite propaganda overtones. Barely three weeks after the announcement of the French alliance, Sir William Howe in one of his famous flanking movements would envelop and seize France's chief spokesman in America and carry him back to England a state prisoner. It would not only mortify the French, it would silence General Howe's numerous critics in and out of the English government.

Orders went out to generals, colonels. Howe was so certain of success, he invited his brother the admiral along to enjoy the show. (He rode in a carriage.) Sir Henry Clinton, intimidated by the prospect of a Howe comeback, glumly agreed to go along as another spectator. By this time British engineers with the help of knowledgeable loyalists had long since mapped the countryside around Philadelphia. Howe gave General James Grant five thousand men with orders to take the road through White Marsh, get behind Lafayette, and cut off his retreat to Valley Forge. Another strong detachment under General Charles Grey of Paoli Massacre fame was to seize the ford nearest to Barren Hill. General Howe and the rest of the main army would advance up the Ridge Road and assault Lafayette from the front.[33]

Grant and Grey with their orders to envelop the Marquis' rear set off early on the night of May 19–20. Howe, who had a shorter route, waited several hours so that everyone would be in position to attack simultaneously. Virtually the entire British army in Philadelphia was on the march—something General Washington would have paid a spy many dollars to know. It was also evidence of how much importance Howe and his generals attached to capturing or killing Lafayette.

What happened next has many versions, a not infrequent happenstance in reporting through the fog of war. In this case, there was a literal fog shrouding the meadows and woods. At the head of General Grant's column rode a troop of dragoons. The sound of their hoofbeats supposedly awakened a captain of the Pennsylvania militia in the town of White Marsh. He peered out his window and glimpsed the red coats of the horsemen. Soon the tramp of thousands of feet became audible. The captain leaped out his back window in his nightshirt and ran through meadows and woods toward Barren Hill, some two miles away. He was on the brink of collapse when he met a wandering surgeon from Lafayette's army, who raced the rest of the way to Barren Hill to warn the Marquis.[34]

At first, Lafayette was undisturbed by the news. He thought the red-coated dragoons were Pennsylvania militia horsemen, who also wore red uniforms. He was still under the illusion that the militia was guarding the road through White Marsh. However, he sent one of his aides to reconnoiter the situation beyond the camp's perimeter. It did not take the aide long to discover that Grant and his men were almost in Lafayette's rear.

Private Joseph Plumb Martin soon learned the bad news. He was part of a detachment who had spent the night guarding the officers' horses. The officers' servants ("waiters," as they were called) rushed up to him as dawn was breaking to take the horses. Martin and his friends dashed to join their company, which was in formation, with their guns loaded. The Connecticut soldier thought he "should soon have some better sport than killing bats."[35]

At this moment, the sound of gunfire from the direction of the Ridge Road to Philadelphia reached everyone's ears. Morgan's riflemen and the Oneida braves were on picket duty on that road. As the firing continued, Captain Allan McLane came racing back to Barren Hill to report an immense number of British soldiers were coming up the road. Finally Lafayette realized what was about to happen and saw his only chance was a rapid retreat.

Morgan's men and the Oneidas had encountered Howe's main column in the dawn gloom. They immediately started shooting, and the British lead companies opened into line-of-battle formation to respond to them. For five minutes, the bullets flew furiously. Finally the British perceived that the opposition was only a handful of men and decided to scatter them in a cavalry charge.

A troop of dragoons thundered toward the Americans and Oneidas, sabers raised, roaring death and destruction. The Oneidas responded with their own special brand of defiance. As one voice, they released a tremendous war whoop. Neither the British horses nor the men in the saddles had ever heard anything like it. Horses bolted and dragoons leaped to the ground and ran for their lives. It took the British another five minutes to reorganize and order the infantry to advance with fixed bayonets. The Morgan men and the Oneidas fell back, firing steadily.

By the time they reached Barren Hill, Lafayette's men were on the road to the one ford (Matson's) that the British had not yet blocked. The Marquis could claim some credit for this development. He had sent some men into the woods with two cannon and told them to act aggressively when they met Grant's men, as if there were a whole column of regulars behind them. Grant was a supercautious general. He hesitated, and finally decided the men in the woods were indeed the heads of columns.

He ignored advice from his second in command, General Sir William Erskine, to push as fast as possible for Matson's ford, where Lafayette was unquestionably heading. Instead Grant advanced toward the Barren Hill church, where he thought Lafayette's men were still concentrated. When he got there, he found only General Howe's men looking flustered and frustrated.[36]

Meanwhile, with Morgan's sharpshooters and the Oneidas bringing up the rear of the column, Lafayette's men were legging it to Matson's ford. Their escape had another component: the training they had received from Baron von Steuben enabled them to move swiftly in a compact body, instead of in their previous Indian file formation. If that amateurish style of march had still been the rule, at least half the little army would have been caught on Barren Hill and killed or captured. Almost certainly Lafayette, who commanded the rear guard, would have been one of the victims.

From Valley Forge, as the Americans approached Matson's ford, came the boom of signal guns. Lookouts in watchtowers Washington had erected on Mount Joy had seen the roads swarming with red coats and notified the commander in chief. Within minutes, the brigades were mustering and ready to march. The British heard the guns too, and Howe decided his scattered army was in a vulnerable position. He glumly issued orders to return as swiftly as possible to Philadelphia and the safety of its ring of redoubts.

One British eyewitness in Grant's cavalry got close enough to see the Americans wading through the swift Schuylkill at Matson's ford, which was about four feet deep. He said they looked like "corks on a fishing seine." As soon as they emerged from the icy river, the Americans formed on the opposite shore and exchanged fire with British horsemen who attacked the rear guard, killing or capturing several men. Concentrated fire from the opposite bank soon sent the dragoons flying.

Here is where the Oneidas may have lost some warriors. They were among the last of Lafayette's army to cross the river. Two of them proved their loyalty to Anne-Louis Tousard. As he reported later, his horse bolted and threw him to the ground. The Oneidas seized the dazed Frenchman and half carried, half dragged him across the swift river.[37]

XIV

Unfortunately, neither Lafayette nor many other white eyewitnesses gave the Oneidas the credit they deserved for the skirmish in the woods on the Ridge Road which held up Howe's main column and for their role in the rear guard's fighting retreat. Many commentators tried to make a joke out of the encounter with the British cavalry, claiming that the Oneidas and the dragoons were equally frightened and both ran away. This prejudiced account is contradicted by other witnesses, who reported that after the British retreat began, the Oneidas and Morgan's men recrossed the Schuylkill and skirmished on the royal army's flanks as they trudged back to Philadelphia.

This sort of courage impressed George Washington. The following year, at his recommendation, one of the leading warriors in the frontier war in northern New York, a St. Regis Mohawk, Lewis Atayataghronghta, was given a commission as lieutenant colonel in the Continental Army. Seven Oneidas and two Tuscaroras were also commissioned at lower ranks.[38]

XV

To prove that he was not intimidated by this narrow escape, Lafayette recrossed the Schuylkill the next day. After spending the night at Barren Hill, as if he were daring General Howe to come out for another try, he returned to Valley Forge. There, Washington said nothing about disobeying his order not to set up a permanent camp. To Congress he commended the Marquis' "timely and handsome retreat." He said similar things to Gouverneur Morris a few days later, though he admitted Lafayette had made a mistake in relying on the Pennsylvania militia to patrol the roads.

President Henry Laurens, acutely aware that it was important to protect Lafayette's (and Washington's) reputation in this adventure, became the Marquis' public relations man. He wrote letters in all directions praising his skillful retreat. On May 27, he sent Francis Hopkinson, author of "The Battle of the Kegs," a detailed account of the clash, including the Oneida war whoop that terrified the British cavalry. "The Marquis' retreat has done him more honor than he would have gained by a drawn battle," the president declared. He urged Hopkinson to convert the account into a newspaper story but without Laurens's name on it. "It may be stiled extract of a letter from York," he suggested.[39]

XVI

The day after Lafayette returned unscathed to Valley Forge, General Charles Lee also reappeared in the winter camp, a free man. He had been exchanged for a captured British general. Lee had again stopped in York on his way to Valley Forge and conferred with his friends in Congress. No doubt with their encouragement, he dashed off a letter to President Henry Laurens, suggesting that he ought to be promoted from major general to lieutenant general—giving him equal rank with General Washington.

General Lee pointed out how many people had been promoted to major general during his captivity, making the rank seem rather ordinary, and claimed if he had stayed in the Polish army, he would have long since become a senior lieutenant general—a very unlikely possibility, since his major general's rank was honorary. He also declared that General Washington had assured him Congress would promote him the moment he requested it.

Congress did no such thing. Laurens and other pro-Washington delegates such as Gouverneur Morris pointed out that if anything happened to Washington, Lee would be the army's de facto commander in chief. Having been exposed to his harebrained scheme for reorganizing the army, these gentlemen had no intention of letting this ascension take place.

At the very least it was obvious that Lee was double trouble. He had Conway's arrogance and Gates's inclination to intrigue with backers in Congress. But Washington continued to treat him with the greatest cordiality. When Lee arrived in Valley Forge this time, the commander in chief and his aides met him on the road and massed bands played a welcome. The troops presented arms with the snap and precision they had learned from Baron von Steuben.[40]

Many historians have puzzled over the commander in chief's apparent toleration of this troublesome general. Some have speculated that General Washington was grateful for advice Lee gave him during the battles in and around New York in 1776. Others have wondered if in his own mind the commander in chief was still the inexperienced tyro general of 1775 and was intimidated by Lee's pretensions to genius. This writer is inclined to dismiss such reasoning. In the political context this book has established, and which undoubtedly existed in Washington's mind, it is naive to take all his words and actions literally.

The commander in chief was well aware that he was dealing with another congressional favorite, in some ways more potent than Gates, as Congress's petulant attitude toward Lee's exchange made clear. He was also aware that the standing-army-hating true whigs were eager to renew their war with him. Having defeated General Gates, he was determined to show no hostility to General Lee unless the latter initiated it. Washington was confident that he now had enough backing in Congress to handle the problem child when and if he erupted. Meanwhile, why not go out of his way to welcome and honor him?

XVII

None of the Americans were aware of how chummy Lee had gotten with high-ranking officers in the British army. At one point during his captivity, he had several long conversations with Sir Henry Strachey, another of Lord Howe's secretaries, who persuaded him to ask Congress to send three delegates to discuss "the interests of the public," claiming that "the most salutary effects" would result from it. Congress rightly saw this as an attempt to open unauthorized peace negotiations and demurred.

At the start of the 1777 campaign, Lee submitted to the Howes a proposal to subdue the Americans quickly and relatively painlessly.

He warned against assuming that the capture of Philadelphia would discourage the Americans. Instead, he urged an attack through Maryland to menace the farmers of southeastern Pennsylvania. Control of Maryland would block Virginia's attempts to send troops northward. In two months, Lee promised, the whole American war machine would be "dissolved." Lee claimed he was submitting this plan because he was convinced the Howe brothers would use their influence to win a merciful peace for the Americans.[41]

The Howes ignored Lee's advice in 1777, but the prisoner continued to see himself as a man who could bring peace with honor to both sides. Early in 1778, he wrote to General James Robertson, the military governor of New York, proposing a plan for a reconciliation. The British would withdraw their army and navy, pardon all American rebels, and renounce the power to tax them. The Americans would renounce independence. If the Howes would support these terms, Lee would urge the Americans to accept them.[42]

General Robertson forwarded Lee's letter to General Howe in Philadelphia, who ordered the prisoner transferred to that city, supposedly so Howe could personally administer the oath required for his parole before releasing him. Behind this subterfuge, the two men had conversations in which Howe told Lee about the coming British peace offensive and urged him to join it. Lee was more than willing. No man was more susceptible to delusions of grandeur. He saw himself as the savior who could reconcile the two countries. He apparently dropped some hints about reconciliation when he visited York, but the congressional reception was chilly.[43]

Lee persevered, writing a long letter to Dr. Benjamin Rush, no doubt assuming that any information given to this true whig blabbermouth would be spread far and wide. Lee unabashedly portrayed himself as "an apologist for General Howe." He claimed that he had found him more "friendly candid good natur'd brave and rather sensible than the reverse." Now Howe had seen the light of reconciliation. He had admitted to Lee that he had been "an instrument of wickedness and folly" in the hands of George III and Lord George Germain.[44]

When Clinton succeeded Howe, General Robertson forwarded the new commander a copy of Lee's letter with his peace proposals. Clearly the British saw Lee as a potentially valuable agent on their behalf. Lee's chief biographer has attempted to put a bland face on this performance, noting that there was no mention of money changing hands. There was no need to mention that discomfiting subject. Robertson, Howe, Clinton, and of course Lee were all aware of the British custom of rewarding soldiers who performed some signal service for king and country. Unquestionably, George III would shower riches on the man who got him out of the mess into which he and Lord George Germain had led the country.

A glimpse of Lee's pro-English feelings emerged on June 9 when General Washington administered the new oath of loyalty to the American government that Congress required all officers to take. Lafayette, in his two-month absence from Valley Forge, had also not taken the oath. Washington converted the occasion into a small ceremony, with his aides and other guests on hand. Lafayette completed his oath with no hesitation. When Lee began to read the passage that declared he owed "no allegiance or obedience to George the Third," he lifted his hand from the Bible. Washington noticed this odd movement and asked him why he had removed his hand. "As to King George," Lee said, "I am ready to absolve myself of all allegiance to him, but I have some scruples about the Prince of Wales."

The spectators laughed, assuming it was another bizarre Lee jest. But anyone with a knowledge of English history might have found cause for alarm in the remark. It was common in English politics for ambitious politicians to form a party around the Prince of Wales and oppose the incumbent king. The words suggested that Lee still had a secret allegiance to the British crown and nation.[45]

XVIII

At Valley Forge, Lee renewed his friendship with General Mifflin, who was, of course, delighted to hear his low opinion of Washington and the men around him. The ex-quartermaster was busy playing independent general, creating a training plan for the troops of his division as if Baron von Steuben had never existed, as well as a school where his officers learned mathematics among other things. There was every evidence that these two malcontents were ready to start plotting trouble for Washington at the first opportunity.

With no warning, a resolution from Congress arrived by courier from York. It called for an inquiry into General Mifflin's performance as quartermaster general and insisted on a court-martial if he or his assistants were responsible for "the extraordinary deficiencies" in his department and the "consequent distresses of the army."

The man behind this resolution was General Washington's semisecret ally, President Henry Laurens. He was acting on his challenge to Congressman Francis Dana to name those responsible for the mess in the quartermaster department. Laurens was well aware that he was setting off a political powder keg. In a letter to the president of South Carolina, he reported there was "a violent opposition" to the resolution which raged for "near four hours."

The president declared he could not understand why Mifflin's friends fought so hard to postpone the motion to investigate him. "Tis amazing to me," Laurens wrote with a presumably straight face. "As a man of honor the General [Mifflin] must wish for an investigation to satisfy the public who at present clamor exceedingly upon the subjects of neglect, misapplication [of funds,] peculation etc." Laurens was sure an inquiry would "remove every groundless speculation." [46]

The vote on the motion to postpone showed that the anti-Washington bloc was still more or less functioning as a unit. Samuel Adams, James Lovell, and Richard Henry Lee, along with New England allies such as William Ellery and Roger Sherman of Connecticut, voted to postpone. They lost six states to three, and General Mifflin had to request General Washington's permission to leave the army and rush to York to defend himself.

The commander in chief soberly granted permission, "however inconvenient and injurious it may be to permit the absence of officers in this period." Almost certainly, there were some covert smiles among Washington's aides as this letter was signed.

One of the first things General Mifflin did when he got to York was write to General Gates, telling him he hoped to prove the "malice" that had produced "this well-timed enquiry [sic]." As soon as Mifflin collected his papers, he planned to see Gates and "take your advice on how to proceed." These revealing words suggest that General Gates was not the innocent victim in the get-Washington game as some historians (as well as Gates's contemporaries) have claimed. It seems far more likely that all the chief conspirators were equally involved in this quest for power.

General Mifflin sourly added that their latest recruit, General Lee, "is almost sick of his station he will tell you how matters stand and how every man must act to be of consequence." He meant everyone supposedly had to show deference amounting to idol worship to General Washington.[47]

Alas for General Mifflin, industriously as he collected his papers and wrote angry letters to President Laurens calling for a speedy investigation, Congress somehow never got around to it. Neither was General Washington very cooperative in convening a court-martial, at one point claiming he had heard a rumor that General Mifflin had resigned from the army, which would make court-martialing him moot. Eventually, Mifflin got the message and quit the army to go into politics full-time. He published newspaper articles condemning the "cruel and . . . unjustifiable attack against his character," but he made little progress.

Sam Adams and his friends persuaded Congress to advance Mifflin a million dollars to settle his quartermaster accounts, but in 1780 he was still trying to resolve some of them, suggesting that Henry Laurens may not have been too far wrong when he called Mifflin a crook as well as the "pivot" of the get-Washington group. Thanks to his powerful friends in Congress, no charges were ever brought against the ex–quartermaster general. But Mifflin learned that when it came to playing political hardball, General Washington, with the assistance of Henry Laurens, was in a class by himself.[48]

XIX

General Charles Lee singularly failed to get this message. He continued to criticize the current organization of the Continental Army to anyone who would listen. His latest complaint concerned the lack of intimate connection between a major general and the men he commanded. He felt a general should lead in battle only the men whom he had personally trained. He seemed oblivious of the role of the brigadier generals, who had such an intimate connection and were more than able to fill this spurious gap. A less friendly reading of this demand can view it as another attempt by General Lee to acquire a piece of the army and make it his personal possession—something General Mifflin had also hoped to do.

General Lee also urged Washington to station part of the American army on the lower Susquehanna River because he was sure the British were planning a foray in that direction. Next came a warning that Lee was now convinced the British were going to seize control of the Chesapeake Bay region, rather than retreat to New York, and the Continental Army should do something to counter the threat. The "something" almost certainly involved giving Lee a chunk of the army and an independent command.

Washington finally wrote General Lee a letter, saying he was always ready to discuss his ideas, but he hoped Lee would stop talking about them to all and sundry. The commander in chief preferred his proposals to come "directly to myself." It did not do the army any good to have generals criticizing problems which might simply be "unavoidable."

A soured Lee, obviously annoyed by his failure to overawe Washington, told his friend Benjamin Rush that when he looked back on the war, he saw the whole thing as a series of blunders committed first by the Americans and then topped by the British. Now the Americans had been rescued by the French alliance, or "we were inevitably lost." Not exactly a compliment to his commander in chief.[49]

XX

General Washington was also dealing firmly, even ferociously, with Horatio Gates in the Northern Department. On May 26, he wrote a letter to his erstwhile antagonist that revealed he was far from forgiving the Saratoga hero. Washington had given orders to forward all the available muskets in the Northern Department to Valley Forge as soon as possible. When he got a letter from a deputy quartermaster general in Easton, Pennsylvania, that substantial numbers of guns had arrived there, and then were abruptly recalled by General Gates, the commander in chief was not pleased.

General Washington immediately suspected Gates was up to his old tricks—acting as if the Northern Department were an independent command. In the draft of the letter, there is a revealing sentence crossed out: "What could induce you to give these orders, or how you can justify this countermand, I cannot conceive." Struggling to control his temper, Washington told Gates he now had 2,500 men in camp without guns. An entire regiment had arrived from North Carolina without a single weapon.

"I therefore desire," Washington wrote, that Gates send every available gun in his possession to Valley Forge "without the least delay." Gates's countermand had "greatly disappointed and exceedingly distressed me." Washington crossed out the personal pronoun and instead wrote: "injured the service." He was trying to reduce the personal animosity, but it was a losing fight. The final sentence was as rough-edged as a bayonet thrust: "You will consider the above as an order not to be dispensed with in the present situation of affairs."[50]

It will not surprise readers to learn that General Gates soon persuaded his friends in Congress to transfer him to Boston, where there was nothing to do and therefore no danger of another Washington tongue-lashing.

XXI

The army continued to add recruits. Although welcome, the addition of several thousand men was enough to put an alarming strain on the commissary department. Toward the end of May, John Chaloner, the assistant to Colonel Ephraim Blaine, started to sound like the Chaloner of the December and February starving times. He told the new commissary general, Jeremiah Wadsworth, that there was "not one live bullock or barrel of salt provision in camp." Because of transportation problems, they were getting nothing from the southern states, which meant New England was their only hope. The enlarged army, with its women, children, and civilian wagoners, was now consuming twenty-six thousand rations a day, and the consumption would soon reach thirty thousand. Wadsworth, still relatively new to the job, told Chaloner there was nothing he could do immediately. Part of the shortage was caused by the huge amount of food and rum General Greene had ordered diverted to depots in New Jersey.[51]

On May 30, General Smallwood and the garrison from Wilmington rejoined the army, bringing with them a large number of recruits. Chaloner nervously warned Blaine that this would add another three thousand rations per day to the army. This was "truly distressing" to the commissary department, and Chaloner feared it would have "fatal consequences" for the army.

Chaloner's sole remaining idea was to send for some "poor cattle" being fattened in nearby Pottsgrove. This, Chaloner warned with his usual overkill, "was my last shift betwixt us & death." He added another familiar tune, begging Blaine to return as soon as possible so he could quit this miserable job.[52]

In this crisis, Commissary General Jeremiah Wadsworth soon proved he was not a do-nothing cipher like his predecessor, William Buchanan. He headed for Hartford, Connecticut, where he demanded that the legislature repeal price controls that had been passed with Congress's approval by a group of state representatives who had met in New Haven earlier in 1778. These artificial ceilings were making it almost impossible to buy beef.

Wadsworth went before the Connecticut legislature and told them the grim truth about the army's precarious state. He convinced them that the survival of the nation depended on their repealing the "regulating act" as it was called. The legislature's resistance collapsed and Wadsworth was able to order New England purchasing commissary Henry Champion to buy "fat cattle" at a furious pace, before the price rose. Wadsworth's goal was at least 150 cattle dispatched to Valley Forge every day.

Wadsworth's performance was reassuring evidence that General Washington had chosen the right man to feed the army. At the same time, the emergency atmosphere in which Wadsworth was forced to act was painful evidence that the Continental Army would continue to live a hand-to-mouth existence—what one historian has called "an economy of scarcity." Fortunately, Valley Forge had proven that the army could and would survive such an unnerving regime.[53]

XXII

In Philadelphia, it was soon obvious that the British were going to evacuate the city. Henry Laurens told Francis Hopkinson that a stream of loyalists and deserters were fleeing into the countryside, talking freely of Sir Henry Clinton's plans. Loyalists who came to Valley Forge were received politely by Washington, who told them there was nothing he could do for them. They would have to make their peace with the assembly and ruling council of Pennsylvania, in Lancaster—an unappealing proposition. These radicals still breathed fiery detestation on the "disaffected" and remained determined to confiscate their property down to the last stick of furniture and hang those who had cooperated with the British army in any way.

Complicating matters was the arrival of three British peace commissioners, who had power to negotiate a reconciliation along the lines of Parliament's proposals. They had been told nothing about General Clinton's orders to evacuate Philadelphia. These gentlemen were thunderstruck when they realized that Congress, buoyed by the French alliance and now by the British retreat, had not the slightest motivation to talk to them.

One commissioner, William Eden, former head of the British secret service, suggested that the army should stay in Philadelphia as long as possible, with the implied threat that they might destroy the city if Congress remained intractable. General Clinton testily informed him that the withdrawal would proceed on schedule. With a French fleet approaching America's shores, London had given him no discretion.[54]

XXIII

By June 17, the withdrawal was in its final stages. The British fleet, with the loyalist refugees and the army's heavy equipment, had already sailed. Much of the British army had crossed the Delaware into New Jersey for the march to New York. General Washington summoned his fellow generals to a council of war. General Lee promptly seized the floor and insisted that General Clinton was going to head for the Chesapeake. Washington, who had reports from New York of the British assembling hundreds of small boats to ferry Clinton's army from New Jersey, politely demurred.[55]

The commander in chief wanted to know whether the generals thought they should march parallel to General Clinton's army across New Jersey, betting on the arrival of the French to give them the navy support they needed to assault New York. Or should they attack his rear guard in the hope of achieving a minor victory that would add to the royal army's humiliation? Or should they choose a favorable site and attack with every available man to destroy Clinton and end the war?

It swiftly became apparent that the generals were inclined to see the evacuation of Philadelphia as a victory in itself, and hesitated to risk a major battle that might mar this impression in the public mind. Only Anthony Wayne was in favor of an all-out attack somewhere in New Jersey. He pointed out that Clinton's army had a twelve-mile-long wagon train to protect. Even if the British repulsed an assault, they would be unable to pursue the Americans when they retreated.

General Lee took the floor and declared it would be "criminal" at this point in the war to risk a general action. He did not believe American soldiers could defeat British regulars in the open field. Major General Benedict Arnold, who could still barely stand on the leg that had been shattered by a British bullet at Saratoga, said a partial assault would inevitably turn into a general action, and he did not think the Americans had the numbers to inflict a defeat on the British. Lafayette denounced councils of war because they produced nothing but timid opinions and unrealistic compromises.[56]

General Washington made no comment on these responses. But he had begun to share Lafayette's negative opinion about councils of war and may even have put the idea in the Marquis' head during their many private conversations. Washington the warrior, the man who had routed his political enemies during the winter at Valley Forge, remembered the taunts and sneers at his do-nothing leadership that had emanated from York and Lancaster during those grim months of starvation and nakedness. He wanted to wipe those humiliations from the public record. With Baron von Steuben's help, he had resurrected the Continental Army from disarray and despair. He wanted to give that army a chance to prove itself in battle.

Carefully concealing these intense emotions, the commander in chief took a realistic stance. General Arnold was probably right. The Continental Army's numbers barred an all-out assault. They would follow the British into New Jersey and see how the situation developed. But General Washington's actions spoke far more loudly than his words. If he considered the evacuation of Philadelphia a victory, why didn't he parade the entire Continental Army through the city's streets to the cheers of the liberated citizens? That would have provided material for a dozen triumphant newspaper articles.

Instead, he sent a single regiment under limping General Arnold to keep order in Philadelphia until a civilian government was restored. He ordered a Continental division under General Lee to march immediately and cross the Delaware north of Trenton, where they would be in a position to strike the British if they traversed New Jersey by a central route.[57]

XXIV

On June 19, exactly six months to the day after they arrived, the rest of the Continental Army marched out of Valley Forge, regimental flags flying, fifers shrilling, and drummers beating the step for the slow march. They were a new army, with new pride and new confidence, thanks to Baron von Steuben and the tall man who rode at the head of the column.

George Washington had demonstrated his mastery of a new kind of leadership in those six grim months, a blend of the military and the political, which necessity had forced upon him. He had taken command of the entire army and its support services and placed men of his choice in charge of them. He had testified to his solidarity with his officer corps, the "band of brothers" as he sometimes called them, by winning them higher salaries and half pay for seven years after the war.

He had also established a core of support in Congress, which the extremists around Samuel Adams could not overcome with their true whig rants. In the name of the men who had stayed the bitter course at Valley Forge, General Washington would no longer suffer slanders and insults silently. He was the army's commander in chief, with a new depth and dimension to the title—which he would soon make clear on the field of battle—and in the politics of high command.

ELEVEN

A MOMENT AT MONMOUTH

G ENERAL CHARLES LEE LED his division of the army across the Delaware River at Coryell's Ferry (present-day Lambertville) north of Trenton on June 20. General Washington followed him with the rest of the army on the twenty-first and twenty-second. Washington's detailed orders to Lee reveal his distrust of his second in command. Lee was to follow a route laid out for him by Quartermaster General Greene so the division could take advantage of the magazines established in New Jersey. Washington wanted to know "precisely your situation on every day." The commander in chief even spelled out how long Lee should march his troops each day in the summer heat (from 4 a.m. until noon). He was reminding Lee that Lieutenant General George Washington was in command of the Continental Army.[1]

Meanwhile, Washington did everything in his power to impede Clinton's progress toward New York. He had assigned the New Jersey Continental brigade and over a thousand New Jersey militiamen to harass the flanks of the British column. To these men he added Daniel Morgan and his riflemen, their numbers bolstered by volunteer marksmen from other regiments. Jaeger Captain Ewald wrote in his diary: "Each step cost human blood."[2]

Bridges on the royal army's route were burned, roads were blocked by chopped down trees, buckets and ropes were removed from wells to retard the enemy's march. Already burdened by their immense wagon train and afflicted by hot, rainy weather, the British were slowed to a crawl. In the first seven days, they covered barely forty miles.

The unburdened American army, on the other hand, was capable of far more rapid movement, and they remained in prime condition, thanks to the efficiency of Nathanael Greene's revived quartermaster department. The magazines he had established along their route guaranteed the men ample food. Each night, when they arrived at a campsite, they found latrines dug, straw for bedding, and barrels of vinegar to ward off intestinal diseases. Even when they marched off the route where the magazines were located, Greene's wagon trains soon arrived with the day's rations.[3]

II

On June 24, Washington called another council of war. This time there were no questions about marching parallel to the British. He wanted to know if his generals now thought they should "hazard a general action." If so, should they launch the whole army at Clinton's men? Or should they attempt a "partial attack" on the rear guard and let Clinton decide whether he wanted to fight a winner-take-all battle? That way, the Americans could fight on the defensive, after inflicting major damage on the rear guard.

Once more, General Lee's was the loudest voice. He gave a veritable oration, declaring that if he had the power, he would "build a bridge of gold" to assist the British to New York as swiftly as possible. Moreover, the royal army had never been more disciplined and better prepared for battle. The Americans would never be able to withstand them in a European-style conflict. Washington, several generals noticed, was visibly "disappointed" at Lee's rhetoric. A more accurate word would probably be disgusted.[4]

Lafayette, who again denounced councils of war, vehemently disagreed with Lee, and said the Continentals could handle and win a major battle. When the issue was put to a vote, the majority favored Lee, 6–5, with Nathanael Greene abstaining because he was now a staff officer. The council decided to make a partial attack on the rear guard, but it should be no more than a glancing blow. They gave 1,500 men to Brigadier General Charles Scott, a tough, no-nonsense Virginian who had fought well at Trenton, and ordered him to coordinate the attack with Morgan's skirmishers and the New Jersey Continental Brigade. A disgusted Alexander Hamilton later told Elias Boudinot this outcome "would have done honor to the most honorab[le] society of midwives, and to them only."[5]

That night, Quartermaster General Greene wrote Washington a letter. He lamented his "delicate situation"—as a staff rather than a line officer, he was now disqualified from speaking out in councils of war. Greene told the commander in chief he did not agree with the council's decision. He thought the attack should be in far greater force and the main army should be "in supporting distance" to confront the British if they chose to fight an all-out battle.

Greene was thinking politically as well as militarily. "If we suffer the enemy to pass through the Jerseys without attacking them I think we shall ever regret it." He reminded Washington of how they had "come to our grief " in the struggle for Philadelphia by "marching until we get near the enemy" and then doing nothing. (This was in keeping with Washington's strategy of avoiding a general action.) For Greene, "grief " meant the political malaise that enveloped the army at Valley Forge. "People expect something from us and our strength demands it," the quartermaster general warned.[6]

Greene was saying what Washington was obviously thinking. He needed no more persuasion. He expanded the advance force that was to attack the rear guard until it totaled 4,500 men, almost half his infantry. In command he put the Marquis de Lafayette, with Brigadier General Wayne as his subordinate. These were the two generals who were most in favor of a major attack. As senior major general, General Lee had a right to expect the command of this large force. But the commander in chief persuaded him to step aside; Lee agreed it would be better handled by a "young volunteering general."[7]

Shortly after the troops marched, General Lee appeared at Washington's tent and said he had changed his mind. His honor would be impugned if he stood by while the youngster Lafayette commanded the attack. Washington, obviously unhappy, was forced to write an apologetic letter to Lafayette, asking him to accept Lee as his immediate commander. The Marquis did so with good grace.[8]

III

Sir Henry Clinton, meanwhile, had advanced to Monmouth Court House (now Freehold) where on June 27 he paused to give his troops a badly needed rest. The weather remained insufferably hot. The royal army was now only a day's march from Middletown, New Jersey, high ground where they would be safe from assault. From there they could easily reach the Atlantic coast at Sandy Hook, where the fleet would ferry them to New York.

General Washington sent Lee orders to attack the British rear guard. He added as a matter of course that the final decision belonged to Lee, who would be the best judge of the immediate military situation. Lee, again revealing his reluctance, replied that he was sure that Clinton would immediately counterattack with the bulk of his army.[9]

General Washington was unimpressed with this warning. He was now committed to a serious attack, and was unbothered by the possibility of it becoming a general action, no matter what the council of war had voted. He made it clear that Lee was expected to assault and hold the rear guard in place until Washington arrived with the rest of the army. If the British reinforced the rear guard, so be it. Washington had confidence in his Continentals.

The ever-more reluctant Lee did nothing all day Saturday, the twenty-seventh. He made no attempt to reconnoiter the enemy. He did not consider the possibility of detaching five hundred picked men to assault the enemy's wagon train and throw it into confusion at the right moment. He did not se-lect a jump-off site for his attack. When he summoned Lafayette, Anthony Wayne, and two other generals who would lead the assault for a council of war at 5 p.m., Lee neither gave them a plan nor asked them what they had seen from their forward positions. They were simply told to be ready to advance in the morning.

Lee's actions (or better, inactions) underscore an ironic, seldom considered fact about this self-proclaimed military genius: he had never commanded an army in battle before. He had been a distinguished company commander (captain) in the French and Indian War. But his supposed exploits as second in command of a cavalry regiment the British had sent to Portugal in 1761 do not withstand serious scrutiny. Lieutenant Colonel Lee had conducted a single successful raid on a Spanish army camp, which, with his skill at self-promotion, he had escalated to a decisive victory on a vast scale. His major generalship in Poland was an honorary rank granted by a friendly king. He had never gotten anywhere near a battlefield.[10]

On June 28 at 5 a.m., Washington received a message from the commander of the New Jersey militia, General Philemon Dickinson, that the British army had begun its march toward Middletown and its ultimate destination, Sandy Hook. Washington immediately ordered the main army to begin its march and sent one of his aides, Richard Kidder Meade, to Lee, telling him to begin his pursuit and "bring on an attack as soon as possible." As Meade later recalled it, there was no doubt in his mind that Washington was "anxious to bring on a general engagement between the two whole armies."[11]

The temperature soared into the nineties as Washington's 7,800 men trudged down a sandy road toward Monmouth Court House. He had ordered them to leave their packs behind; many now discarded their shirts. Nevertheless, soldiers began toppling from the heat as they reached Englishtown, about six miles from Monmouth Court House. There Washington scribbled a hasty note to President Henry Laurens warning him that a battle was imminent—if the British did not elude General Lee. The latter remark reveals his lack of confidence in Lee's commitment to an attack.

The commander in chief had scarcely finished this dispatch when a messenger arrived from Lee's headquarters, reporting that he had found a little-used road that all but guaranteed he would cut off the 2,000-man British rear guard. An exultant Washington sent an aide galloping to tell Lee he was on the way with the main army.[12]

By noon Washington was close enough to strain his ears for the sounds of battle—but there were none, beyond a half dozen tantalizing cannon shots, followed by scattered barks of muskets. He sent another aide forward to find out what was happening. A moment later Lieutenant Colonel Alexander Hamilton arrived from the strangely silent battlefront to report that General Lee was about to attack. Next came ponderous, sweaty Henry Knox on a streaming horse. The artillery commander angrily reported that Lee's troops were "confused" and there was grave danger of a dismaying reverse.

Nathanael Greene, who was commanding the right wing of the main army, was ordered to take a side road that would prevent a British flanking movement. The rest of the perspiring Continentals advanced down the main road with General Washington in the lead until he met a civilian who told him Lee's men were retreating. A thunderstruck Washington asked where he had gotten this information. The man pointed to a young fifer, who confirmed the bad news. Washington refused to believe the musician and threatened him with a whipping if he spread the rumor.

The commander in chief had barely ridden another fifty yards when he met three men, one of them wearing the remnants of a soldier's uniform. They told him Lee's whole force was retreating. Washington still refused to believe it. It was impossible. Defeat? After those agonizing winter months at Valley Forge, the weeks of relentless training under Steuben? Wouldn't Lee have sent him word so he could position his troops to make a stand? Why was Lee retreating without a fight?[13]

IV

The general rode to the crest of a ridge that overlooked a large swamp and saw coming down the road two regiments in some disorder, all but staggering with heat exhaustion. Their colonels told the stunned Washington that the whole advanced corps was retreating. Within minutes this was confirmed by columns of men on the road, many looking frightened or bewildered or both.

Washington rode up to Colonel Israel Shreve, commander of the Second New Jersey Regiment, and asked him why he was retreating. Shreve, with a strange smile, half sly, half embarrassed, said he did not know. He had been ordered to retreat and that was what he was doing. There was no sign of wounds or powder-blackened hands or faces; his men had obviously done no fighting.

Finally there appeared the one man who could answer General Washington's questions: General Charles Lee, followed by several aides, his dogs, and hundreds more retreating men. An infuriated Washington rode up to him and shouted: "What is the meaning of this?"

Lee could only goggle in amazement at the enraged commander in chief. "Sir, sir?" he stuttered.

"What is all this confusion for, this retreat?"

For several seconds, General Lee could find no words. Then he exploded in a stream of verbiage. He said there was no confusion "but what naturally rose from disobedience of orders, contradictory intelligence, and the impertinence and presumption of individuals." In other words, there was plenty of confusion but none of it was his fault. Lee named Brigadier Generals Scott and Wayne as two of the culprits who had disobeyed his orders. What Washington heard—and saw—was Lee's ineptitude as a general. He had lost control of his troops; most of them did not know where they were going or why.[14]

Beyond Monmouth Court House, Lee said, he had suddenly found himself "in the most extensive plain in America," where British cavalry could have annihilated his regiments. Why he had not bothered to discover this supposedly dangerous terrain on June 27, when he did nothing all day but putter about his headquarters, was ignored. Therefore "he did not chuse to beard the British army with troops in such a situation." Then came words that explained a great deal. "Besides, the whole thing was against my opinion."[15]

"All this may be true, sir," Washington snarled, "but you ought not to have undertaken it unless you intended to go through with it!"

A moment later, Washington's secretary, Robert Hanson Harrison, rode up to report that masses of British troops were advancing in battle formation, and were less than fifteen minutes away. As if General Clinton wanted to make this point very clear, random cannonballs began plowing the sandy earth in their vicinity.

Washington sat silent in his saddle, totally stunned. He had assumed that the British would be more than satisfied with Lee's retreat and would resume their march to Sandy Hook. Instead, General Clinton was living up to the implied threat in his description of his evacuation of Philadelphia as an "apparent retreat."

With two-fifths of the Continental Army (Lee's men) groggy with fatigue and falling back with no orders to take a position, and Washington's main army coming up the road behind him, also without a plan, the stage was set for a rout that might destroy the Continental Army and would certainly ruin the commander in chief's reputation forever. Was this what General Lee had had in mind when he embarked on this maneuver without giving Washington the slightest hint of what he was doing?

For another long moment General Washington sat on his horse in an apparent daze. He knew next to nothing about the terrain around him. He had expected the battle to take place on the level ground around Monmouth Court House that Lee had found so forbidding. His aide Tench Tilghman, recognizing his plight, told him that Lieutenant Colonel David Rhea, who had been with Shreve's New Jersey regiment when they met, knew the local geography well (his family farm would soon become part of the battlefield) and was eager to help. Washington ordered Tilghman to find him, fast.[16]

With Washington was another aide, Dr. James McHenry, who later summed up the commander in chief's dilemma in a letter: "The enemy, who were advancing rapidly, elated by our retreat, were to be checked—the most advantageous ground seized—the main body of the army to be formed—the enemy's intentions and dispositions to be discovered and a new plan of attack to be concerted—and all this too in the smallest interval of time."[17]

V

A moment later General Washington experienced what might be called a military epiphany. In a letter to his brother John Augustine "Jack" Washington, he told how he suddenly sensed "that bountiful Providence which has never failed us in the hour of distress" had arranged for him to encounter Lee at this place. It was all but perfect for defense. A nearby hedgerow could easily be turned into a rampart, and a wooded hill overlooked the road on the left. The British would have to come up a long slope from the Monmouth plain to attack them. In the American rear was a swampy ravine with a narrow passage over it, which could easily be defended if they had to fall back.[18]

By this time, Lieutenant Colonel Rhea was at Washington's side, telling him that the road continued to slope upward to thick woods, ideal for defense, and there were more well-wooded hills behind them on the left. Washington began giving orders. He put Colonel Henry Beekman Livingston's New York regiment behind the hedgerow and added other regiments as quickly as they materialized. He positioned two cannon to cover the road. He ordered two of the retreating regiments to occupy the fringe of the hilly woods on the left and told their colonels that they must attack the enemy and check their advance, even if it cost them every man in their commands. The two colonels, members of General Wayne's brigade, told him they and their men were ready and eager to fight, after watching General Lee avoid battle all morning. Other more disorderly retreaters Washington sent to the rear for reorganization.

Then came a sight that stirred relief and joy: General Anthony Wayne and the rest of his men, marching in perfect formation as if they were on Valley Forge's Grand Parade. Washington told them he was planning to make a stand at this point and put Wayne in immediate command with orders to fight to the death. Lafayette, riding up with the men he had commanded in the advance force, was swept by admiration at the way Washington was taking charge of the situation. "His presence stopped the retreat," the Marquis said. Alexander Hamilton later wrote that he "never saw the general to such an advantage. His coolness and firmness were admirable."[19]

Turning to General Lee, Washington asked him if he wanted to take command of this first line of defense. Lee said he would be "the last man off the field." Washington rode to the rear to deploy the rest of the army on the advantageous ground Lieutenant Colonel Rhea had described. In swift response to Washington's orders, Major General Lord Stirling soon had twelve cannon supporting his division on the left. Nathanael Greene, with his usual skill, arrayed his regiments to defend the right flank. Washington galloped across the width of the battlefield, checking on these deployments while the boom of cannon and the rattle of musketry announced that the British were assaulting the first line.[20]

British cavalry opened the attack on Anthony Wayne's thin line with a thunderous charge. American cannon raked them at long range and blasts of musketry from the hedgerow and nearby woods sent men and horses plunging to the sandy earth, writhing in agony. The surviving dragoons retreated in disorder.

Now came about 1,500 British infantry, the army's vanguard. Out of the woods swarmed the two regiments Washington had ordered to fight to the death. Their headlong assault threw the British into confusion. A wild melee erupted, bayonet to bayonet. These officers and men "performed what they promised" Washington, Dr. McHenry wrote. Both colonels were badly wounded; one was left for dead on the battlefield.

The swarming British infantry returned to the assault on Wayne's men behind the hedgerow. Soon the king's soldiers began lapping around the flanks of the Americans' exposed position. Just in time, Washington sent word that whenever they needed to fall back, there was succor awaiting them. Soon the survivors of this first line of defense appeared, dragging wounded comrades with them, and re-formed behind a rail fence and around a barn. Washington put himself in command at this center of the battle line and ordered General Lee to the rear to reorganize the regiments from his advance guard that had retreated in disorder.

In the rear General Lee encountered Baron von Steuben, who was already dealing with the demoralized men from Lee's command. Steuben told Lee he was acting on orders from Washington. Lee listened to the Baron's stentorian voice restoring confidence and pride to these regiments and admitted he was glad Steuben had taken charge of the situation. He was tired out. Lee rode into the village of Englishtown and sat on his horse in a disgruntled daze, surrounded by his dogs. Steuben swiftly positioned the regoranized man in a defensive line in case the British broke through the position Washington had chosen.[21]

VI

At the front, General Washington got a dividend on the four or five hundred daily rations he sometimes groused about issuing to the camp followers in Valley Forge. A woman who has never been identified was close enough to the fighting to see her soldier husband struck down by a British bullet. She raced to his side, seized his gun, and in the words of an eyewitness, "like a Spartan heroine [began] discharging the piece with as much regularity as any soldier present."

Elsewhere, another unnamed woman whose husband belonged to the artillery, stood beside him, a member of the gun crew. Whether she was swabbing out the red hot barrel or ramming home the powder, no one seems to know. While she was hard at work, a British cannon ball came whistling over the nearby swamp and passed between her legs, taking away a good portion of her skirt. She looked down and remarked that it was lucky the shot did not pass a little higher—it might have carried away something else. Whereupon, according to Private Joseph Plumb Martin, who was an eyewitness, she went back to work on the gun.[22]

Over the course of the next century, with some help from that mythmaker extraordinary, George Washington Parke Custis, the two women blended into the legend of Molly Pitcher.

VII

After a ferocious artillery duel, the British infantry opened their assault on the main American line. Even today's soldiers find it hard to grasp how fearful this wall of advancing red coats looked to those on the other side of the battle line. Three deep, drums beating, they came forward with grim-eyed determination. In the front rank were the grenadiers, their high brass-fronted busbies adding to their fearful appearance. Beside them were the British Foot Guards, the elite of the royal army. Would Lee be proved right? He had repeatedly declared the Americans could never stand up to such troops in open combat. On they came, shouting blood and slaughter, their bayonets lowered.

Scarcely a Continental wavered. Blasts of musketry and cannon fire tore through the closely packed British ranks. It was more punishment than flesh and flood could endure. The first attack on the American left wing faltered and fell back. Another division, under Lord Cornwallis, assaulted the American right wing, where Greene's men met them with more death and destruction from muskets and cannon.

In the center, Lieutenant Colonel Henry Monkton of the Foot Guards, after two repulses, turned his back on the Americans and made a speech to his shaken soldiers. Whirling, he led them a third time toward Anthony Wayne and his Pennsylvanians behind their rail fence. At Wayne's orders, his men aimed their muskets at "the king birds," Monkton and his officers. The colonel fell, riddled with bullets, a few feet from the American line. As Monkton's men stumbled out of range, Wayne ordered his Continentals to abandon their fence and attack them, bayonet to bayonet.[23]

"The officers of the army," Washington later told Henry Laurens, "seemed to vie with each other in manifesting their zeal and bravery." As for the men in the ranks, their behavior "could not be surpassed."[24]

A glimpse of the officers' bravery and the Steuben-instilled confidence of the men in the ranks was reported by Dr. James McHenry. Two or three American companies were ordered to occupy a piece of high ground before the enemy reached it. "In rising the hill our infantry received an unexpected charge from the grenadiers that threw them into confusion," McHenry said. "But recovering themselves, they formed under the enemy's fire, advanced, and very gallantly made themselves masters of the post."[25]

The ground in front of the American battle line had become carpeted with dead and dying British infantry. General Clinton decided he had better start thinking about survival rather than conquest. He ordered a retreat behind the swampy ravine they had crossed to make the first attack of the day. Washington ordered Steuben to bring up the regiments he had reorganized, and the commander in chief sent a New England brigade to assault the British right flank and Virginia troops to assail their left.

When Alexander Hamilton saw these men appear on the road from Englishtown, he was amazed by their transformation from ragged retreaters to confident attackers. Later he told one of Steuben's aides it was the first time he grasped the deeper meaning of the word "discipline."[26]

As Steuben passed through Englishtown on the way to the front, he again met General Lee, who asked him where he was going. Steuben replied that Washington had sent him word that the enemy was retreating in confusion and it was time to throw his rested men into the battle.

General Lee reacted almost angrily to the word "confusion." He could not tolerate such a description of the royal army. He told Steuben the British were "only resting themselves" and warned the Baron that he must have misunderstood his orders. He wanted Steuben to hold his men in place in the defensive position the Baron had chosen. It was another illustration of Lee's defeatist attitude toward the American soldiers' ability to fight the British on equal terms.[27]

Steuben's reinforcements moved out to make the attack with "great spirit," Washington later said. But the combination of the suffocating heat and the oncoming darkness aborted the assault. The men had been marching and maneuvering since dawn, and their weary legs had trouble matching their willing spirits. British artillery was an equally formidable obstacle. Washington ordered the army to rest for the night in their forward positions and prepare to resume the offensive in the morning.[28]

The general spread his cloak on the ground and slept among his troops. Before he closed his eyes, he spent several hours discussing Charles

Lee's behavior with Lafayette. The Marquis was now convinced Lee was a coward and possibly a traitor. Washington apparently remained noncommittal on the latter point. But he too was unhappy with the army's second in command.

When the Continentals awoke in the morning, they found General Clinton and his army had vanished. After giving his men several hours to recover from the heat of the day, the British commander had put them on the road at midnight. General Washington ordered Colonel Daniel Morgan and his riflemen to pursue them with harassing tactics. But there was little hope of overtaking them with the rest of the army. The heat continued to be murderous and water was in short supply. Washington saw no point in wearing down his men. They had done their job. They had proven they could meet the best of the British army and fight them to a standstill.

VIII

For the first few days after the battle, General Washington seemed determined to avoid any further quarrel with General Lee. On June 30, he selected the Englishman as executive major general for July 1. The commander in chief was satisfied with the battle's outcome and was inclined to continue the policy of avoiding a public clash with Lee. In a long letter describing the battle, which included an eyewitness account of Lee's indecision and confusion, John Laurens told his father he thought Lee "must be tried for misconduct," but he urged the president of Congress to say nothing about it, because no decision had been made.[29]

Lee's vanity and uncontrolled temper soon aborted this temporary truce. Even as he was leaving the Monmouth battlefield, he denounced Washington to various officers he met along the road. That evening, he wrote to Richard Henry Lee—an interesting choice of a presumably sympathetic ear. Only a fragment of the letter has survived, but it amply sets the tone. "What the devil brought us into this level country (the very element of the enemy) or what interest we can have (in our present circumstances) to hazard an action, somebody else must tell you, for I cannot."

Lee said he had retreated because his "flying army" was outnumbered and the withdrawal was made in perfect order. "I can demonstrate that had I not acted as I did, this army, and perhaps America, would have been ruined." What did he get for it? "Thanks ... from His Excellency ... of a singular nature." [30]

Obviously, General Lee was borrowing a leaf from General Gates's tactics and taking his quarrel to Congress. Three days later, he made this clear to General Washington. In a furious letter, he declared that only "misinformation from some very stupid or misrepresentation of some very wicked person" could have inspired Washington's "very singular expressions" on June 28. He said Washington had accused him of "disobedience of orders" or "want of conduct" (mishandling his troops) or "want of courage." He desired to know with which of these crimes he would be charged, so he could prepare his justification "to the Army, to the Congress, to America and to the world in general."

Ranting on, Lee insisted he had saved the army from destruction by his retreat and accused Washington of being guilty of a "cruel injustice" to a man who had a right to "some pretensions to the regard of every servant of this country." However, he could not bring himself to believe that General Washington would have spoken and acted in such insulting fashion if his mind had not been poisoned by "some of those dirty earwigs who will forever insinuate themselves near persons in high office." When General Washington acted "from himself," no man in the army "would have reason to complain of injustice." [31]

There it was, the same tactic General Mifflin and his confreres in Congress had used throughout the winter at Valley Forge. General Washington was a wonderful man but he was seduced by the sycophants around him into blunders and hesitations and now into an act of gross injustice to a fellow patriot who had the misfortune to disagree with him. It was another sign that General Lee was egregiously out of touch. He seemed to think he could walk over the commander in chief with this tired combination of insults and threats.

On the same day, June 30, Washington replied in a letter that was as terse as it was angry. He denied using singular expressions. What he had said was "warranted by the occasion." He was only too happy to give Lee a chance to justify himself "to the army, to Congress, to America and to the world in general." But he would first have to convince them that he was not guilty of "a breach of orders, and of misbehaviour before the enemy . . . in not attacking them as you had been directed, and in making an unnecessary, disorderly and shameful retreat." [32]

Lee replied that he looked forward to the opportunity of "shewing [sic] to America the sufficiency of her respective servants." He only hoped the "temporary power of office and the tinsel dignity attending it" would not enable Washington to "obfuscate the bright rays of truth." [33]

Later the same day, Lee wrote yet another letter, in which he insisted on a court-martial rather than a court of inquiry, a proceeding which simply attempts to establish the right and wrong in a conflict of military opinion, with no penalty attached to the judgment. A court-martial would settle things. Its decision came with a guilty or innocent verdict and the possibility of severe punishment.

General Lee said a court of inquiry might bring on "a paper war" between the two sides, all of whom "were not my friends or all your admirers." Here was another implied threat: to spread the story of dissension in the high command of the American army throughout the country. [34]

IX

What General Lee had in mind was amply demonstrated by a letter he wrote on July 3 to Isaac Collins, the editor of the *New Jersey Gazette*. Lee told Collins that an article the editor had run on July 1, describing the battle at some length, was "a most invidious, dishonest and false relation," and he urged Collins to tell his readers it was fiction. Lee claimed he and "the brave men under my command" had been "robbed of the credit due to us." Worse, an "atrocious attack" had been made on his conduct, inflicting injuries "so gross" he had demanded a court-martial.

General Lee was obviously close to hysteria. He was described in the article, which was written by Governor William Livingston of New Jersey with some help from Joseph Reed, as attacking the British and being forced to fall back on Washington and the main army, where the Americans met Clinton's soldiers and forced them to retreat. There were no aspersions cast on his conduct.

What enraged Lee was the line "Our success, under heaven, is to be wholly attributed to the good disposition made by His Excellency." In another letter on the same day, Lee told Collins that "to call the affair a complete victory would be a dishonorable gasconade" and demanded that Collins print both his letters and forward them to papers in Philadelphia.[35]

A victory was exactly what Monmouth was being called, not only in the newspapers, but in Congress and in the army. At first, President Henry Laurens called it "a partial victory," since it was indubitable that the British army had escaped to fight another day. But Congress had no hesitation in promoting it as a victory worthy of celebration. By a unanimous vote, the politicians sent General Washington their congratulations and soon published Washington's report to them as the official account of the battle. That must have doubly enraged Lee. The commander in chief described him as retreating without making any opposition to the oncoming British, to Washington's "great surprise and mortification."[36]

That same day, Lee, continuing his literary rampage, wrote a letter to Robert Morris, apparently on the assumption that he too was an enemy of Washington. It was another indication of how out of touch Lee was. As we have seen, Morris's vote in Congress had swung Pennsylvania into backing the half-pay measure. He was now one of Washington's strongest allies. Lee again ranted about being forced to fight the "flower of the British army" on the "most extensive plain in America" and claimed he had tricked the British into pursuing him into wooded hills where the Continental Army was able to batter them into retreat. "By all that's sacred, General Washington had nothing to do but strip the dead!"

General Lee liked this line so much that he repeated it toward the end of his diatribe and asked Morris to show the letter to Richard Henry Lee, William Duer, and "what others you think prudent." The letter leaves no doubts about Lee's strategy: to force Congress to choose between him and Washington.[37]

X

In a letter to his son, President Henry Laurens went further than calling Monmouth a victory. He told John he now thought General Washington and the army had escaped "a snare." Like Lafayette, Laurens was convinced that Charles Lee had attempted to commit treason at Monmouth. He had thrown his advanced corps into a panic with his sudden decision to retreat and led them into a collision with Washington's army without sending a word of warning and with the British army fifteen minutes away. Was Lee a "Judas"? Laurens wondered. Perhaps—but he had inadvertently given Washington an opportunity to shine, which made the bemused Laurens almost "indebted to the man." [38]

By this time, the Continental Army had marched out of the stifling summer heat of south Jersey to New Brunswick, where the troops drank their fill of fresh water and bathed in the Raritan River. On July 4, they celebrated the second anniversary of the Declaration of Independence. The army's good cheer was enlarged by a double ration of rum from General Washington. No matter what General Lee said, the soldiers' ebullient mood made it clear they thought the Continental Army had won a victory at Monmouth.

XI

Back in Philadelphia, on the Fourth of July, General Conway fought a duel with Pennsylvania militia general John Cadwalader, the man to whom Tench Tilghman had written an incendiary letter at the height of the winter intrigue against Washington. Lately, Conway had spent most of his time being a nuisance. He had visited York and tried to deny he had resigned, blaming Henry Laurens for forwarding his April letter to Congress. As we have seen, Gouverneur Morris put an end to that maneuver with a blunt speech. In a whining letter to General Gates, Conway complained that almost every congressman treated him as if he had smallpox.

Only Richard Henry Lee and Samuel Adams greeted him with any warmth, and they told him "it was vain to oppose the torrent" in favor of General Washington.[39]

General Cadwalader had encountered the discredited ex-brigadier in Philadelphia and had apparently accused him of cowardice at the battle of Germantown. He repeated an old story that Conway had cringed in a barn and refused to rejoin the battle, claiming his horse was wounded. It was a deliberate attempt to provoke a duel. Conway challenged him, and the antagonists met near Philadelphia. Conway missed and Cadwalader shot the brigadier through the mouth. When told it was probably not a fatal wound, Cadwalader growled: "I've stopped the damned rascal's tongue anyway."[40]

It was a brutal but effective reminder of the link between the imbroglio with Lee and the winter conspiracy to destroy Washington. Lee's vituperative assault was utterly blatant, with none of the subtlety displayed by Lovell, Mifflin, and Gates. But the tactics—the appeal to selected congressmen, the letters to the newspapers—were essentially the same. Perhaps hoping to underscore this point, Cadwalader attempted to lure Mifflin into a duel, but that dexterous gentleman proved elusive.

One army officer, Gershon Mott, made the connection in a letter to a friend: "The devils are . . . flattering themselves that they shall now have it in their power to ruin G. Washington on acct of his arresting Lee. . . . Now Gates and his tools will work like the children of hell."[41]

XII

Charles Lee's court-martial, with General Lord Stirling presiding, began on July 3, in New Brunswick. It continued for over a month as the army marched from New Jersey to White Plains, New York, and Washington began trying to cooperate with the French fleet that had arrived off the coast. Lee faced three charges. The first two were lifted almost verbatim from General Washington's letter to Lee: disobedience of orders in not attacking the enemy on June 28, agreeable to repeated instructions, and misbehavior before the enemy on the same day by making an unnecessary, disorderly, and shameful retreat. The court added a third charge: disrespect to the commander in chief in the two insulting letters Lee wrote to Washington and misdated July 1 and June 28—interesting evidence of his hysteria.

From their numerous contacts with General Lee on the day of the battle, Washington's aides provided the prosecution with a wealth of testimony about Lee's inaction and failure to communicate a plan of attack to his troops. They were joined by Generals Wayne and Scott, both of whom had demanded a court of inquiry the day after the battle. They described how Lee let them advance willy nilly, without a scrap of guidance, and then retreated without bothering to inform them. General Lee's aides defended him with vigor and were joined by several artillery officers who had been part of Lee's advance corps.[42]

On August 11, 1778, the court found Lee guilty of failing to attack the enemy as ordered and of disrespect to the commander in chief. They also found him guilty of the second charge, leading a shameful and disorderly retreat, but the court altered General Washington's overheated language. They eliminated the word "shameful" and described the retreat as unnecessary and "in some few instances . . . disorderly." They sentenced Lee to be suspended from the army for a year.[43]

XIII

The next stage in the struggle with Lee shifted to Philadelphia, where Congress would have to decide whether to ratify the verdict. For a long time, the politicians did nothing. Part of the reason was the reluctance of Lee's supporters to confront the issue. They espoused a policy of delay in the hope that the impact of his literary vitriol would diminish over time.

Another reason for delay was Philadelphia's battered physical condition and turbulent politics. The British had left the city a wreck. The statehouse, that symbolic building, exuded a stench that made it impossible for congressmen or anyone else to go near the place. The British soldiers' habit of using it as an oversized toilet had apparently become a deliberate desecration in the final weeks of the occupation. Next to the building the British had, in the words of a contemporary, "opened a large square pit . . . a receptacle for filth into which they also cast dead horses and the bodies of men." Congress was forced to retreat to the College of Pennsylvania.[44]

Filth, looted houses, the ruins of burned houses, were everywhere. The few houses left untorched in the northern section of the city were stripped of doors, windows, even roofs. On almost every side street were piles of garbage and excrement. One returning resident, Board of War secretary Richard Peters, said "the foul and abominable atmosphere" made him ill for three days.

Worsening matters were swarms of flies feeding off the filth. When Baron von Steuben invited his aide, Peter Stephen Duponceau, for a cup of tea in his new quarters, the insatiable flies literally drowned in their teacups and they had to flee.

Richard Peters was not the only one that the stinking city made ill. When Benjamin Rush returned on July 21, a full month after the evacuation, he found dozens of frightened, feverish patients writhing in the summer heat. In September, Rush contracted "a malignant bilious fever" from one of his patients and was reduced "to the brink of the grave." He made his will and "took leave of life." On the eleventh day the fever broke and he recovered.[45]

Only when most of the refugees returned did the scale of the British looting become apparent. The newspapers were crowded with lists of property stolen from private houses. They included beds, walnut dining tables, and Windsor chairs. Artisans reported missing tools and machinery. One man reported four tons of "blistered steel" missing from his factory. A minister reported the loss of a thousand books from his library.

Some of this thievery was committed by locals. The victims published fierce warnings that if the property was not returned, the thieves would be prosecuted. One man hastily advertised two eight-day clocks he was eager to restore to their owners if they would pay "the trifling charges" it had cost him to obtain them. For a final touch, the city fathers estimated British officers had departed owing local businessmen at least ten thousand pounds.[46]

One of the worst thieves was Captain John André. He stole books, scientific instruments, even a portrait of his absent host, from Benjamin

Franklin's house. André's contempt for Americans was never more visible. He gave the portrait to his immediate commander, General Grey; it took 150 years to recover it. Grey wangled his devoted aide an appointment on General Clinton's staff, where the handsome captain flattered his way into Sir Henry's esteem. He was promoted to major and became director of intelligence.[47]

André's callousness did not extend to all Americans. In the the midst of packing his stolen goods, he found time to say farewell to Peggy Chew with a plaintive poem.

> If at the close of war and strife
>   My destiny once more
> Should in the varied paths of life
>   Conduct me to this shore:
> Should British banners guard the land
>   And factions be restrained;
> And Cliveden's mansion peaceful stand
>   No more with blood be stained—
> Say! Wilt thou then receive again
>   And welcome to thy sight,
> The youth who bids with stifled pain
>   His sad farewell tonight?[48]

No one could foresee that in two years, thanks to Peggy Shippen and Benedict Arnold, John André's ascent to power and preferment would become a death sentence. Only then would these melancholy rhymes seem to foreshadow it.

XIV

Adding to Philadelphia's sense of chaos was the return of the Pennsylvania state government. The radicals had only one thing on their minds: vengeance. They began gathering evidence against the "notorious" and "rich and powerful" loyalists who had served as "pilots, guides, kidnappers, and other assistants of the British army." By far the greatest proportion of these collaborators had fled with Clinton's army. But a grand jury soon indicted eighty-seven men for assisting either Joseph Galloway or Sir William Howe during the occupation. Joseph Reed, who aspired to be president of Pennsylvania's executive council (in effect governor), was named prosecutor.

The loathing most Philadelphians felt for the radical government of the state soon played a part in the judicial proceedings. Reed was nonplussed when the city's judges dismissed fifty-seven of the eighty-seven indictments, leaving him only thirty loyalists to prosecute. Merchant Tench Coxe was a typical example of how a well-connected loyalist could beat the game. He had made thousands of pounds doing business with the British. Indicted for high treason, Tench promptly took the oath of allegiance to the rebel government of Pennsylvania. In mid-July, Coxe's wealthy father assured him he need have no fears of jail or disgrace.

Some of the young merchant's numerous relatives had sided with the rebels (Washington's aide Tench Tilghman was a first cousin). They had an inside track to Pennsylvania's chief justice, Thomas McKean. When Coxe appeared before this gentleman, he was pleasantly surprised to find his behavior "much more friendly than I could have expected & genteel." Coxe's case was soon among the dismissed.[49]

Of the 30 cases of supposed treason prosecutor Reed presented to a jury, he was able to convict only two men—and these convictions led to more political turmoil. The defense lawyer for the first man, Abraham Carlisle, was James Wilson, a signer of the Declaration of Independence. Carlisle was found guilty for working as supervisor of the northern gates in the British outer entrenchments, where his chief task was issuing passports to those leaving the city. Wilson showed in the trial that Carlisle, a Quaker who never bore arms for either side, had enabled a number of rebels, some of them possibly spies, to pass through his gates unscathed. Yet Carlisle was condemned to death.

Even more egregious was the fate of John Roberts, the Quaker miller who had concealed the journals of the Continental Congress when they were given to him by panic-stricken Congressman James Lovell. He was sentenced to death for making "verbal utterances" against the state government, something four-fifths of the citizens of Pennsylvania did regularly. He was also accused of recruiting loyalists for the British army and guiding foraging parties into Chester County. Other witnesses from the county said he had warned them of the raiding parties and enabled them to hide their cattle and grain. It was obvious that Roberts and Carlisle were genuine neutrals who showed humanity to both sides.

No fewer than forty state militia officers and a thousand other Philadelphians, including the judge and jury that convicted Roberts, appealed to the Supreme Executive Council of Pennsylvania for clemency. Conspicuous by his absence among these pleaders for mercy was Congressman Lovell, who could have made a powerful statement on Roberts's behalf by testifying to the way he had protected the vital journals of Congress until they were recovered by General Washington. This bold denouncer of the Continental Army and its commander chose to remain silent, rather than reveal his pusillanimous conduct. First Carlisle, then Roberts were hanged before a crowd that included the latter's weeping wife and nine children.[50]

These mean-spirited executions produced a backlash against the so-called Constitutionalist government in the October elections. Led by Robert Morris, the anti-Constitutionalists, who called themselves Republicans, elected their entire local slate to the state assembly. The radicals remained in control of the government thanks to their support in the western counties. But the prevailing antiradical mood in Philadelphia undoubtedly influenced the Continental Congress, where Sam Adams and his friends grimly backed the Constitutionalists, whom they had helped install in the summer of 1776.

XV

During these same turbulent weeks, Sam Adams did not win many friends in Philadelphia when he denounced some Continental Army officers who attempted to revive the Southwark theater to continue producing the series of plays they had begun in Valley Forge. On October 12 Congress passed a resolution declaring, "True religion and good morals are the only foundation of publick [sic] liberty and happiness" and urged the states to "prevent stage playing and such kinds of diversions as are productive of vice, idleness, dissipation and a general depravity of principles and manners."

The officers ignored the resolution, and on October 17 Congress passed an even tougher resolution, which decreed: "Any person holding an office under the United States who shall attend a theatrical performance shall be dismissed from the service." In a letter to a Massachusetts correspondent, Sam Adams added a sneer at that preeminent playgoer, George Washington, which left no doubt about the chief target of this ukase. Adams hoped that "gentlemen of the first rank who deny themselves the pleasures of domestick [sic] life and expose themselves to the hardships of a camp in the glorious cause of freedom show as much good sense and attention to the cause of virtue" by staying out of playhouses in the future.[51]

XVI

This was the political atmosphere in Philadelphia when Congress, having ordered the proceedings of General Lee's court-martial printed so each member could read it, began debating whether to confirm the verdict. Lee hurled himself into the contest, writing a letter to President Laurens, urging that "the doors of Congress be thrown open"—he wanted "the whole world or at least the whole military world" to "form an audience."[52]

This demand was another example of Lee's megalomania. He saw himself competing with General Washington not only on the floor of Congress but with the people at large. The mere idea was ludicrous, and his supporters in Congress knew it. Lee had already disgusted the majority of the public with his vicious attacks on Washington. Opening the doors and revoking Congress's rule of secrecy was the last thing his backers would ever do. One of Lee's aides, Major Evan Edwards, whom Lee sent to Philadelphia to present his case to selected congressmen, complained that he was "almost mob'd" when he attempted to defend Lee to local citizens.[53]

Lee soon came to Philadelphia and personally tried to line up congressional support. Joseph Reed reported to Nathanael Greene that Lee was "making his court" to the "Reading Junto"—the party Thomas Mifflin had formed to push Gates and Conway during the winter. Reed also reported that Lee's supporters were circulating "slander on [Washington's] private character, viz great cruelty to his slaves in Virginia and immorality of life." These virtuous descendants of the Puritans were not above taking the low road when it suited them.[54]

When Congress began debating the court-martial on October 23, Samuel Adams, James Lovell, Richard Henry Lee, and their followers did everything in their power to set the verdict aside. Henry Laurens, Gouverneur Morris, Robert Morris, and their circle called for an immediate vote confirming it. The two sides were almost evenly divided. "General Lee's affair hangs by the eyelids," Gouverneur Morris told Washington on October 26, 1778.

The problem, Morris explained, was the argument Lee's supporters were advancing: "Granting him [Lee] guilty of all charges it is too light a sentence . . . and if he is not guilty, there would be an injustice in [delegates] not declaring their opinion." There was a good answer to this contention. The court martial board had issued their judicial decision with an awareness of the trial's political context. Lee was the second-ranking general in the American army. Hanging him or putting him before a firing squad would have shocked and bewildered civilians who had no idea of the real dimensions of the clash. The British would have seized upon such a sentence as proof that dissension was tearing apart the American army. Their newspapers and pamphleteers would have run wild with ugly rumors of worse to come. The judges were hoping that Congress would understand the delicacy of the situation and approve their course with a minimum of oratory.[55]

Washington's ideology-driven opponents chose to ignore this clear and present danger. They pretended that abstract justice was their only interest, ignoring the insults Lee had flung at Washington, which had made his return to the army an impossibility. Washington's supporters, led by Laurens and Morris, had an answer to this reckless course. They flatly stated that approving the verdict was a political necessity.

One fervent Lee supporter, Dr. Benjamin Rush, watching from the sidelines, noted sourly that many congressman had begun to "talk of *state necessity* and in making justice yield in some cases to policy.[56] Rush was, of course, putting the Washingtonians' case in the worst possible terms. Nevertheless, his words return us to the political dimension of the struggle between Washington and his enemies that this book has delineated. The choice the congressmen were being forced to make was: Lee or Washington?

Lee was the last battleground between the Washington haters and fearers in Congress and the general's supporters. There was no one else on the horizon to challenge his leadership. The Lee-Adams junto's only hope was to keep General Lee in the army, where he could be a counterweight (as they saw it) to General Washington's excessive power. Washington's supporters, buoyed by his victory over Gates and Mifflin, had no intention of letting this political disaster occur.

XVII

Richard Henry Lee became the chief spokesman for the defense. According to George Lux, a wealthy Marylander who had served as secretary to a congressional committee and had friends in Virginia who detested Congressman Lee, the Virginian had "always" been for replacing Washington with General Lee.[57]

The congressman and his New England allies resorted to the same mix of parliamentary tactics they had used to defend Thomas Mifflin—delays, postponements, ploys such as calling for a vote on each charge separately. Washington's supporters remained united and ever more grimly determined to prevail. Finally, Congressman Lee saw defeat looming and announced he was going home to attend to family business. That was the signal for several other anti-Washington delegates to absent themselves from Congress when the court-martial finally came to a vote on December 5, 1778.

Like Richard Henry Lee, these absentees did not have the courage to put their names on a negative vote which almost everyone would see as an insult to Washington. Six states voted to confirm the verdict and two voted against it. In four states, delegations were evenly divided, and Delaware was absent, as usual. Samuel Adams, James Lovell, and other New England radicals such as William Whipple of New Hampshire remained pro-Lee to the end.[58]

For a final flourish, the victorious majority ordered Congress's recent vote approving the verdict of the court-martial of General Philip Schuyler to be published. For over a year the ideologues had badgered a reluctant Washington to try Schuyler and his chief subordinate, General Arthur St. Clair, for their supposed criminal failure to stop General Burgoyne's invasion in 1777. The court-martial boards appointed by General Washington had found both men innocent of any wrongdoing. The commander in chief's rout of the Lee-Adams junto was complete.[59]

XVIII

No one felt the totality of this defeat more bitterly than that inveterate military politician, General Horatio Gates. Early in January 1779, General Conway, recovered from his wound, was about to sail back to France and asked his fellow conspirator for a letter praising his service in the American army. Gates replied that he had left the letter in his Virginia house; even if he had it, he would be reluctant to send it, lest it be opened in the mail and "without trial we would be found guilty of dissuading the true believers from the divine worship due the Alexandrine statue." To Gates, Washington remained the stupid figurehead whom Congress had chosen in 1775 because he was from Virginia.[60]

As noted earlier, with the help of his friends in Congress, General Gates had transferred himself to Boston. Major General Alexander McDougall, who commanded the defenses in the Hudson Highlands and often had to deal with Gates, wished him an unfond farewell in a letter to Governor George Clinton of New York. McDougall said he found Gates "exceedingly impatient under command" of General Washington. The Scottish-born McDougall opined that "Gates prefers being the first man in a village to the second in Rome." But "the service will not suffer" from Gates's absence. He had "the weakest mind" McDougall had ever seen in a soldier. "God avert so great a judgment to America as his having the chief command of her armies."[61]

In the summer of 1780, Congress appointed General Gates the commander in the Southern Department, hoping he could cope with the British invasion of South Carolina. At Camden, Gates confronted an army led by Lord Charles Cornwallis. Ignoring the lessons Washington had learned the hard way about the unreliability of the militia, Gates put 1,500 amateurs in the front line beside two regiments of Continentals under Baron de Kalb. The militia fled at their first glimpse of oncoming British bayonets.

Grabbing the fastest available horse, the hero of Saratoga joined the militia in headlong flight. In his panic General Gates abandoned Baron de Kalb and his Continentals. They fought to the death. De Kalb, who had warned Gates he was risking disaster, reportedly suffered eleven bayonet wounds before he fell.[62]

XIX

Infuriated by Congress's confirmation of his court-martial verdict, General Charles Lee again took his case to the newspapers, becoming more and more strident and insulting. Eventually he turned his vituperation on Congress, who voted to change his one-year suspension to dismissal from the army. John Laurens added to Lee's woes by challenging him to a duel, claiming that his insults to General Washington also insulted him. The two met and exchanged shots, leaving Lee with a slight wound in his side. Though General Washington seems to have known nothing about the duel, thereafter Lee claimed the commander in chief was plotting to assassinate him.

Watching all this from the sidelines, Dr. Benjamin Rush was appalled. In August, just after the court-martial found Lee guilty, the heroic doctor had sent the Englishman one of his patented unsigned letters, asking him why and how he had blundered at Monmouth. Lee recognized Rush's handwriting and replied that the letter made him wonder if he should laugh or cry. He assured Rush that "G. Washington saw, knew and was almost as little concerned in the affair of the 28th [the battle of Monmouth] as he was in the battle of Philippi."[63]

After Congress confirmed the Lee verdict, Rush declared that George Washington now had as much influence over the nation's legislature as George III had over the British Parliament. "CONWAY, MIFFLIN and Lee were sacrificed to the excessive influence and popularity of one man," this quintessential true whig moaned. "Where is the Republican spirit of our country?"[64]

It would take this befuddled ideologue several years to realize that the Revolution was alive and well in its reasonable rather than its extremist version under the leadership of that consummate politician, General George Washington.

EPILOGUE

TWO VISITS TO
VALLEY FORGE

I N THE SUMMER OF 1796, John Woodman was working on his small
farm in Valley Forge. Born in North Carolina, Woodman had been a
member of the Continental Army and spent the winter of 1778 in his
brigade's freezing huts. Discharged in 1782, he and two friends hiked for
home. Their route carried them near Valley Forge, and they decided to
visit the "old encampment."

They found little trace of the huts and trenches. The farmers who
owned the land had returned to their plots and torn down the huts for
firewood and fence posts, and were soon producing bumper crops from
the fertile soil. Woodman became ill during the visit, and a friendly
Quaker took him into his house. During his recuperation the soldier fell
in love with the farmer's daughter and married her. The fond father gave
the couple part of his farm, on which Woodman was toiling when a voice
from the road interrupted him.

He looked up as a big gray-haired man dismounted from a fine horse.
He was dressed in formal black clothes. The stranger was asking him what
crops he had planted this year. Woodman told him, and the visitor began
asking questions about yield and fertilizer and growing time that made it
clear that he too was a farmer, even though he was not dressed like one.

Woodman told him he was not an expert in the science of agriculture. He had become a farmer by accident. He had started out his life as a Continental soldier.

"This gave a different turn to the conversation," Woodman recalled. The stranger introduced himself as George Washington and said he was pleased to see one of his men had turned farmer, an occupation he held in high regard.

Woodman gasped and probably whipped off his broad-brimmed hat. He may have apologized for not recognizing the president of the United States. Washington brushed away the apology with a wave of his hand and explained that he had been in the mood for a canter and decided Valley Forge was a good destination. He may have added that it was a relief to escape the humid air of the nation's temporary capital, Philadelphia.[1]

They reminisced for a few minutes about the winter ordeal. Woodman may have reminded his former general of the trouble the North Carolinians had had with their huts, which never seemed warm enough for them. Perhaps the ex-soldier asked the whereabouts of Baron von Steuben. The president sadly reported his death in northern New York two years earlier. The last letter Washington wrote before resigning as commander in chief in 1783 was to the Baron telling him how much he valued his "services."[2]

They may also have mentioned the Marquis de Lafayette. He had tried to export the American Revolution to France and was forced to flee the resulting Reign of Terror, ending up in an Austrian prison. General Horatio Gates? He was living comfortably in New York City. After his first wife died, he had married a wealthy widow.

II

The president rode back to Philadelphia, leaving Woodman with a memory he treasured and passed on to his children. One of them published it in a book forty years later. Did it happen? No one is certain. Some skeptics say Woodman confused the encounter with a visit Washington made to Valley Forge in 1787, during the Constitutional Convention. That day, his purpose seemed to have been fishing with Gouverneur Morris in Valley Creek. But Washington soon left the angling to Morris and rode off to examine the ruins of the encampment.

There are persuasive arguments for both visits. In 1787, Washington had been presiding over the Constitutional Convention, a task that was charged with high anxiety for him. In four years of peace he had become convinced that the Articles of Confederation, the constitution that Congress wrote during the war for independence, was worthless.

The articles gave the federal government no meaningful power. When rebellious farmers led by a hothead named Daniel Shays revolted against the state of Massachusetts in 1786, Congress could not send a single soldier to restore order and peace. The Continental Army had been disbanded and the federal government was bankrupt. Washington had decided that without a new constitution, the American republic was doomed to disunity and dissolution.

There was also alarming evidence that the ideologues General Washington had confronted at Valley Forge were still at work in the Constitutional Convention. Their old bugaboo, fear of power, led to strenuous debates about the office of the president. Should he be chosen by Congress or the people? Would it be better to have a three-man chief executive? As the presiding officer, Washington could not participate in the debates. But offstage, at dinner parties and informal meetings in coffeehouses, he pushed for a one-man presidency, elected by the people, with enough power to deal as an equal with Congress and even to veto legislation when necessary.

Ignoring the lessons of the war of independence, the ideologues also revealed their morbid hostility to a regular army. At one point, one of Sam Adams's allies in the Continental Congress, dapper, argumentative Elbridge Gerry of Massachusetts, proposed a clause in the new national charter limiting the regular army to three thousand men. From the president's chair, Washington murmured sotto voce to the delegates in the first row that he thought this was a wonderful idea if Mr. Gerry could guarantee that the United States would never be attacked by more than three thousand men.[3]

No more was heard of Mr. Gerry's brainstorm. The final version of the federal constitution was a product of James Madison's genius and George Washington's unwavering support.

III

In 1796 President Washington, in the final year of his second term, was under savage attack in the Philadelphia newspapers by another group of ideologues, the worshippers of the French Revolution, led by Thomas Jefferson. They accused him of betraying France and the ideals of the American Revolution by proclaiming the United States neutral in the war that was raging between the French revolutionists and England. Jeffersonian newspapers sneered at the accomplishments of Washington's presidency and his pretensions to being a great man. Washington was wounded and infuriated by this abuse.

What better source of spiritual renewal during both these periods of emotional turmoil than a visit to the place where Americans had confirmed their trust in him, in spite of the sneers of Thomas Mifflin, James Lovell, and their allies? Here was a place where he had experienced the presence of that "benevolent Providence" that had protected and reassured him so often.

IV

"I would cherish those dear ragged Continentals, whose patience will be the admiration of future ages, and glory in bleeding with them." John Laurens had written these words at Valley Forge in a letter to his father. Four years later, with the war almost over, this young idealist had died in a minor skirmish in South Carolina, breaking Henry Laurens's heart.[4]

Other men of talent and dedication had survived the war but died before they could play a part in the new republic. One of the most gifted was aide Tench Tilghman, to whom Washington gave the honor of carrying the news of the climactic 1781 victory at Yorktown to Congress.

The most painful of these premature losses was Nathanael Greene. He died of sunstroke in 1786, while toiling on the rice plantation the grateful state of Georgia had given him. In the closing years of the war, General Greene had rescued the South from the disaster that Horatio Gates's ineptitude and cowardice had inflicted on the region at the battle of Camden. With only a remnant of an army, Greene doggedly persisted unto victory. "We fight, get beat, rise and fight again," he told a French friend.

Who but a witness of Valley Forge could summon such determination and pride? All the senior officers had drawn strength from the men in the huts, whose only eloquence was their patience and endurance. No one drew more spiritual meaning than their commander in chief. Remember his eyes brimming with tears as he talked with the soldiers who came to headquarters to respectfully report their hunger?

V

In late December 1783, when General Washington resigned as commander in chief, he visited the Continental Congress for the last time. The politicians were sitting in Annapolis. They had been run out of Philadelphia by radical mobs. The president was, of all people, Thomas Mifflin, who had become a power in Pennsylvania politics. It is not hard to imagine the rueful thoughts that swirled through the handsome head of "the pivot" during this ceremony.

General Washington read a brief statement praising the officers and soldiers of the Continental Army for their eight years of service. He also commended "our dear country to the protection of Almighty God." As he said these words, his voice broke and tears streamed down the general's cheeks and he was unable to speak for a full minute. If any further evidence of George Washington's religious faith is needed, it can be found here.

Two visits to Valley Forge when events seemed to be threatening this faith do not seem implausible to this historian.

VI

George Washington was not the last American to find spiritual meaning in Valley Forge. Throughout the nineteenth century the place attracted more and more visitors, and its significance grew in the American public mind. With this popularity came one of memory's favorite historical tricks: the simplification and sentimentalizing of the story. Forgotten were the deserters, both those caught and hanged and the 1,500 who made it to British Philadelphia. Gone were the 2,500 men who died in their huts or froze or starved in the abominable hospitals.

Erased were the desperate commissaries, Ephraim Blaine and John Chaloner and Thomas Jones, fearing sudden death from the infuriated soldiers they were failing to feed. The bloody footsteps in the snow were explained by inexplicable temporary shoe shortages rather than by Congress's ineptitude and indifference to the soldiers' sufferings. The undercover campaign to make Washington resign also faded into history's shadows.

There is no need to be surprised or outraged by this process. One of our best historians has concluded that it takes a minimum of a hundred years to begin telling the truth about most of our wars. For the Revolution, with its overlay of complex meanings to old and new Americans, it has taken more than two hundred years.[5]

Contemporary Americans can face the whole truth about Valley Forge—and find a different kind of spiritual renewal at the site of the old encampment. It is an inspiration that goes beyond the nineteenth century's reverence for the mute endurance of the suffering Continentals. It combines their story with the political thoughts and words and acts of the tall Virginian who led those men to ultimate victory.

Telling the whole truth means a readiness to blame as well as praise, to see the revolutionists of 1776 as all too human in many respects— not so different from the mix of politicians of mediocrity and ability, self-interest, and vision, who have presided over the nation's destiny in every generation since 1776. It also means a readiness to recognize greatness when that rarest of blessings emerges inexplicably from history's depths.

Valley Forge tells us that a great leader's gifts are not instantly admired by everyone. Passions such as envy, ambition, and prejudice distort the vision of men and women in every generation. Those who fret about the various controversies that seem to be disuniting contemporary Americans may find some comfort—and even a little wisdom—in this dolorous observation. For this writer, it makes a visit to Valley Forge more, not less inspiring.

VII

On July 4, 1976, during the nation's bicentennial, President Gerald Ford came to Valley Forge to preside over the transfer of the encampment and its surrounding acres from the state of Pennsylvania to the National Park Service. On the world scene, it was another time of crisis for the United States of America. Communist enemies were exulting in their victory in Vietnam. A president and vice president had left office in disgrace, elevating this unassuming veteran congressman from Michigan to the White House.[6]

President Ford found words that confronted these troubled times and summed up much of Valley Forge's meaning for twentieth- and twenty-first-century Americans: "The patriots of Valley Forge send us a single, urgent message. Though prosperity is a good thing, a nation survives only so long as the spirit of sacrifice and self-discipline is strong within its people. . . . When our Tri-Centennial celebration rolls around, grateful Americans will come to this shrine of quiet valor, this forge of our Republic's iron core."[7]

Quiet Valor. Those words tell us this modest president grasped the essence of Valley Forge's importance. They sum up not only the soldiers in their huts but also the steadfast man who led them with a courage and compassion that still shine in the soul of the American republic.

Notes

CHAPTER ONE. **General George Washington: Loser**

1. Now West Coshocken, Pennsylvania. For date of Gulph Road, see Philander Chase et al., ed., *Papers of George Washington* (hereafter *PGW*), Revolutionary War Series (Charlottesville, Va., 2003), vol. 13, 191n.

2. Hugh F. Rankin, ed., *Narratives of the American Revolution*, Albigence Waldo's Diary (Chicago, 1976), 180.

3. Richard Buel Jr., *In Irons: Britain's Naval Supremacy and the American Revolutionary Economy* (New Haven, Conn., 1998), 3, 9–10, 107–16. Jacqueline Thibaut, Valley Forge Report, vol. 2, *This Fatal Crisis: Logistics, Supply and the Continental Army at Valley Forge* (Valley Forge National Historical Park, 1979), 17–18. Gary B. Nash, *The Urban Crucible: The Northern Seaports and the Origins of the American Revoltion* (Cambridge, Mass., 1979), 202–03. In 1774 alone, Philadelphia built more new houses than Boston raised in the previous decade.

4. Joseph Plumb Martin, *Private Yankee Doodle: Being a Narrative of Some of the Adventures, Dangers and Sufferings of a Revolutionary Soldier*, ed. George E. Scheer (Boston, 1962), 99.

5. Henry Dearborn, *Journals of Henry Dearborn, 1776–1783*, Pamphlets in American History (Cambridge, Ma., 1887), 13.

6. Boyle Files, Valley Forge National Historical Park Library (hereafter BF). This designates the letters and diaries gathered from many sources by Joseph Lee Boyle, librarian of Valley Forge National Historical Park. This entry cites "Samuel Armstrong Diary," New England Historical and Genealogical Society, ms C 1058, Dec. 18, 1777.

7. Martin, *Private Yankee Doodle*, 100–101.

8. *PGW*, vol. 12, General Orders, Dec. 17, 1777, 620–21.

9. A. E. Zucker, *General De Kalb, Lafayette's Mentor* (Chapel Hill, N.C., 1966), 163.

10. Joseph Lee Boyle, ed., *Writings from the Valley Forge Encampment of the Continental Army*, 5 vols. (hereafter *WFVF*) (Bowie, Md., 2003), vol. 4, 6–7.

11. BF, Citizens Icon, Duportail to Count de St. Germain, Minister of War, Nov. 12, 1777, citing John F. Reed, ed., *Picket Post, The Magazine of the Valley Forge Historical Society*, third quarter, 1977, 23. Duportail was promoted to brigadier a few days after he wrote this letter.

12. *PGW*, vol. 12, Lafayette to Washington, Dec. 30, 1777, 68.

13. *PGW*, vol. 13, Washington to Lafayette, Dec. 31, 1777, 83.

14. *PGW*, vol. 13, Lafayette to Washington, Dec. 31, 1777, 84.

15. Richard K. Showman et al., eds., *The Papers of Nathanael Greene* (hereafter *PNG*), vol. 2, Jan. 1, 1777–Oct. 16, 1778 (Chapel Hill, N.C., 1980), Varnum to Greene, Feb. 11, 1778, 280. The full quotation is: "I have from the beginning viewd this situation with horror."

16. *WFVF*, vol. 4, Jedidiah Huntington to Jabez Huntington, Dec. 20, 1777, 1.

17. George Washington Parke Custis, *Recollections and Private Memoirs of Washington by his Adopted Son* (New York, 1860), 208–10.

18. *PGW*, vol. 12, Weedon to Washington, Dec. 1, 1777, 491; Sullivan to Washington, Dec. 1, 1777, 486; Stirling to Washington, Dec. 3, 529; Greene to Washington, Dec. 3, 1777, 517; Mease to Washington, Dec. 16, 1777, 614–15: Mease's report, "Sketch of Clothing on Hand," is in George Washington Papers, Library of Congress. Martin, *Private Yankee Doodle*, 88–89.

19. Joseph Lee Boyle, ed., *"Their Distress Is Almost Intolerable": The Elias Boudinot Letterbook, 1777–1778* (Bowie, Md., 2002), Boudinot to Pickering, Oct. 19, 1777, 37.

20. Calvin Jilson and Rick K. Wilson, *Congressional Dynamics: Structure, Coordination and Choice in the First American Congress, 1774–1789* (Stanford, Calif, 1994), 93–97.

21. Edmund C. Burnett, ed., *Letters of Members of the Continental Congress* (Washington, D.C., 1923) (hereafter *LMCC*), vol. 2, Morris to the Commissioners at Paris, Dec. 21, 1776, 183–84.

22. Paul H. Smith et al., eds., *Letters of Delegates to Congress, 1774–1789* (Washington, D.C., 1981) (hereafter *LDC*), vol. 8, Henry Laurens to John Laurens, Oct. 16, 1777, 125.

23. William Duane, ed., *Extracts from the Diary of Christopher Marshall, 1774–1781* (1877; New York, 1969), 159.

24. *PGW*, vol. 12, Sullivan to Washington, Dec. 1, 1777, 486, Varnum to Washington, Dec. 1, 1777, 488, Weedon to Washington, Dec. 1, 1777, 491.

25. Harold C. Syrett, et al., eds., *The Papers of Alexander Hamilton* (New York, 1961), Washington to Hamilton, Sept. 21, 1777, vol. 1, 330–31.

26. *PGW*, vol. 12, Henry Laurens to Washington, Nov. 13–15, 1777, 244–46, and 247n9.

27. BF, Citizens Icon, Arthur St. Clair to Robert Morris, Nov. 13, citing St. Clair Papers, vol. 1, 458–59. For the army's size see *PGW*, vol. 12, 687 n.2. The exact number is 12, 484 men.

28. Syrett, ed., *Hamilton Papers*, vol. 1, 330–31. *PGW*, vol. 12, Washington to Henry Laurens, Dec. 14–15, 1777, 606.

29. *PGW*, vol. 12, Putnam to Washington, Dec. 16, 1777, 616–17. Also note, 616–17.

30. *PGW*, vol. 12, Clinton to Washington, Dec. 209, 1777, 645–48.

31. *PGW*, vol. 12, Washington to Shippen, Dec. 12, 1777, 602; Washington to Burgoyne, Dec. 17, 1777, 621–22.

32. *PGW*, vol. 12, Galloway to Washington, Dec. 18, 1777, 630; Washington to Galloway, Dec. 20, 1777, 649.

33. *PGW*, vol. 12, Washington to Peters, Dec. 14, 1777, 607–8.

34. *PGW*, vol. 12, Hopkinson (and John Wharton) to Washington, Dec. 17, 1777, 622.

35. *PGW*, vol. 12, Clark to Washington, Dec. 19, 1777, 635–36.

36. *PGW*, vol. 12, Clark to Washington, Dec. 18, 1777, 628–30.

37. *PGW*, vol. 12, Clark to Washington, Dec. 19, 1777, 635.

38. *PGW*, vol. 12, Armstrong to Washington, Dec. 19, 1777, 632–34.

39. *LDC*, vol. 8, Harvie to Jefferson, Dec. 29, 1777, 493–94.

40. BF, citing "Extract of a letter from an officer in the Army, dated Wilmington, December 25, 1777," *Maryland Journal and Baltimore Advertiser*, Dec. 30, 1777.

41. *PGW*, vol. 12, General Orders, Dec. 18, 1777, 626–28.

42. *PGW*, vol. 12, From a Committee to Inspect Beef, Dec. 20, 1777, 648–49.

43. John F. Reed, *Valley Forge: Crucible of Victory* (Monmouth Beach, N.J., 1969), 9.

44. *WFVF*, vol. 2, Henry Beekman Livingston to Robert R. Livingston, Dec. 14, 1777, 2.

45. Jacqueline Thibaut, Valley Forge Report, vol. 3, *In the True Rustic Order* (Valley Forge National Historical Park, 1982), 55.

46. Ibid., 59–60.

47. Ibid., 56.

48. *PGW*, vol. 12, Proclamation on Threshing Grain, Dec. 20, 1777, 655–56.

49. *PGW*, vol. 12, Clark to Washington, Dec. 22, 1777, 666; Clark to Washington, Dec. 23, 1777, 680–81; Washington to Henry Laurens, Dec. 23, 1777, 683–84. Also see: *WFVF*, vol. 4, Charles Stewart to William Buchanan, Dec. 22, 1777, 5: "The troops will not march without provisions and how they will be furnished God only knows." Stewart was commissary general of issues, Buchanan commissary general of purchases.

50. *WFVF*, vol. 1, Varnum to Washington, Dec. 22, 1777, 2–3.

51. *PGW*, vol. 12, 671n.2.

52. Joseph Lee Boyle, ed., *"My Last Shift Betwixt Us and Death": The Ephraim Blaine Letterbook, 1777–1778* (Bowie, Md., 2001), 61–63.

53. Thibaut, *The Valley Forge Report*, vol. 2, 23–24.

54. *PGW*, vol. 12, Washington to Henry Laurens, Dec. 22, 1777, 667–68.

55. *PGW*, vol. 12, ibid., 669–70.

56. *PGW*, vol. 12, Armstrong to Washington, Dec. 23, 1777, 678–79.

57. *PGW*, vol. 12, Morgan to Washington, Dec. 23, 1777, 690–91.

58. *PGW*, vol. 12, Potter to Washington, Dec. 23, 1777, 691.

59. *PGW*, vol. 12, Washington to Laurens, Dec. 23, 1777, 683–87.

60. *PGW*, vol. 12, Morgan to Washington, Dec. 24, 1777, 694–95.

61. Reed, *Valley Forge*, 12.

62. *PGW*, vol. 12, Clark to Washington, Dec. 25, 1777, 704–5. Charles S. Lesser, ed., *The Sinews of Power: Monthly Strength Reports of the Continental Army* (Chicago, 1976), 55–56n.G. Lesser's report for December 30 has figures slightly higher than the field report Washington cited in his letter to Laurens.

63. Reed, *Valley Forge*, 12.

64. *PGW*, vol. 12, Washington to Gerry, Dec. 25, 1777, 705–6.

65. Frank Moore, ed., *Songs and Ballads of the American Revolution* (New York, 1855), 150–52.

66. *PGW*, vol. 12, Plan to Attack Philadelphia, 701–3.

67. *PGW*, vol. 12, Stirling to Washington, Dec. 25, 1777, 712, including note 1.

CHAPTER TWO. **Revels and Redcoats**

1. "A Letter of Miss Rebecca Franks, 1778," Feb. 26, 1778, *Pennsylvania Magazine of History and Biography* (hereafter *PMHB*), 16 (1892): 216–18.

2. James Thomas Flexner, *The Traitor and the Spy* (New York, 1953), 20–37, 137–47.

3. Thomas J. Maguire, *Battle of Paoli* (Mechanicsburg, Pa., 2000), 95ff. This is by far the best account of the brief battle.

4. John André, "Particulars of the Mischianza, Preface by Sophia Howard Ward," *Century*, 47 (1893–94): 686.

5. Robert D. Bass, *The Green Dragoon: The Lives of Banastre Tarleton and Mary Robinson* (New York, 1957), 37–37, 44.

6. John W. Jackson, *With the British Army in Philadelphia, 1777–78* (San Rafael, Calif., 1979), 103–4.

7. Judith Van Buskirk, "They Didn't Join the Band: Disaffected Women in Revolutionary Philadelphia," *Pennsylvania History* 62, no. 3 (Summer 1995); Mary Beth Norton, *Liberty's Daughters: The Revolutionary Experience of American Women, 1750–1800* (Boston, 1980), 204.

8. Robert Morton Diary, *PMHB* 1 (1877): 25, 30. Morton's father was one of the Quaker leaders exiled to Virginia.

9. Ibid., 34–35.

10. Elizabeth Forman Crane, ed., *The Diary of Elizabeth Drinker* (Boston, 1991), vol. 1, 258ff.

11. Ibid.

12. Ira D. Gruber, *The Howe Brothers and the American Revolution* (New York, 1972), 56–57.

13. When George Washington became president and Philadelphia was the temporary capital, he too took over this house, which then belonged to merchant Robert Morris. See Edward Lawler Jr., "The President's House in Philadelphia: The Rediscovery of a Lost Landmark," *PMHB*, 126, no. 1 (Jan. 2002): 13, 23ff.

14. Philip Young, *Revolutionary Ladies* (New York, 1977), 76–80; John Alden, *The American Revolution* (New York, 1969), 503–5.

15. Johann Ewald, *Diary of the American War*, trans. and ed. Joseph P. Tustin (New Haven, Conn., 1979), 120.

16. Piers Mackesy, *The War for America, 1775–1783* (Cambridge, Mass., 1964), 55.

17. Gruber, *The Howe Brothers*, 253–54.

18. Ibid., 255.

19. Ibid., 256; BF, citing Richard Fitzpatrick Papers, Manuscript Division, Library of Congress (hereafter LC), *Revolution in America: Confidential Letters and Journals, 1776–1784, of Adjutant General Major Baurmeister of the Hessian Forces*, trans. and annotated Bernhard A. Uhlendorf (New Brunswick, N.J., 1957), Baurmeister to Baron von Jungkenn, Jan. 20, 1778, 145.

20. BF, citing Loftus Cliffe Letters, William Clements Library, University of Michigan.

21. BF, citing William Dancey Letters, Delaware Historical Society.

22. Moore, ed., *Songs and Ballads of the Revolution*, 209–16.

23. BF, citing Johnn Conrad Doehla, *A Hessian Diary of the American Revolution*, trans. and ed. Bruce Burgoyne (Norman, Okla., 1990), 70; Ewald, Diary, 118.

24. Ewald, *Diary*, 121.

25. Ibid., 119.

26. Morton Diary, *PMHB*, 35.

27. John E. Ferling, *The Loyalist Mind: Joseph Galloway and the American Revolution* (University Park, Pa., 1977), 35–44.

28. Joseph Lee Boyle, ed., *"Their Distress Is Almost Intolerable": The Elias Boudinot Letter Book* (Bowie, Md., 2002), 68.

29. Burnett, *LMCC*, vol. 3, "Elias Boudinot Reminiscences," 356–57.

30. *PGW*, vol. 12, Washington to General Howe, Nov. 14–15, 1777, 257n.

31. Jackson, *With the British Army in Philadelphia*, 122.

32. *PGW*, vol. 12, letter from Peletiah Webster, addressed to "Any officer of Genl Washington's army to be forwarded to the General," Nov. 19, 1777, 325–26. Also see Jackson, *With the British Army in Philadelphia*, 122–24.

33. Jack D. Marietta, *The Reformation of American Quakerism, 1748–1783* (Phildelphia, Pa., 1984), 222–40.

34. Helen R. Yalof, "British Military Theatricals in Philadelphia During the Revolutionary War" (Ph.D. diss., New York University, 1972), 35–37.

35. Ibid., 90–91, 98.

36. Ibid., 133–34.

37. Ewald, *Diary*, 121.

CHAPTER THREE. **Ideologues Front and Center**

1. *LDC*, vol. 8, John Adams to Abigail Adams, Sept. 30, 1777, 27. Eighty-eight miles was the distance stated by Adams, describing the trip to York.

2. Douglas Southall Freeman, *George Washington, a Biography*, vol. 4, *Leader of the Revolution* (New York, 1951), 542–43.

3. William Fowler Jr., *The Baron of Beacon Hill: A Biography of John Hancock* (Boston, 1980), 216.

4. *LMCC*, vol. 2, Robert Morris to John Hancock, Dec. 16, 1776, 176.

5. *LMCC*, vol. 2, Henry Laurens to John Lewis Gervais, Sept. 18, 1777, 497–98.

6. Harold C. Syrett, ed., *The Papers of Alexander Hamilton*, vol. 1 (New York, 1961), Hamilton to John Hancock, Sept. 18, 1777, 326–27.

7. Morton Diary, *PMBH*, 3–4.

8. John C. Miller, *Sam Adams, Pioneer in Propaganda* (Boston, 1936), 342–44. When John arrived in France in 1778, he almost choked when he was asked whether he was "the famous Adams."

9. *LMCC*, vol. 2, Benjamin Harrison to Robert Morris, Jan. 8, 1777, 208.

10. *LMCC*, vol. 2, Excerpt from John Adams Diary, Sept. 18, 1777, 497; Miller, *Sam Adams*, 344–46.

11. *LDC*, vol. 8, John Adams Diary, Sept. 19, 3; John Adams to Abigail Adams, Sept. 30, 1777, 27.

12. Howard Swiggett, *The Great Man* (Garden City, N.Y., 1953), 150–57. *LDC*, vol. 8, Lovell to Washington, Dec. 31, 1777, 509–10.

13. Charles H. Metzger, *The Prisoner in the American Revolution* (Chicago, 1971), 207; *LDC*, vol. 8, James Lovell to Samuel Adams, Jan. 20, 1778, 618–19; David Freeman Hawke, *Honorable Treason: The Declaration of Independence and the Men Who Signed It* (New York, 1976), 205–6.

14. Fowler, *The Baron of Beacon Hill*, 219–20.

15. Miller, *Sam Adams*, 26–27.

16. Ibid., 345–47.

17. H. James Henderson, *Party Politics in the Continental Congress* (New York, 1974), 230.

18. David Freeman Hawke, *In the Midst of a Revolution: The Politics of Confrontation in Colonial America* (Philadelphia, 1971), 103–4.

19. William Duane, ed., *Extracts from the Diary of Christopher Marshall* (New York, Arno Press, 1969), Dec. 25, 1777, 151, Dec. 28, 1777, 153.

20. Hawke, *In the Midst of a Revolution*, 190. Other quotes from Gordon Wood, *The Creation of the American Republic* (New York, 1969), 86–87.

21. Paul Starr, *The Creation of the Media: Political Origins of Modern Communications* (New York, 2004), 71.

22. David Freeman Hawke, *Paine* (New York, 1974), 70–73.

23. Helen E. Royer, "The Role of the Continental Congress in the Prosecution of the American Revolution in Pennsylvania" (Ph.D. diss., Pennsylvania State University, 1960), 216.

24. Ibid., 190.

25. Ibid., 205.

26. Ibid., 222.

27. *PGW*, vol. 13, Pennsylvania Executive Council to Washington, Jan. 15, 1778, 249–50.

28. *WFVF*, vol. 2, Thomas Craig to Thomas Wharton Jr., April 12, 1778, 107. Also see Royer, *The Role of the Continental Congress*, 221.

29. *Marshall Diary*, 153. The petition is in the Dreer Collection, Historical So-

ciety of Pennsylvania. Also see Royer, *The Role of the Continental Congress*, 219–20. The assembly took the petition very seriously. After much discussion, it sent the proposal to Congress, who forwarded it to General Washington. He gave it short shrift.

30. John C. Fitzpatrick, *The Writings of George Washington*, 39 vols. (Washington, D.C., 1931–44), Washington to Hancock, Sept. 8, 1776, vol. 6, 27–33.

31. E. Wayne Karp, *To Starve the Army at Pleasure: Continental Army Administration and American Political Culture, 1775–83* (Chapel Hill, N.C., 1984), 40–42.

32. Ibid., 44–45.

33. J. Bennett Nolan, *George Washington and the Town of Reading* (Reading, Pa., 1931), 70.

34. James Thomas Flexner, *George Washington*, 4 vols., 1965–72, vol. 2 (Boston, 1968), 253.

35. Ibid., 255.

36. Nolan, *George Washington and Reading*, 67, 72.

37. David R. Chesnutt et al., eds., *The Papers of Henry Laurens* (Hereafter *PHL*) (Columbia, S.C., 1990), vol. 12, Kalb to Laurens, Jan. 7, 1778, 267–68.

38. Karp, *To Starve the Army*, 45; Christopher Marshall Diary, Dec. 28, 1777, 152–53.

39. Hawke, *Honorable Treason*, 68–70.

40. Ibid., 68.

41. Hawke, *In the Midst of Revolution*, 104–5.

42. L. H. Butterfield, ed., *Letters of Benjamin Rush*, vol. 1, *1761–1792* (Princeton, N.J., 1951), 152–53.

43. *LDC*, vol. 8, Lovell to Adams, Dec. 20, 1777, 451.

44. Butterfield, ed., *Letters of Rush*, Rush to Adams, Oct. 1, 1777, 154–57.

45. Ibid., Rush to Adams, Oct. 21, 1777, 159–62.

46. Ibid., Rush to Adams, Oct. 13, 1777, 158; Freeman, *George Washington*, vol. 4, 595.

47. Douglas Southall Freeman, *George Washington*, vol. 3, *Planter and Patriot* (New York, 1951), 520.

48. Flexner, *George Washington*, vol. 2, 37.

49. J. Kent McCaughey, *Richard Henry Lee of Virginia: A Portrait of an American Revolutionary* (Lanham, Md., 2004), 20, 130–33; *PNG*, vol. 2, George Lux to Nathanael Greene, April 28, 1778, 366.

50. Jonathan Gregory Rossie, *The Politics of Command in the American Revolution* (Syracuse, N.Y., 1975), 181, 183.

51. *LDC*, vol. 8, Lovell to William Whipple, Nov. 21, 1777, 302; Lovell to Samuel Adams, Dec. 20, 1777, 450–51; Lovell to John Adams, Jan. 13, 1778, 578.

52. Rossie, *Politics of Command*, 183. Sargent had become attorney general in the radical-dominated government of Pennsylvania.

53. L. H. Butterfield, ed., *The Adams Papers* (Cambridge, Mass., 1961), series 1, Diary of John Adams, Sept. 21, 1777, 265.

54. *LDC*, vol. 8, John Adams to Abigail Adams, Oct. 26, 1777, 187.

55. *LDC*, vol. 8, Mifflin to Gates, Nov. 17, 1777, 314–15n.5. For two centuries this letter was attributed to James Lovell. That persuaded many historians to claim there was no evidence linking Mifflin to the anti-Washington bloc.

56. *LMCC*, vol. 2, Henry Laurens to John Laurens, Oct. 16, 1777, 521–22.

57. Rossie, *Politics of Command*, 99.

58. Kenneth R. Rossman, *Thomas Mifflin and the Politics of the American Revolution* (Chapel Hill, N.C., 1952), 97–98.

59. Ibid., 98.

60. Harry Alonzo Cushing, ed., *The Writings of Samuel Adams*, 4 vols. (New York, 1904–8), vol. 4, 1–2.

61. *Dunlap's Pennsylvania Packet, or, The General Advertiser*, Jan. 14, 1778.

CHAPTER FOUR. **Playing the Insult Card**

1. BF, Tilghman to Cadwalader, Jan. 18, 1778, citing Military Papers of General John Cadwalader, *PMHB* 32, no. 2 (1908): 168–70. Also see L. G. Shreve, *Tench Tilghman: The Life and Times of Washington's Aide-de-Camp* (Centreville, Md., 1982), 34–36, 41, 209–10.

2. Shreve, *Tilghman*, 98.

3. Joseph Ellis, *His Excellency, George Washington* (New York, 2004), 117.

4. Charles Lee, *The Lee Papers*, 4 vols. (New York, 1872–75), vol. 3, Lee to Gates, Mar. 29, 1779, 319–21.

5. Paul David Nelson, *General Horatio Gates, a Biography* (Baton Rouge, La., 1976), 37.

6. Ibid., 55.

7. Ibid., 60.

8. Freeman, *George Washington*, vol. 4, 297, 309.

9. Nelson, *General Horatio Gates*, 77.

10. Ibid., 84–85.

11. Ibid., 143.

12. *PGW*, vol. 12, Washington to Lee, Oct. 28, 1777, 41.

13. *PGW*, vol. 12, Stirling to Washington, Nov. 3, 110–11. Also see Butterfield, *Letters of Rush*, vol. 1, 162n. The quotation was common gossip before Wilkinson

got to Reading. It is not inconceivable that Stirling had heard it and ordered Major McWilliams to try to confirm it from Wilkinson. Dr. Rush used it in a letter he wrote to John Adams on October 21. Wilkinson, vainly trying to defend himself, pointed out the already widespread circulation of the comment in a letter to Washington on March 28, 1778. The source of this circulation was probably General Conway, who was as indiscreet verbally as he was on paper.

14. *PGW*, vol. 12, Washington to Conway, Nov. 5, 1777, 129.

15. *PGW*, vol. 12, Conway to Washington, Nov. 5, 1777, 130–1.

16. *PGW*, vol. 12, 131n.

17. *PGW*, vol. 12, Gates to Washington, Dec. 8, 1777, 576–77.

18. Freeman, *George Washington*, vol. 4, 559.

19. *LDC*, vol. 8, Richard Henry Lee to Samuel Adams, Nov. 23, 1777, 313.

20. Freeman, *George Washington*, vol. 4, 560.

21. Ibid., 548–49.

22. *PHL*, vol. 12, John Laurens to Henry Laurens, Jan. 1, 1778, 229–31.

23. *PHL*, vol. 12, Gates to Laurens, Dec. 8, 1777, 135–36.

24. *PGW*, vol. 13, Conway to Washington, Dec. 31, 1777, 77–79.

25. *PGW*, vol. 13, Washington to Henry Laurens, Jan. 2, 1778, 119.

26. *PHL*, vol. 12, John Laurens to Henry Laurens, Jan. 3, 1778, 245–47.

27. *PHL*, vol. 12, Henry Laurens to John Laurens, Jan. 8, 1778, 269–71.

28. Ibid., 272.

29. Ibid., 275.

30. John McAuley Palmer, *General von Steuben* (New Haven, Conn., 1937), 86.

31. Ibid., 115–16; *PGW*, vol. 13, Washington to Steuben, Jan. 9, 1778, 193–94.

CHAPTER FIVE. **Enter the Committee in Camp**

1. BF, citing Diary of Lt. Samuel Armstrong, New England Genealogical Society, and Diary of Colonel Israel Angell, Massachusetts Historical Society.

2. Ray Raphael, *Founding Myths, Stories That Hide Our Patriotic Past* (New York, 2004), 92–3.

3. Sandy Bauers and Dan Hardy, "Park Ranger Takes a New Look at Valley Forge Winter," *Philadelphia Inquirer*, Feb. 3, 2004.

4. Thibaut, *The Valley Forge Report*, vol. 2, 524.

5. Boyle, ed., Blaine Letterbook, 67–68.

6. Ibid., 69–70, 85.

7. *WFVF*, vol. 1, John Brooks to Unidentified, Jan. 5, 1778, 16–17; Miller, *Sam Adams*, 146–47.

8. Wayne Bodle, *The Valley Forge Report*, vol. 1, *The Vortex of Small Fortunes: The Continental Army at Valley Forge* (Valley Forge, Pa., 1980), 162.

9. Boyle, ed., Blaine Letterbook, 75.

10. Ibid., 85.

11. Ibid., 85.

12. Oscar Reiss, *Medicine and the American Revolution: How Diseases and Their Treatments Affected the Colonial Army* (Jefferson, N.C., 1998), 190–91, 196–97, 199–201.

13. Martin, *Private Yankee Doodle*, 110–11.

14. Boyle, ed., Blaine Letterbook, 82.

15. Ibid., 84–85.

16. Ibid., 86.

17. BF, Citing Diary of Israel Angell, 20–21, 23.

18. Ibid., Dec. 31, 1777, 16.

19. "Diary of Lieutenant James McMichael," *PMHB* 16 (1892), 157. This is an edited version of the diary. In BF, there is a more complete version, describing McMichael's trip to New Jersey to see Susanna.

20. BF, McMichael Diary, Feb. 4, 1778, 2–3.

21. BF, Armstrong Diary, Dec. 19, 1777.

22. Ibid.

23. Ibid., Feb. 23, 1778; March 11, 1778. On the latter day the officers had "business" with the sutlers who camped on the other side of the Schuylkill. But "falling into company," they were soon making another "frolic."

24. McMichael Diary, *PMHB*, 158.

25. WFVF, vol. 1, John Cropper to Margaret Cropper, March 13, 1778, 80–81.

26. Charles P. Neimeyer, "No Meat, No Soldier: Race, Class and Ethnicity in the Continental Army" (Ph.D. diss., Georgetown University, 1993), 22–23.

27. Ibid., 50.

28. Ibid., 95–96.

29. Ibid., 109.

30. John B. B. Trussell Jr., *Birthplace of An Army, A Study of the Valley Forge Encampment* (Harrisburg, Pa., 1983), 107. Trussell notes the story may be apocryphal but it has "the ring of practical truth."

31. Ibid., 164.

32. Ibid., 212–13.

33. George Quintal, unpublished independent research. Mr. Quintal has been working on a book about the blacks at Valley Forge for many years. He has explored pension applications and numerous other sources to confirm his data. He has generously shared some of his research with me. With each man he

provided ample documentation. Thus far he has identified slightly more than five hundred African Americans at Valley Forge.

34. Ibid.

35. Ibid. The petition for a citation for bravery is in the Massachusetts State Archives, Boston, Archives 180 241.

36. Neimeyer, "No Meat, No Soldier," 225–26.

37. BF, citing Todd pension application, National Archives, RG15, M806, roll 1561.

38. Holly A. Mayer, *Belonging to the Army: Camp Followers and Community during the American Revolution* (Columbia, S.C., 1996), 133.

39. Ibid., 144–45.

40. Butterfield, ed., *Letters of Rush*, Rush to Washington, Dec. 26, 1777, 180–82.

41. *PGW*, vol. 12, Washington to Rush, Jan. 12, 1778, 210.

42. Butterfield, ed., *Letters of Rush*, Rush to Henry, Jan. 12, 1778, 182–83; *PGW*, vol. 13, Henry to Washington, Feb. 20, 1778, 609.

43. *PGW*, vol. 13, Washington to Gates, Jan. 4, 1778, 138–39.

44. *PGW*, vol. 13, Lafayette to Washington, Jan. 5, 1778, 146.

45. Boyle, ed., Blaine Letterbook, 94.

46. *PGW*, vol. 13, Craik to Washington, Jan. 6, 1778, 160–61.

47. *PGW*, vol. 13, Gordon to Washington, Jan. 8, 1778, 173–75. Richard Henry Lee was not related to Charles Lee.

48. *PGW*, vol. 13, Gordon to Washington, Jan. 12, 1778, 205–6.

49. *PGW*, vol. 13, Washington to Gordon, Jan. 23, 1778, 322–23; Washington to Gordon, Feb. 15, 1778, 545–46.

50. *PNG*, vol. 2, Clark to Greene, Jan. 10, 1778, 249–51.

51. Don Higginbotham, *Daniel Morgan, Revolutionary Rifleman* (Chapel Hill, N.C., 1961), 83.

52. *PGW*, vol. 13, Gates to Washington, Jan. 23, 1778, 319–21.

53. BF, Gates to Laurens, Feb. 2, 1778, citing Papers of the Continental Congress. Nelson, *General Horatio Gates*, 12.

54. *PHL*, vol. 12, Laurens to Isaac Motte, Jan. 26, 1778, 347–48, including note 18.

55. *PGW*, vol. 13, Lee to Washington, two letters dated Jan 20, 292–94; Bass; *The Green Dragoon*, 38; Ewald, *Diary*, 121; Charles Royster, *Light Horse Harry Lee and the Legacy of the American Revolution, 1775–1783* (New York, 1981), 26–27.

56. Robert F. Jones, *William Duer: King of the Alley* (Philadelphia, 1992), 45.

57. BF, citing Wayne to Thomas Wharton, April 10, 1778, *PMHB* 24 (1900): 387–88.

58. Johann Charles Philip von Krafft, *Journal of Johann Charles Philip von Krafft,*

1776–1784, Collections of the New-York Historical Society for the Year 1882 (New York, 1882), vol. 12, 10–29. In Philadelphia, von Krafft enlisted as a sergeant with a promise of elevation to lieutenant.

59. Hugh F. Rankin, ed., *Narratives of the American Revolution* (Chicago, 1976), Albigence Waldo's Diary, 193–94. Also see Trussell, *Birthplace of an Army,* 85–87.

60. *PGW,* vol. 14, Washington to John Bannister, April 21, 1778, 574. Washington added that he had been "creditably informed" that the captaincy of a troop of dragoons had been sold for four thousand guineas.

61. *The Lee Papers,* Collections of the New-York Historical Society, 1872 (New York, 1873), vol. 2, 294.

62. *LDC,* vol. 8, Lovell to Samuel Adams, Jan. 20, 1778, 618–19.

63. *PGW,* vol. 13, Washington to Henry Laurens, Jan. 31, 1778, 419.

CHAPTER SIX. "Congress Does Not Trust Me"

1. Stanley J. Idzerda, ed., *Lafayette in the Age of the American Revolution, Selected Letters and Papers, 1776–1790,* vol. 1 (Ithaca, N.Y., 1977), 250n.

2. Ibid., Gates to Lafayette, Jan. 23, 1778, 249–50.

3. *PGW,* vol. 13, Washington to Gates, Jan. 27, 1778, 361.

4. Idzerda, ed., *Lafayette,* Laurens to Lafayette, Jan. 24, 1778, 252–53.

5. Ibid., Lafayette to Laurens, Jan. 26, 1778, 254.

6. Ibid., Lafayette to Laurens, Jan. 27, 1778, 259; Laurens to Lafayette, Jan. 28, 1778, 262.

7. Idzerda, ed., Laurens to Lafayette, Jan. 28, 1778, 262.

8. *PHL,* vol. 12, Laurens to Washington, Jan. 27, 1778, 359; "Thoughts of a Freeman," 359–62.

9. *PGW,* vol. 13, Washington to Laurens, Jan. 31, 1778, 420–21.

10. *PHL,* vol. 12, Lafayette to Laurens, Jan. 27, 1778, 363.

11. Harlow Giles Unger, *Lafayette* (Hoboken, N.J., 2002), 64–65.

12. *PHL,* vol. 12, Laurens to Rutledge, Jan. 30, 1778, 375.

13. Idzerda, ed., *Lafayette,* Lafayette to Gates, Feb. 7, 1778, 283–84.

14. Ibid., 271n.

15. Freeman, *George Washington,* vol. 4, 575–76.

16. William Cresson, *Francis Dana: A Puritan Diplomat at the Court of Catherine the Great* (New York, 1930), 46. Dana's son, who first published the story, maintained that this encounter became the proudest recollection of his father's life.

17. Freeman, *George Washington,* vol. 4, 587.

18. *PGW*, vol. 13, To a Continental Congress Camp Committee, Jan. 29, 1778, 376.

19. *PGW*, vol. 13, ibid., 377.

20. *PGW*, vol. 13, ibid., 377–78.

21. *PGW*, vol. 13, ibid., 390–3.

22. *PGW*, vol. 13, ibid., 393–96.

23. *PGW*, vol. 13, ibid., 402–4.

24. *PGW*, vol. 13, Washington to Ephraim Blaine, Jan. 31, 1778, 418.

25. Thibaut, *Valley Forge Report*, vol. 2, 140ff.

26. Ibid., 170.

27. BF, Morale icon, Reed to Henry Laurens, Feb. 12, 1778, citing William B. Reed, *Life and Correspondence of Joseph Reed* (Philadelphia, 1947), vol. 1, 361–62.

28. Thibaut, *Valley Forge Report*, vol. 2, 169–70.

29. Ibid., 172.

30. Ibid., 111.

31. *PGW*, vol. 13, Continental Congress Camp Committee to Washington, Feb. 11, 509–10, including notes.

32. Flexner, *George Washington*, vol. 2, 277.

33. *PHL*, vol. 12, Laurens to Dana, Feb. 20, 1778, 472.

34. *PGW*, vol. 13, Washington to Gates, Feb. 9, 1778, 484–87.

35. Swiggett, *The Great Man*, 312–13.

36. *PGW*, vol. 13, Greene to Washington, Feb. 15, 1778, 546–47; *PNG*, vol. 2, Varnum to Greene, Feb. 13, 1778, 280.

37. Nelson, *Wayne*, 73–74.

38. Thibaut, *Valley Forge Report*, vol. 2, 189–90.

39. *PGW*, vol. 13, Fitzgerald to Washington, Feb. 16, 1778, 555–56.

40. *PGW*, vol. 13, Henry to Washington, Feb. 20, 1778, 609–10. As late as 1784, Washington still sought confirmation of his suspicion that Rush was the author. He found it from William Gordon, the first historian of the Revolution, who visited Mount Vernon that year and instantly recognized Rush's handwriting when Washington showed him the letter. *PGW*, vol. 13, 610–11 (notes).

41. Flexner, *George Washington*, vol. 4, 489–90 (for Washington's religious practices while president).

42. Fred Anderson, ed., *George Washington Remembers: Reflections on the French and Indian War* (New York, 2004), 126–31.

43. *PGW*, vol. 12, Washington to Landon Carter, Oct. 27, 1777, 125–27.

44. *PGW*, vol. 14, Washington to Fairfax, Mar. 1, 1778, 9–10.

45. Paul K. Longmore, *The Invention of George Washington* (Berkeley, Calif., 1988), 204.

46. Alan S. Everest, *Moses Hazen and the Canadian Refugees in the American Revolution* (Syracuse, N.Y., 1976), 58–59.

47. Idzerda, ed., *Lafayette*, Lafayette to Washington, Feb. 9, 1778, 287.

48. Ibid., Lafayette to Henry Laurens, Feb. 19, 1778, 296.

49. Ibid., Hazen to Lafayette, Feb. 18, 1788, 289–91.

50. Ibid., 312: also see 301n, for Conway's letter to Gates.

51. Ibid., 297–98n.

52. Ibid., Lafayette to Laurens, Feb. 19, 1778, 295–96.

53. Ibid., Lafayette to Washington, Feb. 19, 1778, 299–301.

54. Karp, *To Starve the Army at Pleasure*, 45–46.

55. Ibid., 46–47.

56. Ibid., 49–50.

57. *PHL*, vol. 12, Laurens to Dana, Mar. 1, 1778, 489–92.

58. *PGW*, vol. 13, Washington to Fitzgerald, Feb. 28, 1778, 694.

59. *PHL*, vol. 12, Henry Laurens to John Laurens, Feb. 3, 1778, 393; John Laurens to Henry Laurens, Feb. 9, 1778, 431.

60. *PGW*, vol. 13, Gates to Washington, Feb. 19, 1778, 590.

61. *PGW*, vol. 13, Washington to Gates, Feb. 24, 1778, 654–55.

62. Nelson, *Gates*, 182–83.

63. *LDC*, vol. 9, Smith to Reed, Feb. 21, 1778, 157–58.

64. *LDC*, vol. 9, Lovell to Adams, May 16, 1778, 687.

65. Hawke, *In the Midst of a Revolution*, 201–2; *LMCC*, vol. 3, Dyer to Williams, Mar. 10, 1778, 122. Some historians, such as Bernard Knollenberg, have quoted Dyer as proof that there was no plot against Washington. See his *Washington and the Revolution: A Reappraisal* (New York, 1940), 72.

66. Burnett, *The Continental Congress*, 270.

67. *LDC*, vol. 9, Sam Adams to James Warren, May 25, 1778, 745.

68. Cushing, ed., *Writings of Samuel Adams*, vol. 4, 246–47.

CHAPTER SEVEN. Discipline from a Baron

1. Palmer, *Steuben*, 121.

2. Friedrich Kapp, *The Life of Major General Frederick William von Steuben, Major General, United States Army* (1859; Gansevoort, N.Y., 1999), 105.

3. Palmer, *Steuben*, 54–64.

4. Ibid., 98–99.

5. *PGW*, vol. 13, Washington to Laurens, Feb. 27, 1778, 686–87.

6. *PHL*, vol. 12, John Laurens to Henry Laurens, Mar. 9, 1778, 530–35.

7. Palmer, *Steuben*, 137–38.

8. Kapp, *Life of Steuben*, 115–16.

9. Ibid., 118–19.

10. *PHL*, vol. 12, 531n, citing Charles H. Lesser, ed., *The Sinews of Independence* (Chicago, 1976), 59.

11. *PHL*, vol. 12, John Laurens to Henry Laurens, Mar. 9, 1778, 531.

12. BF, Valley Forge National Historical Park Library, "The Valley Forge Fish Story"; Harry Emerson Wildes, *Valley Forge* (New York, 1938), 174–75. Mr. Boyle's research exploded this myth.

13. Friedrich Wilhelm von Steuben, *Regulations for the Order and Discipline of the Troops of the United States, Part I* (Philadelphia, 1779), 10–11. Steuben's complete manual was published by order of Congress in 1779.

14. Palmer, *Steuben*, 144–45.

15. Steuben, *Regulations for Order and Discipline*, 25.

16. Ibid., 134–35. The author first heard these words quoted to him in 1965 when he was writing a history of West Point. The quoter was Major (later Colonel) Harry S. Maihafer of the Class of 1949.

17. Palmer, *Steuben*, 147–48; Kapp, *Life of Steuben*, 130.

18. Palmer, *Steuben*, 148.

19. Ibid., 149.

20. *PNG*, vol. 2, Greene to Abeel, Mar. 11, 313; Greene to Smallwood, Mar. 16, 316; Greene to Biddle, Mar. 23, 319.

21. *PNG*, vol. 2, Greene to Laurens, Mar. 26, 1778, 321–22.

22. *PNG*, vol. 2, Greene to Biddle, Mar. 30, 1778, 327–28.

23. *PNG*, vol. 2, Greene "To The Inhabitants of the United States," Mar. 28, 1778, 324, 325, including the note, which discusses how these certificates fared in practice.

24. Paul David Nelson, *Anthony Wayne, Soldier of the Early Republic* (Bloomington, Ind., 1985), 73; *PNG*, vol. 2, 282, note. Also see John P. Stegman and Janet A. Stegman, *Caty: A Biography of Catherine Littlefield Greene* (Athens, Ga., 1977), 10, 51–59.

25. Cresson, *Francis Dana*, 51; *LDC*, vol. 8, Lovell to Adams, Jan. 20, 1778, 618.

26. *LDC*, vol. 9, "Delegates Pledge of Order," 403.

27. *LDC*, vol. 9, Laurens to Duane, Apr. 7, 1778, 381.

28. *PGW*, vol. 14, Washington to Laurens, Apr. 10, 1778, 460.

29. *LDC*, vol. 9, Lovell to Adams, Apr. 18, 1778, 436. Also see Cresson, *Francis Dana*, 52. Gouverneur Morris admitted the importance of Dana's role. "A majority of our house has been agreed to a certain point ever since Mr. Dana arrived here."

30. *PHL*, vol. 13, Laurens to Lafayette, Mar. 24, 1778, 29.

31. Rossman, *Thomas Mifflin*, 148.

32. Ibid., 135–36.

33. Ibid., 149.

34. Martin, *Private Yankee Doodle*, 117–18.

35. Palmer, *Steuben*, 152–53.

36. *PHL*, vol. 13, John Laurens to Henry Laurens, Apr. 1, 1778, 68.

37. Palmer, *Steuben*, 154–55, 157.

38. *PHL*, vol. 13, Conway to Laurens, Apr. 22, 1778.

39. Palmer, *Steuben*, 157.

40. Ibid.

CHAPTER EIGHT. **From Anxiety to Exultation**

1. *PGW*, vol. 14, Washington to Bannister, Apr. 21, 1778, 575–79.

2. *PGW*, vol. 14, Washington to Laurens, Apr. 10, 1778, 459–62; Washington to John Bannister, Apr. 21, 573–79. For lack of clothing, vol. 14, 541n. On April 17, Washington wrote a ferocious letter to Clothier General James Mease, demanding his immediate appearance at Valley Forge. Mease did not even bother to answer it.

3. *PGW*, vol. 14, Bannister to Washington, Apr. 16, 1778, 531; Washington to Bannister, Apr. 21, 1778, 574–77; Burnett, *The Continental Congress*, 314, 317.

4. Ewald, *Diary*, 119–21.

5. Ibid., 120–21.

6. *LDC*, vol. 9, Reed to Wharton, Feb. 1, 1778, 4–6.

7. Higginbotham, *Daniel Morgan*, 82: *PGW*, vol. 14, Washington to Lacey, Apr. 11, 1778, 476–77.

8. *LDC*, vol. 9, Reed Wharton, Feb. 1, 1778.

9. *PGW*, vol. 14, Wharton to Washington, Mar. 2, 1778, 43; Lacey to Washington, Mar. 3, 1778, 46–47.

10. *PGW*, vol. 13, Jameson to Washington, Feb. 2, 1778, 440; vol. 14, General Orders, Mar. 25, 1778, 298. Another man, Abel Jeans, was convicted of passing counterfeit money supplied by the British, as well as trading with them, received one hundred lashes, and was ordered confined to a prison somewhere in Pennsylvania and kept at hard labor until the war ended.

11. *PGW*, vol. 13, 441n.

12. *PGW*, vol. 14, Washington to Lacey, Apr. 11, 1778, 476–77: Lacey to Washington, Apr. 9, 1778, 435.

13. *PHL*, vol. 13, Rodney to Laurens, Apr. 14, 1778, 183–84. Also see 175n.

14. Leonard Lundin, *Cockpit of the Revolution: The War for Independence in New Jersey* (Princeton, N.J., 1940), 375–76.

15. *PHL*, vol. 13, Rawlins Lowndes to Henry Laurens, Apr. 13, 1778, 113–15.

16. *PGW*, vol. 14, 547–48n.

17. *PGW*, vol. 14, Washington to Laurens, Apr. 18, 1778, 546–48, including note 6.

18. *LDC*, vol. 9, Chase to Johnson, Apr. 20, 1778, 451–52; Henry to Johnson, Apr. 20, 454–55.

19. *PHL*, vol. 13, John Laurens to Henry Laurens, Apr. 20, 1778, 156–57.

20. *PHL*, vol. 13, ibid.

21. *PHL*, vol. 13, Laurens to Rawlins Lowndes, May 1, 1778, 227–28.

22. Burnett, *Continental Congress*, 325.

23. *PGW*, vol. 14, Laurens to Washington, Apr. 27, 1778, 664.

24. Burnett, *Continental Congress*, 328.

25. *LDC*, vol. 9, McKean to Rodney, Apr. 28, 1778, 520–21. Also see John M. Coleman, *Thomas McKean, Forgotten Leader of the Revolution* (Rockaway, N.J., 1975), 220–21.

26. *LDC*, vol. 9, Lovell to the Commissioners, Apr. 30, 1778, 546–47. Also see *LDC*, vol. 9, 560–64, for Folger's examination before Congress on January 12, 1778.

27. *LDC*, vol. 9, Lee to Jefferson, May 2, 1778, 566.

28. BF, Lacey report to Thomas Wharton Jr., president of the Pennsylvania Ruling Council, May 4, 1778, citing Stauffer collection, No. 617, HSP. Also see Jackson, *With the British Army in Philadelphia*, 223–25.

29. Burnett, *Continental Congress*, 332.

30. Unger, *Lafayette*, 71: *PHL*, vol. 13, Lafayette to Laurens, May 1, 1778, 235–37.

31. Reed, *Valley Forge: Crucible of Victory*, 54.

32. Thomas Ewing, ed., *George Ewing, Gentleman Soldier of Valley Forge* (Privately printed, Yonkers, N.Y., 1928), 47.

33. Freeman, *George Washington*, vol. 5, 1.

34. Palmer, *Steuben*, 162–64; Flexner, *George Washington*, vol. 2, 290.

35. Palmer, *Steuben*, 165–66.

36. Flexner, *George Washington*, vol. 2, 290–91.

37. Ibid., 291.

CHAPTER NINE. **The Follies of Spring**

1. Jackson, *With the British Army in Philadelphia*, 227; Ewald, *Diary*, 123.

2. Gruber, *The Howe Brothers*, 297.

3. Ewald, *Diary*, 123.

4. Yalof, *British Military Theatricals*, 121–22. Also see John Peebles, *John Peebles' American War: The Diary of a Scottish Grenadier, 1776–1782*, ed. Ira D. Gruber (Mechanicsburg, Pa., 1998), 171–72.

5. Jackson, *With the British Army in Philadelphia*, 173.

6. George Winthrow Gelb, "A History of Philadelphia, 1776–1789" (Ph.D. diss., University of Wisconsin, 1969), 75–76.

7. Ibid., 85–87.

8. Jacob E. Cooke, "Tench Coxe, Tory Merchant," *PMHB*, 96: Jan. 1972, 48–62.

9. Gelb, "History of Philadelphia," 78–80.

10. Ibid., 80–81.

11. Peebles, *John Peebles' American War*, 162.

12. Jackson, *With the British in Philadelphia*, 174; Gelb, "History of Philadelphia," 85.

13. Gelb, "History of Philadelphia," 83, Jackson, *With the British Army in Philadelphia*, 173.

14. Jackson, *With the British Army in Philadelphia*, 193–94.

15. Peebles, *John Peebles' American War*, 171.

16. Jackson, *With the British Army in Philadelphia*, 178.

17. Ferling, *The Loyalist Mind*, 40–41.

18. Ewald, *Diary*, 126.

19. BF, *Citizens*, citing Eleazer Oswald to John Lamb, May 15, 1778, John Lamb Papers, New-York Historical Society.

20. Jackson, *With the British Army in Philadelphia*, 225–26; Gruber, *The Howe Brothers*, 296.

21. Jackson, *With the British Army in Philadelphia*, 231; Gruber, *The Howe Brothers*, 287.

22. Yaloff, *British Military Theatricals*, 145–46.

23. "André's Description of the Mischianza," *Century* 47 (1893–94): 687–88.

24. "André's Description of the Mischianza," 689–91; Yaloff, British Military Theatricals, 167–184. Yaloff adds details from other sources.

25. Jackson, *With The British Army in Philadelphia*, 248, 144–45.

26. Ibid., 249.

27. Gruber, *The Howe Brothers*, 349; Ferling, *The Loyalist Mind*, 57–59.

28. *PHL*, vol. 13, Laurens to Lowndes, May 17, 1778, 316.

29. Young, *Revolutionary Ladies*, 84–86.

30. William B. Willcox, *Portrait of a General* (New York, 1964), 226–27.

31. Ibid., 227.

CHAPTER TEN. **General Double Trouble**

1. Lesser, *The Sinews of Independence*, 69.

2. *WFVF*, vol. 1, Samuel Ward Jr. to Phebe Ward, 130–32.

3. *WFVF*, vol. 1, John Cropper to Margaret Cropper, May 10, 1778, 134–35.

4. *WFVF*, vol. 2, John Cropper to Margaret Cropper, May 29, 1778, 139–41.

5. Yaloff, *British Military Theatricals*, 140.

6. Jason Shaffer, "Great Cato's Descendants: A Genealogy of Colonial Performance," *Theatre Survey*, May 2003, 9–13.

7. Joseph Addison, *Cato*, in *Eighteenth Century Plays*, intro. Richard Quintana (New York, 1952), 48, 27.

8. Flexner, *George Washington*, vol. 1, 199.

9. Thibaut, *Valley Forge Report*, vol. 3, 115; Reed, *Crucible of Victory*, 57; Yaloff, *British Military Theatricals*, 139–40.

10. *PHL*, vol. 13, 305n, 321; Fitzpatrick, ed., *The Writings of Washington*, vol. 11, Washington to Morris, May 18, 1778, 413.

11. *LMCC*, vol. 3, Morris to Washington, May 21, 1778, 260.

12. *LDC*, vol. 9, G. Morris to R. Morris, May 11, 1778, 650–51. Also see Henderson, *Party Politics*, 120–24, which includes a table showing how delegates voted.

13. *WFVF*, vol. 1, Samuel Ward Jr. to Phebe Ward, May 5, 1778, 130–32. The final form of the half-pay compromise was not achieved until May 15, but Ward must have heard assurances that it was as good as settled when he wrote this letter.

14. Trussell, *Birthplace of an Army*, 86–87, 133 (appendix 3).

15. *PHL*, vol. 13, Laurens to Washington, May 5, 1778, 28; Washington to Laurens, May 29, 1778, 367.

16. John Richard Alden, *General Charles Lee, Patriot or Traitor?* (Baton Rouge, La., 1951), 36–37.

17. Flexner, *George Washington*, vol. 2, 17, 23.

18. Neimeyer, *No Meat, No Soldier*, 100–101.

19. *Lee Papers*, vol. 2, Lee to Gates, Oct. 14, 1776, 261; Lee to Gates, Dec. 13, 1776, 348.

20. *PGW*, vol. 13, Laurens to Washington, Apr. 14, 1778, 411n6. Also see Henderson, *Party Politics in the Continental Congress*, 111, and Burnett, *The Continental Congress*, 268–69. As early as February 1777, Burke wrote: "There appeared . . . a great desire in the delegates of the Eastern States . . . to insult the general."

21. *PHL*, vol. 13, Henry Laurens to John Laurens, Apr. 9, 1778, 94.

22. *Lee Papers*, vol. 2, 383–89.

23. Ibid.

24. Elias Boudinot, *Journal, or Historical Recollections of American Events During the Revolutionary War* (Philadelphia, 1894), 75–79.

25. *Lee Papers*, vol. 2, 390.

26. *LMCC*, vol. 3, Laurens to James Duane, Apr. 17, 1778, 169–70.

27. Idzerda, *Lafayette in the American Revolution*, vol. 2, Washington to Lafayette, May 18, 1778, 53–54.

28. Louis Gottschalk, *Lafayette Joins the American Army* (Chicago, 1937), 145–46.

29. Idzerda, *Lafayette in the American Revolution*, vol. 2, Lafayette to McLane, May 18, 1778, 55.

30. Gottschalk, *Lafayette Joins the American Army*, 187.

31. Martin, *Private Yankee Doodle*, 118–19.

32. Unger, *Lafayette*, 75–76.

33. Ibid., 76.

34. Gottschalk, *Lafayette Joins the American Army*, 189–90.

35. Martin, *Private Yankee Doodle*, 120.

36. Unger, *Lafayette*, 76.

37. Gottschalk, *Lafayette Joins the American Army*, 192.

38. Anthony Wonderley, "Oneida Iroquois at the Barren Hill Fight, Revolutionary War: A Cautionary Tale of Historical Bias," Oneida Indian Nation Web site, http://oneida-nation.net/bhill.html. 1–16. For commissions, see Francis J. Sypher Jr. ed., *New York State Society of the Cincinnati: Biographies of Original Members and Other Continental Officers* (Fishkill, N.Y., 2004), 10–11. Colonel Atayatghronghta was a St. Regis Indian of the Iroquois nation, who married an Oneida woman. He was also known as Louis Cook.

39. *PHL*, vol. 13, Laurens to Hopkinson, May 27, 1778, 345–47.

40. Alden, *General Charles Lee*, 189–90; Flexner, *George Washington*, vol. 2, 294.

41. *Lee Papers*, vol. 2, 361–66.

42. Alden, *General Charles Lee*, 186–87.

43. Ibid., 191.

44. *Lee Papers*, vol. 2, Lee to Rush, May 3, 1778, 397–98.

45. Alden, *General Charles Lee*, 201–2.

46. *PHL*, vol. 13, Laurens to Rawlins Lowndes, June 12, 1778, 447.

47. Rossman, *Thomas Mifflin*, 151–52.

48. Ibid., 155–60.

49. *Lee Papers*, vol. 2, Lee to Rush, June 4, 1778, 399.

50. Fitzpatrick, ed., *The Writings of Washington*, vol. 11, Washington to Gates, May 26, 1778, 458–60.

51. Boyle, ed., Blaine Letterbook, Chaloner to Jeremiah Wadsworth, undated, frame 1267, 200.

52. Ibid., Chaloner to Blaine, May 30, 1778, 204–5.

53. Thibaut, *Valley Forge Report*, vol. 2, 225–26, 243.

54. Willcox, *Portrait of a General*, 229–30.

55. Flexner, *George Washington*, vol. 2, 296; Alden, *General Charles Lee*, 205.

56. Alden, *General Charles Lee*, 205–7.

57. Flexner, *George Washington*, vol. 2, 297.

CHAPTER ELEVEN. **A Moment at Monmouth**

1. Flexner, *George Washington*, vol. 2, 297–98.

2. Ewald, *Diary*, 139.

3. *PNG*, vol. 2, 446n.

4. Alden, *General Charles Lee*, 108–9.

5. Syrett, ed., *Papers of Alexander Hamilton*, Hamilton to Elias Boudinot, July 5, 1778, vol. 2, 510.

6. *PNG*, vol. 2, Greene to Washington, June 24, 1778, 446–47.

7. *Lee Papers*, vol. 2, Lee to Washington, June 25, 1778, 417–18.

8. *Lee Papers*, vol. 2, Washington to Lafayette, June 26, 1778, 422–23.

9. *Lee Papers*, vol. 3, 6 (in testimony from the Lee court-martial).

10. Alden, *General Charles Lee*, 6–11, 22–23; Dave Richard Palmer, *The Way of the Fox: American Strategy in the War for America* (Westport, Conn., 1975), 151–52.

11. *Lee Papers*, vol. 3, 7–9 (Meade's testimony in the court-martial of General Lee).

12. Flexner, *George Washington*, vol. 2, 302–3; Freeman, *George Washington*, vol. 5, 24–25.

13. Freeman, *George Washington*, vol. 4, 26.

14. Palmer, *The Way of the Fox*, 153.

15. *Lee Papers*, vol. 3, 81, testimony of Tench Tilghman at Lee court-martial.

16. Freeman, *George Washignton*, vol. 4, 28–29.

17. Thomas H. Montgomery, "The Battle of Monmouth Described by Dr. James McHenry," *Magazine of American History*, vol. 3, 360.

18. Fitzpatrick, ed., *Writings of Washington*, vol. 12, Washington to John Augustine Washington, July 4, 1778, 156–57.

19. Flexner, *George Washington*, vol. 2, 308–9; Unger, *Lafayette*, 79.

20. Flexner, *George Washington*, vol. 2, 308–9.

21. *Lee Papers*, vol. 3, 96.

22. Martin, *Private Yankee Doodle*, 132–33.

23. Rupert Hughes, *George Washington* (New York, 1930), vol. 2, 375–76.

24. Flexner, *George Washington*, vol. 2, 309.

25. Montgomery, "The Battle of Monmouth," 359.

26. Palmer, *Steuben*, 187.

27. *Lee Papers*, vol. 3, 96.

28. Flexner, *George Washington*, vol. 2, 309–10.

29. Alden, *General Charles Lee*, 229; *PHL*, vol. 13, John Laurens to Henry Laurens, June 30, 1778, 532–37.

30. *Lee Papers*, vol. 2, 430.

31. *Lee Papers*, vol. 2, Lee to Washington, misdated July 1, 1778 [June 30], 435–36.

32. *Lee Papers*, vol. 2, Washington to Lee, June 30, 1778, 437.

33. *Lee Papers*, vol. 2, Lee to Washington, misdated June 28, 1778 [June 30], 437–38.

34. *Lee Papers*, vol. 2, Lee to Washington, June 30, 1778, 438.

35. *Lee Papers*, vol. 2, Lee to Collins, July 3, 1778, 452, 456.

36. Fitzpatrick, ed., *Writings of Washington*, vol. 12, Washington to Henry Laurens, 139–46. Also see *Lee Papers*, vol. 2, Joseph Reed to Lee, July (undated) 1778, 475–77.

37. *Lee Papers*, vol. 2, Lee to Morris, July 3, 1778, 457–59.

38. *PHL*, vol. 13, Henry Laurens to John Laurens, July 6, 1778, 549. Some historians have agreed with President Laurens. Kemble Widmer, who has written widely on the Revolutionary War in New Jersey, argued at a symposium on the Battle of Monmouth that Lee was a traitor since 1776, when he "arranged" to be captured by British cavalry to escape hanging because he thought the Revolution was collapsing. Mary R. Murrin and Richard Waldron, eds., *Conflict at Monmouth Court House*, proceedings of a symposium on the 200th anniversary of the Battle of Monmouth (Trenton, N.J., 1983), 57–58.

39. *LMCC*, vol. 3, 278n.

40. *Hughes, Washington*, vol. 2, 404–5.

41. Alden, *General Charles Lee*, 141.

42. *Lee Papers*, vol. 3, Proceedings of a General Court Martial &c, 1–208.

43. *Lee Papers*, vol. 3, 208.

44. Charlene Mires, *Independence Hall in American Memory* (Philadelphia, 2002), 24; Jackson, *With the British Army in Philadelphia*, 267.

45. Jackson, *With the British Army in Philadelphia*, 267; Butterfield, ed., *Letters of Benjamin Rush*, vol. 1, Rush to David Ramsay, Nov. 5, 1778, 219.

46. Jackson, *With the British Army in Philadelphia*, 268–71.

47. James Thomas Flexner, *The Traitor and the Spy* (New York, 1953), 215.

48. Ward preface, "Major André's Story of the Mischianza," 687.

49. Cooke, "Tench Coxe, Tory Merchant," 62, 85–87.

50. Winthrop, *History of Philadelphia*, 135–39. Also see Swiggett, *The Great Man*, 156–57, and John High, "The Philadelphia Loyalists" (Ph.D. diss., Temple University, 1974), 227–28. Lovell's performance prompted Swiggett to write: "Such were the qualities of the men who preferred Gates to Washington."

51. *LMCC*, vol. 3, Samuel Adams to Samuel Philipps Savage, Oct. 17, 1778, 451–52.

52. *Lee Papers*, vol. 3, Lee to Laurens, Oct. 29, 1778, 243.

53. Alden, *General Charles Lee*, 148.

54. *Lee Papers*, vol. 3, Joseph Reed to Nathanael Greene, Nov. 5, 1778, 250.

55. *LMCC*, vol. 3, Gouverneur Morris to George Washington, Oct. 26, 1778, 465.

56. Butterworth, ed., *Letters of Benjamin Rush*, vol. 1, 220.

57. *PNG*, vol. 2, George Lux to Nathanael Greene, Apr. 28, 1778, 366.

58. *Journals of the Continental Congress*, vol. 12, Dec. 5, 1778, Internet edition, Library of Congress, image 1195, http://memory.loc.gov/ammem/amlaw/lwjc.html. Also see Alden, *General Charles Lee*, 254–55. Thanks to no votes by Sam Adams and James Lovell, Massachusetts backed Lee. The other Lee state was a wild card, Georgia. Edward Langworthy usually voted against the radicals, and he was the only Georgia delegate present. In 1795, Langworthy published a sympathetic sketch of Lee.

59. *Journals of the Continental Congress*, vol. 12, Dec. 5, 1778.

60. Swiggett, *The Great Man*, 218.

61. *BF*, McDougall to Clinton, Nov. 5, 1778, citing Charles S. Hall, ed., *Life and Letters of Samuel Holden Parsons* (Binghamton, N.Y., 1905), 199.

62. George F. Scheer and Hugh F. Rankin, *Rebels and Redcoats* (New York, 1957), 470–72.

63. *Lee Papers*, vol. 3, Lee to Rush, Aug. 13, 1778, 228–29.

64. Butterfield, ed., *Letters of Benjamin Rush*, vol. 1, Rush to David Ramsay, Nov. 5, 1778, 219–20.

EPILOGUE. Two Visits to Valley Forge

1. Lorett Treese, *Valley Forge: Making and Unmaking a National Symbol* (University Park, Pa., 1995), 7–8.

2. Charles Royster, *A Revolutionary People at War* (Chapel Hill, N.C., 1979), 214.

3. George Athan Bilias, *Elbridge Gerry, Founding Father and Republican States-man* (New York, 1976), 191.

4. *PHL*, vol. 12, John Laurens to Henry Laurens, Mar. 9, 1778, 532.

5. Michael Kammen, *The Mystic Chords of Memory* (New York, 1991), 590–610.

6. Treese, *Valley Forge*, 186.

7. Gerald R. Ford, *Public Papers of the Presidents of the United States* (3 vols) vol. 2, April 9 to July 9, 1976 (Washington, D.C., 1979), 644.

Index